Lydgate's Siege of Thebes

Early English Text Society.
Extra Series, No. CXXV.
1930 (for 1920).

Bvt / ȝe may reden in a Tragedye
Of moral Senyk fully his endynge
His dool his meschief / and his compleynynge
How with sorow / and vnweldy age
This Edippus / fille into dotage
Lost his wit and his worldly delit
And how his sonnes / had hym in despit
And of disdeyn tok of hym no kepe
And bookes seyn his eyen out he wepe
And as myn auctor liketh to devise
As his sones rebuke hym and despise
Vpon a day in a certeyn place
Out of his hede / his eyen he gan race
And cast at hem / he can non other bote
And of malice / they trad hem vnder fote
ffully devoide / both of love and drede
And whan Edippus / for meschief was thus dede
With inne a pytte / made in the erth lowe
Of crueltè his sones han hym throwe
Werse than serpent / or eny tigre wood
Of cursid stok / cometh vnkynd blood
As in story / ȝe may rede her to forn
Al be the roos / grow out of a thorn
Thus of Edippus whan he was blynd and old
The wrecched ende / I haue ȝou pleynly told
ffor which therfore / to man and child I rede
To be wel war / and to taken hede
Of kyndely riȝt / and of consience
To donne and dien reuerence
To fader moder / of what estat thei be
Or certeyn ellis they shul neuer the

MS. Arundel 119 (British Museum), fol. 17 front (ll. 994–1024)

Royal MS. 18. D. II (British Museum), fol. 148 front, 2nd col.

The Party of Pilgrims.

(The second person from the left is Lydgate. See further, p. 55.)

Lydgate's
Siege of Thebes

EDITED

FROM ALL THE KNOWN MANUSCRIPTS AND THE TWO OLDEST EDITIONS

PART II.—INTRODUCTION, NOTES, RHYME-LISTS, AND A GLOSSARY, WITH AN APPENDIX

BY

AXEL ERDMANN, Ph.D.†

LATE PROFESSOR OF ENGLISH IN THE UNIVERSITY OF UPSALA

AND

EILERT EKWALL, Ph.D.

PROFESSOR OF ENGLISH IN THE UNIVERSITY OF LUND

LONDON:

PUBLISHED FOR THE EARLY ENGLISH TEXT SOCIETY

BY HUMPHREY MILFORD, OXFORD UNIVERSITY PRESS

AMEN CORNER, E.C. 4.

Great Clarendon Street, Oxford OX2 6DP
United Kingdom

Oxford University Press is a department of the University of Oxford. It furthers the University's objective of excellence in research, scholarship, and education by publishing worldwide. Oxford is a registered trade mark of Oxford University Press in the UK and in certain other countries

First Edition published in 1930

Published in the United States of America by Oxford University Press
198 Madison Avenue, New York, NY 10016, United States of America

British Library Cataloguing in Publication Data
Data available

Library of Congress Cataloging in Publication Data
Data available

Extra Series, 125

ISBN 978-0-85-991718-6

PREFACE

The first part of the *Siege of Thebes* (the Text) was published in 1911. The intention was probably that the second part would follow soon. In fact, it is announced among the works from which the publications of the Early English Text Society for 1911 and 1912 were to be chosen. The second part appears to have occupied Professor Erdmann's attention all through the decade following the publication of the first part. The description of the MSS. seems to have received its final shape in 1914. The genealogy of the MSS. was under work in 1920–21 and was partly finished, when in 1921 Professor Erdmann fell ill of a serious malady, which for a long time prevented him from too strenuous work. No doubt it was owing to ill-health that he was never able to finish the work. He slowly recovered, but he did not regain his former strength.

By 1925 Professor Erdmann had come to doubt if he would be able to complete the book, and when I visited him in May that year he consulted me as to the possibility of finding someone to continue it. The upshot was that I undertook to do so myself, if necessary, and the arrangement was that in the autumn the collections and drafts were to be sent to me. Meanwhile he was to undertake the final revision of the Glossary. But the confident hope that his book would be finished and his engagements to the Early English Text Society fulfilled, as he wrote to me in a letter dated August 31st, 1925, gave him new strength. He took up the work again, hoping that after all he would be able to bring it to a conclusion, and he continued working at it till the end of the year. In his last letter to me, dated December 18th, 1925, he writes that the work had again taken more time than he expected, but that the introductory chapters, the Notes and Glossary were almost completed, except for the final revision. He says he is going to take a well-earned Christmas holiday, but hopes to start afresh in the New Year. This hope was probably not fulfilled. There is nothing to show that any further work was done on *Thebes* after December 1925. After Professor

Erdmann's death the unfinished MS. and the collections referring to *Thebes* were handed over to me.

It remains to give a brief account of the state of the book at the time when I took over the completion, and of the work done by me. In reality the work had progressed so far that it ought to have taken its original author comparatively little time to give it its final form, had he been in possession of his full strength. To me, who had first to make myself familiar with the text and with Professor Erdmann's methods and intentions, it has naturally offered far greater difficulties.

I have used Professor Erdmann's drafts and notes as far as possible, and have generally refrained from making additions of my own except when this was necessary. I may add that I was given a perfectly free hand and was authorised to make any alterations that I thought desirable. Most of the chapters of the Introduction were finished, or nearly so, except for the final revision. But the general plan of the Introduction was not definitely settled. The arrangement adopted is in accordance in the main with that contemplated by Professor Erdmann at a somewhat earlier stage of the work. A rough draft of a plan dated May 14th, 1925, shows some changes, but it includes sections that were never even begun.

Some chapters of the Introduction were so nearly completed that my work could be limited chiefly to the final revision, the verification of references and the like. Here belong Chap. I, Chap. II, except § 3, 7, for which a good deal of material was found among the collections, and Chap. III, § 2, Vocabulary, which, however, has been slightly revised with the help of the new Concordance to Chaucer's works by Tatlock and Kennedy. In Chap. V a few details only wanted addition and verification. I have not found it necessary to check all the data concerning the various MSS. Professor Erdmann told me this would be supererogatory, and the collation of the references from MSS. in the British Museum and the Bodleian Library undertaken last summer revealed only some slight inadvertencies.

Chap. VI has given me most trouble. The general arrangement was not fixed, and the various drafts of a plan for the chapter found among Professor Erdmann's papers do not agree in all respects. For the paragraph on MS. Lb., undoubtedly that most difficult to place, only some rough notes and collections were to be found. I had to work through the whole of Chap. VI in order to check references and to familiarise myself with the whole problem, before I could do anything with MS. Lb. As a result of my study of the whole genealogical question I have found it advisable to make a few slight modifications or additions in the other parts. I have generally made a distinction between readings (" faults ") peculiar to a certain MS. or group of MSS. and such as are to be found also in other more remotely related MSS. It is obvious that such a distinction is useful, and in an earlier very full draft of Chap. VI (dated 1911) a similar distinction is made by Professor Erdmann himself. In this draft to each fault is appended a list of the MSS. in which it is found. Evidently this arrangement was found too cumbrous, and the references were cancelled.

For Chap. III, § 1 I am mainly responsible myself. My instructions were that this chapter, as well as that on metre, was to be brief, and that the chapter on language should be limited chiefly to matter that might throw light on versification. To the versification and metre of *Thebes* Professor Erdmann devoted much time and interest, and his collections contain a good deal of material for a full treatment of the question. Chap. IV has mainly been pieced together from odd notes written by Professor Erdmann at various times.

The Notes, to which Professor Erdmann gave a great deal of time and work, are printed almost exactly as they were written by him. I have verified all the references, including the copious extracts from Lydgate's sources, and filled in a few gaps.

I have no reason to suppose that Professor Erdmann intended to include the Rhyme-lists. Instead he contemplated a section dealing systematically with Lydgate's rhymes, favourite rhyme-words and rhyme-vowels and the like. No draft of such a section was made, and I have thought it best to print Professor Erdmann's full list of rhymes, though in a somewhat systematised form.

The Glossary was finished. I have checked all the references and added a few items that had been accidentally missed out.

After the Introduction was already in type, I discovered a MS. of *Thebes* that had been overlooked by Professor Erdmann, MS. Ch. (= MS. Christchurch Library 152). I had an opportunity of collating the MS. last summer and give the results in an Appendix. I take this opportunity of offering my sincere thanks to the Dean of Christchurch and the Librarian for the facilities extended and the courtesy shown to me.

It is a matter for regret that Professor Erdmann could not complete the book himself and undertake the final revision of the whole. The present writer by no means possesses his intimate familiarity with the text and with Lydgate generally, and no doubt many details would have looked different, had he been able to add the final touches himself. However, by far the greater part of the volume is in the form in which it left Professor Erdmann's pen. I have done my best to complete the work in the spirit of Professor Erdmann, and it is a source of satisfaction to me that I have been able to contribute to it that this important work of my old teacher and friend is now at last (more than forty years after it was first planned) going to be given to the world.

Lund, September 1929. E. E.

AXEL ERDMANN

A MEMOIR

Axel Erdmann was born at Stockholm on February 6th, 1843. He was the son of Axel Joachim Erdmann, the famous geologist. He matriculated at Upsala in 1861 and took his degree of Ph.D. in 1871. In the same year he became a " docent " in Old English in the university. In 1892 he was appointed to the newly-founded chair for Germanic philology at Upsala, and in 1902, when separate professorships for English and German were instituted, he chose the English chair, which he held till the end of 1909, when he retired with a pension. He died at Upsala November 8th, 1926, nearly 84 years old.

Axel Erdmann's range of study was unusually wide. He was primarily a student of Germanic languages, but he was widely read in the whole field of comparative philology. In fact, in the years of waiting for a professorship in his particular subject he was for long periods reader and examiner in Sanskrit and comparative philology. In Romance philology he did independent research work. Swedish dialects from an early period aroused his keen interest, and he left behind large manuscript collections for the dialects of Uppland, his native province. What is more, he was one of the chief originators of the systematic survey of the Swedish dialects, which has been going on for many years on a large scale and given highly important results. His warm interest in his home province also led to his taking part as one of the chief editors in a monumental description of Uppland, which began to appear in 1902.

Teaching and examining work claimed a very large share of his time and energy, especially after he had got his professorship. It was no small task in itself to keep abreast of the constantly growing literature in the two fields of English and German philology. He gave the utmost care to the preparation of his lectures. His store of learning and his sound criticism were always at the disposal of his students. His influence as a university teacher has perhaps not always been sufficiently acknowledged. It is not too much to say that Axel Erdmann inaugurated the study of Germanic; notably English, philology on modern lines at Upsala. Many able scholars issued from his school, and if at the present day the standard of English and Germanic philology in Sweden may be said to be high, the credit is to a great extent due to his stimulating influence. Erdmann was also one of the pioneers of the movement for the reform of the teaching of modern languages in schools, and in his university teaching he gave much prominence to the modern languages.

It is not to be wondered at that the published work of a scholar with such a wide range of interests should not have been very extensive. Moreover, in his research work Erdmann was as conscientious and careful as in his teaching. He was never content unless he went right to the bottom of the problem he was investigating. Some of his published works were never finished according to the original plan. At least one finished work was never published. In a study on *Doublets in English* he refers more than once to a forthcoming treatise to be published in Upsala Universitets Årsskrift for 1887 under the title *Om de gutturala och palatala c-, ȝ- och h-ljuden.* This treatise was never published.

Erdmann's first work was his doctor's dissertation : *Essay on the History and Modern Use of the Verbal Forms in -ing in the English Language.* I. *Old Anglo-Saxon Period* (Stockholm, 1871). A continuation never followed. The treatise deals with the present participle in Old English, especially its periphrastic use in combination with the verb *to be.* The study has hardly received the attention it deserves. It is a very valuable piece of research work and is characterised by stringency of method and a feeling for subtle shades of meaning. His next work, *Dubbelformer i den moderna engelskan* (Doublets in Modern English), was published in the *Transactions of the Språkvetenskapliga sällskapet i Uppsala* for 1882–1885, pp. 129–62. The part published deals with words of Germanic origin. A sequel dealing with Romance words was projected, but never appeared. Being written in Swedish, this study, which gives evidence alike of sound judgment and ripe scholarship, is probably unknown outside Scandinavia. In 1889 was published an edition of an Old French text : *La vie Seint Edmund le Rey, an old-French Poem by Denis Piramus* (Gothenburg, 1889). Next followed the important treatise *Über die Heimat und den Namen der Angeln* (Upsala, 1890). The main thesis of this penetrating study has not been generally accepted by critics, but everybody will ackowledge the learning displayed and the masterly presentation of the evidence. Besides, the book gives much more than the title promises: it is an important contribution to the study of Germanic tribal names generally.

The problem discussed in *Die Grundbedeutung und Etymologie der Wörter Kleid und Filz im Germanischen* (Upsala, 1891) is limited in scope, but the solution proposed has been universally accepted. As a piece of etymological research the paper is a model performance.

After Erdmann's appointment to his professorial chair his teaching and other work claimed most of his time, and it was not until after his retirement that the next more extensive work appeared, *Lydgate's Siege of Thebes*, I. This work had occupied his attention for many years. I do not know exactly when the plan of the edition was formed, but a note-book, which contains notes on MSS. of *Thebes* and the like, bearing date 1888 shows that it cannot have been later than that year. There are among Professor Erdmann's papers a good many notes concerning Lydgate's *St. Edmund*, and I have the impression that at one time he contemplated a study of this work rather than of *Thebes*. Some notes containing a comparison between Lydgate's *St. Edmund* and Denis Piramus' poem *Seint Edmund* may indicate that it was the work on the Old French Life of St. Edmund that brought him into contact with Lydgate and eventually led to the edition of *Thebes*. Probably it was in the course of his long stay in England in the years 1888–89 that the plan was formed. The visits to England in the summers of 1892, 1896, 1897, 1904 and 1907 were probably undertaken mainly in the interest of the edition of *Thebes*. On the edition itself this is hardly the right place to speak. It may be said, however, that few text-editors have been so well equipped for their task as Axel Erdmann. His wide learning, his stylistic sense, his inexhaustible patience, his meticulous care were assets of first-rate value for such a task as that of editing a text from twenty-three MSS.

The range of Axel Erdmann's interests was by no means exhausted by his philological and teaching work. He was a humanist in the broadest sense of the word. He was a lover of music. Natural scenery had a strong appeal to him. He was an intense patriot. He did not take an active part in the politics of the day, but he took a lively interest in all that was going on and had very definite opinions of his own. Personally he was warm-hearted and enthusiastic in a quiet way. He was an unselfish friend and wa always glad when he could help others. Should I sum up my impression of Axel Erdmann, I know of no better formula than a quotation which is perhaps somewhat worn, but which is singularly applicable to him: He was a scholar and a gentleman.

E. E.

BIBLIOGRAPHY

Boccaccio's *Genealogia deorum.* Quoted from the printed edition of 1481 in the British Museum (=*G.D.*).

The Works of Geoffrey Chaucer, ed. by W. W. Skeat. Oxford, 1894–97. *The Student's Chaucer,* ed. by W. W. Skeat. Oxford, 1897.

Constans, Léopold: *La Légende d'Œdipe.* Paris, 1891.

Hystoire de Thebes. In *Les Histoires de Paul Orose traduites en François.* Printed in 1491 (=*HT*).

Koeppel, Emil: *Lydgate's Story of Thebes. Eine Quellenuntersuchung.* München, 1884.

Lydgate's Fall of Princes, ed. by H. Bergen. E.E.T.S., Extra Series CXXI–CXXIV.

Lydgate's Pilgrimage of the Life of Man, ed. by Furnivall and Miss Locock. E.E.T.S. LXXVII, LXXXIII, XCII.

Lydgate's Reson and Sensuallyte, ed. by E. Sieper. E.E.T.S. Extra Series LXXXIV, LXXXIX.

Lydgate's Saint Edmund and Saint Fremund. In *Altenglische Legenden,* Neue Folge. Heilbronn, 1881 (=*St. Edmund*).

Lydgate's and Burgh's Secrees of old Philisoffres, ed. by R. Steele. E.E.T.S. Extra Series LXVI.

Lydgate's Temple of Glas. ed. by J. Schick. E.E.T.S. Extra Series LX.

Lydgate's Troy Book, ed. by H. Bergen. E.E.T.S. Extra Series XCVII, CIII, CVI.

A New English Dictionary. Oxford, 1884, ff. (=*Oxf. Dict.*).

Le Roman de edipus. Printed early in the sixteenth century in Paris and reprinted in the *Collection Silvestre* in 1858 (=*RE*).

Le Roman de Thèbes, publié par Léopold Constans. Paris, 1890.

Tatlock, J. S. P., and Kennedy, A. G.: *A Concordance to the Complete Works of Chaucer,* 1927.

ten Brink, Bernhard: *Chaucer's Sprache und Verskunst.* 2nd ed. Leipzig, 1899.

Ward, H. L. D.: *A Catalogue of Romances in the Department of MSS. of the British Museum.* London, 1883, ff.

CONTENTS

? ★

The Siege of Thebes

INTRODUCTION

CHAPTER I

§ 1. *The Title of the Poem.* § 2. *The Frame.* § 3. *The Contents.* § 4. *The Sources.* § 5. *The Date.*

§ 1. *The Title of the Poem.*

LYDGATE in his poem twice mentions the name or rather the contents of the poem. In the beginning of Prima Pars he says, turning to Chaucer's pilgrims:

> I wol reherce a story wonderful,
> Towchinge the siege and destruccioun
> Of worthy Thebees the myghty Royal toun (ll. 184–86),

and towards the end of Tercia Pars, addressing the pilgrims for the last time, he reminds them:

> At the gynnyng I took no mor on honde
> Be my promys, in conclusioun,
> But to reherce the destruccioun
> Of myghty Thebes shortly, and no more (ll. 4604–7).

The colophon of MS. Ar. is: "Here endeth the destruccioun of Thebes." Nine MSS. and the two printed texts (Bo. T_1. L_1. Lb. M. Ra. E_1. P. E_2. L_2. Ro.) have substantially the same colophon as Ar.; four MSS. (Di. S. C. T_2.) have: "Here endeth the Sege of Thebes"; MS. I. has: "Heere endith the laste tale of Canterbury maad and told bi Dan Iohn Lidgate Mon" (the rest has been cut away). MSS. Ad_1. and G. have no colophon. In MSS. Ad_2. Ap. Ba. Du. the end of the poem is lost.

Lately the poem has usually been spoken of as "The Story of Thebes," and it is mostly thus referred to in the great Oxford English Dictionary. This change of title was probably due to a misunderstanding of l. 184 quoted above. The "story" mentioned there, which Lydgate says he is going to "reherce," *i.e.* repeat, recite (something heard or read), is the same "story" that he cites again and again in the course of the poem, viz. his chief source, the French prose "roman" (see § 4).[1] His own poem he always alludes to as "my tale" (see ll. 176 and 4716). As a matter of fact, the question of the title has been settled by Lydgate himself, who in his *Fall of Princes* calls our poem "The Sege of Thebes" (see Part I, Temporary Preface, § 1).

"The story" in our poem, as pointed out above, in the great majority of cases refers to the French prose "roman." Exceptionally it refers to other sources drawn upon by the poet, most often to Boccaccio; see *Notes* to ll. 199, 307, 3154–3204.

§ 2. *The Frame of the Poem.*

The *Siege of Thebes* was written by Lydgate to form an additional link in the famous series of the Canterbury Tales composed by Chaucer. As Chaucer never finished the series according to the plan proposed by the host of the Tabard inn and accepted by the pilgrims in the evening before they start on their pilgrimage, but has given us only twenty-four tales of the more than hundred planned, so that the story-telling breaks off even before the pilgrims arrive at Canterbury, there was ample room for an addition. Lydgate did not choose to tack his tale on to the last tale of his admired master: he has preferred to represent it as the first tale on the pilgrims' return journey. As to his meeting with the host and the other pilgrims at Canterbury, and the evident incongruity between the time of their pilgrimage and his own age, see Temporary Preface, § 2 in Part I.

The Prologue is, of course, addressed to the readers of the poem. It is for a great part modelled on Chaucer's Prologue. In the tale itself Lydgate several times alludes to the circumstances in which it is supposed to be told. In three places these allusions are quite explicit: in the opening lines of the first part, 177–86 (182, Of ȝow echon ridyng her beside), towards the end of the third part,

[1] E_1., on the second leaf (a ii) of the first gathering, has: "Prologus. Here begynneth the prologue of the Storye of Thebes." On the second unmarked leaf (originally the sixth leaf) of the same gathering: "Here begynneth the Story of the destruccyon of the Cyte of Thebes." In the title-page of E_2. the poem is designated "the siege and destruccion of the worthy Citee of Thebes." In the Table of Contents the editor speaks of "The Prologue of the storie of Thebes," of the first, second, and third parts of "the siege of Thebes." About the colophons of E_1. and E_2., see above. H. Ward, in his *Catalogue of Romances*, calls our poem "The romance of Thebes." Constans, *La légende d'Œdipe*, p. 367, says "le Siège de Thèbes."

4603–7, and 4520–24, where he refers the pilgrims, with regard to "the gentyllesse of Theseus," to the Knight's Tale, which they have heard "at Depforth in the vale" (cf. *Notes*). See also ll. 316–27. 1043–46. 1057–59. 3519. 3536–37. 4619. Sometimes, however, Lydgate forgets his imaginary surroundings and inserts remarks quite inappropriate to the motley company of pilgrims, *e.g.* ll. 3193–3202, where he tells them to read a work written in Latin by Boccaccio.

§ 3. *The Contents of the Poem.*

The *Siege of Thebes* has 4716 lines, divided into the Prologue and three parts. Lines 1–176 contain the Prologue. The first part, 177–1046, relates the foundation of Thebes by king Amphioun, or, according to other old authors, by Cadmus; the accession of Layus to the crown of Thebes; the exposing of his new-born son; the rearing of the child, who was given the name of Edippus, by king Polyboun of Archadye; Edippus' journey to Thebes to discover his true lineage, during which journey he happens to slay his own father in a disorderly kind of tournament and afterwards encounters and kills the terrible Spynx; his election to be king of Thebes and marriage with the widowed queen Iocasta, his mother; the disclosure of his birth; the unfilial conduct of his two sons Ethiocles and Polymyte, and his (Edippus') miserable death.

The leading subject of the second part (1047–2552) are the disputes of the two brothers about the supremacy in Thebes. Two new actors of great importance are introduced into the tale, Tydeus, the brave and courteous son of the king of Calydoyne, and Adrastus, the mighty king of Arge. A temporary compromise is brought about by the Theban lords, according to which the two brothers are to reign in Thebes alternately, interchanging year by year. Ethiocles, being the elder, remains in power, while Polymyte is obliged to leave the town at once. Riding alone by unknown and deserted paths he comes at night to the palace of Adrastus. The same night Tydeus, who has been banished from Calydoyne, seeks quarter in the courtyard of the palace. Polymyte brusquely refuses to admit him, and the two young men have a regular fight, which calls up king Adrastus. He commands them to deliver up their swords, and on learning their names receives them hospitably. Next day they are, by the good offices of the king, not only reconciled, but made fast friends, true to each other for life. They are married to Adrastus' two beautiful daughters, and he gives up half his kingdom to them. As to Ethiocles, he resolves never to let his brother return to Thebes. At the end of the first year Tydeus goes to Thebes to crave, on the part of his brother-in-law, that the conditions of the compromise shall be fulfilled. In plain and angry terms Ethiocles declines to do so. Every chance of a peaceable agreement is destroyed by his dispatching fifty knights to waylay Tydeus and to slay him. By wonders of bravery, strength, and skill Tydeus kills all these knights except one, who is sent back to Ethiocles to tell him of the defeat of his men. Severely wounded, Tydeus gets upon his horse, and riding on comes in the night to the castle of king Lygurgus. The king's daughter, on the following morning, finds him asleep in the garden of the castle and sees to it that he is taken care of by her women and by the best physicians. Nevertheless he leaves next day, and after a difficult journey reaches Arge, to the great joy of all his friends, and especially of his wife Deiphyle.

The third part (2553–4716) begins with an account of the great preparations for war made by Adrastus for the purpose of assisting his son-in-law, Polymyte, to recover his right, and of the measures of defence busily undertaken by Ethiocles. Both of them collect troops and military stores. Ethiocles strengthens the walls of Thebes. Adrastus calls together a council of war. They decide to ask the advice of the old and prudent bishop Amphiorax as to their chances of victory. Amphiorax, in the strongest terms, warns them not to go to war, because the result would be disastrous to them as well as to himself. He tries to hide himself in a tower, but is betrayed by his wife and taken by the Greeks, who carry him with them on their march. The army is on the point of perishing from want of water. Tydeus and king Campaneus reconnoitring happen to enter a garden, where they find a fair lady nursing a baby, the only son and future heir of king Lygurgus of Trace. Persuaded by Tydeus, she leaves the child, well wrapped about, asleep in the grass and guides him to a river with plenty of water. By Tydeus she is presented to Adrastus, who thanks her and promises to be always at her service. The name of the fair lady is Isyphile, she is the daughter of a king (in the isle of Crete), and had been obliged to flee from her own country, because she had, against the common resolution of the Cretan women, rescued her father from being slain. Now, returning to the garden, she finds the child killed by a venomous serpent. Full of despair and dreading the vengeance of Lygurgus and his queen, she seeks out Tydeus. He immediately repairs to Adrastus. The king, accompanied by all the princes and dukes of his army, rides to the palace of Lygurgus to intercede for Isyphile. His pleading is one of the finest passages of the poem, and he succeeds in obtaining for Isyphile the king's and the queen's pardon. The Greeks then continue their march and at last (l. 3560) pitch their tents in a green meadow under the walls of Thebes. Fresh negotiations are set on foot and carried on between Adrastus and Iocasta, who comes to the Greek camp with her two beautiful daughters, Antigone and Ymeyne. Owing to the stubbornness of Ethiocles these negotiations fall through, and so the fighting begins. Fortune favours, now the Thebans, now the Greeks, but the final issue of the battles and the assaults on the walls quite makes good the prophecy of Amphiorax. The old bishop falls down to hell with his people, the ground opening and closing over them. Tydeus and all the Greek kings and princes, except Adrastus and Campaneus, are slain together with most of the knights. Ethiocles and Polymyte kill each other. The Thebans then elect Creon to be their king. Adrastus sends a wounded knight to Greece to announce the irreparable losses suffered by the Greek army. This calls up his daughters, Argive and Deiphyle, and all the other noble widows to assemble in the town of Arge and to go in procession, barefoot and in black clothes, to Thebes for the purpose of burying their husbands. Creon, however, does not allow the corpses to be buried or burnt, which, of course, doubles the grief of the poor widows. Fortunately Theseus, duke of Athens, returning from a victorious war on Femenye, passes by with his chivalry. On the humble prayers of Adrastus and the ladies he espouses their cause, kills Creon and all his people, thoroughly destroys the town of Thebes and sends Iocasta and her daughters as prisoners to Athens. Even Campaneus is now slain in an assault on the walls. Then at last the obsequies of the Greek princes and knights are performed with due solemnity, and Adrastus and the widowed ladies return to their country. Then follows the peroration.

The third part contains nearly as many lines (2164) as the first and second parts together (2376). From the above short survey it appears that it is only the second half of the third part (from 3560) that answers strictly to the title of the whole poem, "The Siege of Thebes." The first and second parts and, in a more direct way, the first portion of the third part describe the events that in their gradual development lead up to the final catastrophe.[1]

§ 4. *The Sources of the Poem.*

The ultimate medieval source of Lydgate's *Siege of Thebes* (LT) is the French *Roman de Thebes* (RT), written about 1150 in more than 10,000 octosyllabic lines. From this poem are derived several prose versions, varying in length and other respects. One of these versions was printed in Paris by Pierre Sergent in the beginning of the sixteenth century with the title of *le Roman de edipus* (RE) and reprinted in 1858 in the Collection Silvestre. It belongs to the branch of shorter redactions (Constans, *Roman de Thebes*, vol. ii, p. cxxiii ff.). Although in a few unimportant particulars it does not agree with Lydgate's poem, it may be rightly considered as the nearest immediate source extant. Another prose version, also belonging to the shorter redactions (Constans, *op. cit.*, ii, p. cxli), was printed in 1491 with the title of *Hystoire de Thebes* (HT) as part of the first folio volume of *Les histoires de Paul Orose traduites en françois* (see also Koeppel, *Lydgate's Story of Thebes*, p. 52). Koeppel, who had no opportunity of seeing RE, regards this version (HT) as the source of our poem. In a foot-note, p. 60, however, he refers to RE and says it may possibly be still more closely related to LT than HT is. HT cannot be the source of Lydgate's poem. It deviates from RE and LT in several respects. Very many passages are more fully developed in HT than in RE; the expressions are in general unlike those of RE and LT, even where the extent and the meaning of the passages are alike. HT uses *oratio directa* in many passages where RE has *oratio obliqua*. Pious reflexions and warnings are a prominent characteristic of HT as against RE and often form separate paragraphs superscribed "Le translateur." There is plenty of moralisation in Lydgate's poem, but it is of the poet's own manufacture. The numerous extracts from RE given in the

[1] Lydgate in the prologue of his rhymed translation of Guido de Colonna's Latin prose work, *Historia Destructionis Troiæ*, designates this work as the Troy Book (Book I, l. 148, Troye Boke), which title has stuck to his own poem. Towards the end of the fifth book he speaks of his poem as the Siege of Troy, saying that he will pray day and night for Henry V (3462–64):

> þat whylom gaf me in commaundement,
> Nat ȝore a-go, in his faderes tyme,
> þe sege of Troye on my maner to ryme.

The first book and two-thirds of the second are devoted to events prior to the beginning of the siege.

Notes will make it easy to verify the close resemblance, not seldom the literal agreement between the French redaction and Lydgate's poem. A few instances of coincidence in single words or phrases may be added here: l. 1439 Tweyne mantels: RE deux manteaulx; 1618 in wodes and Ryverys: RE en bois et en riuiere; 2188 That nervaile was: RE que cestoit grant merueilles a veoir; 2194 gret prouesse: RE grant proesse; 2263 anguysshous: RE angoisseux; 2330 she . . . touched hym ful softe: RE elle le crolla vng petit. HT has nothing to correspond. Still there are undoubtedly in LT passages which agree more closely with HT than with RE. To some of these attention has been directed in the Notes (741–46, 1807–10, 3757–63, 4022–46). A remarkable instance is apparently "Polimites" in HT, "Polymyte(s)" in LT, against "Policenes" in RE. But it is possible that Lydgate's French original followed the HT redaction on this point, or, what is still more reasonable, Lydgate, who knew the name and story of Polymite(s) from Chaucer's *Troilus*, V, 1488, 1507, may have substituted the name for Policenes. We must not forget that the redaction of the poem preserved in the print of Pierre Sergent is not the identical version that Lydgate had before him. This was a redaction, which in the main agreed very closely with that of the print, but at the same time presented some points of coincidence with HT. This redaction was the immediate source of Lydgate's poem.[1]

From the redaction of the French "roman" referred to, Lydgate has taken nearly two-thirds of his poem. About one-third is occupied by Lydgate's additions. These are of two kinds, independent additions drawn from his own creative imagination or his experience and general store of knowledge, about a quarter of the poem, and additions derived from the Bible and authors such as Seneca, Martianus de Capella, Boccaccio, Chaucer, about one-fifteenth of the poem.

Lydgate's most important source of the latter kind is Boccaccio's *De genealogia deorum* (G.D.): 186–243, 293–315, 855–66, 1272–79, 3171–87, 3510–35 (cf. 3537–43). The two other Latin works of the Italian author are rarely quoted: *De claribus mulieribus* 3188 ff., 3193–207, *De casibus virorum illustrium* 1753–55. The *Bible* is quoted seven times; the Old Testament four times: Esdre (Neemye)

[1] It is possible that one of the numerous MSS. of *Roman de Edipus* (cf. Constans, *op. cit.*, and note on l. 1716) will be found to come near Lydgate's actual source.—E.E.

1729–36, the Proverbs of Salamon 1743–46, the Books of the Kings 1753–55, Isaiah 4660–67; the New Testament three times: St. Luke 794–801, 4679–82, Revelations 4660–67. Chaucer is Lydgate's source four times: 1377–86, 3188–92, 4463–4540, 4562–64; Marcian de Capelle, *De nuptiis Philologiæ et Mercurii*, once: 826–42; Senyk once: 994–1001 (see *Notes*). There is a difficulty in exactly separating Lydgate's independent additions from the other two sources of his poem, because the different elements are sometimes inextricably interwoven with each other.

§ 5. *The Date of the Poem.*

The *Siege of Thebes* was a work of Lydgate's mature manhood. In the prologue he states (l. 93) that he was "nyȝ fyfty ȝere of age" when he met with the pilgrims at Canterbury and was called upon by "her gouernour, the host" to tell a tale on their return journey. Lydgate is held to have been born about 1370 (see Schick, *Temple of Glas*, p. lxxxvii). If this is right, the date of the pilgrimage would be about 1420, and the date of the beginning of the poem would no doubt be about the same as that of the pilgrimage. But the date of the poem can be determined much more accurately by the help of allusions in it to historical events. The *terminus a quo* for the finishing of the poem is May 1420, when the treaty of Troyes was concluded between England and France. It is quite evident that Lydgate, when he wrote ll. 4690–4703, had learnt not only the fact that there was peace between the two countries, but also the exact terms of the important 24th paragraph of the treaty, as he was enabled to translate and insert it into his poem. Cf. Thebes 4702 f.:

> Forto reforme a-twixe Regyouns
> Pees and quyet, concord and vnytè,

with the words of the said paragraph: "Item, ut Concordia, Pax, & Tranquillitas inter prædicta Franciæ & Angliæ Regna perpetuo futuris temporibus observentur," and 4690 ff.:

> But the venym and the violence
> Of strif, of werre, of contek, and debat
> . . . .
> Shal be proscript and voyded out of place,

with: "& obvietur Occasionibus et Principiis, ex quibus inter eadem Regna, quod absit, Debata, Dissensiones seu Discordiæ futuris possent temporibus exoriri." Also in the peroration of the *Troy*

Book Lydgate refers to the terms of the said treaty. Cf. V, 3410–12:

> To maken oon þat longe hath be tweyne:
> I mene þus, þat Yngelond and Fraunce
> May be al oon, with-oute variaunce,

and V, 3435 f.:

> Pes & quiete, boþe nyȝe and ferre,
> With-oute strife, debat, or any werre.

The *terminus ante quem* is determined by the death of Henry V on August 31st, 1422, for it is evident that Lydgate could not possibly have composed the fourteen above-mentioned lines, so full of joy at the happy ending of the war and of hopefulness for the future, if the bright political outlook had been already darkened by the sudden death of England's youthful king. And if the poem had been still in his hands at that time, we cannot but suppose that he would have struck out or altered the passage in question. As this has not been done, he was evidently no longer in a position to do so. Copies must have been made and issued. Accordingly, some time must have elapsed between the finishing of the poem and the king's death. These arguments lead to the conclusion that the greater part of the *Siege of Thebes* was written before the end of 1421. See Temporary Preface, § 6, in Part I.

The time when the poem was begun cannot be fixed with certainty, for it is, of course, impossible to say how many months it took Lydgate to compose it. He was now at the height of his training and skill as a versifier, having just completed his *Troy Book*, a poem of 30,117 lines. The *Siege of Thebes* was not, like the *Troy Book* and the *Fall of Princes*, made to order, for the pleasure of some noble patron; it had its origin in a happy idea of his own and associated him, as it were, with his venerated, never-forgotten master. On both these grounds its composition must have been a labour of love to its author. The probability would seem to be that the composition of the poem did not extend over a very long period. On the other hand, we may suppose that *Thebes* was not begun until after the completion of the *Troy Book*. This poem was finished in the eighth year of Henry V (cf. V, 3366–76), and after the treaty of peace in May 1420 had been concluded (cf. *supra*), and after the marriage on June 2nd between Henry V and "Kateryne," daughter of King Charles of France (cf. V, 3420–26), *i.e.* in "the summer, or early fall, of 1420" (Bergen, *Troy Book*, Part I, Introductory Note, p. ix). It seems probable that Lydgate allowed himself some breathing-space after the completion of a poem of more than 30,000 decasyllabic lines, and that his *Siege of Thebes* was begun not earlier than the autumn of 1420. The conclusion would be that at least the greater part of the poem was written in the course of 1421.

The statement in the Prologue that Lydgate was nearly fifty in the middle of April of the year when the pilgrimage was undertaken helps to determine more exactly the date of Lydgate's birth. We may assume that the poet refers to the April of the year in which the poem was begun, or, what is the same thing, when the Prologue was written, for undoubtedly the Prologue was the first portion written. If the poem was begun in the autumn of 1420, we may conclude that the April of 1420 is meant. But if Lydgate was nearly fifty (*i.e.* forty-nine) in April 1420, it is safe to assume that his fifty-first birthday fell before the end of the year, *i.e.* that he was born in 1370. If the *Siege* was begun in or after the middle of April 1421, which is not impossible, the year of his birth would be 1371.

CHAPTER II

§ 1. *Lydgate's Treatment of his Sources.* § 2. *His Independent Additions.* § 3. *His Composition and Style.*

§ 1. *His Treatment of his Sources.*

HIS French source (RE), the identity of which he never reveals, Lydgate treats with great freedom, very often enlarging or shortening its text, and omitting particulars that he regarded as unimportant. A detailed comparison of Lydgate's *Thebes* with RE shows that the passages of the poem which offer considerable enlargements, are of nearly the same extent as those in which Lydgate follows his French text more literally, *c.* 1570 against *c.* 1660. His method of working in *Thebes* is in marked contrast to that maintained by him in his immediately preceding poem, the *Troy Book*. Here he follows his French original much more closely, abstaining in general from enlargements as well as from independent additions (cf. Sidney Lee in *Dict. Nat. Biogr.*, s. Lydgate). The contributions drawn from Boccaccio and other openly acknowledged sources he handles much more tenderly. The words of the writings quoted are rendered much more faithfully. Altogether, they take up no great space in the poem, *c.* 310 lines, but they are not unimportant, because they add to its variety.

Lydgate shows his cultured taste in altogether omitting some features of revolting brutality that he found in his sources. RE relates, in conformity with the old French poem *Roman de Thebes*, that Edippus' sons threw their father alive into a pit, leaving him to die there. According to Lydgate the unfilial deed was not committed until after Edippus' death (see 1010–12 and *Notes*). When Tydeus was mortally wounded by an arrow, he demanded of his companions that they should bring him the head of his slayer, and (says Boccaccio, *G. D.*) when he got the gory head in his hands, sank his teeth into the neck and devoured it like a wild beast. This disgusting detail, which is, besides, in glaring contrast with the character of Tydeus as depicted in the poem, is not mentioned by Lydgate (see 4235–39 and *Notes*). In other cases incidents or speeches are toned down by the poet so as to agree better with the higher standard of his own time. For examples see *Notes* to 533–44 and 4463–90. The statement of RE and HT that the rush of the soldiers into the river was such as to cause an inundation is wisely omitted by Lydgate (l. 3117 ff.).

On the other hand, the poet occasionally leaves out details, the graceful or tender import of which makes them worthy, it seems, of being preserved; see *e.g.* 1468–72 with *Notes*. The poet is profuse in praising the beauty of the young princesses, but that womanly trait—their modest embarrassment at meeting the two strange knights which calls forth blushes doubling their beauty—has escaped his notice or not awakened his interest. In Pars Secunda 2254 ff., Lydgate describes, in close agreement with RE, the painful ride of the wounded Tydeus after he had successfully fought with the Theban knights sent out by Ethiocles to kill him, but he passes by one detail very characteristic of his hero, the valiant and tender-hearted Tydeus. RE continues: Tydeus fears he is dying, and thinks with regret of his wife Deiphile, his companion Policenes, and his father (-in-law) Adrascus, whom he loved much, and as he rode on, his thoughts went out to one after the other.

Sometimes Lydgate, forgetting that he is writing a poem, speaks like a chronicler who feels bound accurately to register conflicting information on a detail under debate, *e.g.* 3188 ff. He has spent thirty lines (3154–83) on the early fortunes of Isyphile, which are of small importance to the subject of the poem; nevertheless, he cannot abstain from adding twenty lines (3188–207) in order to relate an episode of her life taken from another source and irreconcilable with what he has already told, and to discuss the irrelevant question of her father's name, which is of no consequence whatever. The same objection holds good with regard to 293–304, although this ancient variant of the origin of Thebes may pass notice more easily, as it contains the medieval etymological explanation of the name Boece. And in ll. 3822–3915 Lydgate has seized upon and treated at length the silly episode of the tame tiger, the favourite of the Thebans and especially of king Ethiocles, the death of which at the hands of the Greeks is made the immediate cause of the outbreak of active hostilities.

§ 2. *Lydgate's independent additions*, i.e. those not drawn from an acknowledged source, form an important part of the poem. Most of them contain moralisations of different kinds.

1. Again and again the author inculcates the idea that truth, in the long run, is always stronger than falseness. Out of the struggle between the two, truth will, in Lydgate's firm opinion, always issue as victor; see *e.g.* ll. 2077–78:

> For this the fyn: falshede shal not availe,
> Ageynes trouth in feeld to hold batayle,

and 1763–70:

> It (truth) may be clipsed and derked be disceyte,
> . . . .
> But at the last it wol clerly shyne,
> . . . .
> For it in soth of kyngdames and of Reawmes
> Is berer vp and conseruatrice
> From al Meschief . . .

For other moral reflexions see ll. 1019–46 (on the duty of children towards their parents) and 3414–51 (reflexions on life and death).

2. Of particular importance are the poet's repeated admonitions to kings and princes to bear themselves with affability and kindness towards their subjects; disdain and haughtiness breed hatred, although the subjects may not dare show it openly in the king's presence; see *e.g.* ll. 244–61. In ll. 258–61 Lydgate pictures simply but graphically a scene from contemporary public life, which he may himself have witnessed, perhaps more than once in his youth, with inward disapproval:

And thus ful ofte gendred is Envye
In folkes hertes, of soleyntè and pryde,
For swich as list nat onys loke a-syde
To Reward hem whan they lowe loute.

Cf. also the following lines (262–71):

And ageyn kynde it is, out of doute,
That eny hed, be recorde of the wyse,
Shuld the foot of disdeyn despyse,
Which bereþ hym vp, who so can take hede,
And Susteneth in his moste nede
As his Pyler and his sowpowayle.
For fynaly, ne were the porayle
her berer vp and Supportacioun,
Farwel lordshyp and domynacioun,
Thorgh-oute the world, of euery hegh estat!

Neither should kings squander the nation's means on their pleasures, oppressing their subjects by heavy taxation; see *e.g.* ll. 2688–94:

And in a prince it is ful gret offence,
As clerkes seyn, and a gret repreef,
Suffre his puple lyven at mescheef.
It is ful hevy and greuous in her thoght
ȝif he habound and they han right noght.
he may not both possede good and herte,
He to be riche and Seen his puple smerte.

These reproaches probably refer chiefly to Richard II, whose character and administrative as well as political measures caused so much discontent and at last brought about his ruin. They may, however, also have some bearing on Henry IV, seeing that Lydgate specially emphasises the duty of "conquerors" to practise liberality and bounty. See ll. 2701 ff.:

For which eche prince, lord and gouernour,
And specialy euery Conquerour,
Lat hym be war, for al his hegh noblesse,
That bountè, Fredom, plentè, and largesse,
Be on accord that they his brydel lede,
Lest of his puple, whan he hath most nede,
He be defrauded; whan he is but allone,
Than is to late for to make his mone.

Cf. the proclamation of Henry IV at his landing in England to make war on Richard II, promising that though he is a conqueror, he shall deprive no man of his property: "It is not my will that no man think that by way of conquest I would disinherit any man of his heritage" (Stubbs, *Const. Hist.*, iii, p. 13).

The allusions to temporary events, to which may be added those in ll. 3425–32, 3655–73, and 4690–703 (see *Notes*), give Lydgate's poem an added interest to us and they may help to explain the popularity it enjoyed among the poet's contemporaries. They show us Lydgate as a patriot and as a man with a warm heart and sympathy for the humble and the oppressed. It sometimes looks as if the story did not interest Lydgate so much in itself as for the opportunities it gave him to plead the cause of truth, justice, and clemency.

3. Astrological expositions form a third—very subordinate—class of independent additions. The principal specimen of this kind occurs in the first part of the poem (ll. 358–99), where king Layus consults "dyvynoures, phylosophres wise, famous physiciens, and wel expert Astronomyens" as to his unborn child's future fate, and receives the crushing verdict "that with his swerd his fader shal be slawe" (398). A great number of astronomical terms Lydgate may have learnt from Chaucer's *Astrolabe*, but it is evident from the last two lines of the passage quoted that he had also studied some astrological work. Also the unfortunate magician (2815), prophet (2808), and bishop Amphiorax dabbles in astrology (2816–18, 4052–54), although he is certainly represented by Lydgate as having more dealings with the devil and other infernal powers than with the celestial bodies and their dominances.

4. Classical mythology of a sort is a favourite subject of Lydgate's pen. Part of his disquisitions are derived from his own store of classical learning, other scraps are borrowed from Boccaccio (853–74) and Martianus (826–43). Pluto and Proserpina are said to reign in hell (4042–44), whether as co-regents or as subordinates of the devil ("devel" 4039) or Lucifer (4662) we are not told.

§ 3. *Lydgate's Composition and Style.*

1. Lydgate's style has been very severely criticised by some modern editors. Professor Schick in the Introduction to his excellent edition of the *Temple of Glas*, in which he breaks so much new ground in the field of Lydgate research, says, p. cxxxiv: "Drawled-out and incompact, are the first epithets one would most readily apply to the style of the monk's productions. His sentences run on aimlessly, without definite stop, and it is often difficult to say where a particular idea begins or ends. . . . He knows little of

logic connection, or distinct limitation of his sentences, and the notion of artistic structure . . . is entirely foreign to him." Sieper, *Reson and Sensuallyte*, ii, p. 44, quotes this statement and fully endorses the description, which is indeed well founded. However, it is too sweeping. Not all the passages of the monk's productions are constructed in the faulty manner described, not all of them are equally open to the above severe judgment. There are unimpeachable sentences in all of them. Sieper, *l.c.*, remarks that "the natural prolixity of the monk and the inconsistency of his syntactical constructions are less prominent in our poem (*Reson and Sensuallyte*) than in some of his other works." The same remark holds good also with regard to *Thebes*. This poem is on several accounts the most readable of Lydgate's epic poems. It is much shorter than the *Troy Book* or *Fall of Princes*, being little more than a sixth of the former and an eighth of the latter. The tiresome repetitions that weigh down the longer poems are for the most part absent in *Thebes*. And the variety of the story of Œdipus and his sons, containing elements tragic and heroic, keeps up the interest in the poem. There certainly are also in *Thebes* long and loosely constructed passages (see *infra*), but they are on the whole exceptions. And the logical connection of the sentences being decidedly superior to the syntactical, there is generally not the slightest difficulty in following and appreciating the ideas presented. The poetical sentiments may be scattered and far between and their expression not always artistically happy, but the verdict formulated by Sieper, *op. cit.*, ii. p. v ("it cannot be too clearly asserted that as poetry Lydgate's works are absolutely worthless,") is severe even to downright injustice.

Ten Brink, *Geschichte der englischen Litteratur*, ii, p. 232 f., and even Schick, in spite of their strictures, acknowledge that Lydgate possesses some poetical merit. Ten Brink says: "Lydgate besitzt eine grosse Leichtigkeit des poetischen Ausdrucks und trifft nicht selten das richtige Wort. . . . In seinen Dichtungen findet sich manches Tüchtige, ja in seiner Art Treffliche. . . ." Schick says, *Temple of Glas*, clvi: "There is certainly many a felicitous line and many a poetical sentiment or piece of imagery to be found in his works that would not deface the finest page of a true poet." And the admiration of Lydgate's contemporaries and later generations must be remembered. In his lifetime he enjoyed the encouragement of noble patrons and he was undoubtedly highly valued. The great number of MSS. of his works bears witness to his popularity. The comparison with the incomparable Chaucer has been the bane of Lydgate's reputation as a poet. Of the difference between himself and his master, Lydgate was only too well aware, and he is doubtless sincere in his humble confession, *Troy Book*, V, 3528 ff.:

> Was neuer noon to þis day alyue
> To rekne alle, boþe ȝonge & olde
> þat worþi was his ynkhorn for to holde.

2. Lydgate has been reproached for his want of humour. Humour is a rare, very rare gift of the gods. Many poets of acknowledged rank have been without it. Certainly Lydgate was not one of the favoured recipients. Neither did he altogether lack it. The character of his larger works affords little scope for humour. With regard to *Thebes* the reproach is palpably unjust. There is an immense difference between the drastic stories, sarcastically told by uncultured or half-cultured persons, in which Chaucer's humour is so brilliantly displayed, and the sad history of Edippus and his sons, in which the principal actors are kings and queens, princes and princesses. It is pathos, not humour, that tragic drama calls for, and the poet cannot fairly be denied the merit of having brought into his tale more than one pathetic touch. The Prologue—without comparison the best part of Lydgate's own work in the poem—is the only portion fit for a lighter and merrier treatment. Lydgate has done his best to adapt his style to the situation. Of course he takes his cue from Chaucer. The situation being quite analogous to that pictured so admirably by the master, what better could the disciple do than imitate him? But he has not copied him. His sketch of the Host, while in perfect conformity with the portrait painted by Chaucer, adds new and original characteristics of the man in question. Our monk's reception on his arrival at the Canterbury inn is well drawn. The Host, with his usual self-importance and assurance, speaks and acts as if he stood in his own inn-yard in Southwark. His instincts as an innkeeper are at once stirred by the appearance of a new guest, who looks "so pale, al deuoyde of blood", and he rolls off a long bill of fare for his choice. Unbidden, he adds hints as to his accommodation for the night and concludes by mentioning several household remedies to be used in case the guest should feel physically indisposed. This officiousness and all-round wisdom is quite in keeping with the character of the

Host, whose acquaintance we have made in *C. T.* On popular terms employed by him see Chap. III, § 2.

3. Lydgate has been, in our times, represented as a sincere admirer of womankind and as a champion always ready to enter the lists against her detractors. And indeed in his writings he praises the virtues of woman in no measured terms. His *Reson and Sensuallyte* has the following three passages:

6164 ff.:

To declare, thus I mene,
That youthe in his grene age
Varieth ofte of corage,
Redy for to chaunge sone
After the nature of the mone;
But of chaunge the properte
Longeth nat, in no degre,
Vn-to woman of Nature,
They be so stable and so sure
In ther trouthe to persever,
For ther hertys chaunge never.

6343 ff.:

And who considereth euerydell,
Ther is no wyght kan do so well
To holde A Mene in euery thing,
As women kan in ther werkyng.
They be so prudent and so wyse,
What euere thing they shal devyse,
And in what thing they shal procede,
A Mene dooth her brydel lede.

6361 ff.:

Her counsayl ys of swych noblesse,
And touchinge also secrenesse
Ther is no wight more prive,
And what ye lyst to ha secre,
Tel yt a woman boldely,
And thow maist truste feythfully
Thow shalt never here yt more,
Thogh at hir herte yt sitte sore.

His translation of Guido's *Troy Book*, made for Henry V, offered many opportunities, and he seized them. In a work meant for the reading of ladies of the highest rank he could not let the author's malicious and ill-natured remarks pass unnoticed. He answers them in all three places.

Troy Book, I, 2098–2135:

Allas, whi wolde he so cursedly write
Ageynes hem, or with hem debate!
I am riȝt sory in englische to translate
Reprefe of hem, or any euel to seye;

. . . .

Þei ben so gode and parfyte euerechon,
To rekne alle, I trowe þer be nat on,
But þat þei ben in wille and herte trewe.
For þouȝ amonge þei chese hem lovis newe,
Who considreth, þei be no þing to blame;
For ofte tyme þei se men do þe same.

. . . .

Troy Book, II, 3562 ff.:

To alle women I am so moche bounde:
þei ben echon so goodly and so kynde,
I dar of hem nat seyen þat·I fynde
Of Guydo write þoruȝ-out Troye book.

Ib., III, 4361 ff.:

For I dar wel affermen by þe rode,
Ageyn oon badde ben an hundrid gode;
And þouȝ som oon double be & newe,
It hindreth nat to hem þat be trewe.

In *Thebes* there are two passages in praise of woman, ll. 2843–44 and 4448–57. The former refers to Amphiorax's wife:

She was so trewe, as wommen ben echon,
And also cloos and mwet as a ston.

The second treats of the Greek widows, princesses and other noble ladies, who walked barefoot to Thebes to bury their husbands.

In the passages quoted from the three poems, all written before 1422, Lydgate spends his praises for truth, faithfulness, prudence, moderation, secrecy on womankind in general, urging repeatedly that they apply to every woman. In *Reson and Sensuallyte*, 6164 ff., he compares young men with young women, reproaching the former with being ready to change "After the nature of the mone", whereas the latter are by nature "so stable and so sure In her trouthe to persever". In *Reson and Sensuallyte*, 6361 ff., he advises whoever wishes to keep something secret to tell it to a woman, as he may then be sure never to hear of it. This is, of course, irony and was certainly accepted as such by an intelligent contemporary reader. But it is irony of so ingenuous and delicate a kind that it may almost be called humour. A similar remark may be made concerning *Thebes*, 4448–57, where the poet utters some surprise, saying that it was "an vncouth thyng" not to find among one or two thousand women a single one who was not true-hearted. His ever-recurring "echon" is his little joke. In *Thebes* Lydgate discovers his real opinion of woman by saying of Amphiorax (2869–70) that he was a fool to endanger his life by disclosing his plan to his wife.

Lydgate is no partial champion of the fair sex. He was wise enough on the whole to see that men and women are much the same sort of human beings, both showing a mixture of good and bad qualities.

4. Lydgate has a copious vocabulary, which often leads him to indiscriminate profusion. The use of two synonymous words to enforce an idea is a frequent and quite legitimate stylistic feature in ancient as well as in modern literature. It is not rare in Chaucer. But Lydgate carries it to excess, employing it even where there is no logical stress on the idea. It has become a mannerism and a prominently characteristic feature of his poetry. A long list of instances is given by Sieper, *Reson and Sensuallyte*, ii, 49 ff. Here are some select examples from *Thebes*; many combinations are met with more than once in our poem: "paleys and mansioun" 11, "wonder and merveil" 195, "wild and rage" 431, "serch and seke" 439, "werre or stryff" 677, "whisper neither rowne" 695, "grounde and cause" 943, "counsel non nor rede" 953, "in quyete and in pees" 1083, "quyete and reste" 1107, "maat and wery" 1170, "chief and principal" 1244, "trist and mournyng" 1869, "wood and furious" 1961, "vntrouth and falsnesse" 2056, "rehercen owther telle" 2426, "wisdam and sapience" 2883, "clamour and noyse" 2933, "pur and clene" 3628, "worship and honour" 4124, "parte nat nor seuere" 4143, "slaughter and occisioun" 4204, "thought and sorowe" 4614, etc. Sometimes one of the doublets is of English and the other of French origin; sometimes both are English or both are French. Occasionally combinations of three synonyms occur, as "contek, werre and striff" 1035.

5. Lydgate shows much inventiveness in varying his expressions in referring to his principal source, the French *Roman de Edipus* (RE), whose title he never mentions.[1] For aught his readers learn, it may just as well be a Latin or Italian as a French work. The variations in expression are connected with the poet's want of a rhyme-word. The most usual references are (the) story and myn autour: "the story seith certein" 341, "the story can devyse" 361, "in storie as is tolde" 535, "Thow the story writ not the maner howh" 582, "in story as I fynde" 614, "in story as is kouth" 1197, "the story specifies" 1507, "as the story lerys" 1547, "In the story as it is conprehendid" 1637, "the story can ȝou teche"

[1] Lydgate is here in accordance with the custom of his time, followed also by Chaucer, for literary men to keep the secret of their literary dependency from their readers.

1995, "the story telleth vs" 2608, "the story maketh mynde" 3146, "the story doth expresse" 3862, "And as the story liketh to declare" 4437, etc., "And as myn autour writ in wordys pleyn" 877, "And as myn auctour liketh to devise" 1003, "As seith myn autour" 1266, "And her myn autour makeþ rehersaille" 3154, "As myn Autour wel reherce kan" 4232, "And as myn Autour doth clerly certifie" 4426, "as myn auctour liketh to compyle" 4611, "As writ myn auctour and bochas both two" 199, etc. Then there are more general references: "And bookes seyn" 1002, "For it is nat declared in my boke" 1505, "as bookes specifye" 2809, "But as I fynde" 1506, "as mad is mencioun" 3005, "lik as it is founde" 4391, "lik as I rede" 4417, etc. Most of these references are formed so as to rhyme with the preceding or following line. But there is, besides, a number of rather meaningless, empty phrases, in the second half of lines, inserted for the sole purpose of rhyming, pure expletives: "in sentence" 197, 366, 794, 2976, etc., "in sentement" 1903, 2467, 4399 (both phrases are characteristically Lydgatean), "who that can aduerte" 251, "be recorde of the wyse" 263, "who so can take hede" 265, "in conclusioun" 69, 285, "to speke in special" 396, "platly this no les" 1777, "platly this no phage" 453, "ȝif I shall not feyne" 4345, etc.

6. Lydgate sometimes embodies his practical wisdom in proverbial sayings, *e.g.*

1014.	Of Cursid stok cometh vnkynde blood.
1016.	Al be the Roose grow out of a thorn.
1790 f.	But lete his brother blowen in an horn, Wher that hym lyst, or pypen in a red.
2961 f.	But ȝouth allas be counsail wil not wyrke, For which ful ofte he stumbleth in the dyrke.
4458 f.	For seelde in feldys groweth eny corn, But ȝif some wede spryng vp þer-among.

7. Lydgate's long rambling sentences and loose syntax have often been criticised, and they have already been mentioned in this chapter. One sentence may do service as principal and subordinate at the same time. Anacolouthia are frequent. It is not always easy to say under what heading a construction should be placed; sometimes we may hesitate whether the copula has been omitted or the poet has lost his thread and we have an anacolouthon before us.

A typical instance of a long loosely constructed sentence is the passage ll. 1–65, in which no full-stop is marked in the printed text. Almost as good an example is offered by the following ll. 66–91.

Other examples are found in Tydeus' speech to Ethiócles, ll. 1906–31, 1932–44, and in Ethiocles' reply, ll. 1965–87.

Cases of anacolouthia are pointed out in the notes to ll. 253, 726 ff., 1032–38, 1728–41. Other examples are 79–82, 837–42, 1143–50, 1252–57, 2495–500, 2965–70, 4704–9. Not rarely a present participle is used (in a very loose way) instead of a clause, though there is no antecedent to which it can be referred. For examples see note to l. 98. A similar case is found ll. 3316 ff. ("Ȝe be welcome to ȝoure owne place, Thankyng hertly . . ."). In other cases a present participle is co-ordinate with a clause, as in ll. 2832 ff., 3270, 3867.

Sudden change from direct to indirect speech or *vice versâ* occurs; *e.g.* ll. 92 ff. ("I answerde my name was Lydgate . . . Come to this toune to do my pilgrimage, As I haue hight"), 1341 f. ("And shortly seide, it geyneth not to stryve; That of force he shal devoide blyve"). See also ll. 652–56 and 3794–99 (with note). Change from present to preterite also occurs, as ll. 1844 f., 2633 (see *Notes*), 3739 ff. ("she made first hir went . . . And they receyve her"). Of examples of sudden change from singular to plural may be mentioned ll. 3553–54 ("warned euery man To be redy in al the hast they kan") and 3669 f. ("many a-noþer that is her present, Of ȝoure trespas that ben Innocent").

Omission of the copula is frequently met with. See notes to ll. 18–19, 2220 and 3212.

Absolute constructions are of common occurrence. Combinations of a present or a past participle or (more rarely) an adjective and a noun or pronoun are so used, *e.g.* "The fyn concludyng" 792, "They requeryng" 2857, "aforn y-rekned his hondes" 707, "wounded the feet" 973, "barbyd þe visage" 4440, "tournyd vp the white" 4482, "with bitter teeres dewed al her face" 1867, "beerdlees al his Chyn" 33.

Lydgate's word-order frequently differs from what we may suppose to have been the natural one in ordinary prose. Sieper, *Reson and Sensuallyte*, ii, 58 f., calls attention to the common occurrence of "inversion"; especially often an adverb or adverbial phrase or sometimes some other part of the sentence, as the object, is moved to a place before the conjunction introducing the clause to which it belongs. This kind of inversion is very common in *Thebes*, e.g. "Bexperience as it is ofte kouth" 706 (cf. 721), "For a tyme in Ioye thogh they floure" 852, "And, in bokes as sondry clerkes write" 880, "Of þe clok that it drogh to nyne" 1050, "To the gardyne til she is repeyred" 3211. Cf. also 342, 737, 738, 1059, 1218–20, 1887, 3511–13, 3939, 4545, etc. The object is placed before the conjunction in 2283 ("The goodly place whan that he byheld").

Similarly, an adverb or adverbial phrase is placed before a relative pronoun, *e.g.* "with lyf or deth which we shal dareyn" 656, "To Athenes that kam with Palamoun" 3521, "Of ȝoure trespas that ben Innocent" 3670. Cf. also the following cases: "Out of the Cyte But lyve in exile" 1097 f., "After lygurgus born forto ben hayr" 3366, "He vnto hir be ordre wold not spare his auenturis fully to declare" 2371 f., "And ageyn kynde it is out of doute, That eny hed, *be recorde of the uyse*, Shuld . . ." 262 ff.

A few isolated instances of abnormal word-order may be added: "of Mercurye þe soote sugred harpe" 273, "with his pylled nolle The pardowner" 32 f., "at the hil of the woode Rage" 2374 (cf. *Notes*), "Til that he fond a tyme for to preye Conuenyent for ysyphilee" 3452 f. (for "a tyme conuenyent").

CHAPTER III

THE LANGUAGE OF "THEBES"

§ 1. *Phonology and Accidence.*

As no MS. of *Thebes* is the author's autograph, no certain conclusions can be drawn from the spellings. If the object is to determine Lydgate's own forms, an examination of the language must be based on rhymes and metre.

1. *Phonology.*

e-sounds.

Lydgate as a rule keeps the close and the open variety of the long *e* (ẹ̄ and ę̄) apart. The lists of rhymes in -*ē*, -*ēre*, etc. sufficiently prove this. There are no doubt a few rhymes which must be classed as impure, but similar examples are found also in Chaucer's works. Thus there are seven rhymes between O.E. (O.Fr.) ẹ̄ and *ēa* (*hēde* "heed": *dede* "deed,"[1] etc.) and two between O.Fr. ę̄ and O.E. *ē*

[1] For references see the rhyme-lists.

(*mene* "means" : *grene*, etc.). But *leve* s. "leave" : *greve* v. is to be compared with similar rhymes in Chaucer (ten Brink, § 26, note).

O.E. ǣ^2 (W. Germ. *ā*) as a rule rhymes with itself or with ẹ̄ (O.E. *ē*, etc.). In fourteen cases it rhymes with O.E. *ēa*. In two of these, however, the rhyme word is *leue* s. "leave." The normal sound in Lydgate's pronunciation was no doubt ẹ̄. The open sound may be due to influence from Chaucer.

O.E. ǣ^1 (W. Germ. *ai* with *i*-mutation) rhymes with ę̄ and ẹ̄. Chaucer occasionally rhymes ǣ^1 with ẹ̄. The pronunciation of ǣ^1 varied a good deal in Middle English. In Lydgate's dialect it may have been close. Lydgate uses the close variety to a greater extent than Chaucer.

The rhyme *ek* : *Grek* proves ẹ̄ for *ek*.

There is in *Thebes* one rhyme between ẹ̄ and *ī* : *desyris* : *Ryveris*. On this typically Lydgatean rhyme see Schick, p. lxi f.

Shortening of ǣ^1 has given *a* in *ladde* pret., *lad*, *shad* pp.; *e* in *smette* (: *mette*).

Shortening of ǣ^2 has given *a* in *adrad* pp. (: *mad*), *rad* pp. (: *sad*).

A remarkable form is *lyst* "lest," which does not occur in rhyme, but is so common in the MSS. that it would seem to go back to Lydgate's own MS.

The word *die* appears twice in rhyme with *ey* (*deye* : *leye*, *seye*), once with *ī* (*dye* : *replie*).

There are in *Thebes* two rhymes between Fr. *-ende* (*diffende*, *descende*) and *wende* pret. "thought," three between *ende* s. and *wende* inf. or pres. We may perhaps conclude that the *e* of *ende* and *wende* (to wend) was long, while that of the pret. *wende* was short.

-ę̄we and *-ẹ̄we* are not rhymed together. There are three *ę̄we*-rhymes, twelve *-ẹwe*-rhymes. Evidently the two diphthongs were kept apart. There are nine rhymes between French words such as *due*, *eschewe*, *swe*, *remwe*, etc., but none between these French words and English words in *-ę̄we*. We must conclude that *trewe*, *newe*, etc. did not rhyme with *dewe* "due," *eschewe*, etc.

o-sounds.

The close and the open variety of the long *ō* are generally kept apart. Some rhymes between ọ̄ and ǭ (as *do* : *fro*, *to* : *fro*) occur. Lydgate seems to allow himself this liberty more often than Chaucer. The words *so* and *two* rhyme with ọ̄ and ǭ. The pronunciation varied. Chaucer rhymes them with ọ̄ and ǭ. Rhymes such as *cold* : *gold*, *tolde* : *sholde* are probably not quite pure, but Chaucer uses rhymes of the same kind.

The rhyme *wors* "worse" : *hors* "horse" is probably impure.

u-sounds.

The numerous rhymes *-ūs* : *-us* (as *furious* : *Tydeus*) are noteworthy. The same type of rhyme occurs in Chaucer.

The forms *contune*, *discure*, *recure* (continue, discover, recover), which are found in other works of Lydgate's, are often found in rhymes in *Thebes*.

y-sounds.

O.E. *y* (short or long) nearly always appears as *i* in *Thebes*, as in the rhymes *hille*: *wille*, *fille*: *ille*, *bylt*: *spilt*, *hide*, *pride*: *abide*, *kynde*: *finde*, *fire* : *desire*, etc. *Dry* adj. appears (written *dreye*) in rhyme with *seye* once. Once *drye* rhymes with *malencolye*. Further, *shette* "shut" rhymes thrice with *lette* v., *mette* "met"; *sherte* "shirt" once with *smerte* adj. On this point Lydgate's dialect shows remarkable difference from Chaucer's. As *e* is a common development of O.E. *y* in East Anglia, we might have expected to find *e* commonly in *Thebes*.

Unstressed *-e*.

Schick concludes from an examination of *Temple of Glas* that final *-e* is sounded by Lydgate in nearly all the cases in which Chaucer sounds it. This conclusion is borne out by an examination of *Thebes*.

At the end of a line an historically correct *-e* is normally sounded. It is very rare to find an early M.E. monosyllabic word bound in rhyme with a disyllabic one. A reference to the rhyme-lists (e.g. *-ad*, *-adde*; *-aid*, *-aide*; *-as*, *-ace*; *-ein*, *eine*; *-ent*, *-ente*; *-our*, *-oure*) will show how well monosyllables and disyllables are kept apart. There is in *Thebes* not one rhyme between *-ī* and *-īe*. Some exceptions are only apparent and have their counterparts in Chaucer.

Adjectives in the plural and the definite form generally have the ending *-e*. But the ending is sometimes absent. Romance adjectives such as *disconsolaat*, *infortunat*, *evident*, *present* do not get the ending in all cases. Predicative adjectives are often unchanged in the plural, as *war* (: *dar*), *derk* (: *werk*), *wis* (: *avis*, *devys*), *stronge* (: *wrong*, *among*). This is in accordance with Chaucer's usage.

The plural preterite of strong verbs and the plural present of verbs such as *can* sometimes show a form identical with the singular, as *abood*, *rood*, *ran* pret. plur., *can*, *shal* pres. plur., which occur in rhyme with monosyllables. Forms of this kind, which are found also in Chaucer, have not lost a final *-e*. The plural form has been supplanted by the singular.

Nouns after prepositions often appear in the old dative form in *-e*, as *on londe*, *be nighte*, *vnder fote* (really from *fōtum*). These forms make their appearance also in adverbial phrases, such as *al my lyve*, *al the weie*.

Sometimes *-e* is absent where Chaucer has it. Chaucer often rhymes pres. participles or nouns in *-inge* with words such as *singe*. No such rhymes occur in *Thebes*, where words in *-ing* rhyme with *kyng*, *thyng*, etc. Chaucer has these forms too, but Lydgate carries them through consistently.

The words *drede*, *quene* sometimes rhyme with monosyllables, while Chaucer seems to have only disyllabic forms. *Queen* is an old monosyllable (O.E. *cwēn*), and *dred* may have been a monosyllable originally. Possibly Lydgate in these cases followed other models than Chaucer and used the words as monosyllables in verse. The East Anglian *Genesis and Exodus* has the form *quuen*.

But there is no reason to try and explain away rhymes between original disyllables and monosyllables, for there are some indubitable cases, e.g. *hed(e)* s. "heed" (: *renomed* pp., *rede* s. "advice," *dede* adj "dead"), *chas* s. "chase" (: *pas* s.), *grace* s. (: *trespace* s.), *cheer* s. (: *ȝer*), *rewme* s. (: *Ierusalem*), *mouth* v. (: *couth* adj.), *tent* s. (: *spent* pp.), *Ymeyne* (: *souereyn* adj.).

In Lydgate's pronunciation final *-e* was probably silent. Its preservation in verse is no doubt traditional and chiefly due to imitation of Chaucer. Under the circumstances it may be said that Lydgate has been very successful in keeping up the old distinction between disyllables and monosyllables.

Also in the interior of the line final *-e* is generally sounded when historically correct, and in many cases it should be added where the MSS. have not got it. It is true there may be some doubt whether it should always be pronounced (or inserted) before the cæsura. Thus in l. 3 *old* may be altered to *oldë*, in which case the line would get its normal structure. Or else *old* may be kept, and the verse is of the "waistless" type. The final *-e* is to be sounded, for instance, in *briȝte* 1, *bole* 2, *virgyne* 4, *mone* 7, *newe* 14, *make* 26, *hadde* 41, *ȝoue* 46, *with-oute* 54, *trewe* 56, *tyme* 58, *reherce* 63.

The *-e* is mostly silent when the next word begins with a vowel or an *h*, as *Aprille* (and) 2, *thoposicioun* 6, *take* (his) 11, *tyme* (and) 12, *braunch* (and) 16, *tyme* (in) 18, *some* (of) 22, 23, *some* (also) 24, 25, *acquytte* (hemsilf) 29, *ywrite* (and) 38, *sentence* (haue) 54, *tale* (as) 63.

The final *-e* of words that are frequently unstressed is often silent, as in *ȝoure* 96, etc., *hadde* 31, *haue* 85, etc., *were* 484, etc. Final *-e* likewise often disappears after a syllable with weak or medium stress, as *prouerbe* 51, *siknesse* 72, *execute* 414, *forest* 416, etc.

The imperative is often monosyllabic even in weak verbs, as *wrappe* 109, *make* 171, *telle* 170, etc. Final *-e* is silent in *forȝete* pp. 373, *come* pp. 94.

In all these cases Lydgate is in accordance with Chaucer's usage.

The remaining cases are not very numerous. Probably Lydgate drops the *-e* to a somewhat greater extent than Chaucer does, but the difference is not very marked. Examples are: *myrth* 134, *fressh* (def. adj.) 12, *loke* (pres. plur.) 89, *lye* (pres. conj.) 111, *seye* (pres. conj.) 127, *make* (inf.) 161, 164.

Sometimes it is doubtful how a verse should be read. Thus l. 35 ("Tellyng a tale to angre with the frere") may be read with monosyllabic *tale* or with disyllabic *talë* and contraction of *to angre* to *tangre*. In 154 "Fully in" may be run together into two syllables, and "purpoos" may be stressed on the second syllable. The line may then be read: "Fúlly in purpoós to cómë tó dynére," which really gives the sentence a more natural stress.

An unstressed *e* before a consonant is usually sounded, as in the endings *-es*, *-ed*, etc. In accordance with Chaucer's usage the vowel is often dropped after a syllable with weak or medium stress, as in *pylgrymes* 59, 78, *dyvynoures* 362; further, before the *n* in past participles such as *leyn*, sometimes in other verbal forms, as *bern* inf. 247, *seyn* 295, *weren* 156, etc.

Also in other cases an *e* is occasionally dropped, as *bereþ* pres. 265, *sirs* plur. 177, *lordes* 283, etc. It is doubtful if in rhymes such as *touns* : *barouns*; *souns* : *Clarions*; *flours* : *predecessours* we should read *tounës* : *barounës* or *touns* : *barouns*.

Final *-n*.

In rhyme the final *-n* of the infinitive, pres. plur., pret. plur. and pp. is always lost except in forms where the vowel before the *n* had been dropped, as in *ben*, *goon*, *sen* inf., *sayn*, *gon* pres. plur., *seyn*, *slayn*, *gon*, *lorn*, *sworn* pp. Loss of *-n* is proved by rhymes such as *embrace* inf. (: *face*), *take* pres. plur. (: *sake*), *slawe* pp. (: *lawe*). Also forms such as *do* inf., pp., *se* inf. occur.

In the interior of the line an *-n* is occasionally found, but it may have been introduced by a scribe. However, in some cases it may have been put by the poet in order to avoid hiatus, as l. 70 ("to entren into toun,") 432 ("token her viage,") 462 ("to maken hym his hayr,") 491 ("founden and vnknowe;") cf. also 555, 937, 963, 984, 1020.

2. *Accidence.*

Nouns.

The plural forms *foon* (: *on*, etc.), *myle* (: *while*) and *pound* (: *hound*) are proved by rhymes.

Dative forms in *-e* are common after prepositions; cf. 1. We may add *to wive.*

Adjectives.

The ending *-e* is common in the plural and in the definite form. Cf. 1.

Verbs.

The following forms of the preterite are proved by the rhyme:

brak, spak, cam with short *a.*

chę̄s (chose).

faught (: *draught*).

awoke (with ǭ), to judge by the rhyme with *shoke.*

slēp, fil (: *hil*).

hightë.

On plural preterites such as *rood, ran* see 1.

The present 3rd singular in *-s* occurs in two rhymes: *lerys* (: *banerys*), *specifies* (: *fantasies*). The form in *-th* is also proved by rhyme: *goþ, doth* (: *soth*). Contracted forms occur occasionally. The rhyme proves *lyst* (: *vnwist*). The metre shows that *writ* "writes" is sometimes the poet's form.

§ 2. *Vocabulary.*

Editors and other philologists have remarked that Lydgate's language is more modern than Chaucer's. French and Latin loan-words, most of them still in use, are met with in greater numbers in Lydgate's works. Thus his language makes a more familiar impression on the reader than Chaucer's works, which, in spite of their great indebtedness to the above-mentioned two languages, bear a more genuinely native English stamp. A detailed comparison of the vocabularies of the two authors has never been undertaken. This will be done here, although the members of comparison must be so widely different in extent as Lydgate's poem, *The Siege of*

Thebes, and the whole body of Chaucer's poetical and prose productions.

None of the words registered in the following paragraphs as used in *Thebes* are to be found in any of Chaucer's works.

1. Lydgate uses several colloquial or slang words, not admitted by Chaucer, referring to parts of the human body. All of these are put into the mouth of the Tabard Host, and no doubt chosen for the express purpose of characterising his speech. Chaucer's mastership, throughout the Canterbury Tales, in his description of the Host is well known, but he seems to have shunned drawing from a domain of the colloquial language which we cannot but regard as very typical of the subject: *bekke* s. nose, *crop* s. throat, *koyse* s. body, *nolle* s. head, *roppys* s. plur. entrails.

A series of culinary terms is also mentioned by the Host, who is, of course, at home in this department: *franchemole* s. a sort of haggis, *froyse* s. a kind of pancake, *hagys* s. haggis, *puddyng* s., *tansey* s. a sort of pudding, *annys* s. anise, *coriandre* s. coriander.

2. Military terms. Such terms are more numerous in Chaucer's works than in Lydgate's, as is quite natural in regard to Chaucer's courtly service and his taking part, though only for a short time, in the French war. Not a few of these terms were known to and are used by our monk, but he offers, besides, a score of his own. Weapons and armour: *ablaster* s. cross-bow, *brake* s. winch of a cross-bow, *cusshewes* s. plur. armour for the thighs, *geseran* s. a light coat of armour, *greues* s. plur. armour for the legs below the knee, *quarel* s. bolt, *sabaton* s. armoured shoe, *vyser* s. visor. Fortifications: *barbykan* s., *barrer* s. palisade, *bulwerk* s., *crest* s. top line of a fortified tower, *crestyd* adj. Other terms: *forey* s. foray, *forraye* v. intr. (Ch. *forage* s.), *hosteye* v. intr. make a warlike expedition, *maskowe* v. tr. machicolate, *rest* s. (for the lance), *route* s. disorderly retreat, *sawdyour*, *soudeour* s. soldier, *vnbrace* v. tr. undo the armour (of).

3. Common English words, still living in modern English: *ado* s., *blunt* adj., *froward* adj. adverse, unfavourable, *hyde* s. hide (of a bull), *myrk* adj. dark, *nye* v. intr. neigh, *nyinge* s., *sigh* s., *sighen* v. intr. (Ch. *syk*, *syken*, once, *sigh* sing. once, *syghes* s. plur.), *ther-at* adv., *thong* s., *toward* adj. favourable, auspicious, *wher-up-on* adv.

4. English words, now obsolete: *aforn*, *afore* adv., *bywelde* v. refl. move about freely, *forwounded* adj., *kyndle* s. the young (of a tiger), *myd*, *mydde* prep. in the centre of, *out-korve* pp., *out-mete* v. tr., *out-*

ringe v. intr., *ouerleyd* pp., *ouermore* adv. moreover, *ouerslyde* v. intr. pass unnoticed, *parbrake* v. tr. shatter.

5. Scandinavian loan-words : *bleyk* adj., *drowne* v., *ille* adv. (Ch. has *il* adj. only as a characteristic of the speaker's North-English birth), *lugge* v. tr. pull, worry, *lynke* v. tr. link, join, *sale* s.—all still living ; *geyn* s. expedient, resource, *geynpath* s. short cut, are obsolete or dialectal.

6. Latin loan-words, all still living : *adiacent* adj., *circumspecte* adj., *deiecte* adj., *patere* v. intr. repeat the paternoster, *repelle* v. tr., *supersedyas* s. (law-term).

7. French loan-words, living in modern English : *admit* v. tr., *ambicioun* s., *ame* v. intr. aim, *antiquytè* s., *avoyde* v. tr., *breefly* adv., *brose* v. tr. bruise, *calculacioun* s., *certefie* v. tr., *commoditè* s., *concelen* v. tr., *concours* s., *contradiccioun* s., *controover* s. contriver, inventor, *conuencioun* s., *conuersaunt* adj., *cremysyn* adj. crimson (Spanish), *damask* s., *demur* adj. grave, serious, *depende* v. intr., *devoyde* adj., *differre* v. tr. defer, *dilusioun* s., *disapere* v. intr., *disclose* v. tr., *dyuerte* v. intr. and tr., *engroce* v. tr. write out in legal form, *enrolle* v. tr. register, engross, *exortacioun* s., *expectaunt* adj., *expedient* adj., *faute* s. fault, *fyret* s. ferret, *genologye* s., *hermyn* s. ermine, *incantacioun* s., *inportune* adj. persistent, *inspeccioun* s., *interrupte* v. tr., *monstre, mostren* v. intr. muster, come together (an army), *nutritif* adj., *obscure* adj., *paganysme* s., *panter* s., *periur* adj., *pillage* s., *predecessour* s., *prerogatif* s., *preserve* v. tr., *promys* s., *provide* v. intr. provide, prepare, *prouidence* s. foresight, *pyrat* s., *rampaunt* adj., *ratefye* v. tr., *reedifye* v. tr., *reforme* v. tr., *registrer* s. registrar, recorder, *relacioun* s., *reuolue* v. tr. turn over mentally, *sage* adj., *seuere* v. intr. part (from) (Ch. *disseveren*), *soyle* s., *tedious* adj., *transgressioun* s. offence, *trist, trest* adj. sorrowful (Ch. has only *Tristitia* sadness), *trye* v. tr. try (Ch. has only *trye* adj. choice, excellent), *vndermyne* v. tr. (Ch. *myne* v. tr.), *vndiscreccioun* s. (Ch. *discrecioun*), *vngracious* adj. (Ch. *gracious*), *vnperturbed* adj. (Ch. *perturbe* v. tr.), *vnrepreuyd* adj. irreproachable (Ch. *repreve* v. tr.), *vnsicrenesse* s. (Ch. *sikernesse* s.), *vnsupported* adj., *vow* s. (Ch. *avow* s.).

8. French loan-words, now obsolete : *allure* s. a walk in a garden, *amaat* adj. (Ch. *mat, maat*), *amervaylyd* pp. (Ch. *mervelinge* pres. part.), *apport* s. bearing, demeanour (Ch., Lydg. *port* s.), *asselyd* pp. attested by a seal (Ch. *seel* s.), *bestaylle* s., *burlyd* adj. striped, *busshement* s. ambuscade, *caarte* s., *carecte* s. mark, scar, *coarte* v. tr. enforce,

coerce, restrain, *compas* prep. round, *contune* v. tr. and intr. (Ch. *continue*), *devoide* v. tr. and intr. expel, go away, *disamayed* pp. (Ch., Lydg. *dismaye* v.), *disespeyre* v. intr. (Ch., Lydg. *dispeire* v. intr.), *distracte* adj., *dool* s., *enarched* pp. adj. arched over, *enchace* v. tr. chase, *enhaste* v. refl., *eure* s. luck, *eurous* adj., *fage* s. idle talk, lie, *fallas* s. deceit, *gendre* v. tr. (Ch. *engender* v.), *maylle* s. halfpenny, *noyeng* s. annoyance (Ch., Lydg. *anoy* s.), *occisioun* s. slaughter, *odyble* adj. odious, hateful, *possede* v. tr., *pourpartie* s. proportion, share, *priket* s. small wax candle, *race* v. tr. tear away, pull out (Ch. *arace* v.), *rayle* v. tr. array, adorn, *raylle* v. intr. flow, gush, *recur* s. succour, remedy, *recure* v. tr. and intr. recover (Ch. *recovere*), *repleveshed* pp. filled, *sayllyng* s. attack (Ch., Lydg. *assaile* v.), *sowpowayle* s. support, *trayn* s. trickery, guile, *vnpes* s. warfare, *vayle* v. intr. avail (Ch., Lydg. *availe* v.), *voluntè* s. (Ch. has *voluntarie* adj.).

9. English and Scandinavian words used by Lydgate and Chaucer in different senses:

a. still living: *besette* v. tr. surround, invest (Ch. employ), *draught* s. bowshot; drawbridge (Ch. drink, move at chess), *liklynesse* s. comeliness (Ch. probability), *piked* adj. cleared of husks (Ch. pret. stole), *pyhte* pret. pitched (tents) (Ch. *pighte* pitched, fell), *ryve* v. intr. (Scand.) break, burst (Ch. pierce, tear), *shrowde* v. tr. hide (Ch. *shrouded* clad), *spryng* s. spring, well (Ch. first beginning, dawn);

b. obsolete: *abrayde* v. intr. break forth (Ch. awake), *chese* v. tr. choose; see, perceive (Ch. choose).

10. French words used by Lydgate and Chaucer in different senses:

a. still living: *amendement* s. correction (Ch. compensation), *atteyne* v. intr. suffice, be sufficient (Ch. attain, succeed in), *atteynt* pp. convicted (Ch. experienced), *charge* v. tr. care about, trouble oneself about (Ch., Lydg. command), *cloos* adj. reticent, discreet (Ch. hidden, shut up), *desolat* adj. disconsolate (Ch. *desolate* adj. waste, lonely, evil), *distille* v. intr. trickle down (Ch. v. intr. melt), *fygure* v. tr. imagine (Ch. signify), *mynistre* v. tr. furnish, give (Ch. govern, manage), *note* v. tr. take note of (Ch. s. mark, musical note), *pervers* adj. unpropitious (Ch. self-willed), *preferre* v. tr. prefer, favour (Ch. v. tr. precede, take precedence of), *reenge* v. tr. go over searching (Ch. range, place in rows), *reste* v. intr. take one's stand on, rely on (Ch. remain, repose), *soleyn* adj.

sullen, morose (Ch. solitary, unmated), *sotyltees* s. plur. exquisite dishes (Ch. *soteltee* s. subtlety, device);

b. obsolete: *chevysaunce* s. remedy, shift (Ch. borrowing), *dyvynaile* s. problem, riddle (Ch., Lydg. divination).

11. English words not used by Chaucer but having in his language nearly related forms, differing only in suffix or grammatical category:

a. still living: *brasyn* adj. (Ch. *bras* s.), *brotherhode* s. (Ch., Lydg. *brotherhede*), *brotherly* adj., *dewe* v. tr. to wet (with tears) (Ch., Lydg. *dewe* s.), *fresshly* adj. (Ch., Lydg. *fressh* adj.), *kyngly* adj., *lothsom* adj., *lowlynesse* s., *manful* adj., *moderly* adj., *mouth* v. tr. utter, tell, *name* v. tr., *sleghty* adj. (Ch., Lydg. *sleight* s.), *want* s. (Ch. v.)—*angre* v. tr. (Ch. s.), *give* v. tr., *gift* s. (Ch. *yeve, yive, yift*)—*craggy* adj. (Ch. *crag* s., Gaelic);

b. obsolete: *beheeste* v. tr. promise (Ch., Lydg. *biheste* s.), *ferdful* adj. frightened (Ch. *ferd* s. fear), *manlihede* s.

12. French loan-words, not used by Chaucer, but having in his language nearly related forms, differing only in suffix or grammatical category:

a. still living: *abstene* v. intr. (Ch. *abstinence* s.), *adverte* v. intr. and tr. (Ch. *advertence* s.), *allaye* v. tr. (Ch. s.), *attendaunt* adj. (Ch., Lydg. *attendaunce* s.), *avail* s. (Ch., Lydg. v.), *cankered* adj. (Ch. *cancre* s.), *chas* s. (Ch. *chase* v.), *comowner* s. (Ch. *commune* adj.), *compyle* v. tr. (Ch. *compilatour* s.), *conspiracioun* s. (Ch. *conspiracye* s.), *correcte* adj. (Ch. v.), *cristalyn* adj. (Ch. *cristal* s.), *declyne* s. (Ch. v.), *diffiaunce* s. defiance (Ch., Lydg. *diffye* v.), *doolful* adj. (Ch. *dolor*), *eclipse* tr. (Ch. s.), *excelle* v. intr. and tr. (Ch., Lydg. *excellence* s.), *except, exceptid* pp. (Ch., Lydg. *excepcioun* s.), *wel-fauoured* adj., *fraternal* adj. (Ch. *fraternitee* s.), *indurat* adj. (Ch. *induracioun* s.), *lyneal* adj. (Ch., Lydg. *lyne* s.), *opportune* adj. (Ch. *oportunitee* s.), *orloger* s. horologer (Ch. *orloge* s.), *perturbaunce* s. (Ch. *perturbacioun* s.), *progenitours* s. plur. (Ch. *progenie* s.), *propoos* s. purpose (Ch. *proposicioun* s.), *proscript* adj. (Ch. *proscripcioun* s.), *recompense* s. (Ch. *recompensacioun* s.), *solempnyze* v. tr. (Ch., Lydg. *solempne* adj.), *support* s. (Ch. *supportacioun* s.);

b. obsolete: *apoynt* s. resolution (Ch. v.), *coniurisoun* s. (Ch. *coniuracioun* s.), *disencrees* s. decrease (Ch. v. intr.), *habounde* adj. (Ch., Lydg. v. intr., Ch. *haboundant* adj.), *rage* adj. wild, savage (Ch., Lydg. s.), *scarshed* s. (Ch. *scarsetee* s.), *surplusage* s. (Ch. *surplus* s.).

CHAPTER IV

LYDGATE'S METRE AND RHYMES

§ 1. *The Metre of "Thebes."*

LYDGATE could write good verse, easy-flowing, harmonious, regular verse, and there are in his works, not least in *Thebes*, many passages that can be read with real pleasure. His constant occupation as a versifier gave him a great skill in handling the English language metrically, but, on the other hand, the strain exercised on his composition by the number and in some cases the extraordinary length of his poems had an unfavourable influence on his poetic art. Haste in composition led to carelessness. Hence the great number of hard and rugged lines. Going over a work already done, correcting and polishing, was apparently a task seldom performed. Lydgate himself was well aware of his deficiencies in this respect, and, far from trying to conceal them, confesses them more than once with great candour. In his *Troy Book*, for instance, he says:

For wel wot I moche þing is wrong,
Falsly metrid, boþe of short and long.
(Bk. V, 3483–4. See Bergen, *Troy Book*, Introductory Note, p. xvi.)

A careful study of the metre of *Thebes*, however, shows that at any rate in this work the verse is on the whole far better than it may look at first sight. No manuscript preserves Lydgate's original text intact. In many cases a final *-e* has been omitted by a scribe, which should undoubtedly be added. It is not quite clear if hiatus in the cæsura should be assumed to be a liberty admitted by Lydgate, but this may well be so.

Lydgate made use of the same metrical liberties as Chaucer and other contemporary poets. The place of the chief stress of many words both English and French varied, at least metrically. In *Thebes* variable stress is found in words with suffixes such as *-esse*, *-nesse*, *-ing*, *-y*. The first or the second syllable takes the stress as the case may be in *power*, *honur*, *pyler*, *cite*, *royal* and many others. The accentuation of proper names is very variable. *Adrástus* and *Ádrastus*, *Bóchas* and *Bochás*, *Cádmus* and *Cadmús*, *Edíppus* and *Édippus* are used interchangeably. *Ethíocles* and *Polymýte* are the usual forms, but also *Ethiócle(s)* and *Polýmytes* occur.

A trochaic foot often replaces an iambic one at the beginning of a line and after the cæsura. In some cases it is doubtful if a trochaic foot or change of stress should be assumed, *e.g.* in l. 2648 ("Redy to don what hym list devise"). In many other cases it is impossible to determine exactly how a line should be read, especially because of the comparative freedom with which a final *-e* may be sounded or not.

It is a reasonable conjecture that many metrically deficient lines are corrupt in the extant MSS. and should be restored by a slight alteration. A large number of lines that are faulty when judged by the strict standard of Chaucer's heroic verse could easily be made perfect by replacing some form of a word by another that is found in other lines of similar build, or by inserting some word (a pronoun, preposition, adverb or the like) that is of frequent occurrence in similar instances. In several cases (*e.g.* l. 760) the form *-selven* (*-silven*) instead of *-self* (*-silf*) would set the line right. In l. 1338 ("To suffre me it shal litil greue") a *you* before *litil* would make the line perfect. No doubt this method of restoring is justifiable up to a certain point. There is no reason to suppose that Lydgate went out of his way to write faulty lines; at least he ought to have the benefit of the doubt. But there are many lines that cannot be altered and must be allowed to stand as they are. Lydgate's verse is not in all respects that of Chaucer. Lines without a thesis at the beginning of the line or after the cæsura cannot be interfered with. Lydgate's "headless" and "waistless" lines are characteristic of his versification.

The lines of *Thebes* may be classified as follows.

1. Full, regular lines :

◡ ⁄ ◡ ⁄ | ◡ ⁄ ◡ ⁄ ◡ ⁄ (◡)

e.g. l. 18. The tyme in soth / whan Canterbury talys.

This type is varied in certain ways. The cæsura may be placed after the third thesis :

e.g. l. 1 : Whan briȝte phebus / passëd was þe ram.

The first foot or the foot next after the cæsura may be a trochee :

e.g. l. 40. Floure of Poetes / thorghout al breteyne.

l. 22. Some of desport / some of moralitè.

This is by the far the most common type. In the Prologue at least 100 lines out of 176 belong to it.

2. "Headless" lines :

⁄ ◡ ⁄ | ◡ ⁄ ◡ ⁄ ◡ ⁄ (◡)

l. 16 : Braunch and bough / wiþ red and whit depeynt.

l. 15 : with her flourës / craftyly ymeynt.

The following lines in the Prologue belong to this type : 4, 15, 16, 20, 31, 34,[1] 37, 50,[2] 58, 59, 61, 66, 73, 74, 84, 91, 92, 108,[3] 111, 114, 128,[4] 135, 137, 144,[5] 148, 149, 153, 157, 164, 165, 168, 173.

3. " Waistless " lines :

⌣ ⁄ ⌣ ⁄ | ⁄ ⌣ ⁄ ⌣ ⁄ (⌣)

e.g. l. 10 : And Iubiter / in the Crabbës Hed.

l. 48 : Chief Registrer / of þis pilgrimage.

The following of the lines in the Prologue belong or may belong here :

3(?),[6] 10, 21, 29, 32, 33, 39, 42(?),[7] 45, 47(?),[8] 48, 55, 68, 71, 76, 81, 86, 97, 100, 102, 104, 105, 112, 117, 119, 120, 122,[9] 126, 136, 142, 143, 144, 146, 147, 158, 159(?),[10] 160, 163(?),[11] 167, 169.

4. Head- and waistless :

⁄ ⌣ ⁄ | ⁄ ⌣ ⁄ ⌣ ⁄ (⌣)

l. 30 : Boystously / in her teermës Rude.

l. 53 : Of eche thyng / keping in substaunce.

There are only these two certain cases in the prologue. But 98 may belong here. See Errata. Cf. also 2316, 4583, 4590, 4662.

5. Double-waisted :

⌣ ⁄ ⌣ ⁄ ⌣ | ⌣ ⁄ ⌣ ⁄ ⌣ ⁄ (⌣)

l. 85. Thogh ȝoure bridel / haue neiþer boos ne belle.

But *bridel* may be read with elision of *e*. At least in Chaucer's verse elision of this kind before a word beginning with a vowel or *h* occurs, according to ten Brink (§ 269). Some lines that might

[1] " Glasy-Eyed / and face of Cherubyn." Probably *-eyed* should be read as one syllable.

[2] " Feynëd talis / nor þing Historial." Professor Erdmann suggested that the line is headless and double-waisted. But *talis* may be monosyllabic.

[3] Aftere soper / Slepe wil do non ille." Professor Erdmann seems to have stressed *soper* on the second syllable and places the line among waistless ones. But *sóper* is at least equally probable.

[4] " For to-morowe, anoon / as it is day." The *-e* of *morowe* may be elided. Professor Erdmann gave the line as a double-waisted one.

[5] " But, for al this / be of hertë liȝt." The line may be read also as a waistless one. This was Professor Erdmann's opinion.

[6] But more likely *old* should be altered to *oldē*.

[7] Perhaps *rethorikē* with hiatus in the cæsura.

[8] Perhaps we should read *wel-seyingē*, which makes the line full.

[9] *My-silven* instead of *my-silf* would set the line right.

[10] " And to me seide / as it were in game." Perhaps we should read "seidë."

[11] " It ís no dísport / só to pátere and séie " is a possible way of reading the line.

belong here are more probably to be read differently. In l. 67 (At Canterbury / wel loggëd on and all) *-bury* should be read *-bry* as in Chaucer's *C. T.*, Prol. 16. In l. 128 (For to-morowe, anoon / as it is day) and l. 150 (And touarde morowe anon as it was light) we should surely read *to-morwe anon* with elision of the *-e* before the vowel. But see 2307, 4562, 4579, 4622, 4631, 4650.

6. Headless and double-waisted:

´ ⌣ ´ ⌣ | ⌣ ´ ⌣ ´ ⌣ ´ (⌣)

l. 2383: To a chambre / she ladde hym vp alofte.

Few lines can be with certainty referred to this type. See 2423, 4677. On l. 50 see p. 34 foot-note. On l. 34 see p. 34 foot-note. L. 27 (" Ech admitted / for non wold other greve ") may belong here, but it is possible that Lydgate read *admitted* with the first syllable stressed. Cf. l. 179: " And admitted / a tale for to telle ".

§ 2. *The Rhymes.*

Lydgate had no small skill in handling the rhyme. Of course many of his rhymes are conventional. Derivative suffixes such as *-nesse*, *-ing*, *-oun* commonly occur in rhyme. Stopgap phrases are not rarely resorted to in order to supply a rhyme. Yet these cheap rhymes are not so numerous that they produce a general impression of monotony.

The rhymes are on the whole good. Impure rhymes occur, but not very frequently. Open and close *ē* and *ō* are sometimes rhymed together. Rhymes between a long and a short vowel (as *cas* : *was*) are few. Assonances are rare. The only examples in *Thebes* are *bekke* : *effecte* 169/70, *take* : *shape* 1247/8.

A characteristic feature of Lydgate's rhymes, and one which contributes to giving variety and force to the verse, is the fact that generally sections (long passages) end in the middle of a rhyming couplet, there being a full-stop and an obvious pause after the first line of the couplet. Typical instances are 261/2, 327/8, 353/4, 399/400, 495/6, 523/4, 531/2, 557/8, 639/40, 749/50, 801/2, 911/12, 953/4, 967/8. But the Prologue and the three Parts end with rhyming couplets.

For details of Lydgate's rhymes in *Thebes* a reference is made to Chapter III, and especially to the rhyme-lists. The latter will give the best idea of the poet's favourite rhyme-words and rhyme-vowels.

CHAPTER V

DESCRIPTION OF THE MSS. AND PRINTED EDITIONS[1]

§ 1. Ad_1. = *Additional* 18632. British Museum.

Select MS., vellum, 101 leaves, 12¾ × 8¼ inches. Double columns of 42 lines. Gatherings of eight leaves, with catchwords. Maroon morocco binding. The MS. also contains Hoccleve's *De Regimine Principum*. *Thebes* begins fol. 5 front and ends fol. 33 front, first column. Besides the gap 785–88, only one line is missing, 1732. No colophon. At the beginning of the Prologue and the three Parts are fine initials and ornamental borders. No rubrics before fol. 21 front; from there short rubrics in Latin, far between, written in the outer margin of the leaf. The cæsura is marked in the two first pages (= fol. 5 front and back) by a low point; from fol. 6 front by a low point with a small curve or hook above it; from fol. 24 back by a kind of hook alone; from some way down col. 1. in fol. 29 front the low point re-enters into use. Instead of initial *wh*, *w* is often written; this *w* has often been corrected by *h* being added above the line. Instead of *-ign-* is always written *-ingn-*; *-us* for *-es* is not rare; *is* for *his* is not seldom found. Date of the MS. about 1440. See Ward, *Catalogue*, vol. i, p. 89, *Catalogue of Additions to the MSS. of the British Museum in the years* 1848–1853, p. 124.

§ 2. Ad_2. = *Additional* 5140. British Museum.

Vellum and paper, 423 leaves, 11 × 7½ inches. Single columns of 33 or 34 lines. Gatherings of twelve leaves (one vellum, four paper, two vellum, four paper, one vellum), with catchwords. Bound in olive morocco. The volume contains the *Canterbury Tales*, which end fol. 357*b* at the middle of the page. "Explicit narracio Rectoris et ultima inter narraciones huius libri de quibus composuit Chauucer cuius anime propicietur deus. AMEN." Then, after a short interval, follows: "Incipit ultima de fabulis Cantuarie translata et prolata per Dompnu*m* Iohannem Lidgate monachu*m* in redeundo a Cantuaria. Incipit p*r*ologus." The text itself begins fol. 358*a* and goes to bottom of fol. 423*b*, which is the last of the volume. At the end of the Prologue, fol. 360*b*, is: "Sequitur

[1] In order to facilitate references, the MSS. are arranged alphabetically, *i.e.* according to the initial letters used as abbreviations in the foot-notes of Part I. Then the early printed editions are added.

Fabula eiusdem dompni I. L. monachi. de obsessu Ciuitatis de Thebes." The text is imperfect at the end, the last line being 4503, and there is a large gap 4094–4158 (one leaf lost here). Besides this, 785–88 are missing, and so are 601–2, 1343–44, 2005–6, 2013–14, 2021–22, 2027–28, (2074), (2802), 2927, (3414), (3504), 4289–90. Sum-total of lines missing 301 (inclusive of lines entirely re-written). Red and blue initials at the beginning of the Prologue and three Parts. No rubrics. No colophon. The cæsura is marked by a slanting stroke. In the upper right-hand corner of the front pages is written "Lydgate" (underlined red or blue on alternate pages). þ is not used, only *th*. Date of the MS. end of the fifteenth century.

§ 3. Ap. = *Appendix* XXVII. British Museum.

Paper, 51 leaves, the original size of which was 11 × 7½ inches; the leaves having been mounted on larger paper, their present size is 12⅜ × 9¼. This MS. once formed part of a bigger volume, old Appendix XXVII, bound in brown Russian leather, which was cut up about twenty-five years ago. The leaves 14–62, which contain the text of *Thebes*, were taken out and now form the new Appendix XXVII. The latter part of the present MS., from fol. 39, was much damaged in the fire of 1731. *Thebes* begins fol. 14 front and ends fol. 62 back. The end of the poem, from 3409, is lost, and so is one leaf (1681–1746) between fol. 38 and 39, making together 1374 lines lost. Several lines, especially top-lines, have been wholly or partially burnt off, as 1747–52, 3026, 3269, 3339. In two places about half a dozen lines, which have been already given in their right sequence, are found to be repeated, viz. 2367–71, wrongly inserted again at the top of fol. 49 front between 2440 (bottom line of fol. 48 back) and 2441, and 2813–19 also wrongly inserted again at the top of fol. 55 front between 2846 (bottom line of fol. 54 back) and 2847. No mark of cæsura. No rubrics. Often "whyt" for *with*, "wych" "wech" for *which*, *th* for *gh* and *ght*, e.g. "thorth" "thoruth" for *thorgh*, "myth" for *myght*, "nouth" for *nought*, also "abouht" for *about*. Date of the MS. sixteenth century. See Ward, *Catalogue*, vol. i, p. 91.

§ 4. Ar. = *Arundel* 119. British Museum.

Vellum, 80 leaves numbered with pencil in the upper right-hand corner, 10⅞ × 7⅜ inches. The text ends fol. 79 front, line 4, with the colophon in line 7. The MS. contains only *Thebes*. The text is perfectly complete. Single columns of 32 lines from fol. 1 to 9 front, 31 lines fol. 9 back to fol. 24 back, and 30 lines fol. 25 to the end. Date of the MS. 1425–30.

Gatherings of eight leaves. The catchwords, enclosed in a rectangular frame of lines drawn with the pen, are in the lower right-hand corner of the last leaf of the gathering. They do not always agree in spelling with the opening words of the following page. Ruling on both sides of the leaf with the pen, from prickings at the edge of the leaf. In fol. 1–5 of the first gathering and in the third gathering (fol. 17–24) these prickings have been cut off by the binder. The text is confined on both sides by vertical lines, and at the top and the bottom by horizontal lines, all of which extend across the four margins to the edge of the leaf. The ruling for the text does not go beyond the vertical side-lines just referred to. Rubrics, of varying frequency and length, are found throughout the poem. They are written, without any ruling, in the outer side-margins. In fol. 46–61 they are darker than elsewhere, of a dark violet colour.[1]

The writing of MS. Ar. is a clear and regular court-hand. It resembles rather closely that of Harley MS. 7334 (early fifteenth century), given in Plate 101 of Thompson's Facsimiles. The two MSS. differ, however, in a number of minor points. The initial letters of the lines are mostly capitals or enlarged minuscules (printed as capitals); some letters, as *h*, *k*, *l*, *v*, *y*, ȝ, are found also as small minuscules or as minuscules with a tick at the left side (these are printed as capitals). Initial *w* presents the three first-named forms. There are three different forms of *r* and *s*. Sometimes in the first line of a page one or more letters have their stems elongated upwards, whereas in the last line of the page they are drawn out downwards.

Tags are pretty numerous in MS. Ar., of various shapes and sizes. The long-vexed question of how they ought to be treated in print has been generally decided in the negative, most editors now taking no notice of the tags in their MSS. Towards the end of the last century opinions varied, but Dr. Furnivall, the founder and for many years secretary of the Chaucer Society and the Early English Text Society, favoured the opinion that tags had in many

[1] Probably the rubricator's (= the copyist's) store of red ink was giving out, and he had to manage as well as he could, mixing his red ink with ordinary black, until a fresh supply arrived.

cases a phonetic value, and in his editions reproduced them conscientiously. In the text of the present edition [1] all clear tags are marked either as tags or—where the metre or grammar demands it—as final *e* (italicised in contradistinction to final *e* written in the text). This translation of a tag into an italic *e* is here a matter of practical convenience, "heght*e*" 194, for instance, being printed instead of "heghtë" or "heght[e]." Cf. "Sparë" 112, where in MS. Ar. the *r* has no tag. Tags vary in length. Some are very small, others equal to a long cæsura-stroke, and between these extremes all intermediate gradations are to be seen. In most cases the tag is evidently only an idle ornament, being added to the last letter of words that never had a syllabic final *e* and the rhyme-words of which may be tagless, as 97 : 98, etc. In not a few instances the copyist has altered a tag into *e* by writing *e* upon the tag so as to partly cover it. Such words are, of course, printed with final *e*, *e.g.* "caste" 529, "herte" 1961, "longe" 2151, "a-lofte" : "softe" 1053–54, etc., also "counsaillinge" 4002, where certainly neither Lydgate nor the copyist pronounced final *e*. The letters *h* and *ll*, which are never tagged, often bear a cross-stroke, straight or curved; this stroke, in the present edition, is treated just as the common tag, *e.g.* "which*e*," "hill*e*." Exceptionally the cross-stroke of *ll* stands clearly for *-es*, e.g. "wall*es*" 2029. The downward loop, which generally stands for *-es*, as kyngg*es* 418, knyght*es* 1360, 2393 : 94, etc., is not seldom used as a mere ornamental flourish and is then printed as a common tag, *e.g.* kyng' 189, 973 : 4, 1191 : 92, etc. It is most often added to the letter *g*, especially in rhyme-words.

The cæsura is marked in the great majority of the lines. In the first 500 lines there are only twenty exceptions. In some lines (eight in the first 500 lines) we find two marks of cæsura. The usual mark is a slanting line (pause-bar); much more rarely occurs a middle point, or a slanting line preceded by a middle point, or an inverted semicolon. Occasionally the pause-bar is quite or nearly vertical. The marks of cæsura have been kept in the printed text, because it seemed to be a matter of no small interest to know how Lydgate's lines were recited by the scribe who copied his poem a few years after its composition. Although this scribe may not have been a nice judge of versification, his careful copying proves him to have

[1] In the rubrics, which, in order to distinguish them from the side-notes, are printed in small Clarendon, the tags are not given, because tagged letters were not to be had in the Clarendon type.

been a well-trained reader, who had probably gone through a good deal of Middle English poetry.

The usual abbreviations occur, as p*ar*cel 913, p*er*aunter 1248, p*ro*vyde 3088, gouerno*ur* 79, p*re*serue 431, man*ere* 514, vng*ra*cious 4348, v*ir*gin*e* 3 (rubric), pilg*ri*mage 94, obseru*au*nces 1556, remembrau*n*ce 38, conclusiou*n* 69, so*n*ne 153, Lygurg*us* 2308, deor*um* 3542 (rubric), þ*at* (*passim*), kyngg*es* 418, wall*es* 2029.

A whole word or one or more letters of a word either underdotted or struck through by the copyist are simply omitted in the printed text, but the omission is always mentioned in the foot-notes. On the other hand, a letter (letters) or word written by the copyist above the line with the old sign of caret (two thin vertical parallel strokes) under the line is in the printed text inserted in its place.

The spelling of MS. Ar. agrees in the main with that of Lydgate as ascertained by the poet's rhymes and by certain texts, especially by MS. Harl. 2278 of his life of Saint Edmund, the presentation copy of which was made directly from Lydgate's own original MS. and probably under his supervision. A few peculiarities show, however, that the language of the copyist (or of some preceding copyist) was not quite the same as that of the author. Generally "puple" for *peple* (cf. Behrens, *Paul's Grundriss* I, p. 977), "hegh" for *high*, *hy*. Rarely *ay* for *a*: "wayst" 1034, "layt" 2251, *a* for *ay*: "lade" 4560, "male": "mervale" 1365–6. Initial *h* prefixed: "hayr," "hamyng"; *wh-* for *w-*: "whisshing" 4490; *-oyre* for *-orye*: "memoyre": "gloyre" 45 : 46, "victoyre": "memoyre" 2239 : 40. Generally "dieu" for *due*.

Ornamentation. The first page of MS. Ar. is adorned with a large (six-line) initial W, containing a rather badly designed picture of a man in a black cloak and hood riding a white horse on a greensward, no doubt meant to represent the author himself (cf. l. 73 seq.). The initial itself is very well executed in gold and blue, the background being brown with very fine scrollwork in gold. An ornamental border of foliage and flowers in gold, blue, red, brown, and white encompasses the page on all four sides. The front page of fol. 4 is ornamented in the same manner. The (six-line) S contains a coat of arms held by white doglike beasts. The front page of fol. 18 is provided with a fine initial P (six lines) and a pretty ornamental border of red and blue flowers and foliage along the inner, upper, and lower margins. The front page of fol. 43 is embellished in the same way as that of fol. 18; the initial O, however, is not quite so large, occupying only four lines (see pp. 1, 10, 45, 106 of the printed edition). Throughout the volume, though of varying frequency in different parts (see edition), there are initials of two lines, in gold on a ground of blue and violet, from which fine foliated ornaments extend to each side along the margin. Besides this and much more frequently, although now and then with rather long intervals, is to be found the usual mark ¶ before a line, alternately in gold with black or violet flourishes, and in blue with red flourishes.

MS. Ar. has been taken as basis of the present edition, every deviation from it being marked by asterisks in the text, or, in the case of pause-bars, only mentioned among the *variæ lectiones*. Final *-e* as well as *e* in the endings *-es*, *-ed*, *-eth*, mute in modern English, but pronounced by Lydgate and forming a syllable metrically, is distinguished by two dots over *e*, as "passëd" 1, "bolë" 2, etc. In some cases this, by inadvertency, has been neglected. Italicised final *-e* is of course always meant to be sounded.

Two or more parts of a compound word, written separately in the MS., are in the printed text united by a hyphen, as "to-forn," "with-oute," "with-drawe," "y-Ronne," "thred-bar," "Wher-vp-on," etc. The same is done with the syllables of a simple word divided in the MS., as "shorte-ly," "straun-gers," etc.

Punctuation. No signs of punctuation in MS. Ar. In the printed text modern punctuation has been used, but in many cases where no ambiguity seemed to be possible, the pause-bar has been allowed to serve as comma.

Fol. 79 front, after the colophon, are ll. 4709–14 copied by a late (sixteenth-century) hand:

> "and lat vs pray to hym þat is most gud
> whiche for mankande shedde hes preshus blud
> thogth besicheyng of þat euenly whene
> wyffe and muder *and* madin clene
> to send vs pes her in thes lyue present
> And of oure synnys pa*r*fit amedment."

Fol. 80 front, at the top of the page, are some glosses: "Lere, tell" (the rest of this line has been cut off by the binder) "Orloger, a clocke keper" "parde, truly" "a portoos is a book that holy mattens and evensong in It" "Iape, a iest" "full yoor agone, ful long ago" "to his lyeges, to his lordes" "Surquedry," (not explained) "lorne, lost" "Surquidous" (not explained). Fol. 80 back, in the upper part of the page, are some scribblings in Latin.

About the middle of the page is written "Beuellus ball est verus possessor huius libri Domine Domine noster quam admirabile nomen in vniversa terra tuum est."

MS. Ar. is bound in calf. The outsides of both covers are stamped with the mark of Bibliotheca Arundeliana. The title on the back of the volume is "Lydgate's Destruction of Thebes. Mus. Brit. Bibl. Arundel. 119. Plut. CLXIV. C." See Ward, *Catalogue*, i, p. 87 ff.

§ 5. Ba. = *Marquis of Bath's MS.* 257. Longleat.

Vellum, 212 leaves (and one front fly-leaf, not numbered),[1] 12 × 8¼ inches. Single columns of 46 lines. Gatherings of eight leaves. No catchwords, but the first four leaves of each gathering are marked A 1, A 2, A 3, A 4, B 1, etc. in the right-hand margin near the bottom. These marks have in many cases been cut off by the binder. Olive morocco binding.

Thebes, fol. 1–27 (fol. 28 lost), fol. 29–48. The text is incomplete at the middle, 2490–2580 (= fol. 28) being lost, and at the end, 4431 being the last line. Besides, a considerable number of single lines is missing: 294, 299, 318, 416 f., 498, 504, 699, 750*b*–751*a*, 829, 1286, 3104, 3105*b*–3106*a*, 3232, 3446, 3447, 3550, 3944, 4146, 4294. Sum-total of lines missing 396. The mutilated lines 750 and 751 are contracted into one meaningless line, 3446 and 3447 clumsily reconstructed (see foot-notes). There are large illuminated initials fol. 1 front, fol. 2 back, fol. 12 front; the fourth initial, at the beginning of the third Part of the poem, was in the lost fol. 28 and was probably the cause of the loss. The same three pages are also surrounded with richly ornamented borders. The initials and other ornaments are in colours (red, blue, green, opal; no gold) and represent foliage or flowers. According to Dr. Henry Ward they are the work of a South French or Italian artist. The writing of the MS. is English. No rubrics. No mark of cæsura.

Sometimes *ei* for *e*, as "reid" : "heid" for *red* : *hed*, "wheyn" for *when*; *ay* for *a*, as "tayle" : "payle" for *tale* : *pale*; "boykes" 761 for *bookes*; *c-* for *ch-* in "Caloun" 1196, "caumbre" 1247, "*carge*" 1281; þ is not used, only *th*. The English plural forms *her*, *hem* are everywhere replaced by "their," "theim."

[1] The whole MS. was examined by Mr. Henry Bradshaw in 1878, and "several leaves found to be wanting," 25 in all. Accordingly, the actual number of numbered leaves is 186 + the original fol. 108, now misplaced as fly-leaf before fol. 1.

Date of MS. Ba. latter half of fifteenth century. In the margin of fol. 5 front is an astrological diagram. This diagram and the Latin words inscribed in it are not written by the copyist of MS. Ba., but by a later hand, which seems, however, to belong to the fifteenth century.

§ 6. Bo. = *Bodley MS.* 776. Oxford.

Vellum, 71 leaves numbered + 4 fly-leaves at the beginning, 1 at the end, all unnumbered, 10 × 6¾ inches. Single columns of 34 lines. A very good MS. Date about 1430–1440.

Gatherings of eight leaves, with catchwords in the right-hand bottom corner of the back of the last leaf of each gathering. The volume is bound in calf and contains only the text of *Thebes*. The first eight lines of fol. 1 front and the corresponding lines 31–40 on fol. 1 back have been cut off altogether or in part, no doubt for the sake of the illumination once adorning the front page of the MS. Between leaves 68 and 69 is a gap of two leaves, ll. 4456–4586. Sum-total of lost lines 149. The rubrics are written in red in the column of the text (not in the margin), and are counted in the 34 lines of the column as stated above. In some pages the letters are half effaced and filled in with darker ink. Ornamental border (gold, blue, green, vermilion), resembling those of MS. Arundel 119, on fol. 1 front, stretching along left side and bottom (upper part cut off). Large initials (in red and blue), with scrollwork extending along margin, at the beginning of Pars prima, Pars secunda, and Pars tercia. Ornamented initials of the same kind but smaller are to be found on leaves 25 to 34, one on each leaf, either on front or back.

The cæsura is marked in the majority of the lines, except in the Prologue, where it is often missing. The mark varies very much. It may be a curve (the commonest mark in fol. 4–9), or a middle point, or a slanting stroke, or point and stroke (on the whole the most usual mark, especially in the latter part of the volume), or a sort of curve resembling a 7. Colophon (in red): " Here endeth þe Destruccion of Thebes " (the last eleven letters almost effaced). Between l. 4716 and the colophon stand two lines (cf. 185 and 186):

> " Here is now ended a fynal destruccioun
> of mighty Thebes þat strong and roial toun."

§ 7. C. = *Cambridge University Library, MS. Addit.* 3137.

Vellum, 48 leaves, single columns of 33 lines. The leaves are at present 8¾ × 5 inches, but the volume has been mutilated by a binder, who has cut its top edge and outer edge (the bottom is less cut) so much as to carry away not only much of the foliate border but sometimes even the first letter or part of the first letter of lines in back pages. The fourth leaf front has in the right-hand margin a kind of armorial bearings showing three black shields encompassed by red lines on three sides; this has been the means of preserving the original breadth of the leaf ($6\frac{1}{2}$ inches), the binder, instead of cutting the margin as usual, folding it inwards against the text column. How much has been cut off at the top and bottom cannot now be ascertained. The MS. was written in the second half of the fifteenth century.

Gatherings of eight leaves, with catchwords. Ruling with the plummet. Cæsura frequently marked (in about four or five lines in each page, on an average), either by middle point or by slanting stroke; occasionally both marks are to be found in the same line. Rubrics in the column, preceded by a small ornamental scroll, alternately blue and gold.

MS. C., which contains only *Thebes*, originally had 74 leaves; of these no less than 26 are now lost, viz. fol. 1–13 (ll. 1–822), fol. 15 (ll. 886–951), fol. 17 and 18 (ll. 1017–1142), fol. 23 (ll. 1403–1468), fol. 30 (ll. 1858–1922), fol. 58–63 (ll. 3668–4060), fol. 69 and 70 (ll. 4386–4515). Altogether 1668 lines are missing.

Leaves 1 and 2 had been misplaced by the original binder (they are fastened together by a small piece of parchment), but they have been detached and put in their right place by the University Librarian, Mr. Jenkinson.

C. is a good MS.; the spelling is very good. Final *e* is sparingly used, except where it was pronounced. Tags are frequently, but not at all regularly, used. MS. C. was bought of a Birmingham bookseller in 1894.

The colophon runs thus:

> "Here endith the Sege of Thebes the cite
> Example yevyng to lyue in rest. loue and charite."

§ 8. Di. = *Digby* 230. Bodleian Library, Oxford.

Vellum. Large folio, 223 (written) leaves, $15\frac{3}{4} \times 11$ inches. Double columns of 45 lines. The late experts, Mr. Madan of the Bodleian Library, and Mr. Macray, author of *Codices Digbeiani*, who discussed the relative age of Digby 230 and Bodley 776 in my presence, disagreed in opinion; Mr. Madan considering Digby 230 to be younger than Bodl. 776, Mr. Macray regarding the two as contemporaneous (between 1440 and 1450), or, if anything, the former as older than the latter. Mr. Bergen, in his edition of Lydgate's *Troy Book*, Introduction, p. xiv, says, "late fifteenth century, 1470(?)."

Gatherings of eight leaves, with catchwords. The original first leaf of the first gathering has been cut off; this was evidently done pretty long ago, as the front side of the leaf, which is at present the first, is so much worn that several words are scarcely legible, while others have been filled in by a later hand (not always correctly).

The text of *Thebes* occupies fol. 1 front—27 back, but on account of the loss just mentioned it is incomplete at the beginning. The present fol. 1 begins with l. 154. Besides this, the latter half of l. 1537, l. 1538 and the former half of l. 1539 have been carelessly omitted by the copyist. Sum-total of lines missing 155. At the bottom of the second column of fol. 27 back stands the colophon: "Here endith the Sege of Thebes." The next line is: "And bigynneth the Sege of Troye."

No mark of cæsura. Tags occur, but not regularly, except in *g*, where a tag is the rule. At the end of each line there is, with few exceptions, either a middle point or a rather comma-like hook. Rubrics in the columns. þ is used alternately with *th* in all positions; "wiche" for *whiche* is the rule; ȝ always for *y* in *ȝe*, *ȝoure*, *ȝit*, etc., and for *gh* in *brouȝte*, *siȝt*, etc.

The text of *Thebes* is beautifully ornamented with large initials and foliate borders in gold and blue on fol. 1 (Pars Prima), fol. 6 (Pars Secunda), and fol. 15 (Pars Tercia). The original first leaf, if quite filled with text, would have contained 180 lines; as it held only 153, the space of 27 lines was left for ornamentation. There are also some smaller illuminated initials (in gold, blue, violet). At l. 1901 space was left for an initial of two lines, which was not executed.

Brown leather binding with clasps. On the front cover are the Digby arms with the circumscription: "Insignia. Kenelmi. Digby. Equitis. Aurati."

§ 9. Du. = *Prince Frederick Duleep Singh's MS.* Old Buckenham Hall, Norfolk.

Vellum, 83 leaves (unnumbered), 71 of which contain the text of our poem, while 12 are blank. Size of leaves 10⅜ × 7 inches.

Single columns of 30 lines. Rubrics in the columns. Old binding (but probably not the original one), boards covered with brown calf. On the back LIDG ATES POEM is stamped in black. Date late fifteenth century.

The volume is constituted as follows: three blank paper leaves, two blank vellum ones (on the front page of the first a late hand has written "The Story of Odipus by Lydgate Monk of Bury disciple of Chaucer"), ten gatherings of eight leaves (nine of which leaves are lost) with catchwords, six blank vellum leaves, one blank paper leaf. The paper leaves were put in when the volume was rebound; on this occasion leaves were cut down a little, as is proved by the lower half of the catchwords of the ninth gathering "Marked hym wiþ" being gone. The first page of the Prologue, from its somewhat soiled condition, appears to have been for some time the coverless front page of the MS. volume.

The text has several large gaps, viz. 111–337 (= four leaves), 4284–4340 (= one leaf), 4459–4572 (= two leaves), and 4630–4716 (= two leaves); besides these losses (nine leaves = 485 lines + the rubrics) 1537*a*–39*b*, 1799–1800, 2901–4, 3973–74, 4260*b* and 4261*a* are omitted (= 10 lines). Sum-total of lines missing 495 + rubrics.

The rubrics, which are very like those of Arundel 119, are alternately blue and red. In some cases Du. has an extra rubric in Latin, *e.g.* before l. 1569: (blue) "Verba regis Adrasti ad Polimite atq*ue* Tide*um* milites strenuissi*m*os." The cæsura is marked in almost every line by a middle point and a slanting stroke. At the end of every line is a middle point. Every other or third line begins with a capital letter, exceptionally two lines in succession; thus as a rule capitals and small letters alternate here. *y*, never ȝ; þ and *th* interchange; long open *ē* is regularly written *ea*, as "reason," "ease," "please," etc.; "berth" for *birth*.

The first page of the text (Prologue) is beautifully illuminated in gold and colours, the text being enclosed on all four sides by a border in gold, blue, and violet, surrounded with fine foliate ornaments in gold, blue, pink, and green. The initial W is of four lines. The initial letter at the beginning of Secunda and Tercia Pars (of four lines), and in a few other places, *e.g.* l. 1569 (of three lines), are only in the blue and red of the rubrics. The beginning of Prima Pars is lost. On the inside of the front cover are the names of four prior owners of the MS. Then comes the book-plate of the present owner, showing his arms, with the motto: "Prodesse quam Conspici. Ex libris Principis Frederici Duleep Singh."

§ 10. G. = *The Gurney MS.*

This MS.,[1] which contains only Lydgate's *Thebes*, belongs to Mr. J. H. Gurney, of Northrepps, Norwich. It gives the text almost without any gaps; only 2714, 3142, 4149, 4184 are omitted.

Paper, 75 leaves, 11 × 8¼ inches. Single columns of 28 to 30 lines, except in the last six or eight leaves, which have about 35 lines in each page. Rubrics are very scarce, only at large intervals a word or two, as "Thebes," "kyng Amphion," "Edippus," etc. being written in the margin by the copyist. There are also here and there some words written in black in the margin by a later hand, as "Lidgate munk of Burye" (l. 92), "to auoyd the Collyke" (l. 118), etc.

The MS. is cleanly and clearly written. No mark of cæsura. Occasionally a fairly large letter (of two or three lines) appears in blue and red, with a little scrollwork in red. In some pages the first letter of each line is touched with red. In leaves 1 to 15 front each pair of rhyme-lines is marked by ═══] in red to the right of the column. In the first part of the MS. many proper names are underlined with red. The MS. dates from the fifteenth century. Original binding, wooden boards in deerskin.

After the last line of the text: "And Ioye eternal whan we hens wende," a sixteenth-century hand has written: "And of my bok thus I make an ende," while another sixteenth-century hand has added: "ffinis q^{d} J Lidgat." Inside the front cover are names of (seemingly) two former owners of the MS.: "Antonius Morellus Parrhisiensis medicus" and "William Rookes." Inside the book cover is the name Thomas Radclyffe.

§ 11. I. = *the late Sir H. Ingilby's MS.*, now at Compton Hall, Staffs.[2]

"Paper, 350 leaves, 4to shape. It contains Chaucer's *Canterbury*

[1] It was, through the good offices of Dr. Furnivall, collated for me by Mr. Henry Littlehales, who also, after consulting Mr. F. Bickley in the MSS. Department of the British Museum, sent me much information, of which use has been made in the description of the MS. Later on, coming to London myself, I had an opportunity of looking over the MS., which by the liberal courtesy of Mr. Gurney was allowed to go up to my private London address.—A. E.

[2] This MS., while in the possession of Sir H. Ingilby, Bart., of Ripley Castle,

Tales (ending fol. 301 front) and Lydgate's *Thebes* (fol. 301 back to fol. 350 at the foot of the front page)." Single columns of 45 to 48 lines in *Thebes*. No rubrics. Date second half of fifteenth century. Bound in brown calf. "The leaves to cclxxii are numbered by the text-copier. . . . No leaves seem to be missing from the *Cant. Tales*. I have numbered the leaves 273–350 in pencil." In the *Thebes* part of the MS. are two large gaps, 3935–4116 (two leaves = 182 lines) and 4582–4676 (one leaf = 95 lines). 785–8 are omitted, and so are 118, 601–2, 1343–44, 2005–6, 2013–14, 2021–22, 2027–28, (2074), (2802), 2927–8 (3414), 3504, 4289–90 (= 25 lines). Sum-total of lines missing 302 (inclusive of the lines replaced by new ones).

The cæsura is marked in almost every line by a slanting stroke. No illuminated letters or other ornaments. At the beginning of the Prologue and the three parts of the poem space is left for large capitals (of four, three, two and two lines respectively), but none have been executed. At the end (fol. 350 front) is this colophon: "Heere endith the laste tale of Canterbury maad and told bi Dan John Lidgate Mon" (the rest has been cut off).

§ 12. L_1. = *MS. Laud. Misc.* 557. Bodleian Library, Oxford.

Paper, 66 (written) leaves, 11¾ × 8 inches. Single columns of 35 or 36 lines, including the rubrics, which are in the text column. Written in the second half of the fifteenth century. The text of *Thebes* is perfectly complete. The volume contains five gatherings, three of 20 leaves with catchwords, one of 20 leaves, and one of 26 leaves, both without catchwords. There are some enlarged (two line) initials in blue and red with scrollwork down the margin of the page. The rubrics are preceded by the common two-stroke mark in varying colours, red, or blue, or blue and yellow, or violet and yellow. At the bottom of the first leaf is written: "Liber Guilielmi Laud Archie*pisco*pi Cantuar*iensis* et Cancellarij Vniuersitatis Oxon*iensis*. 1633." There are three fly-leaves at the beginning and as many odd leaves at the end. No marks of the cæsura. Large

Yorkshire, was most kindly collated for me by Dr. Furnivall, who also wrote down and sent me many particulars (quoted above between inverted commas) about the MS. At a visit to London some time afterwards I had myself an opportunity of there examining the MS. through the courtesy of its then owner, Mr. Lawrence W. Hodson, Compton Hall, near Wolverhampton. The collation of Dr. Furnivall had then already been entered among the foot-notes: otherwise the MS. would here be designated by the name of the Hodson MS. of *Thebes*.—A. E.

tags are frequent, especially in *s* and *t*. In the former part of the volume there is no point or other mark at the end of the lines, but from fol. 49 front, l. 11 (= l. 3431 of the text) to the end the copyist has made a point and a hook at the end of every line, except l. 3537–49, which lack such a mark. The *z*-like form of *r* is the only one used.

Thebes begins fol. 1 front ("The prolog*us* off Thebes") and goes to fol. 66 front, where is the colophon:

> "Here endith now þe fynall destruction,
> Of myghty Thebes þe roiall toun."

Then follows:

> "O bona fortuna cur non es omnibus vna,
> Es bona diuitibus es mala pauperibus.
> Constat Rogero Thorney m*ercer*.
> John Stowe."

On the first fly-leaf is written:

> "Constat Rogero Thorney m*ercer*."

Then (by another hand):

> "Qui in rota altius cedet, is proximus est ruine
> Illa casta, quam nemo rogauit.
> Infida est custos, castitatis necessitas.
> Omnis n*ost*ra actio, subiecta est mille casibus."

(by yet another hand)

> "Laud 557.
> This is John Stowes boke."

The next leaf is of vellum. At the top of the front page of the third fly-leaf is written on a scroll bordered with red: "The calender off Thebes."

The covers are flexible, made up of six layers of linen cloth, covered with rose-coloured parchment.

§ 13. L_2. = *MS. Laud. Misc.* 416. Bodleian Library, Oxford.

Paper, 289 leaves, 12 × 8½ inches. The MS. has no fly-leaf and is imperfect both at the beginning and at the end. The *Siege of Thebes* is written in double columns of 43 lines fol. 227 front to fol. 254 front, ending at about three-fourths down the first column, with the colophon (in black ink): "Here endith þe distruccion of thebes." The second column of fol. 254 front and the whole of fol. 254 back are blank. Lines omitted in the text of *Thebes* 139–40, 849–52, 1300, (3628) = 8 lines. The volume contains, amongst other texts, an English translation of Vegetius' *De re militari* (for the other contents, see Coxe's *Catal.*).[1] This translation was copied in our MS. in 1459, as witnessed by the note written fol. 226 back: "Here endith the boke that clerkis clepyn in latyn Vegecii de re militari which was translate out of laten in to Englesh at the ordinaunce *and* byddyng of the worthy *and* worshipfull lord Sir Thomas berkeley . . .; by (*sic*) turnyng of this boke in to English was endid in the vigill of alle hallowyn the yere of our lord MCCCC *and* VIII . . ., Amen. Script*um* Rhodo p*er* Joh*anne*m Neuton die 25 Octobris 1459." As *Thebes* is written in the same hand and with the same ink (though not on the same paper, the water-marks differing, as was kindly pointed out by the librarian, Mr. Nicholson), its date may be regarded as pretty well settled.

The rubrics are few in number and written in the outer margins with the same somewhat pale ink as the text. The poem fills two gatherings, the former of 12 leaves, with catchwords "Such opyn wrong," the latter of 16 leaves. No mark of cæsura. There are no ornamental initials in *Thebes*. At the first three lines of the Prologue and of the three Parts of the poem there are small spaces left, but these spaces have not been filled in. As a rule, proper names (personal, geographical, mythological) are underlined by the copyist.

The volume is bound in wooden covers, with clasps (broken), and leather back. At the bottom of the first leaf is the same inscription as in L_1, viz. Liber Guilielmi Laud, etc.

§ 14. Lb. = *Lambeth MS.* 742. Lambeth Palace Library, London.

Vellum, 68 leaves, 11 × 7 inches. Single columns of 32 to 34 lines. *Thebes* begins fol. 1 front and ends fol. 68 back, with the colophon: "Here endith the destruccion of Thebes by J. Lydgate Monke of Bury qd Lȝ." The first page as well as the last is very much soiled, these leaves having evidently during a long time been on the outside of the volume, which had then no cover. The text of these pages is, however, perfectly legible. There is a gap 65–392 (328 lines = five leaves) and another 4597–4658 (62 lines = one leaf). Besides, 814 and 3654 are omitted. Sum-total of missing lines 392. The date of MS. Lb. is about the middle of the fifteenth century.

Gatherings of eight leaves, with catchwords. No ruling for the lines, but the text of each page is enclosed within a rectangular

[1] *Catalogi Codd. MSS. Bibl. Bodl.* II.

frame of a single line. Tags are common in *t*, *f*; only *y*, not ȝ; generally *th*, þ only here and there in *þou*, *þanne*, *þe*, etc. Mark of the cæsura common, a slanting stroke. No rubrics in the first two-thirds of the poem. Rubrics begin fol. 48 front and are in the column. They agree, though not wholly, with those of Ar. The first rubric of Lb., corresponding to the rubric at l. 3312 in Ar., is found after l. 3341 of the poem, where the copyist has first written "How Adrastus and alle thestat*es* of" with his black ink, as if it were a line of the text, then added in red the two lines, "How Adrastus and alle þe astat*es* of Grekes/prayden Ligurgus for þe liff of Isiphile"; this is succeeded by l. 3342 of the poem: "for we be come for non othir thynge," written in red like a rubric. Then comes l. 3343 in black.

At the beginning of the Prologue is a large (seven-line) illuminated initial W in red, blue, and gold, with foliate ornaments on three margins of the page. In the same manner the initials of the three Parts of the poem are decorated. Besides, enlarged blue initials with red ornaments occur here and there. Proper nouns are often underlined by a later hand.

Fol. 2 front at the top is the following memorandum: ("Mem. That this *Siege and Destruccion of Thebes* in *English* verse by *John Lydgate* is amongst the Manu-scripts which with many other Books Printed were given by *Henry* Duke of *Norfolk* . . . to the *Royal Society* at *London* for the Promoting Natural Knowledge) See page 134 of þe Catalogus therof Printed at London 1681. in 4to." The last page of the volume, after the colophon, has "Bibliotheca Lambethana" (stamped) and "Ex dono Joh*ann*is Keyti de Wodstocke et de Grays Inne socius tempore visitac*io*nis Oxon. 1624." Under this, in another hand, probably Keyt's own, is written "Gi: Keyt hospit*ii* Grayensis socius."

Fol. 36 front to 38 front are a number of scribblings in the outer margin, done by a later (sixteenth-century?) hand, partly words repeated from the text (where they are underlined) in a more modern form or spelling, as "warryoure" for *werreour*, "laye on them" for *ley on hem*, etc., partly explanatory glosses, as "he wold nothinge kepe back" for *hym list nothyng restrayne* (2685), "lyue in scarcitye" for *leuyn at myschef* (2690), "riches and faithfull hartes" for *good and hert* (2693), "them withdrawe from their libertye" for *hem cohercen from here liberte* (2699), etc.

The volume is bound in red morocco.

§ 15. M. = *Lord Mostyn's MS.* Mostyn Hall, Flintshire, N. Wales (Gloddaeth Library, MS. No. 258).

Vellum, 61 leaves (not numbered), 10½ × 7 inches. Single columns of 39 lines. Rubrics in the column. The end of the Prologue and the beginning of Pars Prima are lost, ll. 147–222 (76 lines = one leaf, the third of the first gathering). The text ends:

> "Of my tale thus I make an ende. Deo gracias."

with the colophon:

> "Now is here ended the fynal destrucoyon (*sic*)
> Of myghty Thebes that strong and roial toun."

The MS. is a good one, written in the second half of the fifteenth century. It contains only Lydgate's *Thebes*.

Seven gatherings of eight leaves, with catchwords. As a rule the cæsura is marked, usually by a small middle curve or a middle point, in some lines by a slanting stroke, in some by a combination of both. Tags are not unfrequent; always *th*, never þ, except in the rubrics towards the end of Pars Tercia.

Fol. 1 front (l. 1) has a large (six-line) initial W in blue, violet, green, and red, with a foliated border round all the four margins; fol. 13 back (l. 1047) has a beautiful P of six lines and fol. 33 back (l. 2553) a six-line O in the same colours with a foliated border along three sides of the page. The initial S of Pars Prima (l. 177) is gone together with its leaf, the initial S (of four lines) on fol. 20 back (l. 1569) has been cut off.

Modern binding of white parchment. On the back is: "Destruction of Thebes by Lydgate, Manuscript."

See *Fourth Report of the Royal Commission on Historical Manuscripts.* Part I, Report and Appendix. London 1874. fol., p. 361 of Appendix.

§ 16. P = *Pepys MS.* 2011. Magdalen College, Cambridge.

This MS., once the property of Samuel Pepys, is now in the library of the above-mentioned college. Vellum, 76 numbered leaves + 6 fly-leaves, 11¼ × 7¼ inches. Contains only Lydgate's *Thebes*. Single columns of 32 lines, with rubrics in the column. The text of the poem is complete except for 1669–72, 2386, 2396, 3093, (3646), 3654, 4662 (= 10 lines), omitted by the copyist. It ends fol. 76 back and is followed by the colophon: "Here endeth the distruccion off Thebes Secundu*m* lidgate Monke off Bury." Gatherings of eight leaves, with catchwords. Ruling with the plummet from prickings in the margin. The cæsura is occasionally marked by a comma; this is used just as often also at the end of the line; here the slanting stroke is also in use, and even the colon. *y*, not ȝ; þ and *th*; *m* at the beginning of a line is as a rule written as a capital, but of small size; "doith," "goith"; a later hand has occasionally altered *ou* into *ow*, as "mowthe" 4407. There are large initials of three to six lines (in violet, blue, green, and gold) with foliated borders at the beginning of the Prologue and the three Parts of the poem. Even in some other pages enlarged coloured initials are to be found. Date of the MS. second half of fifteenth century.

The front fly-leaves are two; on the back of the first and the front of the second a late hand has written the rubrics (in black) under the heading of "The Table." There are four back fly-leaves; on the first is written (in red): "A lenvoye to all prynces that be disposid to be lecherous"; on the second (in red): "This is the letter that dau*n* John Lidgate Monke of Bury sent to Humfrey duke of Gloucester for mony for making of Bochas"; then follow eight stanzas, ending in fol. 3 front (in red): "Explicat l*ite*ra de dàn John Lidgate." Fol. 3 back has at the bottom two lines (black ink):

> "Wyne, wemen, and tonges inconstant
> Mayke of þe Sapient an yngnoraunte."

Fol. 4 front, at the top (black ink): "Edwardus sextus dei gr*aci*a Anglie. ffraunce et hiberne rex fidei defensor et in terr*is* eccl*es*ie Anglicane et hibernice sup*re*mu*s*."

The volume is bound in calf; on the outside of the front cover "Sam Pepys" is stamped in gold.

§ 17. Ra. = *MS. Rawlinson C.* 48. Bodleian Library, Oxford.

Vellum and paper, 136 leaves, 8¼ × 5¾ inches. Single columns, generally of 33 lines. Lydgate's *Thebes* occupies fol. 5 front to 78 front; on this page are the last five lines of the poem; then follow these four lines:

> "Off this seege / nowe is no more
> Where thoruh eue*ry* part / greuyd was sor.
> And thus eendith the fynal destruccіou*n*
> Off worthi Thebes / the myhti Roiall tou*n*."

Then:

> "**Explicit finalis destructio**
> **Ciuitatis Thebanorum.**"[1]

The rubrics are written in the margin with the same black ink as the text, but in letters of somewhat smaller size; in the first 37 leaves Latin and English rubrics alternate more or less regularly; fol. 38–41 (see below) have no rubrics; fol. 42–78 the rubrics are in Latin. Throughout the MS. rubrics are far between. Date of the MS. about 1450.

Gatherings of twelve leaves, viz. one vellum, four paper, two vellum, four paper, one vellum, with catchwords in the right-hand bottom corner. The cæsura is generally marked by an oblique stroke. Only *th* and *y* are used, not þ and ȝ. The first letter of the Prologue is a large (seven-line) capital W, beautifully drawn with ink (no colouring); the top of this letter forms a crown inscribed with the word "Magister." The initials of the three Parts of the poem and of l. 1569 were meant to be two-line capitals, but the spaces left blank for this purpose have not been filled in. Accordingly those letters (S, P, O, S) are wanting. At intervals a line is somewhat drawn in and a mark of two strokes shows that the copyist intended to put the usual ¶ as the sign of a subdivision. But in no case is this sign there. The MS. was never completely finished. It is bound in boards covered with white parchment.

The lines 2099 to 2294 (196 lines = three leaves) having been lost, the gap was filled in by a later (sixteenth-century) hand, that copied from a MS. of the same type as Ra. (Ad_1. Ad_2. I. Ba.). They now occupy the four leaves 38 to 41. The lines 416, 417, 2281–2, 3446, 3447, 4304 (= seven lines) are omitted. In the former portion of the poem, fol. 5 back to 36 front, there is an unusually great number of alterations and insertions made by a later hand, as 518 "And him coniured," 520 "that he wolde," etc.

§ 18. Ro. = *Royal MS.* 18. D. II. British Museum.

Large folio, vellum, 211 leaves + one front and one back fly-leaf, $15\frac{3}{8} \times 11$ inches. *Thebes* begins fol. 147 back, second column (modern numbering with lead-pencil) and ends fol. 162 front, halfway down the first column, with the colophon (in red):

> "Here now endeth as ȝe maye see.
> The destruccyon of Thebes the Cytee."

[1] As to the other contents of the volume, see *Catalogus Codd. MSS. Bibl. Bodl.* Pars v. Fasc. ii. Codd. Rawlinson, ed. Macray, p. 14 seq.

Fol. 146 back and 147 front are blank. Double columns of about 54 lines (50 to 58 lines). Rubrics in the column. Ruling with the plummet. Date about 1460.

Gatherings of eight leaves, with catchwords at the right-hand bottom corner. The cæsura is usually marked by a small point, middle or low; sometimes this mark is wanting, sometimes we find two points. At the end of the lines there is no point, except in fol. 149 front, where all the lines of the first column have a point (generally low) at the end, and fol. 160 front to the end of the poem, in which three leaves there is a point or small curve at the end of all the lines. þ is rare: *þe, þat, þi*; only *y*, not ȝ (in the text itself); the usual form of *r* is the *z*-shaped one, but in the latter portion of the poem the *r*-shaped one comes in more frequently and in the last two leaves is on a par with the other. Consonants, especially liquids, are sometimes doubled, as "storrye," "holle" (N.E. *whole*), "lynne" (N.E. *line*), "sownnes" (N.E. *sounds*), "Segge" (N.E. *siege*), etc.

The text, which is incomplete, is adorned with fourteen most exquisitely painted miniatures. The first of these, fol. 148 front, second column, between Explicit Prologus and Prima pars, represents the party of pilgrims leaving Canterbury; in the background is the town with towered wall, cathedral, and houses, and in the upper left corner outside the wall is a large light grey church; six persons of the party are to be seen on horseback clad in gowns of various colours; the second one from the front is Lydgate, speaking, with right hand outstretched; he has a rose-coloured gown and a blue bonnet, and is mounted on a white horse with trappings, blue with gilt ornaments (cf. his description of himself in the Prologue, ll. 73–75 and see Plate 2). The last miniature, fol. 162 front, col. 1, shows the armorial bearings of some noble family. There are numerous enlarged initials (one or two on almost every leaf) in gold, blue, and mauve, with foliated ornaments going a couple of inches up and down the outer margin or the middle of the page.

Many leaves of this fine MS. have been torn out, and thus there are now five considerable gaps in the text of our poem, viz. 618 lines (513–1130) between the present leaves 149 and 150, 414 lines (1987–2400) between fol. 153 and 154, 200 lines (3011–3210) between fol. 156 and 157, 184 lines (3407–3590) between fol. 157 and 158, and 352 lines (3989–4340) between fol. 159 and 160. Besides, l. 3628 is supplied by a new line and 4422*b*–23*a* have been omitted.

Sum-total of lost lines 1770, considerably more than a third of the poem.

The fictitious connection of Lydgate's *Thebes* with Chaucer's *Canterbury Tales* is twice referred to. Fol. 147 back, col. 1, at the top (in red ink): "In this preambile shortly is comprihendid A Mery conseyte of Iohn lydgate Monke of Bury declarynge how he aionyde þe sege of Thebes to the mery tallys of Caunterburye." Fol. 148 front, col. 2, after the miniature described above, follows in red ink:

"Prima pars
Here begynneth the Segge of Thebes ful lamentably tolde by Iohn lidgate Monke of Bury anneyynge it to þe tallys of Canterbury."

The volume is bound in calf.

See *Catalogue of Western MSS. in the Old Royal and King's Collections* (1921), vol. ii, p. 308 ff.; Ward, *Catalogue of Romances*, i, p. 90 f.; H. Bergen, *Lydgate's Troy Book* (E.E.T.S.), Introduction, p. x.

§ 19. S. = *the Stowe MS.* British Museum, *Additional* 29729.

Paper, 288 leaves, $10\frac{5}{8} \times 7\frac{1}{2}$ inches. The volume is chiefly in the handwriting of John Stowe, the historian. *Thebes* goes from fol. 17 front to 83 front, ending at the middle of this page with l. 4716: "Of my tale thus I make an ende / lawes deo." followed by the colophon (in red): "Her endyth the sege of worthy Thebes / by Iohn lydgatt monk of bwry on hos sowll god have marcy wretyn by Iohn Stowe." Single columns of 34 to 39 lines. Ruling with the plummet. Rubrics in red ink in the outer margin, in many instances cut off by the binder.

Only a few lines are omitted, viz. 1455*b*–59*a*, 1732, 1840 (six lines).

The cæsura is marked by a slanting stroke, which, however, occurs only seldom, many pages being without a single pause-bar. y is 1. (sometimes dotted) = *y*; 2. = þ in þe, þat (elsewhere *th* is written); often *w* for *u*, as "fwll," "crwely," "thowght," etc.; not seldom *-ar* for *-er*, as "nevar," "aftar," "nethar," etc. As a rule *theyr ther*, *them* (rarely *her*, *hem*).

The volume is bound in dark violet morocco.

The date of the MS. is settled by this note on the last page: "This boke perteynythe to Iohn Stowe, and was by hym wryten in þe yere of owr Lord 1558."

See *Catal. Codd. MSS. Brit. Mus.*; Sieper, *Reson and Sensuallyte* (E.E.T.S.), Introduction, p. xiii seq.

§ 20. T_1. = *Trinity Coll. MS. R.* 4. 20. Cambridge, Library of Trinity College.

Vellum, 172 leaves, 10½ × 7½ inches. *Thebes* begins fol. 89 front and ends fol. 169 front, about the middle of the page, with the colophon (in red): "⁖ Heere eendeth the distruccioun of Thebes." Then follows:

> "Here is now eendid the fynal distruccioun
> Of myghty Thebes. that strong *and* royal toun."

Single columns of 28 lines. Ruling with the plummet. Rubrics in the margin. Date about 1440. The writing of T_1. is very formal and set, the letters stiff and, as it were, printed. The cæsura is marked in the majority of the lines by a low point or a small curve (a sort of comma) down to fol. 154 front, and from there by a slanting stroke. Tags occur, of small size.

Gatherings of eight leaves, with catchwords. Only *th* and *y* (no þ and ȝ). There is a gap of two leaves between fol. 99 and 100, ll. 615–726 (= 112 lines), and another of two leaves between fol. 105 and 106, ll. 1061–1172 (= 112 lines). Sum-total of missing lines 224. Except this, the MS. is in a good state of preservation; only the lower parts of some pages, as fol. 101 front, fol. 102 back, a.o., are much rubbed so that the ink of the letters is mostly gone. The text is, however, perfectly legible. In fol. 122 part of the top has been torn or cut off, so that on the front page four lines (ll. 2069–72) have lost their second half, and on the back page four lines (ll. 2097–2100) are almost wholly gone. There are ornamental foliated borders (in gold, blue, red, violet, green) round the whole page at the beginning of the Prologue and of the three Parts of the poem. The six-line initial W of the Prologue contains a miniature representing a town with wall and towers (in red) on a blue ground. Also the initials of the three Parts of the poem are of six lines and in colours. Besides, smaller illuminated initials (of one or two lines) are found here and there.

In the margin of the leaves there are various notes and scribblings, amongst which may be mentioned that of fol. 115 front, along the right-hand margin: "In the laste yeare of kynge Henrye the vii. the sayde kynge Graunted his especyall commissyon vnto Syr Rycharde Empsone knyght, and Edmond Duddelye Esquyer. Whoe were ii. of his grave Counsailours. that they showld especyally inquyre of the offendours of penall lawes, wiche they dylygently prosecuted. But the malyce of the people was so encresed a gaynste them for there endeuour and" (the note breaks off abruptly here). As to the matter, see Holinshed's *Chronicles*, iii, 536 seqq. Fol. 141 back along the outer lateral margin of the page is written: "Richard Crvmpe grocer in newgate market at the syne of The griffin the viiith of marche ao 1571." He seems to have parted with the MS. to his apprentice, who fol. 150 back, at the bottom of the page, has made the following entry: "Be yt knowne to all men by this presents that I Iohn wyke am the trw onar off this bouk in wettenes wheare of I have phillipe. ffylken *and* yf I it lowse *and* you it fynde I praie you be so good *and* kinde as be (*sic*) to bringe it whome agin I am now a prentes with won Rychard Crowmp a grosor dwellinge at the sine of the greffen in newgate market anno domene 1571 the seconde of September."

The volume is bound in whole calf.

§ 21. T_2. = *Trinity Coll. MS. O.* 5. 2. Cambridge, Library of Trinity College.

Vellum, large folio, 211 leaves (numbered with pencil), 17¼ × 12 inches. Double columns of 48 lines. *Thebes* begins fol. 191 front and ends fol. 211 back, at the middle of the first column. Rubrics in the outer margin and in the open space down the middle of the page. Ruling with the plummet. The MS. was written in the second half of the fifteenth century.

Gatherings of eight leaves, with catchwords at the foot of the page in the right-hand corner. No mark of cæsura. No tags. *r* shows the three forms. The writing is very like that of *Royal MS.* 18. D ii. Besides Lydgate's *Thebes* the volume contains the romance of *Generydes* (fol. 1–37) and Lydgate's *Troy Book* (fol. 38–190). It has lost several leaves. In the *Thebes* portion there is a gap of one leaf (ll. 2485–2671 = 187 lines, including the beginning of Pars Tercia) between fol. 203 and 204, and another of three leaves (ll. 3633–4209 = 567 lines) between fol. 208 and 209. Sum-total of lost lines 754.

Large illuminated initials (gold, blue, violet) at the beginning of the Prologue (four-line W) and of the first (three-line S) and the second Parts (four-line P) of the poem. Besides, smaller initials (of two lines), illuminated, are occasionally found. Fol. 199 back, in the left margin, is an escutcheon, bearing a cross and a slanting bar; the escutcheon is silver-grey, the cross is red with seven white lilies, the bar is of the same colour as the escutcheon, with three red lilies. Other escutcheons occur in the volume. At the end of the volume is twice written the name "Henry Thwayts" "Henry Thwaites."

The copyist seems to have enjoyed writing verse. He has delivered himself of several (bad) specimens. The Prologus begins with six lines (in red) composed, probably, by him and inserted before Lydgate's opening line, viz.

> "Who so euere on this story list to behold
> Of a sege shall he heren dou*n* be dayes old
> That first gonne was atwene two brothern
> Whiche of condicions diuers and m*a*rvellous wern
> Ethiocles that on hight sone to king Edipp*us*
> Polymite that other as this auct*our* tellith vs."

Then follows: "Whanne that Phebus passid was þe ram," etc. After the Prologue, fol. 191 back, col. 2, the copyist has written (in red):

> "The prologe here is fully now att anend
> And to the first part anoon shall we wend
> And ther in to trete of the first fundaciou*n*
> Of Thebes and by whom it was begonne."

Pars Secunda is introduced by four lines (in red):

> "Now shewid is clerly the ground of our mat*er*
> Of diuers other werkinges hastyly shall yow here
> And of the brethren that to strive now begynne
> Who þe crown of Thebes reuÿssh shall and wyn*n*e."

And at the end of the third Part, to the last line of which is added "Deo gr*aci*as," there is a colophon of six lines (in red):

> "In this wise endith the sege of Thebes
> Ensample shewiñg for to leuen in pes
> To all men that wiln it distinctly rede
> And clerly se what they gete þ*er* to her mede
> As seith this story to Grekes was it gret confusion
> And to that strong Cite vtter ruyn and distruccion."

At the foot of the column we read this prayer (in red):

> "Scriptoris anime: te χρ*iste* precor ut miserere."

The three above-mentioned texts are in old binding, wooden boards covered with originally white parchment.

See Aldis Wright, *Generydes*, 1878 (E.E.T.S.), Preface; H. Bergen, *Lydgate's Troy Book*, 1909–10 (E.E.T.S.), Introduction, pp. xii–xiv.

§ 22. E_1. = *Wynken de Worde's Edition.* British Museum.

The volume, which is marked C.13.a.21, contains Lydgate's *Thebes*, *Assemble de dyeus*, and Lydgate's *Temple of Glas*. *Thebes* is in 8vo (not in 4to, as stated in the Catalogue of the Museum); the first four leaves of each sheet (gathering) have the signatures a i, a ii, a iii, a iiii, b i, b ii, b iii, b iiii, etc. to l i, l ii, l iii, l iiii; the last four leaves of each sheet are unsigned. The original number of leaves in this edition of *Thebes* was 87; three being lost, the present number is 84. The size of the leaves is 7 × 5 inches. Single columns of 28 lines. Rubrics printed in black in the margin. The cæsura is marked by a point (full-stop). No punctuation. In the Catalogue the print is hesitatingly dated at 1500. Schick (*vide infra*) mentions 1498 as, perhaps, a more probable date.

The first leaf (a i) has woodcuts on both sides. That on the front side represents a knight in full armour on horseback; a late hand has written: "Edipus by name"; but it is more likely to be meant for Tydeus. The woodcut of the back side of a i shows a town, the wall of which is in course of building; in the foreground within the wall is a man with a harp in his hand (Amphion); in the background, outside the wall, a man is seen standing with his foot on a dragon and swinging on high a curved sword (Edippus). Underneath is printed: "This is the Royall Cyte of Thebes."

The Prologus begins a ii: "Here begynneth the prologue of the Storye of Thebes." On the second of the unsigned leaves of the first (a) sheet, front, at the top: "Here begynneth the Story of the destruccyon of the Cyte of Thebes." On the first of the unsigned leaves of the third (c) sheet, back: "Explicit prima pars istius Codicilli. Inmediate sequitur secunda pars eiusdem." On the last (fourth) of the unsigned leaves of the sixth (f) sheet, back: "Explicit pars Secunda. Sequitur pars Tercia." On the third of the unsigned leaves of the eleventh (l) sheet, front:

> "And Ioye eternall. whan we hens wende
> Of my tale. thus I make an ende
> AMEN"

with the colophon:

> "Here now endeth as ye maye see
> The destruccyon of Thebes the Cytee."

Underneath is Wynken de Worde's device, about which see Schick, *l.c.*

There are two gaps in *Thebes*, one of two leaves (a iiii and the first of the unsigned leaves) comprising ll. 107–176 of the Prologue (= 70 lines), the other of one leaf (l i) with ll. 4363–4418 (= 56 lines). Single lines missing: 1537*b*–38*a*, 1732, 4422*b*–23*a*. Sum-total 129. The volume is bound in calf.

See Ward, *Catalogue* i, p. 88; Schick, *Lydgate's Temple of Glas* (E.E.T.S.), p. xxvi; Triggs, *The Assembly of Gods* (E.E.T.S.), Introduction, p. x. Cf. Sieper, *Lydgate's Reson and Sensuallyte* (E.E.T.S.), ii, p. 2.

23. E_2. = *Edition in folio*, 1561. British Museum.

The volume has the mark 641. m. 10. It consists of 5 + 9 + 378 leaves (fol. i–ccclxxviii), 12¾ × 8½ inches. The first leaf, front, is the title-page: "The workes of Geffrey Chaucer, newlie printed, with diuers addicions, whiche were neuer in print before; with the siege and destruccion of the worthy Citee of Thebes, compiled by Ihon Lidgate, Monke of Berie. As in the table more plainly doeth appere. 1561." Then follows the table of contents, ending on the fourth leaf, front: "Thus endeth the table of all the workes." The nine leaves contain the Prologue to the Canterbury Tales. *Thebes* begins fol. 356 front and ends fol. 378 back, with the colophon:

"Here now endeth, as ye maie see
The destruction, of Thebes the Citee.

Imprinted at London, by Ihon Kyngston, for Ihon Wight, dwellyng in Poules Churchyarde. Anno. 1561."

There are two columns in the page, each of 55 lines. Rubrics in the column. The cæsura is marked by a comma; exceptionally two such commas occur in one line. No punctuation.

There is in the British Museum another folio edition of 1561, marked 83. l. 5, which is quite the same book as 641. m. 10, except for a few small differences in the title-page, as "citee," "dooeth," etc. See Ward, *Catalogue*, i, p. 88.

CHAPTER VI

GENEALOGY OF THE MANUSCRIPTS AND FIRST EDITIONS

§ 1. *General Remarks on the Genealogy of the MSS. + O.*

THE genealogy of the twenty-one MSS. and the two oldest editions is rather complex. Neither of the two editions is printed from any one of the twenty-one MSS.; each edition represents a MS. of its own, so that the actual number of MSS. may be said to be twenty-three. No one of these is an immediate copy of Lydgate's original MS. This original MS. is lost and so is the first (= immediate) copy of it, which is the source of all the existing MSS. The first copy had some faults—due either to Lydgate himself or to his first copyist —which are reproduced in all the MSS. From this first copy, which represents Lydgate's lost original and is designated by O in the genealogical diagram, p. 94, the twenty-three MSS. have branched out, each class and branch dividing into groups united and distinguished by peculiarities (faults) of their own. The transmission of the text by the hands of the copyists has not always been clean and uniform. Not only are in several MSS. different portions copied from different MSS. belonging to different branches, but sometimes copyists who had more than one MS. at their disposal interlarded the text of their principal basis-MS. with scattered more or less numerous extracts (real or imaginary corrections) from their subsidiary MS., according to their own taste or fancy. Besides, faults characteristic of one group of MSS. very often appear in one or more MSS. of another group, the same mistakes or the same attempts at correction being made independently by different scribes.

In this manner the principal relations of the MSS. have sometimes become much involved and confused. However, the main facts of the genealogy can be cleared up, and with regard to the most important MSS. (Ar. Bo. T_1. L_1. M. Ad_1. C.) the degree of affinity seems to be subject to no uncertainty. All the MSS. have a more or less considerable number of faults, amounting in some of them to 200–300, and a complete enumeration of all these faults in every one of the twenty-three MSS. would take up more space than can reasonably be afforded. Thus only necessary examples will be repeated here, with a general reference to the *vv. ll.* With a view to economy of space a reference is often given to the *vv. ll.* instead of repeating an entire line. The most important MSS. will, of course, be treated more liberally, with the exception of MS. Ar., which forms the basis of our text and in which all faults, small as well as great, are distinctly marked by an asterisk.

§ 2. Ad_1. Ad_2. I.

a. These three MSS. form one *group*. They have a great number of faults in common, which are found in no other group of MSS., *e.g.* 55. the] *om.* 78. Wher] Where as. 109. wel] *om.* 122. I wol my-silf be] myself wil be. 138. pleynly] such. 245. and] of þe. 303. Soyle] place. 333. lyneal] lyne of. 458. he] hyt. 533. in hast gan] fast gan to. 538. with-in] yn hit. 567. coraious] curious. 606. in al that euere] in al þe hast. 633 *and* 634 *transposed.* 646. abraydyng] obreidinge. 717. thre] his. 724. ageyn he most in hast] in scth he must agein. 732. mor] with him. 749. that he the monstre hath] þat þe monstre is. 769. manly] famous (*see* 770). 785–88 *missing.* 854. Cerberus] Cerebrus. 929. I] he. 1017. whan he was blynd and old] þat was so bolde. 1125. is come out] is ended. 1193. riche] wis. 1268. the] a. 1462. Incomyng] hom coming. 1572. thorgh] bi. 1652. at the] at her. 1735. and trouthes] and his. 1845. vpon] of. 2120. faste] manly (*see* 2119). 2155. at a] of. 2165. liftyng] heuing. 2166. Eue] heuene. 2273. heghe] þe. 2334. drogh] out drowe. 2350. soroufull] ferful. 2365. aduersite] gret aduersite. 2386. yrayled] trayled. 2404. hem] to hem. 2421. fulle] hol. 2462. his manhood] manhod of him. 2499. and rooted on] vpon. 2528. forto be] to haue be. 2673. lik] logged lik. 2771. erly and ek] boþe erly and. 2782. lese] leue. 2820. *see v.l.* 2846. no worldly] al the wordles Ad_1., alle the worldis Ad_2. I. 3002. was þer] fond þei. 3022. eny] ony where. 3168. in her slepe] while þei slepe. 3246. in a] in such a (in such I.). 3478. her answer] this. 3487. knyght] king. 3517 *and* 3518 *transposed.* 3571 *and* 3572 *transposed.* 3681. fatal] final. 3917. ful] right. 4147. that] and. 4161. happy] *om.* 4278. smette] bar. 4445. To hold her way] Her way to hold in ese. 4549. no man] no þing. 4620. in Arge] *om.* 4644. To los fynal vnto] vn-to gret los of. 4675. Ambicioun] abusioun. 4707. loue] *om.*

Frequently one or more words are omitted, *e.g.* 137, 156, 284, 656, 685, 709, 828, etc. Often a word is added, *e.g.* 705, 784, 833, 1399,

1472, etc. The sequence of words is often altered, *e.g.* 755, 782, 834, 1055, 1150, 1480, etc.

b. Ad_2. and I. form a *sub-group* with common faults, which are not found in Ad_1., *e.g.* 27. Ech] They. 54. hool] of Iobe Ad_2., of Iove I. 55. Voyding] Wyndyng. 68. in soth] in feith. 85. boos ne belle] liste nor belle. 93. nyȝ] nat. 120. *see v.l.* 127. *see v.l.* 162. Shet] leve. 169. bekke] necke. 174. bonde] allowid. 200. it] right. 213. Bochas] bookes. 235. styring] strength. 264. foot] stock. 372. silfe] first. 479. abrayde] chied. 563. syyt] ryite Ad_2., right I. 622. to manace] to his manace. 671. Naturely] namely. 725. remewe] rewe. 746. holy] onely. 811. vnwist he] he wist. 854. Chief porter] a feend. 855. *see v.l.* 961. pleyn] feyne. 1048. chilyndre] chelandir. 1137. gret] full. 1176. grisly] grevous. 1216. trist] trysty. 1230. *see v.l.* 1260. leyde] lenyd. 1320. courte] place. 1424. Enforsyng] In forthryng. 1545. Gypon] gryphoun. 1678. the eeres] ther (*cf.* theres Ad_1.). 1732. *see v.l.* 1734. reward] no reward. 1808. voide] leve. 1861. auayled hem] he sette by. 2005 *and* 2006, 2013 *and* 2014 *om.* 2023. *see v.l.* 2074. *see v.l.* 2141. peyn of] *om.* 2184. hegh] gret. 2186. kylleth] styketh. 2300. gilte] glistred. 2304. stoundemele] in that while. 2399. courte] contre. 2491. on] of oo (*see v.l.*). 2520. *see v.l.* 2535. herde] redde. 2697. louen] lyven. 2802. *see v.l.* 2927 *om.* 2930. kalkyng] talkyng. 2962. *see v.l.* 3035. worldly] worthy. 3041. anon remwe] renne a-weye faste. 3042. swe] swe in haste. 3120. some] sure. 3197. Vermes] Sermes. 3273. disioynte] distresse Ad_2., distreyat I. 3305. ful ryal bylt] wel bilded. 3414. *see v.l.* 3504. *see v.l.* 3537. verryfie] to specifie. 3589. thorpes] thruhuppis. 3623. nede] herte. 3846. rescus] reskewe. 3915. roof] rood. 4190. A fewe dayes] And many dayes. 4276. ranne] rood. 4289 *and* 4290 *om.* 4328. aventaylles] entailes. 4334. percyd] pressid. 4441. burnet] moornyng. 4453. menyng] her meevyng I., her moornyng Ad_2. 4483. herte] *om.* etc.

There are many omissions of words, *e.g.* 96, 97, 136, 239, 474, 740, etc., and additions, *e.g.* 77, 108, 206, 266, etc.; fewer transpositions of words, *e.g.* 107, 647, etc. Several couplets were omitted in the common original of Ad_2. I., viz. 601–2, 1343–44, 2005–6, 2013–14, 2021–22, 2027–28, 4289–90. The copyist could scarcely be expected to feel their absence. But the loss of a single line could not but be remarked, and except in the case of 234, has been supplied by the copyist. In some cases, 120, 1732, 2074, 3414, he has succeeded, guided by the context, in finding the right rhyme-words, in others 2802, 2962, 3504, he has not. As to 127–28 see *v.l.*

c. Neither of the two MSS. Ad_2. I. is derived from the other.

Ad_2. has special faults, *e.g.* 128. *see v.l.* 169. nodde] *om.* 634. soth] sothe is. 1095. Regaly] Regalite. 1141. enrolled] envolvid. 1185. saugh] safe. 1230. be bond] by lawe. 1428. ful] fully. 1731. That] What. 2349. dismayd] disamayed. 2846. Discuren] Disceyven. 3078. to releue] to my releve. 3119. water] *om.* 3924. hom] he. 4187. vncouth] sondry. 4464. Tyl] Alle. 4487. constreyntys] compleyntis, etc. 4094–4158 *and* 4504 *to the end are lost.*

I. has special faults, *e.g.* 2. in-to bole] to the foule. 11. paleys] place. 117. Rede] seed (*from* 118). 118 *om.* 127 *and* 128. *see v.l.* 1055 *om.* 1195. is] was. 1221. hie] *om.* 1230. be bond] by lond. 1341. not] *om.* 1524 *and* 1525 *transposed.* 1669. amerous] aueryous. 1839 *and* 1840 *transposed.* 2068 *and* 2069 *transposed.* 2514. and] of the. 2604. kyng ypemedoun] kyng of Epemedoun. 2822. and to] of. 2928 *om.* 3318. goodly of ȝour] of your good hih. 3684. That] *om.* 3935 *to* 4116 *and* 4582 *to* 4676 *lost.*

d. Genealogical relation of subgroup Ad_2. I. to Ad_1.

Ad_1. has special faults, *e.g.* 75. rusty] lusti. 772. to] *om.* 1709. in a maner drede] a manere in drede. 1763. clipsed] eclipsid. 2067. to] it to. 2354. to] forto. 3152. forto] *om.* 3665. in] on. 4397. al] *om.* 4572. and] *om.* 4707. Troubles] troublenesse. Besides, Ad_1. has a number of faults (against Ad_2. I.) in common with other MSS., *e.g.* 18. whan] whanne þat. 166. not] hit nat. 649. preef] preest. 938. falle] bifalle. 953. nor] ne. 1173. ful] right. 1254. and] and þe. 1385. vpon] of. 1406. his] *om.* 1599. that] *om.* 1732 *om.* 1892. his] this. 1930. this] þe. 2504. lorn] forlorn. 3214. and alle] and. 3425. non] *om.* 3460. falle] befalle. 3723. This] Thus. 4298. loud] land. 4390. by] *om.*

In about a dozen cases I. agrees with Ad_1. against Ad_2., *e.g.* 17. *second* on] *om.* 86. wil] wolde. 295. Cadmvs] Cadinus. 1888. as] as a. 2557. thy] the. 3001. þat] as, etc. In a few cases Ad_2. goes with Ad_1. against I., *e.g.* 2822. And to] and Ad_1. Ad_2., of I.

Ad_2. and I. are, by one or more intermediate links, derived from Ad_1. In Ad_1. the lines 2074, 3414, 3504 were, by inadvertency, omitted by the scribe, who, however, soon perceived his error and inserted them (marked with the usual small blue and red ornament) at the bottom of their respective pages (*see vv. ll.*). It is in this state of things in Ad_1. that the treatment of the lines in question in Ad_2. I. finds its easy and natural explanation, thus providing an almost decisive proof that the latter two MSS. are descended from the former. For ll. 2704, 3414, 3504, which the copyist found omitted in their right places, he has substituted new lines. As to the original 2074, 3414, 3504, coming on them further down in his original, he simply left them out. In Ad_1. l. 1732 is blank, probably because the copyist did not quite understand it (*cf. vv. ll.*); it may have been corrupted in some way or other in his immediate original.[1] In Ad_2. I. an almost new line has been supplied. 2927 is another of the lines that stand alone in Ad_1. The next copyist, perceiving this before he had begun to write it out, did not take the trouble to compose a new line to rhyme with it, but simply omitted it. Arriving at l. 2928, which in Ad_1. stands (with the usual mark) at the bottom of the page after l. 2934, he copied it, but being unable to make a new fitting line, left a blank after it. This state of things is maintained in Ad_2. But the copyist of I. preferred to omit l. 2928 altogether.

ll. 120, 2802, and 2962 seem to prove that there are two intermediate links between Ad_1. and Ad_2. I. In the first the lines were omitted, in the second—the immediate original of Ad_2. I.—new lines were composed to fill up the gap. The treatment of 127–8 in Ad_2. I. (*see vv. ll.*) leads to the same conclusion. As to the special faults of Ad_1., it is to be observed that almost all of them are of a trifling nature and might be easily corrected by a copyist.

§ 3. Ra. Ba.

a. Ra. and Ba. form one *group*, bound together by a great number of faults, *e.g.* 81. sterne] stoor. 139. and se] *om.* 235. styring] termys. 311. riche] riht. 416–17 *om.* 553. The fend anon] He herde a soun. 554. With a vois] That was both. 563 *must have been lost in the common original, its place being taken by an altogether new line.* 946. on thyng] a nodir. 970. atonys] all attonys. 1017–20 *much altered, see v.l.* 1067. Advertyng] Hantyng. 1437. and her sabatons] solieres and haberions. 1438. habergons] Iambisons. 1448. sett] serue. 1669. stole] sutill. 1676. this] this noble. 1731–32 *great alterations, see v.l.* 1982. trewe] *om.* 1992. Of this litil] And put from this. 2057. thy] my. 2078. to hold batayle] to take any batail. 2358. hynder] nat hynder. ȝow no] *om.* 2396.

[1] Note that E_1. S. also omit the line, and cf. the readings of Ra. Ba. in *vv. ll.*

to staunche hem] did hem staunch. 2602. Cylmythenes] Thilmythenes. 2710. couetise] fals couetise. 2876. may last] lastith. 2970 *much altered, see v.l.* 2979. forto] wold. 2988. he sauhe] *om.* 3028. passingly] passandli, *cf.* 3749. 3035. worldly] *om.* 3186. Which in] Withynne. 3317. hegh] *om.* 3385. ny] bi and bi. 3445–49 *much altered, see v.l.* 3465. he hath] ye haue. 3466. Lat hym tak] Receyueth. 3515. intencioun] pitous intencioun. 3519. Than] But that. 3560. in fere] to-gidre. 3628. dempte] deputed Ra., deputith Ba. 3644–45. *cf.* 563. 3698. I haue] I to the have. 3779. first that he] hastli. 4005. at no prys] att nouht. 4006. and so wys] in thouht. 4085. they gan hem to dispeire] seide in wordes fair. 4122. outre] grete. 4248. At the brigge euene] Att briggis eend. 4281. of compassioun] meeued of compassioun. 4298. Thebes] Thebans. shalle] shall fall. 4319. to entren] in entryng to. 4351. shet her gatys] shotte her gonnes. 4352. barrys] baliis. 4369. Antigonee] fair Antigone, etc. (*gap in Ba. from* 4432 *to the end*).

b. Ra. is not derived from Ba., which has many special faults, *e.g.* 129. in the Est to dawe] into the Est to drawe. 294 *om.* 299 *om.* 385. toward] coward. 498 *om.* 504 *om.* 698. tak good hede therto] make goode chere too. 699 *om.* 751. *see v.l.* 753. semly] manly. 829 *om.* 928. the] the kinges. 929. Of the king] In all thing. 1051. also] all. 1286 *om.* 1287. anoy and gret] noo grete. 1318. high constreynt] hih constreynyng Ra., high constrened Ba. 1414. a] oon. 1451. in] their. 1982. feithful] sothefull. 1997. refreyne] restreyn. 2045. vowen] wele avov. 2243. fors or] force of. 2490 *to* 2580 *lost.* 2590. meyne] money. 2630. preued (proued)] proude. 3105–06 *contracted into one line.* 3143. Behotyng] Beseching. 3274 *much altered.* 3305. ful ryal bylt] for royallie bilt. 3330. howsyng] houshold. 3348. gentil lesse] gretnesse. 3445–49 *much altered, see v.l.* 3518. fynde can] can tell. 3777. strengthe] trouth. 3990. ben ago] gan goo. 4392. her] high. 4398. in al manere] in all their. 4412. al be on] by oonlie. 4419. eny (any) man] many man, *etc.* Besides, words are often omitted in Ra., *e.g.* 153. Roos. 262. kynde. 295. famous. 1024. ellis. 2735. allye. 3372. affray. 4095 lost, etc., or added, *e.g.* 43. so. 139. that. 162. in. 245. the. 290. wer. 324. Into. 628. him. 786. thing, *etc.*

c. Ra. has many faults which are not in Ba., *e.g.* 29. shortly] sothly. 72. to] for to. 112. to] *om.* 124. For] And for. 176. shal] *om.* 322. Sith] Syn. 560. haþ] hath hym. 574. Al be that]

And al be that. 712. as] *om.* 714. thorgh] to. 918. tabene] to haue. 1064. debate] bate. 1151. This] Thus. 1196. Chaloun] Thalon. 1318. *see b.* 1368 *much altered, see v.l.* 1594. an] any. 2099 *to* 2294 *lost, see v.l.* 2648. what] that. 3100. and] *om.* 3330. largely] large. 3370. pite] pitous. 3379. in] *om.* 3380. not] *om.* 3398. of] for. 3415. Sith] Such. 3455. his] *om.* 3467. she nat ne dye] she now nat dye. 3773. Rightful] rihtfulli. 3860. whan that] *om.* 3882. assayle] thei saile. 3991. rest] *om.* 4072. that] *om.* 4120. so] *om.* 4304 *om.* 4405. worthy] *om.* 4407. Att] And, *etc.*

Most of the faults of Ra. are unimportant and might be easily corrected by an average copyist. Some are, however, of a graver character. The corrupt state of 1368 and especially the omission of 4304 seem to prove that Ba. is not derived from Ra. And if in 1318 the copyist of Ba. had had before him the reading of Ra., which, though wrong, gives perfect sense, he cannot well be supposed to have altered it into the meaningless reading of Ba. Both the MSS. Ra. and Ba. are descended from a common source of their own. From this source Ba. is probably removed by one or two more links than Ra.

§ 4. Ad_1. Ad_2. I. Ra. Ba.

These five MSS. form one *branch*, characterised by a number of common faults, *e.g.* 61. shortly] sooþli. 163. to] *om.* 397. which] they. 902. forto] to. 1900. thus as] as thus. 1978. right] *om.* 2005. be title of no] bi no title. 2042. he spak] spak he. 2113. no lenger ther] þer no lenger. 2193. ful] *om.* 2396. Ful] And ful. 2631. this] þe. 2678. that] there that Ad_1. Ad_2. I., that ther Ra. Ba. 3225. Now can she nought] But nov she can nought. 3397. Dukes] and dukes. 3532. allay] alaies. 3580. ne] *om.* 3983. not fyne] nat feine. 4179. was chosen] chose(n) was. 4341. saylling] assailing. Besides, these MSS. agree with MSS. belonging to different classes in several faults, *e.g.* 78. were logged] logged were. 116. and her croppys] and croppes. 236. this] the. 504. a] *om.* 1241. ful] *om.* 1256. mor] *om.* 1504. fully] ful. 2132. wil] wolde. 2306. meynt] y-meynt. 2592. *second* with] *om.* 2944. he by] hie. 2954. Make] makith. 3098. a right faire] right a faire. 3560. in] on. 3731. for] on. 3769. in special] in especiall. 4092. shoute] to shoute. 4413. ek] *om.* 4479. not ne] not, *etc.*

§ 5. S. E_1.

a. These two MSS. have a certain number of common faults, and seem to be genealogically more nearly connected with each other than with any other MS. Peculiar to S. E_1. are the following faults: 283. For] Or. 299. hyde] side (+ E_2.). 2944. by meschief] þe meschief. 3742. a] *om.* 3913. To-for] Ther for. They also agree in a number of other cases, where certain other MSS. have the same fault, *e.g.* 185. and] of. 333. lyneal] lyne all (E_1. lyne all the). 379. out] out of. 432. they] *om.* 649. preef] preest. 761. heire] there. 1203. To holde] Be holde. 1426. the] these. 1428. ful] *om.* 1732 *om.* 2178. the] his. 2187. and] and in. 2229. of] of this. 2386. yrayled] arayed. 2604. Ypemedoun] Epymedon. 2633. ful] shal. 4710. shadde] shed (= Ro.).

b. S. has special faults, *e.g.* 20. estatis] estate. 34. Glasy-Eyed] glasid eyen. 48. þis] his. 115. on her] *om.* 146. were to soper] to soper wer. 163. It is no disport] Is it a disport. 176. I gan anon] anon I gan. 183. my] *om.* barayn be] be baryn. 233. hym] he. 234. outward] evar. 235. styring] stermes. 264. foot] fete. 267. sowpowayle] supporaylle. 327. aftere] *om.* 358. perceyved] consitheryd. 372. silfe] fwll. 392. born] Iborn. 471. so] *om.* 531. his] this. 539. collusioun] conclusion. 584. verrely] verily it. 606. he] *om.* 819. among] *om.* 918. likly] like. 1032. on] in. 1033. contrayre] congye. 1034. pleynly and appaire] plenty and appaye. 1044. doune this hil] doune of þis hil. 1146. him] *om.* 1385. vpon] in. 1455*b*–59*a* *om.* 1504. fully] fwlly such. 1653. the] thes two. 1660. many] many a freshe. 1795. hool her tale] talle whole. fyned] Ifynid. 1840 *om.* 1841. thilke] ylke. 1856. preued] prowd. 1966. which that] that. 2259. Worthed] worchid. 2303 *and* 2304 *much altered, with different rhyme-words.* 2374. at the hil] all þe wholl. 2500. sikernesse] sewernesse. 2515. feeres] felowes. 2590. taken] make. 2676. fulsom] fwll. 2690. at] in a. 2862. hadde] had sche. gret] as gret. 2936. lordes] yong lordes. 3100. glad] tho glad. 3628. pure] true. 3684. platly] planly. 3969. into] vnto the. 3978. heuenly] hevy. 4089. eure] owre. 4213. sleyht or some] sum sleight or. 4476. sorful] ferful. 4585. wrastlyng] wraxling.

c. E_1. has special faults. In the first 400 lines it presents several agreements with E_2. (cf. § 15) and from l. 4356 on with Ro. (cf. § 16). In both cases it is E_1. (or the now lost MS. from which the old edition was printed) that has influenced the text of the other MS. Faults peculiar to E_1. are *e.g.* 34. Glasy-Eyed] Glasy eyes (= E_2.). 72. Aftere siknesse my vowes] After my sykenesse vowes (= E_2.). 86. me] *om.* (= E_2.). 87. ȝoure] of youre (= E_2.). 101. Franchemole] Fraunchemoyle (= E_2.). 104. late fed] lette fede (= E_2.). 106. shal] shold (should E_2.). 224. yove] gone. 239. nowher] *om.* (= E_2.). 267. sowpowayle] suppoayle (= E_2.). 271. world] londe (= E_2.). 309. to] for to (= E_2.). 324. vii] an. 332. þe stok] by the stoke (= E_2.). 333. be lyneal discent] by lyne all the d. (= E_2.). 393. deiecte] dyrecte (= E_2.). 432. token] taken. 479. cruelly] truely. 553. with-Innen] wymmen. 698. this] thus. 805. hym] of. 817. seyn] seen. 823. mor therof] and therof more. 829. By on accord] Of oure accord. 853. at this] atte. 932. Percen] Percen they. honge] hangynge. 974. Chershing] serchynge. with] how. 1024. shul] sholde. 1033. to hym and] and to hym. 1063. be ful] by full of. 1106. and] of. 1128. whil] whyle that. 1229. thise] the. 1348. lyvely] lyghtly. 1384. myght of other han] of other myght haue. 1393. wolde] wolde it. 1447. not] nothyng. 1537*b*–1539*a* *om.* 1735. To trouthes] The trouthes. and] *om.* 1786. holde] shelde. 1966. broght] I-brought. 1995. sempte] semeth. 2098. wel] right well. 2102. but] but yf (= E_2.). 2167. Mid] In mynde. 2191. foomen] foon. 2206. his cruelte] his fers cruelte. 2333. adawed] dawed. 2368. she was so kynde] he was kynge. 2523. Thorgh-oute] Thrugh-oute all. 2617. found] I-found. 2625. of which] wherof. 2817. mevyng] meanyng. 2869. fool] grete fool. 2897. contrariouste] contrauerse. 3504. avoided] auoyed. 3582. kyndled] kyndly. 3775. asselyd] essealed. 4177. Terdymus] Tardynyus. 4299. Cry] Cytee. 4338. swowys] swounes. 4356. wastyd hath] hasted (= Ro.). 4421. sownys] bale (= Ro.). 4422 *and* 4423 *made into one line, see v.l.* (= Ro.). 4432. In] I (= Ro.). 4486. se] fele (= Ro.). 4487. fel and] *om.* (= Ro.). 4500. ryve] reyne (= Ro.). 4603. shal] sholde (= Ro.). 4625. Ryal] Royally (= Ro.). 4674. stryve] scryue (= Ro.). 4706. ches] these (= Ro.), *etc.*

The numerous special faults of S. and E_1. show that neither can be derived from the other.

§ 6. Ad_1. Ad_2. I. Ra. Ba. S.

These six MSS. form a *subdivision*, distinguished by a number of common faults, *e.g.* 44. which] þat. 63. as] liche as (lich Ra.; *see*

64). 79. Her] the. the] here (their). 82. which] that (Ra. Ba. *om.*). 141. the same] our. 203. And] Bi. 478. myght His pride not] pride myht nat. 508. the trewe ground] þe soth trouthe. 905. thyng] *om.* 1024. certeyn ellis] elles certein (ellis *om.* Ba.). 1144. hadde thauantage] had tho thauantage (etc., *see v.l.*). 1241. myrk] derke. 1293. grete] strong. 1321. non] of any. 1977. thorgh] of. 1979 *and* 1980 *transposed* (*except* Ra.). 1997. nat no lenger hym] him nat lenger than. 2057. ageyn] vnto. 2113. he] him. 2138. which as] which þat. 2206. in] than in. 2238. nat grounded vpon] grounded nat on. 2324. gan] she gan. 2331. Ther] And þer (*see* 2330). 2396. to bynde] binde. 2433 *and* 2434. *see v.l.* (*very important*). 2478. stood] stood thanne. 2485. hanged] y-honged. 2489. that] though (þat). 2790. helde] he held. 2862. hadde] she had. 2895. and the] and here. 2940. gret] ful gret. 2960. maketh] doth make. 3101. Seyng] seyng wel. 3318. ȝour] your hie. 3372. this] al þis. 3499. parcel] *om.* 3610. And of al this] Of this and. 3666. his lawes] þe lawe. 3708. hool þe fyn] the fyn hol. 3780. deluyere] deliuere vp. 3784. Grek is non] Grek is here noon. 3925. to] *om.* 4093. despit and gret] gret dispit and. 4241. her] the. 4261. whan that] whan. 4298. as eny shalle] as euere it shal (*important*). 4341. of þe wal] atte wal. 4383. han] *om.* 4384. hem] han. 4653. eyther party] boþe parties, *etc.*

In l. 2368 these MSS. and G. alone have the right reading (so kynde, *cett.* kynde).

§ 7. Ad_1. Ad_2. I. Ra. Ba. S. E_1.

These seven MSS. constitute a *class* bound together by a number of common faults, *e.g.* 77. which] That (= E_2.). 142. platly] pleinly (= E_2., E_1. *gap*). 297. of the] of (= E_2.). 931. vnto] to. 2409. abyde] to abide. 2695. power] pore *etc.*, *see v.l.* 2793. tapoynt] thapoint (*see v.l.*). 3254. she] he. 3389. the child] it (this Ba.). 3461. nat] and nat. 3666. which] that. 4187. They don for him] Don for him. 4319. As] Atte. 4426. doth clerly] clerely doth (= Ro.). 4490. his] her (= Ro.). The seven MSS. share several faults with MSS. belonging to other classes, *e.g.* 51. prouerbe] prouerbes. 203 *and* 204 *transposed*. 234. outward] after. 458. ne] *om.* 499. forgat] feyned. 1462. thoo] the. 1670. oute] doun. 1943. vnto] both to. 2009. enforth] hens forth. 2029 *and* 2030 *transposed*. 2045. best] lest. 2190. whette] y-whette. 2224. lay] *om.* 2282. alighte] lighte. doun] a-down. 2358. nor] ne. 2436. of] *om.* 2437. forwounded] soor wounded. 2480. and his] and in his. 2523. of] and. 2944. lorn] born. 3086. yet] that. 3251. quene] king. 3619. that] *om.* 3865. at] of. 4490. his] her (= Ro.).

§ 8. Genealogical relations of class Ad.–E_1.

This class holds an intermediate position between the Bo.–M. and the Ar. class, and in the genealogical diagram takes its corresponding place. It agrees with the former against the latter class more often than *vice versâ*. For coincidences with the Bo.–M. class, see § 12. Faults common to this class and Ar., G. (against Bo.–M.) are *e.g.* 203 *and* 204 *transposed.* 499. forgat] feyned. 1670. oute] doun. 3086. yet] that. 3251. quene] king.

The positions of Ad_1. Ad_2. I. and Ra. Ba. in the genealogy are clear. All five go back to a common original of their own. S. and E_1. cannot be derived from the special original of the other five. They must have branched off from the common stock at a stage above the common original of Ad.–Ba. In view of the numerous readings common to S. and Ad.–Ba. against E_1., it is obvious that S. stands nearer Ad.–Ba. than E_1. does, and that E_1. must have branched off earlier than S. See diagram, where the relations are clearly brought out.

S. goes with Ra. Ba. more often than with Ad. Faults common to Ra. Ba. and S. are, *e.g.* 724. in hast] *om.* 1378. both] *om.* 1812. wonder] *om.* 1982. trewe] *om.* 2017. supprised] supposing. 3588. sent out] sett out. But the coincidences are neither numerous nor particularly striking.

E_1. often has the correct reading (with Ar. or others) against other MSS. of its class, as in most of the cases in § 6.

§ 9. Bo. Du. T_1. L_1.

a. These four MSS. constitute one *branch,* descended from a common original and with a number of common faults. See also § 11. Du. has many gaps. Special faults of the branch are *e.g.* 168. Gynne] Gyf Bo., yeve T_1., Gyff vs L_1. (Du. *gap*). 192. vnto] into. 249. nat] ne. 735. lyves] lyf is. 1106. high] *om.* 4122. And] at (An L_1.). 4190. A fewe] by fele (And few L_1.). Besides Bo.–L_1. have many faults together with other MSS. but against M. Di., *e.g.* 32. pylled] pallid T_1. Du., ballyd L_1. (Bo. *gap*). 152. oure] þe. 417.

faste] fast þei. 428. þorgh they gan] þei gan þorugh. 1146. hym hastyng] haastyng him. 1157. fals] his fals. 1384. no sight] eny sight. 1520. which] whome. 1624. be] it be. 1756. it] *om.* 1776. walles] wal. 1972. That] as. 2613. Pyrrus] of Pyrrus. 2668. also ben] ben also. 2843. echon] euerychon. 3496. Hent out] Rent out. 3673. shal] shul. 3712. pes] a pes. 3836. the lyoun] to a lyon. 3852. good] gret. 3989. of] on. 4390. by] *om.*

b. Bo. and Du., especially in the second half of the text, form a group with a number of special common faults, *e.g.* 56. piked] pyken. 685. ne] to. 3288. For] Of. 3350. specifye] especifie. 3476. her] his. 3977. nor] ner. 4214. vnwarly] warly. 4240. Thebans] Thebanx. Bo. Du. also agree against T_1. L_1. in many cases where other MSS. have the same fault, as 2713. contune (: fortune)] continue. 2714. of] and. 2988. stood] stonde. 2997. the] his. 3068. I wol] ye wol. 3313. kyngly] knightly. 3324. ouermore] euer more. 3353. touche] touchith. 3389. into the] into. 3475. fynal] finaly. 3537. verryfie] to verrifie. 3591. hom] hem (= 3924). 4228. but that he] that he. 4604. took] take.

c. Bo.

Bo. is one of the best MSS., but it has many special faults, *e.g.* 96. ȝe] þee. 105 *and* 106 *transposed.* 115. men] *om.* 200. ȝe shal] þou shalt. 284. loue] *om.* 290. mad] *om.* 296. Cadmvs] Cadicius. 449. that] *om.* 515. verrely] *om.* 579. all tho] of tho. 661. Is] As. 707. bothe] *om.* 879. also] *om.* 1086. of resoun] of reȝt. 1087. crowned] crownyng. 1171. al the day] alway. 1196. sone] þe son. 1229. shal] *om.* 1230. of] and. 1374. first] *om.* 1491. and] or. 1538. as] þat. 1556. her] his. 1609. oure enmyes] enemyes. 1690. Hadde al] had of. 1856. so wel a preued] a gentil. 1927. put out] pacient. 1952. ȝe] *om.* 1992. Of] as. 2004. lette] *om.* 2078. to hold] to haue. 2167. his] þe. 2182. they] þei gan. 2297. newe] *om.* 2391. whan] *om.* 2427. his] þis. 2435. hym] *om.* 2546. all] *om.* 2641. they] *om.* 2746. his] þis. 2769. hym] *om.* 2817. heghe] *om.* 3017. ful] *om.* 3068. owne] *om.* 3099. of water] *om.* 3128. pyhte] were pight. 3251. this þing] *om.* 3319. ȝou] now you. 3332. haue] hath. 3366. forto ben] to haue ben. 3369. newe] now. 3400. her] *om.* 3533. whan] þere. 3598. hom] hem. 3602. gan] *om.* 3859. it] he. 3897. made] make. 3978. the] tho. 4022. in his] him in. 4109. but in] bouten. 4211. hem] And. 4238. is] was. 4270. hadde] *om.* 4338. That] *om.* swowys] swerdes. 4364. Ther-Inne of gold] ther in golde. 4389. Although] As þough. 4420. descryve] bescryue. 4608. his] *om.* 4664. the] þo. 4689. it] *om.* The majority of the special faults consist in omissions of single words. At the beginning of Bo. 1 to 6 and 31 to 40 are cut away; 7 and 8 are incomplete; 4456 to 4586 lost.

d. Du.

Du. is a rather good MS., but it has many gaps, 111–337, 4284–4340, 4459–4572, 4630–4716, and a number of special faults, *e.g.* 34. Glasy-Eyed] glasy rede. 447. bare hym hom] hym bare home. 527. first how he] hou first he. 586. in hast] *om.* 599. after that] aftreward. 605. ay] *om.* 684. not] *om.* 699. Thilke] This. 907. the kyng] *om.* 1056. attempre] attemperyd. 1085. first] *om.* 1094. he] one. 1186. was] *om.* 1272. writ] wrote. 1321. non] name. 1388. alight] he light. 1537*b*, 1538, *and* 1539*a* *om.* (= Di. E_1.). 1641. that] *om.* 1708. lyve in] haue. 1734. comparison] comparacion. 1799 *and* 1800 *om.* 1895. kyngly] kyndely. 2133. euere] euel. 2368. she] *om.* 2572. recure] rekouere. 2662. of Armyng newe] or armoure new. 2717. loue] and loue. 2892. entryked] entrikled. 2901–04 *om.* 2944. Til] to. 3018. hom] han. 3077. al] *om.* 3167. warly] verraly. 3333. ȝour] his. 3361. whilis] *om.* 3564. grene] grete. 3612. grete] *om.* 3652. how] haue. 3758 *and* 3760. hool] holde. 3856. was] *om.* 3941. anon] he none. 3973 *and* 3974 *om.* 3975 *and* 3796 *transposed.* 4151. knyghtly] kyndely. 4260*b* *and* 4261*a* *om.* 4368. ȝonge] *om.* 4420. ȝif] *om.* 4428. *second* of] othre. 4617. al] *om.*

e. T_1.

T_1. is a very good MS., perhaps even better than Bo. Special faults are *e.g.* 29. hemsilf] hem wel. 97. ȝe be soul] it be so. 200. ȝe shal] ye shulen. 231. ther was] was ther. 412. To] And. 467. by] in. 577. he] *om.* 615–726 *lost.* 902. brast] barst. 911. ferde] fere. 1047. on] of. 1061–1172 *lost.* 1177. were] *om.* 1786. And] *om.* 2099 *almost wholly cut away.* 2140. or] *om.* 2234. sured] *om.* and] *om.* 2479. wex] was. 2609. hadde] hath. 2645. and her] and. 2714. Ay] As. 2760. and some] *om.* 2833. saue] haue. 3119. so] *om.* 3235. may be] is. red] drede. 3254. wil] shall. 3361. entreten þus] thus entretiden. 3373. wist] wist than. 3477. Shortly] sothly. 3773. putte] putte hym. 4054. or] and. 4423. facys] her faces. The copyist of T_1. clearly regards the prefix *y-* of the pp. as obsolete, for he omits it at the risk of spoiling the metre, *e.g.* 38, 212, 837, 1488, 2536, 2655, 3775, 4594. Sometimes the omission even makes a four-beat line out of a five-beat one, *e.g.* 561, 1045, 2032, 4043, 4064.

f. L_1. has a very great number of special faults, *e.g.* 2. Myd] and myd. 4. his] a. 25. also in soth] in soth eeke. 33. The pardowner beerdlees] The berdles pardoner. 55. for to seyn] fro the seyne. 125. ȝou] no. 132. professioun] proffeschoun. 134. founden] *om.* 184. wonderful] full wonderful. 193. preised] preved. 194. weren on heghte] on high were. 231. Eerys] hertis. 253. priuely wol] whilom. 299. out-korve] korve out. 397. sort] force. 517. gan] gan Edippus. 563. syyt] side. 574. ful] sor. 718. withseyn] withstonde. 755. sawh also] se also. 890. plonged] plukkyth. 1011. *see v.l.* 1047. on þe ble] vnder þe ble (*see, however, Notes*). 1102. euerich] eueryche of hem. 1181. refut] resku. 1342. of force] of deuorce. 1346. clene] brith. 1370. with] went with. 1374. first] both. 1428. worthy] riall. 1464. manere] chere. 1491. knyghtes] kynges. 1690. soget] subiecte. 1707. wenyng] *om.* 1724. Centre] Countre. 1790. his] youre. 2180. proudely] myghtly. 2398. *see v.l.* 2479. wex] waxte. 2488. is ȝowe] now is. 2583. sende] wage. 2609. Proued] Provided. 2699. coarten] coverten. 2902. swed] shewid. 2940. werre] verrey. 3009. refut] refuge. 3071. cher] hide. 3305. his paleys] þis place. ful ryal] *om.* 3415. Sith] Sayth. 3426. shour] houre. 3446. torment] tornament. 3466. Lat hym tak] That ye will tak. 3594. with houndes] Woundes. 3665. Marte (: coarte)] Mars (: coars). 3938. trete] tretise. 3969. conduit] conduct. 3975. wilfulnesse] wofullnes. 4014. Tytan] þey. 4213. sleyht] crafte. 4341. sayllyng] sawtyng. 4423. her ofte] Of her. 4498. evyl] well. 4628. contek] contecte. 4640. falle] full, *etc.* The copyist has modernised, or tried to modernise, several old words, *e.g.* 1690. soget. 3969. conduit. 4628. contek.

§ 10. M. Di.

a. M. and Di. form one *group*, held together by a very great number of common faults, *e.g.* [M. 66. while] tyme. 103. han] *om.* 140. wil] forth wil].[1] 241. Reysed first] first reisid. 265. bereþ] beren. 266. susteneth] hym sustenen. 310. this] kyng. 410. ȝonge] *om.* 664. ȝif] *om.* 709. felle] cruel. 753. semly] manful. 786. For which] Wherfor. 1032. of] after. 1166. roches] roges.

[1] Lines 1–153 are missing in Di.

1273 *and* 1274 *transposed.* 1462. thoo] thilk. 1536. enhasted] hasted. 1602. This] That is. 1626. gif] yeueth. 1693. ȝif] *om.* 1759. be sleght] by cause. 1772. Prosperite] gode prosperite. 1864. sure] in sure. 1992. litil pore] litil and poure. 2088. falsly] iustly. 2227. han] had it. 2272. ageyn] by. 2417. goodnesse] greet goodnesse. 2488. is ȝowe] is on you. 2509. both] *om.* 2615. renomed] wel renomed. 2647. Cam] cause. 2653. fynaly] fully. 2699. coarten] coercen. 2862. gret] *om.* 3068. I wol] ye wil now. 3185. child] sone. 3210. gan] gan godely. 3312. Ful wel] Right wel. 3397. kyngges] princes. 3534. the grete] þat stronge. 3585. space] place. 3741. al] there. 3975. nor of no] neither of. 4040. paied] quyt. 4090. recure] to haue recure. 4115. clamour] labour. 4132. eny spotte of blame] spot of ony shame. 4287. handlyng] handeled. 4405. Grekys] knightes. 4501. my maister] myn auctor. 4649 *and* 4650 *transposed.* 4664. werre] syn. 4678. gynnyng] gynner, *etc.* The sequence of words is extremely often inverted. In several lines an adjective is inserted attributively before a noun, in general to the advantage of the metre, *e.g.* 1772, 2417, etc. The copyist frequently omits *y*- in pp. M. has lost 147–222, Di. 1–153.

b. Di.

Di. has a great number of (partly grave) special faults which are not found in M., *e.g.* 224. this] þe. 251. who that] who so. 274. Than] Whan. 352. And] And to. 403. to-forn] final. 617. forby] sothly. 651. sothly] oonly. 684. also] allone. 698. *see v.l.* 929. in] *om.* 1132. haþ] hadde. 1175. hidously] sodeinly (*see* 1174). 1306. brest] hors. 1318. high constreynt] hiȝe conuersaunt. 1596. half] al. 1850. infortunat] fortunat. 1911. conceyve] to knowe. menynge] comyng. 2001. y-made] *om.* 2157. way] day. 2202. her] þe. 2629. beste] worthy. 2710. couetise] foule couetise. 2897. contrariouste] contrauersite. 3257. bille] wille. 3897. That made] To make. 4331. grounde] y-grounde. and whet] *om.* 4348. vngracious] gracious. 4567. Nor] For. 4633. hath] *om.* 4640. falle] brouȝte.

In the gap of M. 147–222 Di. presents several faults, *e.g.* 163. no disport] none sporte. 167. holynesse] hevynesse. 170. draweþ] touchiþ. 184. wonderful] riȝt wonderful, etc.

Di. is derived from M., probably a direct copy. The special faults of M. are both few and unimportant, and the corrections or alterations made by the copyist may be characterised as very easy, he being guided in general either by the context, *e.g.* 772, 890, 3512,

3944, etc., or by the metre, *e.g.* 1451, 1584, 1767, 2530, etc. In l. 3667 (wher ȝe be glad or loth) "wroth" in M. is in Di. altered into "loth" in conformity with the usual wording of the phrase. In 2710, where M. has bettered the metre by inserting "eke," Di has exchanged eke for "foule."

§ 11. Bo. Du. T_r. L_1. + M. Di.

These six MSS. constitute one *class* with special faults, *e.g.* 43. who] whos (*exc.* L_1.). 174. So] *om.* 194. weren on heghte] on height (high) were. 195. wonder and merveil] merueile and wondre. 205. the] his. 222. the] þat (*exc.* L_1.). 230. plesaunt] *om.* 239. was nowher] nowhere was. 244. myche may] moche it may (ȝe may Di.). 248. apport] porte. and] and to. 249. and] *om.* 267. As] As is. 268. For] And. 322. which] *om.* 370. Root ytaken] rote taken. 392. whan] þat. 1368. tolde] tolde þei (= E_1.). 1568. In] And in. 2419. taken] to take (*exc.* L_1.). 3322. That] for. 4187. They don for him] Don þei for him. Besides, the six MSS. have many faults in common with MSS. belonging to other classes, especially with Ad.–E_1. (see § 12) and with MSS. belonging to the class P.–Ro. Agreements are particularly common with Lb.; see further § 21. Examples are 1. briȝte] *om.* 12. The] That. 22. some] and som. 25. also in soth] eke in soth. 42. In] bothe in. 46. ȝoue] ioye. 74. slender long] longe sklendre. 124. afore] bifore. 125. shal] þat shal. 128. anoon as] as sone as. 140. that] *om.* 144. liȝt] right light. 162. Shet] Shet vp. 191. fame] name. 204. whilom] some tyme. 214. Cler] Clerly. 263. eny] the. 269. berer] beryng. 294. Groundyng] Grounden. 300. wyde] ful wyde. 316. vnto] *om.* 327. Regnyng] And regned. 400. sore] *om.* 416. fer] þere. 489. and] if. 539. collusioun] illusion. 894. of] on. 940. lad] had. 1044. And] *om.* 1385. vpon] on. 1568. he gan] began. 1812. was] *om.* 1966. that] *om.* 1997. nat no lenger hym] not him no lenger. 2187. and] and in. 2227. han] it han. 2432. and] ne. 2455. konnyng] konnynges. 2491. hath] *om.* 2884. presence] prudence. 3376. hent] rent. 3447. ȝif that] if. 3449. Is] It is. 3455. offended] *om.* 3473. That] But. 4095. socour] her socour. 4137. ne] ne on. 4373. to gouern hem] hem to gouerne. 4405. worthy] þe worthi.

In l. 1322 this class alone has the right reading ("noyeng" as against "moving" Ar., etc., see *vv. ll.*).

§ 12. Ad_1. Ad_2. I. Ra. Ba. S. E_1. + Bo. Du. T_1. L_1. M. Di.[1]

These MSS. in a great number of cases show remarkable agreement. In nearly all the cases given, except from l. 3286 on (cf. § 21), Lb. agrees with these, and from 4375 on Ro. (cf. § 16). Examples are: 161. manere] *om.* 197. shortly] playnly (platly Ad_1. E_1. T_2. E_2.) 385. ellys] *om.* (+ T_2. E_2.). 535. is] it is (+ T_2. P.). 572. Euerich] eche. 604. retourne] turne (+ G.). 623. sight] of sight (*exc.* S.). 662. hym-silue nat] not himself. 882. the ton] oon. 914. that] *om.* 938. falle] byfall. 946. ay is] is ay. 978. that] *om.* (+ P.). 983. that] þan (+ P.). 1063. be ful] by full of (bee ful of). 1064. For] and for. 1195. Chysoun] Clysoun. 1337. with] by. 1343. a-twen] bitwene. 1400. I-axed] He asked (and asked Di. Ba. L_2.). 1451. word] worke, werk *etc.* (+ Ap., wordes L_1.). 1515. A-twene] Bi twene (+ P.). 1569. ne] *om.* 1624. be] it be (be it). 1644. that] *om.* 1703. his] *om.* (+ Ro.). 1964. vnto] to. 1972. that] as. He] þat he. 1997. nat no lenger hym] not him no lenger (not hym longer, him nat lenger than). 2017. supprised] supprisyng Bo. T_1. Du. L_1. Lb. Ad_1. Ad_2. I. E_1., supposing Ra. Ba. S. 2029–30 *transposed* (exc. Bo. L_1. Lb. Ba.). 2033. ado] to do. 2154. couartly] cowardly. 2167. Mid] In myd, in myddes Lb., In mynde E_1. 2270. which] whome. 2284. voyded] avoidid. 2285. the] his. 2369. benygne] so benigne (*exc.* Ba.). 2386. Yrayled] arayed, *etc.* 2491. hath] *om.* 2492. Brought] hath brought. 2549. þe] *om.* 2679. worthy] *om.* (*exc.* L_1.). 2703. hegh] *om.* 2758. manly] many (+ Ap.). 3076. which] whom. 3097. wolde] wolde she. 3128. they] þere. 3251. þing] *om.* 3260. she] *om.* 3370. that] *om.* 3477. ellis] *om.* 3519. aforn me] me aforn. 3665. put our mater] put it. 3955. which] þat. 4206. lyf] hede. 4375. left] *om.* 4379. dure] endure. 4499. as] *om.* 4501. Chaucer] *om.* 4629. froward] mighti. 4656. felyn] folowe.

The agreements adduced would seem to suggest a fairly close relationship between the two classes Ad.–E_1. and Bo.–M. Perhaps a common original for these two classes should be introduced in the genealogical diagram below O.

[1] The examples are taken from an earlier draft of Chap. VI by Professor Erdmann. A query-mark placed in the margin suggests that he had come to hesitate as to whether the coincidences were worthy of notice. It seems to me, however, that they are so significant that they should be called attention to. In a draft of the genealogical diagram dated 10.7.1911 the thirteen MSS. + Lb. are given as a class or division parallel to Ar. G. and Ap.–Ro.—E. E.

§ 13. C. T_2.

a. C. and T_2. form one *group*, which has a number of faults in common. Where there is a gap in either of the MSS., the group is here represented by the other MS., as shown by this synopsis: T_2. 1–822, C. T_2. 823–85, T_2. 886–951, C. T_2. 952–1016, T_2. 1017–1142, C. T_2 1143–1402, T_2. 1403–68, C. T_2. 1469–1857, T_2. 1858–1922, C. T_2. 1923–2484, C. 2485–2672, C. T_2. 2673–3633, C. 3634–67 (gap in both MSS. 3668–4060), C. 4061–4209, C. T_2. 4210–4385, T_2. 4386–4515, C. T_2. 4516–4716. Faults found only in one of the MSS. are bracketed. Examples are [78. Wher] Ther. 96. ȝe ȝoure] he her. 112. ȝif] And iff. 136. proude] bold. that dar] that day. 163 *and* 164 *transposed*. 176. anon as] so as. 233. list] *om*. 236. bylde] bigge. 274. Than] Thanne is. 318. pith] pitche. 352. And] And ek; *see* 390, 472. 480. felly] fully. 515. verrely] verry. 579. all tho] all hem. 626. by] be somme. 634. platly] shortly. 646. corage] rage. 749. Thorgh] In.] 833. philolegye] Philoloy. [927. men] *om*.] 1269. Calydonye.] Calcidoyne. 1273. to] on. [1435. hem] haue.] 1614. The] The hool C., hool the T_2. 1977. thorgh] be. [2554. thy] *om*. 2648. redy] godely.] 2875. he] she. 3065. al] *om*. 3251. hath this thing] this thing hath. 3313. with] in. 3362. wooful] sorful C., dredful T_2. 3499. aswage] to swage. 3560. in fere] yfere. [4065. vnwarly] sodenly. 4107. such counsayl] *om*. 4166. In stede of whom] In whos stede.] 4228. but that he] but he. 4332. ther was no let] they were nat lette. [4408. whan] whan that. 4505. fourtenyght] fourtene nightes.] 4662. fader] the fader C., that fader T_2. C. T_2. also agree against other MSS. belonging to this class in many cases where MSS. belonging to other classes have the same readings, *e.g.* [1. Whan] Whan that. 128. anoon as] as sone as. 194. on heghte] on heigh. 212. neither] *om*. old] of old. 295. famous] *om*. 308. from] *om*. 461. the] this. 538. with-In] ther with-yn.] 932. Percen] perced. [1086. For which] Wherfore.] 1213. hadde sone] sone had. [1414. not] neuer.] 1793. as] that. 2334. Vp he stert] He vpsterte (+ E_2.). [2608. vs] thus. 2611. sete] se (+ E_2.).] 4696. now] *om*. etc.

b. Neither MS. seems to be derived from the other. Both have special faults. Faults of C. are, *e.g.* 853. platly] plainly (= S. E_2.). 855. to] of. 1157. þorgh] of. 1286. with] of. 1685. Inly] gretly. 1836. spede] nede. 2276. gan] streight gan. 2386. of gold] *om*. 2436. sorowe] gret sorwe. 2701. lord] *om*. 2714. Ay] ever.

2765. Iuellis] yeftes. 3022. ȝif] yf that. 3318. your] your gret. 3380. sighe sobbe and wepe] sorwe sighe and wepe. 3535. dreynt] drouned. 4541. ȝit] And. 4706. sake] loue, *etc.*

Special faults of T_2. are, *e.g.* 1173. ful] right. 1287. also] *om.* 1537. wisly] auisely. 1742. euery] all the. 1772. prosperite] long prosperite. 1923. voyden] be voided. 2004. shal] will. sothly] trewly. 2229. of] for this. 2284. hath] thanne. 2417. thonkyng] towchyng. goodnesse] goodlynesse. 2418. largesse] and largenesse. 3082. but lityl] *om.* 3204. *see v.l.* 3370. lith] *om.* 3380. sighe] *om.* 4298. shalle] shralle. 4324. verray] grete. 4326. amyng] armyng. 4334. to the herte roote] vnto the rote. 4354. grekys fewe] knightis fewe, *etc.*

§ 14. (Lb.) P. E_2.

a. P. and E_2. form one *group*,[1] with which Lb. in its last third (from 3286) is associated. Common faults, *e.g.* 114. Collikes] colles. 967. Fro when] From whense. 1028. And] And hem. 1099. Ful] *om.* 1306. vpon] and on. 2090. how] on howe. 2612. Crete] grece. 2717. loue] but love. 3072. her] his. (Lb. P. E_2.): 3312. ful] *om.* 3670. Innocent] verry Innocent. 3684. this tweyne] you tweyne. 3879. in purpos] purposed. 3920. day] tyme. 4145. Crestyd] crestes. and batailled] Enbatayled (–Lb.). 4230. ȝit was he] yet he was. 4467. Gretly] And gretely. The following readings of P. E_2. (Lb.) which agree with those of MSS. belonging to other classes may also be noticed: 634. platly] pleynly. 752. grete] *om.* 1286. wynde] *om.* 1836. Ful] Fully. 2119. Thorgh-out] Thurgh. 3380. sighe sobbe and wepe] sobbe sighe and wepe. 3660. likly] lightly. 3674. gynnyng] gynner (begynnere (Lb.). 3972. platly] pleynly (plain E_2.). 4051. stood hym stede] stode in stede.

b. P. has a very great number of (partly grave) special faults, of which only relatively very few can be here mentioned, *e.g.* 12. and] that. 13. The noble] That noble. 41. sothly] shortly. 45 *and* 46. *see v.l.* 82. to me] anone. 97. ȝe be soul] ye be seke. 124. parcel a-fore] percas before. 176. I gan anon] began. here] aftir here. 210. ȝoor agoon] many a yeere ago. 214. Cler] Clerkely. 220. non] Man. 450. Of his woundes] Off his sore woundes forsothe. 478. His pride not] not his pres. 537. and] as golde. 718. *see v.l.* 935. hom resort] restored home. 1086. *see v.l.* 1124. ȝerne] *om.*

[1] Except in the first 400 lines; see *d.*

1181. for refut] for fortune. 1203. in his hond] and the Croune. 1254. plees] paleys. 1351. ranne] rydden. 1501. to bedde] *om.* 1565. I] they. 1570. ȝour] my. 1669–72 *om.* 1715. this counsayl] her comynge. 1800. hym to] Or holdeth the. 1856. preued] preferred. 1911. conceyve] toucheinge. 2137. worthy] *om.* 2203. enviroun] newe y-ronne. 2374. woode] worthy. 2386 *and* 2396 *om.* 2519. Hent] Thurgh the whiche he hent. 2834. vttrely] Covertly. 2902. swed] served. 2991. hosteye] haste. 2992. werreye] waste. 3071. verrey] womanly. 3093 *om.* 3094. supprised] she suppressid. 3214. destitut of myrth and alle] restitute of all. 3305. of ston] of lyme and stone (= L_1). 3357. surplus] remnont. 3592. *see v.l.* 3646. *see v.l.* 3684. platly] playnely. 3759. with Sceptre] that Septor. 3876. ronne doune] began to wexe. 3989. mo] Man (: agoo). 4116. euere in on] in euer. 4159. not] doith. 4248. vpon] above. 4456. kowde] coude not. 4547. ouerlade] overthrowe. 4616. deth] *om.* 4625. Ryal] hye. 4654. nowther of hem] neþer party. 4656. felyn] fall to. 4662 *om.*

P. is on the whole carelessly written. The copyist has made many gratuitous alterations. In the immediate original of P. several lines were missing; some of these were supplied at random by the copyist, others by a later hand that wrote in the margin of the MS. It is clear that P. cannot be the source of E_2.

c. Lb. P.

Lb. in its last part and P. constitute a *sub-group*, bound together by a number of common faults, *e.g.* 3286. they] *om.* forto] elles to. 3332. non] ony. 3436. But] But that. 3592. soortes] stoore. 3611. Gan] Wheche ganne. 3645. spede] fare. 3654 *om.* 3660. most] *om.* 3686. euer] euer therof. 3754. opynly] specially. 3920. cessen] cheson. 3944. Than] As. 3965. drow to eve] drewe night to eve Lb., drew nye Eve P. 3983. nyght] *om.* 4036. on which he stood] that they on stode. 4073. swalowen] swolowe. 4159. apalle] enpalle. 4161. mor] *om.* 4260. causer] cause. 4331. grounde and] *om.* 4423. her ofte] With ofte. 4427. Grece] all Grece. 4449. a wonder] a wondyr thynge. 4464. þer as] where. 4472. right] ful. 4476. sorful] woful. 4498. trist and] *om.* 4585. to telle] *om.*

d. E_2.

E_2. has many special faults. In the first 400 lines E_2. often agrees with E_1.; it does so occasionally also in the later parts of the poem. These agreements have been noted under E_1. (§ 5). They are evidently due to E_2. having been compared with the earlier printed edition. Special faults of E_2., *e.g.* 48. of] in. 125. A company] Accompanie. 129. to] *om.* 465. Whether] *om.* 498. a-point] apeinte. 500. his owne] this and aboue. 570. Who] Who that. 676. *see v.l.* 837. Marcian] Matrician. 866. derknesse] Dronkenesse. 902. brast] breste. 1033. Fortune] For the tyme. 1048. chilyndre] kalender. 1177. man and beest] many a beste. 1317. and of] and great. 1367. And] And were. 1614. this] al this. 1851. what so that] whatsoeuer. 2098. vp] was up. 2308. maked] did make. 2517. frat] was. 2527. ryse] arisen. 2648. Redy] Lowly. 2737. a whil] a time. 2824. parte of] blood right of. 2827. *see v.l.* 2841. thar] there. 2948. renne] sterte. 3057. excepting] I excepte. 3178. mordre] matere. 3195. wante] write. 3196. Thoante] Thorite. 3235. ther may be non] none other. 3270. grete] grounde. 3406. sharpe] teary. 3590. ravyn] rauing. 3722. nat but] all but. 3805. apoynt] appointment. 3846. deceyued] destreined. 3893. whil] wise. 3931. ȝolden] yeuen. 3988. tourne] come. 4036. on which he stood] that he on rode. 4075. may] doeth. 4090. wenyng] Sownyng. 4122. outre] after. 4130. renomed] worthi of deede. 4161. for mor happy sped] after beste redde. 4189. stallyd] stabled. 4298. as eny] as soche thing. 4405. worthy] whiche. 4481. stark] straught. 4632. the Cyte] the Thebans cite. 4679. luk] looke, *etc.* Some alterations are clearly modernisations, *e.g.* 10. Jupiter. 252. peoples. 360. Messengers.

The many special faults of E_2. show that it (or rather the MS. from which the old edition was printed) cannot be the source of P.

§ 15. (Lb.) P. E_2. C. T_2.

P. E_2. C. T_2. and Lb. in its last third (from 3286) form one *branch*. In the first 400 lines the faults of the branch are in E_2. very often corrected by referring to E_1. (see § 5). These corrections are not noted in the list below. Common faults of the branch are, *e.g.* 220. to] vnto. 230. plesaunt fauourable] favourable plesaunt. 249. nat to bene] to be not. 345. so] full. 632. opynly] pleinly T_2. P., fully E_2. 647. I haue] Seide I haue. 743. Muet pale and ded] hevy as any lede. 749. that he the monstre hath] þat the monstre was. 762. or] and. 832. On] non. 833. philolegye] philolis P., Philoloy C. T_2., Philolaie E_2. 935. hom resort] resorted home (restored home P.). 970. brak] brast. 1095. Regaly] Bothe regalye. 1264. The worthiest] One the worthiest C. P. E_2., On of the w. T_2. 1318. his] gret. 1348. take] bestride (stride E_2.). 1393. light] hie (highe him E_2.). 1520. I made] made is. 1596. this] my. 1686. after] after tyme (afterward T_2.). 2005. of no bond] of his bond. 2042. spak] seide. 2500. sikernesse] sothnesse. 2590. stuffen] sustene. 2735. Don to] Vnto. 2942. conceytes] coueiting. 3052. speer] *om.* 3160. hooly al the] al the hole. 3161. why] how. 3334. in Tentys] intentifly. 3361. entreten þus] trete thus. 3415. Sith loos of deth] Ayenst dethe. no man may] may be no. 3479. Al] *om.* 3499. her sorowe] *om.* 3507. that] *om.* 3622. which] that. 3628. which] Suche. 4071. frowne] sorowe. 4101. fals] *om.* 4122. vnto] to the. 4292. smote] rof. 4351. Tho of the toun] Of the toun thei. 4532. looke] loke hit. 4563. bonys] bodyes (= M. Di.). 4638. a] ony.

The faults in 3334–4563 (except 3622) are all also in Lb.

§ 16. L_2. Ro.

a. L_2. and Ro. are united into one *group* by a number of common faults. Ro. has many great gaps, viz. 513–1130, 1987–2400, 3011–3210, 3407–3590, 3989–4340. The general agreement of L_2. and Ro., showing itself in many very characteristic common faults and even in spellings, entitles us to suppose that Ro. in general agreed with L_2. also in its numerous gaps, and that L_2. may thus stand as a fair representative of the group L_2. Ro. Special faults of the group, *e.g.* 2. in-to bole] in the bole (= Ra.). 3. old] *om.* 15. her] the. 21. man] *om.* 25. in soth] *om.* 27. for] *om.* 41. of] *om.* 49. noght at al] noght al. 68. I not] I ne wote. 99. mad] *om.* 117. Rede] sede (= I.). 143. to-nyght] this nyght. 174. So] And. 230. plesaunt fauourable] favourable plesaunt. 417. Her] the. 425. ful hygh] fylle L_2., fel Ro. 503. opportune space] oportune and space. [653. wel] *om.* 685. counsel] *om.* 699. herto-forn] to-forn. 743. Muet pale and ded] fully dysmaide. 935. lefte hym ther] Left ther the child. 953. nor] oþer. 1063. be ful mortal] by fell mortal.] 1204. alle] the. 1241. obscure] oscure. 1272. Stace] Stage. 1565. ouerslyde] slide. 1626. What] That. 1719. that] *om.* 1755. her] his. 1911. my] the. [2158. At] And. 2180. proudely] smertly. 2192. allas] naþeles. 2193. gret] sore.] 2421. Beheestyng] Besechyng. 2458. ther. . . ther] her . . . her. 2616. Ther] Thider. 2630. preued] best. 2644. Vnto] And to. 2648. hym list] he wold. 2654. ygadred] Ther gadred. 2765. Iuellis] iowellis

L_2., Iowewelles Ro. 2846. Discuren] Diskevir. 2988. whan that] whan. [3100. But] And. 3107. hem] þer.] 3358. was] not. 3379. myne] gynne L_2., gyne Ro. [3444. tak] tak yt. 3446. *see v.l.* 4016. of assent] of oon assent. 4058. on] of. 4304. in were] in fer.]

In 3838 L_2. and Ro. are right (with Ar. G.) against all the other MSS. (*see v.l.*). On the connection between Ro. with E_1. in the last part of the poem, see *infra*, *c*.

b. L_2. is an extremely valuable MS. It has a number of special faults, which show that it cannot be the source of Ro., *e.g.* 45. alwey] evir. 52. Sugrid] sugir. 66. pilgrymes] pylgrimage. 108. wil do non] well & do noun. 115. greuen] gronyn. 139 *and* 140 *om.* 165. therof] herof. 227. kyng] *om.* 304. Boece] Cyte. 375. eke] þe. 424. But that] That. 426. that] ther. 432. that] *om.* 513–1130. *see a.* 1212. lich] þe kyng. 1213. This worthy kyng] In all his lyf. 1229. Possede] Procede. 1230. His] And his. be bond] hurt. 1241. myrk] *om.* 1300 *om.* 1374. a-sonder] in sonder. 1522. nedeth] nede. 1647. wommanly] wounderly. 1695. of oth] of oþer. 1754. And] *om.* 1987–2400. *see a.* 2517. So frat] So that. 2745. the] his. 2757. Maskowede] Mannyd. 2992. werreye] werry. 3011–3210. *see a.* 3224. Now] nought. wayle] *om.* 3225. sighen] wayle. 3319. ȝou] not. 3395. kyngly] knyghtly. 3399. restreyn] constreyne. 3401. wolde] wyll. 3407–3590. *see a.* 3609. maked] *om.* 3721. tavoyde] to voide. 3757. she] he. 3940. avise] full wyse. 3989–4340. *see a.* 4341. and] of. 4480. in] on. 4565. what] *om.* 4585. wrastlyng] wrostelyng. 4600. they] he, *etc.*

c. Ro. cannot be the source of L_2.; it has many special faults of its own, *e.g.* 16. red and whit] white & rede. 25. Ribaudye] lewed ribaudrye. 33. al] of. 34. Glasy-Eyed] Glasyne Eyde. 49. Al] Of. 99. ȝoure] youre owne. 116. filled] fylled wele. her mawes and] *om.* 118. sede] rede. 136. proude] hardy. 170. to effecte] of to speke. 175. pale] ful pale. 274. whetted] grounde. 299. thong] a whonge. 312. *see v.l.* 324. suppose] deme. vii] sex. 335. To telle forth] Now wole I tele. 346. gret a] moche. 356. wolde] thinke wolde. 425. And anon] Anone thes seruauntis. 427. They henge hym vp] And hynge this childe. 476. specyaly grete] grete and odyǫus. 508. the trewe ground] the treuthe. 513–1130 *lost*. 1242. be] of. 1297. þorgh] for. 1321 *and* 1322. *see v.l.* 1428. worthy] gentyle. 1561. surly] shortly. 1647. to se] of sight. 1648. *see v.l.* 1742. tresour] *om.* 1800. he thoght] they thought it. 1812. wonder longe] passynge longe. 1856. that] *om.* 1979. ȝif] though. 1987–2400 *lost.* 2417. goodnesse] worthynesse. 2517. frat] sat. 2581. liklyest] semblyeste. 2669. clerly] pleynly. 2867. They falle on hym] Allas Amphimorax. 2868. And sette hym vp] Is take and sett. 2954. due] dewe discrete. 3011–3210 *lost.* 3219. burlyd] Curlyde. 3312. good] riche. 3319. ȝou] nowe. 3341. on no parte] percele. 3385. a rowe] A throwe. 3407–3590 *lost.* 3610. And of al this] And all this while. 3638. trye] trete. 3813. or ille] evele. 3838. as eny] lyke A. 3966. taking tho her leve] ther leve toke right. 3989–4340 *lost.*

From l. 4356 to the end Ro. agrees with E_1. in a most remarkable manner, which can only be explained by the supposition that either of the two MSS. has been slavishly copied from the other. For examples see §§ 5, 7, 12. Further examples are: 4445. forth] *om.* 4549. reles hym] hym reles. 4565. any lenger] than lenger. 4681. puple] people. Undoubtedly it is Ro. that has, in the last 400 lines, been copied from the MS. that was the original of the first (known) printed edition of *Thebes*. For in not a few instances Ro. agrees not only with E_1., but also with S. or with S. and the Ad. and Ra. groups; see *vv. ll.*

§ 17. (Lb.) P. E_2. C. T_2. L_2. Ro.

These six, in the last third of the poem seven, MSS. constitute one *division*, held together by common faults. Occasionally some MS. differs from the others, its reading coinciding with that of an unrelated MS. or group of MSS. This is the case particularly with E_2. in the beginning (see § 14) and with Ro. towards the end (see § 16). Such discrepancies must often be due to different side-influences during the series of copyings through which the existing MSS. have come down to us, and are not noticed in the list below. MSS. C. and Ro. have many gaps. Common faults, *e.g.* 517. *see vv. ll.* 837. As] And as. 1051] þe] of (as E_2.). 1196. whylom] som tyme. 1259. surer] sure. 1318. high constreynt] him constreined. 1338. shal] shal but. 1352. Euerich] either. 1776. thenk] thenketh (thynckyth). 1952. ȝe han quytt] ye acquite. 2007. all] *om.* 2030. Fynaly] plainly. 2257. hym-silue tho] tho hymself. 3229. she] *om.* 3330. may largely] largely may. 3385. ny] *om.* 3447. ȝif that] and. 3567. lusty] hasty. 3890. the Thebans] Thebans. 4490. parted] coruen (corvid). 4549. myght] may, *etc.*

Faults common to this division and certain other MSS. are, *e.g.*

2123. ride] riding. 2132. wil] wolde. 2138. *second* most] *om.* 2334. *second* he] *om.* 3399. water] teeres. 3425. nor duk] duk. 3512. this] the. 3667. loth] wroth. 3904. lyoun] a lyon. 4376. vpon] on. 4630. gynne] begynne. 4704. *second* and] *om.*

In the last thousand lines of the poem, this class of MSS., in general of subordinate value, has alone, or in conjunction with some other MS. or group of MSS., in some cases preserved the correct reading against the majority of the MSS. See 3610, 3611, 3649, 3665, 3712, 3788, 3955, 4085, 4095, 4118, 4119, 4553, 4565, 4592, 4629. Cf. a similar list in § 19 (P.–Ap.): It should be noted that lines 3409 to the end are lost in Ap.

§ 18. Ap.

Ap. is a late MS. and has lost nearly a third of the text. Its affinities go in various directions, but on the whole Ap. comes nearest the P.–Ro. class, especially the L_2. Ro. group (cf. 110, 283, 424, 466, 1922, 2060, 2479, 2583, 3219, 3274). Ap. has a number of special faults, *e.g.* 4. In] In þe. 16. wiþ] *om.* 31. dronken] dronkynge. 45. fressh ben] freyshely bene. 124. parcel a-fore] parse aftyr. 169. with] *om.* 358. hath] *om.* 424. the] thys. 586. with-drawe] drawe. 1004. hym] *om.* 1082. Shope] Shape. 1230. be bond] by wey. 1512. Royal] hygh. 1565. lak] lyt lak. 1681 *to* 1746 *lost.* 2232. for a wed] for wed. 2398. tapese] to pese. 2735. sone] sone Polymytes. 2926. controover] contrarye. 2936. her] hygh. 3026 *om.* 3312. ful] ryght. 3385. ny] by. 3409 *to the end lost.*

§ 19. (Lb.) P. E_2. C. T_2. L_2. Ro. Ap.

These seven, in ll. 3286–3408 eight, MSS. form one *class* with a number of common faults. The remarks on occasional differences made § 15 hold good also with regard to this group of MSS. Common faults, *e.g.* 316. vnto] to. 324. as] *om.* 532. wil] wolde (= S.). 741. so] thoo. 752. grete] high. 839. this] his. 894. erthly] hertly. 932. Percen] Persyng (Perced T_2). 1079. as thow] lik as. 1203. To holde] He helde. 1222. high] ofte. 1322. *see v.l.* 1406. soth] cause. 1903. only] hooly. 1987. and] and in (= Lb.). 2045. vowen] vowe it. 2138. which] such (= Lb.). 2331. Ther] Wher. 2504. A parcel] And parcel (= Lb.). 2932. after] by. 2944. he by] he in. 2987. evyl] heuy. 3286. whan] That. 3298. and] and with hem. 3386. grounde] erthe. Ap. 3409 *to the end lost.* The most conclusive lines as to the genealogical connection of these eight MSS.

are 894, 1203, 1406, 3298, 3386. The class in several cases has the right reading together with Ar. against the Bo.–M. class, *e.g.* 370 (Root ytake), 2360 (vnto), 2363 (hool my), 2386 (yrayled), 2389 (they), 2475 (which), 2703 (hegh), 2919 (which). In 1448 (for to), 2633 (ful), 3086 (yet), the right reading is preserved against all the other MSS. In l. 1309 this class with the Bo.–M. class preserves the right reading against the rest (Tydeus); cf. *Notes*.

§ 20. Ap.–Ro. + Bo.–M.

In the first few hundred lines (1–*c.* 550) there are striking coincidences between Ap.–Ro. or groups of MSS. or isolated MSS. belonging to this class and the Bo.–M. class. The remarks on occasional differences made in § 15 hold good also here. On Lb. see § 21.

Ap.–Ro. and Bo.–M., *e.g.* 23. gentillesse] gentilnesse (+ Ad_2. I. Ra. Ba. S.). 165. a] no. 302. Wher-vp-on] There vpon. 444. drowe] drowe hem. 466. lat] I late.

P.–Ro. + Bo.–M., *e.g.* 98. to-nyght] þis nyght. 133. nor] ne (+ S.). 171. make] and make. 204. whilom] some tyme. 298. be compas out] oute by compas. 420. that] *om.* 425. ful] *om.* (fylle L_2. fel Ro.). 428. to] *om.* 469. his] *om.* 592. vayleth] auaileth.

P. (E_2.)[1] T_2. (C. gap) + Bo.–M., *e.g.* 1. briȝte] *om.* (+ Ra. Ba.). 25. also in soth] eke in soth. 43. Rede] Redeth. 53. in] þe. 66. this] in this. 74. slender long] longe slender. 136. non] noon is. 152. oure] þe. 154. fully] ful. 191. fame] name. 214. Cler] Clerly (Clerkely). 263. eny] the. 269. berer] beryng. 294. groundyng] grounden. 306. ther hath longe not] hath not there longe (+ Ra. E_1. S.). 323. oure] youre. 327. Regnyng] And regned. 346. Iubiter] to Iubiter. 400. sore] *om.* 416. fer] there. 426. se] it se. 489. and] if. 539. collusioun] illusion.

T_2. (representing group C. T_2.; cf. § 13) + Bo.–M., *e.g.* 42. In] bothe in. 128. anoon as] as sone as. 212. neither] *om.* 308. from] *om.* 546. To] Vnto.

P. + Bo.–M., *e.g.* 12. the] that. 162. Shet] Shet vp.

§ 21. Lb.

a. Lb. has a fair number of special faults, *e.g.* 2. and] *om.* 8. fro heuene made] made fro heuene. 13. noble] lusty. myghty] *om.*

[1] Cf. § 14, *d.*

27. other greve] ooyr eve. 28. as] *om.* 50. nor] and. 55. sothly] softely. 65—392 *lost.* 403. to-forn] be to forn. 430. þis is no tale] in tale. 486. vnto the] to a. 499. forgat] foryeteth. 503. opportune] tyme and oportune. 537. On] And. 538. ful] right. 574. Al be that] Albe though. 623. odyous] hidious. 626. by] that bi some. 688. Thus] This. 707. bothe] ben. 741. awapyd and amaat] dismayed and dissolaat (= 742). 811. ȝif] yit. 814 *om.* 905. mor and] *om.* 940. lad] haue. 1031. werk] werkus. 1042. thyng] caas. 1056. hoolsom] *om.* 1117. ȝeer] There. 1175. tarise] ganne ryse. 1222. high] hevy. 1322. noyeng ne] no maner. 1362. And reporte] And make reporte. 1458. make] make hem bothe. 1685. Inly] oonly. 1812. wonder] ouer. 1836. mor] moste. 1850. wer it] Whether hit be. 2004. ȝif] and. 2102. Fro] Of. 2167. Mid] In myddes. 2236. opynly] oonly. 2348. distresse] grete distresse. 2543. Euerich] Euery man. 2546. and] and after. 2612. seiþ] telleth. 2661. may] mowe. 2695. *see v.l.* 2841. thar] ther-of. 3051. Kyngges Prynces] knyghtes and squyers. 3054. want] faute. 3092. leyde] *om.* 3251. hath this þing] this hath. 3295. hir] þeyre. 3330. howsyng] haunsinge. 3357. surplus] surplice. 3366. forto ben] to. 3556. way] *om.* 3594. houndes] woundes. 3747. Antigone (: bewte)] Antigon (: beute anon). 3846. rescus] recours. 4136. diffacyd] to faced. 4237. gaf] was. 4369. Antigonee] antygon. 4370. to se] to se on. 4371. sorowes] sorownesse. 4440. barbyd þe visage] barfote the vyage. 4597–4658 *lost.*

b. Lb. presents a rather composite text. In its last third (3286 to the end) it is closely connected with the Ap.–Ro. class, especially with the C. T_2. P. E_2. group, and more particularly with P. (cf. §§ 14, 15, 19). Also in other parts of the poem Lb. fairly often agrees with P. For this reason it is in the genealogical diagram placed nearest to P.

In the first few hundred lines (1–*c.* 550), where Ap.–Ro. and Bo.–M. agree closely, Lb. generally has the same readings as these two classes, where they agree (see § 20). Where these two classes disagree, Lb. generally goes with Bo.–M., as 22. some] and some. 36. *see v.l.* 39. was] *om.* 46. ȝoue] ioye. 63-392 Lb. *gap.* 410. sone] childe. 463. who so] whos. 465. that] *om.* 467. of dayes and of ȝeeris] by dayes and by yeeres. 488. so be] *om.* 517. doune on knees eft a-geyn] dovne eft on knees. 531. forto] to. 564. perteynent] apparteynyng.

Between *c.* 550 and 3286 the affinities of Lb. are more difficult to determine. It continues to agree with Bo.–M. But the majority of cases are those where Bo.–M. go with Ad.–E_1. (see § 12). In most of these cases Lb. agrees with Bo.–M. and Ad.–E_1. Other agreements between Lb. and Bo.–M. are, *e.g.* 606. Towardes] Toward (+ Ad_1). 749. al] *om.* 794. recordeth] recordeth it. 1044. And] *om.* (+ T_2. P. Ba.). 1755. thorgh] for. fro] þorugh. 1767. Who that] Whos. 1997. nat no lenger hym] not him no lenger. 2012. to] *om.* 3086. yet] now.

Special agreements with Ad.–E_1. are few, *e.g.* 1256. mor] *om.* (Lb. + Ad_1.–Ba.).

Faults common to Lb. and several MSS. of the Ap.–Ro. class are not numerous, and in most cases one or more MSS. belonging to other classes have the same reading, *e.g.* 1145. a] þe (+ L_1. M. Di. I. S.). 1707. his] the (+ M. Di. E_1.). 2123. ride] ridyng (+ M. Di. Ad_1.–Ba. S.). 2138. *second* most] *om.* (+ M. Di. Ad_1.–Ba. S.). 2276. ride] to ride (+ Ad_1.–Ba. E_1. S.). 2282. doun] a-down (+ Ad_1.–Ba. E_1. S.). 2421. Beheestyng] Bihotyng (+ T_1. Du. M. Di. Ad_1. Ad_2. E_1. S.). 2735. and] and to (M. Di. Ad_1.–E_1.). 2942. diuersyte] aduersite (+ Di. Ad_2. I.). 3206. hegh] *om* (+ Ad_1. Ad_2. I. S.). 3286. lorn] forlorne (+ M. Di.).

In 2078 Lb. Bo.–M. and P. E_2. C. T_2. have the right reading against the rest.

In some cases, however, Lb. agrees with Ap.–Ro. or several MSS. of this class against the other classes, *e.g.* 1987. and] and in. 2138. which] such. 2504. A] and.

More numerous are coincidences with T_2. and P. Lb. T_2. : 628. besyde] forthe besyde. 658. thus] *om.* Lb. P. : 1013. than] than a. 1322. nor] ne. 1504. knowlecchyng] knowyng (+ Ap.). 1953. al] *om.* 2756. into] to (+ E_2.). 2963. termyne] determyne. 3286. they] *om.* forto] elles to. Cf. also § 12.[1]

[1] The special coincidences between Lb. and Ap.–Ro. or even with P. in the part 550–3286, are neither very numerous nor very striking, and they do not seem to justify the grouping of Lb. as a whole with this class. In earlier drafts of the genealogy Professor Erdmann placed Lb. with the Bo.–M. class, and in the critical apparatus below the text it has its place between Bo.–L_1. and M. Di. There seems to be good reason for this placing of Lb. The numerous faults common to Lb. and Bo.–M. + Ad.–E_1. might suggest that if these two classes go back to a common special original, Lb. is derived independently from the same original. However, in view of the fairly numerous faults common to Lb. and Bo.–M. and the rare occurrence of special agreements between Lb. and Ad.–E_1., it seems more likely that Lb. and Bo.–M. go back to a common original. The genealogy would then be something like this:

§ 22. Ar. G.

a. Ar. and G. form one *group* (*class*) connected by a number of common faults. Some of these are found only in Ar. G. (special faults), in other faults Ar. G. are associated with the Bo.-M. class, and still more often with the Ad$_1$.-E$_1$. class. Besides, there occur, as usual, casual coincidences with other MSS. or groups of MSS. The close relationship of Ar. and G. manifests itself even in unique spellings. Special faults of Ar. G., *e.g.* 110. to] *om.* 165. a] *om.* 282. Outher] Oyther. 333. lyneal] lyne al. 365. Come] Corue. 440. holtes] haltes. 1034. waast] wayst. 1170. til] to. 1256. without] with. 1322. noyeng ne] moving ne Ar., mevyng no G. 1750. vnstabilete] vnstablete. 1811. due] dieu. 2010. al] of. 2162. til] to. 2814. ȝiue] ȝif. 2833. no] to. 3051. be] ly. 3211. To] Til. 3440. Repleneshed] Repleveshed. 3597. tusshy] trusshy. 3663. put our mater] puter Ar., putte G. 4306. ronne] room Ar., roone G. 4378. that] *om.* 4626. departyden] partyd. 4649. Bellona] Belliona.

Faults common to Ar. G. and one or more other MSS., *e.g.* 109. with] *om.* 203 *and* 204 *transposed.* 380. collecte] correcte. 382. hour] tour. 499. forgat] feyned. 508. the trewe ground] the trewe troupe. 649. preef] preest. 1098. But] *om.* 1648. tok than] tok. 1988. high] gret. 2078. in feeld] *om.* 2084. ye lordes] the

---

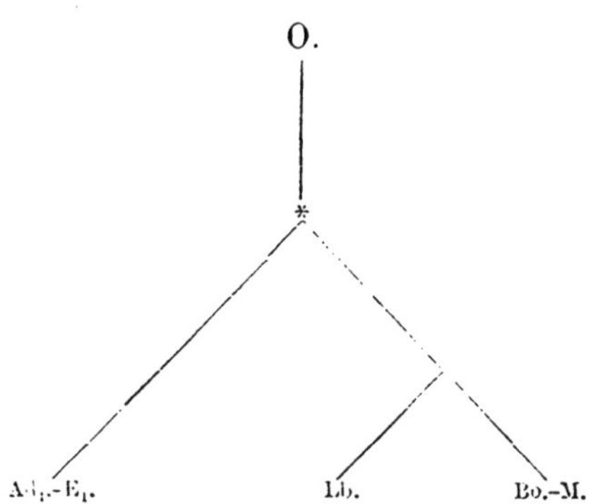

If this is right, the coincidences of Lb. with Ap.-Ro. would be due to some side-influence in the series of copyings. The probability would seem to be that the copyist who wrote Lb. had access to a MS. nearly related to P., from which a number of corrections were introduced into the text. From l. 3286 on he made the MS. of the P. type the basis of his text alone, possibly because the other MS. was defective.—E. E.

lordes. 2437. forwounded] soor wounded. 2555. sperkles] sperkes. 2739. which in] with Inne. 3376. hent] rent. 3496. Hent out] Rent out. 3852. good] gret. 4187. They don for him] Don for hem. 4284. unbrace] embrace Ar., enbrace G. 4298. loud] land.

b. The special faults of Ar. against which G. offers the right reading are few and unimportant, *e.g.* 46. to whom] to who. 95. haue] ha. 185. and] of. 368. fate] face. 445. til] to. 461. purpoos] propoos. 553. The fend] He fond. 752. grete] riȝt. 1130. Til] To. 1132. ascendeth] descendeth. 1203. To holde] Be holde. 1784. flaterye] flatrye. 1909. to] *om.* 2368. so] *om.* 2374. at the hil] al the hil. 2433. Wherto] Wherfor. 2717. loue] gold. 2944. he by] he. lorn] born. 3232. her] ther. 3628. were] that were. 4101. by] *om.* 4389. Al-thogh] Al they. 4679. luk] bok (Luce *in rubric*).

Ar. is the oldest and one of the very best MSS. As has been seen, it presents no inconsiderable number of faults,[1] but it compares favourably with any other of the good MSS. Every deviation, however small, from Ar. being marked in the text by an asterisk, the impression may well be created that Ar. is more faulty than, *e.g.*, Bo. Du. Ad_1. M. C. A glance at the variant readings will immediately show that such an impression is wrong.

Ar. has no definite connection with any of the three other types of MSS. It holds an independent position, agreeing now with the Ad.–E_1., now with the Bo.–M., and occasionally with the Ap.–Ro. type.

Ar. participates with all the other MSS. in the faults which were in the first copy (O.). Ar. has not left any descendant except G.

c. G.

The special faults of G., against which the right reading is preserved in Ar., are not grave but numerous. Many of them are due to mere carelessness on the part of the copyist, as the frequent omission not only of single words but of whole lines, *e.g.* 35. a] to. 61. And fro] at. 73. Cope] Cape. 89. al] and. 100. hagys] hastyng. 126. by] my. 132. a-side] a-doun. 170. to] *om.* 176. shal] may. 251. ofte] of. 266. And] Ashuld. 267. As] And. 284. do] to. 308. from thennys] from Thebes. 371. out] *om.* 376. white] *om.* 402. Agayn] And gayn. 624. I] *om.* 732. mor]

[1] In some miscellaneous notes (undated) found among Professor Erdmann's papers he remarks that there are several alterations of the readings of Ar. which he would wish undone. There is no indication of the passages to which this remark refers, except for some corrected in Errata.—E. E.

no. 743. Muet] *om.* 796. toke] take. his] *om.* 881. ful] *om.* 1023. estat] of state. 1039. Therfor] Ther of. 1044. descendid] condescended. 1136. A-twene] And twene. 1190. londe] long. 1304. proude] *om.* 1364. two] tho. 1440 *om.* 1484. gold] *om.* 1578. liklynesse] liknesse. 1651. For] Of. 1667. louys] louyng. 1692. make] take. 1946*b* *and* 1947*a* *om.* 2003. ȝere] nyght. 2031. bete] fylled. 2075. collusioun] conclusioun. 2121*b* *and* 2122*a* *om.* 2154. leyn] hym. 2329. of] with. 2422 *and* 2423. wolde] wyl. 2512. pitous] poyntes. 2714 *om.* 3016 *om.* 3091. herbes] leues. 3142 *om.* 3312. ful good] a gret. 3955. lightly may] likly many. 3975. nor of no] more of. 4057. swiche] which. 4149 *om.* 4184 *om.* 4267*b* *and* 4268*a* *om.* 4448. they weren alle] euerychon were. 4453. port] thoght. 4655. swich] sewyth. 4656. felyn] fallyn in. 4708. pur] clene.

G. is a direct descendant of Ar., but several faults seem to suggest that G. was not copied directly from Ar., but that there is at least one intermediate link.

§ 23. O.

No MS. of the *Siege of Thebes* written by Lydgate's own hand has come down to our time. We have no means of judging of his handwriting or of his carefulness as a corrector. But from Lydgate's reiterated requests that his readers should kindly correct the slips and mistakes of his writings, we have cause to believe that he was conscious of having not seldom neglected to bestow proper care on the metre or the syntax of his poetical productions. Also on this point he is in strong contrast to Chaucer, who, addressing his future copyists, entreats or rather enjoins them not to alter his texts at all, but to copy them carefully and faithfully.

In Lydgate's case it is probable that the first fair copy of a longer poem of his was, as a rule, written by some professional copyist, and that the first batch of copies sent out to expectant readers was made from this first copy, not from the author's own rough draft. Thus the said first copy supplies the place of the author's original MS. and, besides transmitting possible or probable faults of this MS. (see below, remarks on ll. 289–92 of the poem), may have added other faults of its own. As a matter of fact, there is a number of faults common to *all* the Thebes MSS., whether contemporary with the author or of later origin, which faults can be explained only by supposing that they existed already in the first fair copy above referred to. That some of these faults are due to Lydgate himself and not to his first copyist is extremely probable. The first copy, doing duty for Lydgate's own original draft and being the common source of all the existing MSS., will be in the genealogical diagram marked by a capital O.

Faults of O., the common original, now lost, found in all the extant MSS.

289–92. These four lines are identical with 239–42, with the exception only of the first word: *Noble* (*and riche*) in 289 instead of *Royal* (*and riche*) in 239. Evidently the lines must be struck out in one place. Lydgate having composed and inserted them after 238 thought them better suited to come after 288, so as to form the conclusion of the whole story of the building of Thebes by king Amphioun. He must have forgotten to cross them out in their original place, and his copyist thoughtlessly wrote them out twice. That this mistake was not detected and corrected before further copies were allowed to be made, reveals the significant and rather interesting fact that Lydgate did not take the pains of reading over the first copy of his poem. Bergen, in his edition of Lydgate's *Troy Book*, Introductory Note, p. xvi, calls attention to a similar mistake, though of minor extent, viz. of l. 719 of the Prologue being repeated as l. 727.

324. All the MSS., except Ba., have: "The space in soth as I suppose of vii. myle." Ba. has "for sothe" instead of "in soth." This makes a seven-beat line. "In soth" must be struck out. It was probably added by the first copyist.

927 and 928. All the MSS. have 927 "To certeyn men," and all, except Ar. and G., have 928 "To execute (Texecute)." The first copyist by mistake took the "To" of 928, which is in its right place before the infinitive (M.E. "bidden" may be construed with or without "to" before the following infinitive), and put it before the direct object (certeyn men), where it is misplaced, leaving it also at the beginning of 928. Ar. tried to correct the mistake, unsuccessfully.

1346. It seems probable that the pp. "armed" in all the MSS., instead of y-armed, which is decidedly demanded by the metre, is due to the first copyist. See also 1882, 4022, and cf. 1306.

1357 and 1358 offer another instance of an initial word being wrongly transferred from one line to the preceding or following one, a mistake of rather common occurrence in our MSS. In the present case " And " lost its place in 1357 by being moved down to 1358 (cf. above, l. 927).

1738. The context clearly shows that the reading of all the MSS. " The influence " is wrong. " Neemye " is the subject, " gat " the predicate, " licence " the direct object of the sentence. The influence of truth cannot be anything but an adverbial phrase, denoting the means and properly introduced by the preposition " by."

1901. See *Notes*. Probably " Sir " was not written out by the copyist, a free space being left for the illumination of the initial.

2081. This line, as it stands in all the MSS. except Ra. and Ba., has only four beats. It seems highly probable that the right reading found in Ra. and Ba. is due to a happy correction made by the scribe of the MS. that was the immediate source of Ra. and Ba.

3603. All the MSS. have " occasions " (occasiouns) instead of occisiones. See also 4204. There is no doubt but that it is the first copyist that must be charged with this fault, whether owing to careless copying or to a deliberate attempt at amendment (see *Notes*).

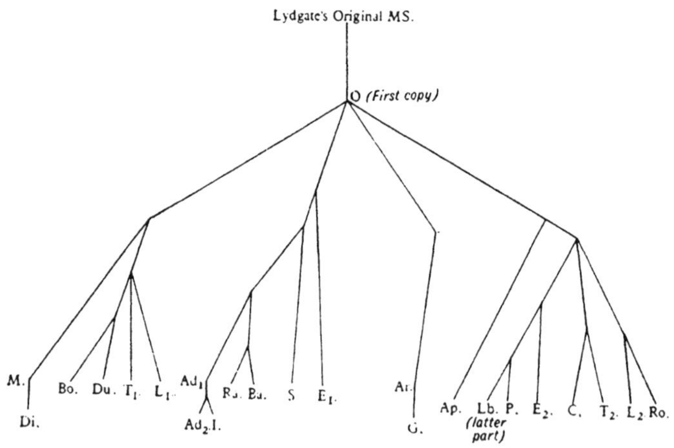

The diagram is dated 12 Nov. 1925

NOTES

1, 2. Cf. *C. T.*,[1] Prol. 7–8: "and the yonge sonne Hath in the Ram his halfe cours y-ronne." Accordingly, Lydgate's meeting with the Host of the Tabard and the other pilgrims at their inn in Canterbury (Prol., 66 ff.) on the eve of their return journey is represented as taking place about a fortnight after the gathering of the pilgrims at the Tabard in London. Wülcker once remarked (*Altengl. Lesebuch*, ii, p. 270) that this shows how much time the pilgrimage from London to Canterbury (+ the stay of the pilgrims in that town) is by Lydgate supposed to have taken. But see Furnivall's computation (founded on medieval statements) in his Temporary Preface to the six-text edition of Chaucer's *Canterbury Tales* (Chaucer Soc.), according to which the pilgrimage from London to Canterbury was done on an average in three days and a half. See also *The Tale of Beryn* (ed. by Furnivall for the E.E.T.S.), i, Prol., l. 675 ff., from which it appears that Chaucer's pilgrims are supposed to stay in Canterbury only half a day and one night and to start on their return journey before sunrise on the following morning. This agrees surprisingly well with the case of Lydgate as stated by himself in the Prologue. One would expect that he, a monk, should devote more time to paying his thanks to "the holy seynt," to whom he was indebted for his recovery from "siknesse." But no, Lydgate does not even try to remonstrate against the Host's peremptory order. He has arrived in Canterbury after dinner and is invited to join the pilgrims at supper. However, he evidently thinks that the afternoon will afford him time enough his "vowes to aquyte," and is quite prepared to start for London (and Bury St. Edmunds) in company with Chaucer's pilgrims next morning "anon as it was light" (Prol., 71–2, 108, 123–4, 150). Such a proceeding was apparently the regular thing. And to many persons their pilgrimages were mere pleasure trips. Lydgate's astronomical notice l. 1 was, of course, never meant to convey an exact date.

3. Adopted by Sackville in his Induction to the *Mirror for Magistrates*: "And olde Saturnus with his frosty face." Cf. Chaucer, *Boethius*, Bk. IV, metrum 1: the olde colde Saturnus.

5. Malencolik] The influence of the planet Saturn was supposed to produce a gloomy and morose disposition and character. Cf. saturnine adj. See also 389: Hevy-chered, malèncolik and loth.

8–9. When there is much moisture in the air, the eastern sky is red at sunrise.

15. Subordinate clause, "y-meynt with her floures" being connected with "grene." Cf. 2306.

18–19. The tyme . . . whan Canterbury talys Complet and told] *i.e.* were told completely. Omission of the copula (was, were) is not rare in *Thebes*, see *e.g.* 65, 136, 395, 1889, 2227, 3183, 4194, 4372.

[1] *Canterbury Tales.* References to Chaucer's works are made to Skeat's *Student's Chaucer.*

19. at many sondry stage] *i.e.* in (during) many different stages of their journey from Southwark to Canterbury.

20. Of estatis in the pilgrimage] Inversion for "in the pilgrimage of estatis," *i.e.* during the journey of the pilgrims who belonged to and represented many different orders and classes of society. Inversions are common in *Thebes*.

22–25. Adjuncts to "talys" in 18.

32. Lydgate is mistaken in describing the Pardoner as having a "pylled nolle." Baldness is a characteristic of Chaucer's Miller,[1] see *C. T.* A 3935 (*The Reves Tale*): "as piled as an ape was his skulle." In his Prologue 675–76 Chaucer says:

> "This pardoner hadde heer as yelow as wex,
> But smothe it heng, as dooth a strike of flex."

33. beerdlees al his Chyn] Inversion: "beerdlees" is an adjunct of "chyn," not of "pardowner." See *C. T.*, Prol. 689.

34. Glasy-Eyed] See *ib.* 684: "Swiche glaringe eyen hadde he as an hare."

and face of Cherubyn] Another mistake of Lydgate's. He has attributed to the Pardoner a characteristic quite incongruous with the man's general appearance as described by Chaucer. It is of the Somnour that Chaucer says (Prol. 624): "That hadde a fyr-reed cherubinnes face."

Lydgate evidently had only a confused and faulty remembrance of his great master's greatest work and was careless enough not to refresh it by re-reading at least the Prologue. At the time of writing the finishing pages of his poem he had procured a copy of the *Canterbury Tales* (cf. *Note* on l. 4463 ff.), but he neglected to use it to revise and correct his own prologue.

35. Tellyng a tale to angre with the frere] *i.e.* to anger the frere with. Cf. *C. T.*, Prol. 791–92:

> "That ech of yow, to shorte with your weye,
> In this viage, shal telle tales tweye."

Lydgate is again mistaken, as was remarked already by Wülcker, *l.c.* 270. In *C. T.* it is the Somnour, not the Pardoner, who, retaliating on the friar for his tale about a somnour, treats the pilgrims to a very drastic tale about a certain friar.

39–57. Praise of Chaucer as the flower of poets, especially as the author of the *Canterbury Tales*.

47. wel seyinge] *i.e.* wel-seyinge (eloquence); cf. "hoom-comynge" 2429.

49. Inversion: "al þat was tolde" is a direct object of "forȝeting."

53–57. Chaucer, omitting the unimportant incidents of each tale, preserved the principal points faithfully and by his poetic art gave them more light and life than they had before. With 54 f. cf. also *Troy Book*, Prol. 148–52:

> "Of Troye Boke, I-made be dayes olde,
> Wher was remembrid, of auctours vs be-forn,
> Of the dede the verreie trewe corn,
> So as it fil seuerid from the chaf."

60. Chaucer's Prologue l. 20.

65. None so hardy] *intellige* "was."

[1] Not the Miller who was in the company of pilgrims, but that of the *Reves Tale*.

70. to entren into toun] toun, preceded by a preposition, sometimes has the definite article, sometimes not. The reading of Ar. L_2. Ro. G. has been kept against that of Bo. and the majority of the MSS. See also 1834, 2540, 2756, 3779, 3927, etc. In two of these lines, 2756 and 3779, Bo. agrees with Ar. In 2540 and 3927 the reading of Bo. and the majority of the MSS. ("into the toun") is, on metrical grounds, inadmissible.

71–2. Cf. *C. T.*, Prol. 18.

73. a Cope of blak, and not of grene] Green was in Lydgate's time regarded as a stately and festive colour. Cf. Chaucer's *Leg. Good Women*, Prol. 214, where the dress of Alceste, the queen of the god of love, is described: "And she was clad in real habit grene."

74. Cf. *C. T.*, Prol. 287 (the Clerk of Oxenford): "As lene was his hors as is a rake."

75. mad nat for þe sale] The bridle was not polished and shining as is usual when the horse is being offered for sale.

76. My man to-forn with a voide male] It is unlikely that the servant should ride in front of his master. Probably we have here a rather strained inversion of the regular word-order, and what the author really means to say, is that his man had his (Lydgate's) empty (scantily filled) wallet before him on his horse. Cf. *C. T.*, Prol. 686: "His (the Pardoner's) walet lay biforn him in his lappe."

79. Her gouernour, the host] Cf. *C. T.*, Prol. 813–14: (and preyden him also . . .)

> "And that he wolde been our governour,
> And of our tales juge and reportour."

79–80. "The same tyme" is adverbial adjunct to "Stonding"; the clause is an absolute one.

Lydgate in his sketch of the Tabard host has somewhat exaggerated the self-confident character and bold manners ascribed to him by Chaucer, *C. T.*, Prol. 751–57. Cf. however *C. T.* B 3998–99:

> "Than spak our host, with rude speche and bold,
> And seyde un-to the Nonnes Preest anon."

82–83. Cf. the Host's words to the Monk, *C. T.* B 3118–20:

> "But, by my trouthe, I knowe nat your name,
> Wher shal I calle yow my lord dan Iohn,
> Or dan Thomas, or elles dan Albon?"

85. Cf. *C. T.* B 3984–85:

> "For sikerly, nere clinking of your belles,
> That on your brydel hange on every syde."

88. "Withoute more shortely" is adverbial adjunct to "telle" in 86.

90. Cf. *C. T.*, Prol. 290: "Ful thredbar was his overest courtepy."

91. Wel araied for to ride late] Because offering no temptation to robbers. With regard to the risk of robbers on the pilgrims' road, even in the vicinity of Canterbury, see *C. T.* H 5–8. "Wel araied" is to be referred to "ȝe" in 88, not to "hood."

92. Lydgate's family had taken their name from Lidgate, a village in Suffolk, about ten miles south-west of Bury St. Edmunds.

96. Daun John, quod he] The Host here suddenly proves to know Lydgate's Christian name, though in 92 Lydgate gives only his family name. This inadvertency is of slight importance. Readers are to under-

stand that Lydgate has mentioned it, but not registered the fact. The same inadvertency, if it may be so called, is found in Chaucer's *C. T.*; cf. the Host's question quoted above in the note to 82—which question remains unanswered by the monk in our text of *C. T.*—with his words *C. T.* B 3982: "Wherfor, sir Monk, or dan Piers by your name."

96. wel broke ȝe ȝoure name] The expression is much older than the earliest example in *Oxf. Dict.*, s.v. Brook (1587 Harrison). *King Horn* (Wissman's ed.) has ll. 209–10: Horn child, quaþ þe king, wel bruc þu þi neuening. But its meaning in this place, as well as in the examples quoted in *Oxf. Dict.*, "may you bear your name appropriately, do credit to it," scarcely seems to suit our passage. It should rather be interpreted in a more general sense: "may you enjoy a good use of your name, may you use your name and enjoy it, may you live and flourish long." ten Brink, *Geschichte der engl. Lit.*, i, 265, translates the Horn passage: Wohl geniesse du deines Namens, Horn.

It may be added that the phrase occurs also in *The Tale of Beryn* (ed. by Furnivall and Stone for the E.E.T.S.), which is held to have been written by a Canterbury monk. The Prologue describes the doings of a party of pilgrims during their afternoon and night in Canterbury, while the Tale is told by a merchant in the early morning soon after their start from Canterbury. In l. 65 the Pardoner says to the tapster at the inn, with whom he wants to ingratiate himself: "And Goddis blessing have þow, Kitt! now broke wel thy name."

98. Preiyng ȝou soupe with vs to-nyght] Lydgate often uses the present participle instead of a finite form to tack on a principal clause to a preceding one, even in cases where such a construction would not be allowed in modern English. Cf. 84–86: "ȝe be welcom . . . besechinge ȝou þat" etc. Cf. Introduction, Chap. II, § 3, 7.

102. Sclender is ȝoure koyse] Chaucer has not the word "koyse," but Gower has. The *Oxf. Dict.* registers it (coise), adding: etymology and meaning uncertain. Macaulay in his Gower glossary does not translate it. Mätzner, *Wörterbuch*, i, p. 452, explains it: ugly woman, monster; Pauli: mistress. Halliwell: body. The last-mentioned translation is evidently right. The word was at home only in the colloquial or vulgar language of the time, and is used here by the Host in a depreciatory or contemptuous sense. See Introduction, Chap. III, § 2, Lydgate's vocabulary.

104. Or late fed in a feynt pasture] Remark the contrast to Chaucer's monk, to whom the Host says, *C. T.* B 3122–23:

> "I vow to god, thou hast a ful fair skin,
> It is a gentil pasture ther thou goost."

106. At the end of the line should be a comma instead of the mark of exclamation.

114. Collikes] Ar. Bo. and the great majority of the MSS. have "Collis" ("colles,") M. and L_2. "collikes," Ro. and S. "collica" ("colica,") Ad_2. and I. "collyk." Nevertheless "Collis" cannot be allowed to stand. A word "col" ("colle") in the sense demanded by our passage does not exist. There is reason to hold "collikes" of M. and L_2. to be the correct reading, because all the other MSS. (except Ro. S. Ad_2. I.) show a genitive, viz. collis (colles), which was probably miswritten for collikes in the common original of all the MSS. "Collikes" was successfully restored by the scribes of M. and L_2. However, with regard to the readings of the inferior MSS. quoted above (collica, colica, collyk) as well as to "collica passio" (Trevisa), "collica passio" (*Prompt Parv.*; see

Oxf. Dict.), it may be called in question whether Lydgate's original version had not, after all, "Collik passioun," which was altered into "Collikes" in the first copy of the author's own MS.

117. fenel Rede] The use of fennel in medicine as well as for culinary purposes is a well-known fact. But "red fennel" as a special variety is, in medieval literature, mentioned perhaps only by Lydgate in this line. Wülcker, *Altengl. Lesebuch*, ii, p. 271, says that "fenell rede auch fenelle the browne genannt, war als mittel zur verdauung im MA. bekannt. Vgl. z. B. Babees B. s. 183, anm. zu v. 191." It is not clear where he got this information as to the identity of the red fennel with the brown. The only authority quoted (*Babees B.*) is not in point. "Holy hokke & yardehok, peritory, and þe brown fenelle" are here (in John Russell's *Boke of Nurture*) prescribed as the ingredients in "The making of a bathe medicinable"; and the note added says, "Brown Fennelle probably Peucedanum officinale, Hog's fennel, a dangerous plant." Th. M. Fries, late Professor of Botany in the university of Upsala, kindly communicated the following dates from seventeenth-century botanical works. Dodonæus, *Herbarius oft Cruydt-Boeck* (Leyden 1608), says (p. 514) that there are three kinds of Venckel: 1. De Eerste heet Gemeyne Venckel; 2. De Tweede Roode Venckel; 3. De Derde Suete Venckel; and that "Venkelsaet ingenomen versterckt de mage, geneest de walginge, versoet de smerte ende crimpinge des buycks, ende verdrijft alle windachticheden." In Caspar Bauhinus' classical work, *Pinax Theatri Botanici* (Basle, 1671), the description of Fœniculum vulgare Germanicum contains (p. 147) this notice: "Variat foliorum colore: nam commune foliis est virentioribus, altera (sic) subnigricantibus, rubentibus, aliàs non differens: quare Fœniculum 1. & 2. facit Dodonæus." Joannes Raius, *Historia plantarum*, vol. i. (Lond. 1686), in treating of Fœniculum vulgare, Common Fennel or Finckle, says (p. 457): "Præterea semen hoc ventriculum roborat, nauseam sedat. . . . Hæc ergo de semine sicco accipienda sunt, quod & flatus discutit secundum tritum illum versiculum: Semen fœniculi reserat spiracula culi; & . . ." Thus it is a fact that in the seventeenth century a certain variety of fennel was known as red fennel, on account of the colour of the leaves. It may very well have been known even in the fifteenth century. The medicinal properties of the seeds as stated by Dodonæus and Raius are exactly such as the Host has in view in recommending "fenel Rede" to Lydgate. This being so, "fenel Rede" in l. 117 is safe; the reading of Ad_1. and Ad_2. "I rede," I advise you, though good in itself, must be regarded as an alteration, due perhaps to the scribes being ignorant of the existence of the red variety of fennel.

124. parcel a-fore Pryme] A little before 6 a.m.

125. A company (apposition to "we" in 124) [that] will do you good.

126. by kokkis blood] A profane asseveration: by God's blood. In *C. T.* H 9 the Host uses "for cokkes bones" in the same way.

154, 155. to come to dynere Vnto Osspryng] Ospringe is a village near Faversham, 10 miles from Canterbury, close to the pilgrims' road. At Ospringe was a hospital, referred to as "Domus Dei et B. Marie de Ospreng," 1465 *Index to the Charters and Rolls in the British Museum.* See also Furnivall, Temporary Preface, p. 13. Early dinner (twelve o'clock) is meant.

Only two other places on the road are mentioned in *Thebes*, Boughton under Blean (l. 1047) and Deptford (l. 4523), the latter only in a reference to Chaucer's *Knightes Tale.*

160. be ȝour Cristene name] a mild kind of adjuration.

163. It is no pleasure [for us to hear] you muttering your paternosters

in that way. [Besides] it will make your lips dry. Cf. *C. T.* B 3981, For ther-in is ther no desport ne game.

165. Tel some tale and make ther-of a Iape] "a Iape" is the reading of T_1. Ad_1. Ad_2. I. Ra. Ba. S. E_2. Ar. and G. have only "Iape." Bo. and the rest have "no Iape." These differences of the MSS. are based on, and explain themselves by, the two different shades of meaning that belong to the word jape (see *Oxf. Dict.* s.v.). Jape means (1) a trick, a device to cheat. If Iape be taken in this sense, the correct reading must be "no Iape," and the Host's words would imply: "tell us some tale, and do not try to trick us out of it by doing it in a perfunctory manner; because you shall not be allowed to escape from it; but mind, we will have no sermon or legend," etc. Jape means (2) a device to amuse, a merry or idle tale, a jest, joke. This is probably the sense Lydgate meant the word to bear here. The sense jest, joke, is found also 634: "This verray soth platly and no Iape." In the *Cant. Tales* "Iape" is repeatedly used in this sense, and it seems probable that Lydgate, when writing 165 ff., had in mind the words of the Host to the Pardoner (C 319): "Tel us som mirthe or japes right anon." Cf. also the Cook's prologue, *C. T.* A 4342–45:

"I wol yow telle as wel as ever I can
A litel jape that fil in our citee.
Our host answerde, and seide, I graunte it thee;
Now telle on," etc.

167. But preche not etc.] Perhaps a reminiscence of *C. T.* E 12 and 15 (Prologue of the Clerk of Oxenford): "But precheth nat, as freres doon in Lente, . . . Telle us some mery thing of aventures."

168. Cf. *C. T.* B 1896: "Tel us a tale of mirthe, and that anoon" (the Host to Chaucer).

169. And nodde not with thyn heuy bekke (bek, beke, beeke)] "bekke" is here "nose," a slang expression well fitting in with the free and humorous language of the Host. Thus it affords an earlier example of "beak" for the human nose than those quoted in *Oxf. Dict.*

170. Telle vs some thyng that draweþ to effecte Only of Ioye] Cf. *C. T.* A 2479–82:

"Now wol I stinten of the goddes above,
Of Mars, and of Venus, goddesse of love,
And telle yow, as pleynly as I can,
The grete effect, for which that I began."

As for the pronunciation of "effecte" in this line (: bekke), it seems safe to assume that the spelling "effek" of Bo. and many other MSS. is phonetic.

174. See 130; "in al thinge" refers to "I obeyed."

188. Vpon the tyme of worthy Iosue] See Boccaccio's *G. D.* lib. ii, cap. 63: "Dicit . . . Eusebius in libro temporum (*i.e.* Chronicorum lib.) anno regni Abantis regis argivorum viii., qui fuit mundi annis m.dccc.xxvii (= 1827) cadmum ab Amphione et Zeto regno pulsum." The creation of the world, according to the Jewish chronology, took place in the year 3761 B.C.

199–227. The reference to "myn auctour" is wrong. There is nothing about Amphion in *Roman de Edipus* (RE) or *Hystoire de Thebes* (HT). Lydgate has taken the legend from "bochas" only. In Boccaccio's *G. D.* lib. v, cap. 30 we read: "Homerus præterea ubi supra dicit, Iovem tres ex Anthiopa suscepisse filios, Amphionem scilicet et Zetum atque Calatum. Hos præterea volunt expositos a matre pulsa a Lynceo rege Thebarum . . ., et demum pulso Cadmo sene apud Thebas regnasse. Ex istis autem secundum Servium Amphion musicæ artes adeo peritus fuit, ut iuxta Lactantium a Mercurio cytharam meruit (206–209), cum qua thebanos muros construxit, ut Seneca poeta in Tragœdia Herculis furentis dicit. Cuiusque muros natus amphion iove struxit canoro saxa modulatu (205) trahens et cætera." And towards the end of the chapter: "Theodontius tamen dicit, Amphionem et fratres . . . aufugerunt in Græciam, et a Cadmo suscepti eum senem regno privaverunt, et se Iovis dixere filios. Floruit enim (ut dicit Eusebius in libro temporum) in musicis Lynceo regnante argis. Eum autem cythara movisse saxa in muros thebanos construendos dicit Albericus nil aliud fuisse quam melliflua oratione (215–27) suasisse ignaris atque rudibus et duris hominibus et sparsim degentibus, ut in unum convenirent et civiliter viverent et in defensionem publicam civitatem mœnibus circumdarent (228–39) quod et factum est. Quod autem a Mercurio cytharam susceperit, est quod eloquentiam ab influentia Mercurii habuerit (215–27), ut Mathematici asserunt." See also Koeppel, *Lydgate's Story of Thebes*, p. 23.

205. the werbles sharpe] See preceding note: "canoro modulatu."

215. Bochas . . . Seith (that) Mercurye . . . ȝaf etc.

225–30. See note 199 seqq.: "melliflua oratione suasisse."

234. His cheer, his port was outward so benygne] Cf. 250: "In contenaunce outward."

239–42. See Introduction, Chap. VI, § 23.

245. "lownesse," which is only in Ar. and G., is proved by the metre to be the right word as against "lowlynesse" in Bo. and the rest of the MSS. Lownesse in the sense of humility is found more than once in Lydgate, e.g. *Reson and Sensuallyte* (ed. Sieper), 1501, "To lownesse and humilyte"; *Fabula Duorum Mercatorum* (ed. Schleich), 489. Also Chaucer has it in the *Persones Tale*.

244–85. A lengthy disquisition on the duties of kings, especially their behaviour towards the common people, which is a subject often returned to in the poem.

253. The subject [they] of "wol rowne" is to be taken out of the genitive "puples" in the preceding line.

260–61. Probably a scene from contemporary life, witnessed by Lydgate. The sovereign that the poet has principally in his mind's eye must have been the late king Richard II. But it is not impossible that his words may refer also to Henry IV and Henry V. The last was England's admired hero, but far from faultless.

263 ff. Lydgate in his *Fall of Princes*, Book II (ll. 806–917), devotes Chapter III to a comparison between the members of the human body and the orders of the state; in stanzas 4–6 he particularly speaks of the relation between the head and the foot.

269. her berer vp and Supportacioun] With regard to the combination of a nomen agentis with an abstract noun, cf. *e.g. Temple of Glas* 325, Causer of ioie, Relese of penaunce; Chaucer, *Leg. Good Women*, 1369 (Jason): "Thou sly devourer and confusioun Of gentil-wommen."

283–85. For, as learned men can tell you, kings will in the end come to nothing, unless supported by the love of their people. In 283 "as" has been put in with Bo. Ad_1. M. and others against Ar. L_2. Ro. Ap., etc., because a parenthetical sentence accords better with Lydgate's general usage. Cf. *e.g.* 319, 2689; also because the syntax ("That, but loue her crowne do supporte, The fyn ys noght") would be rather too complicated for Lydgate's style. As the text stands now it is in conformity with the mode of expression in *Fall*, Book I, ll. 1275–77.

> " But in lordeshipes, as myn auctour seith,
> Withoute that vertu be ther trewe guide,
> In hem ther is surauncc noon nor feith."

293–305. " Some expositours " seems to refer to Boccaccio, and " olde auctours " to Ovidius. See *G. D.* lib. ii, cap. 63 : " Cadmus antiquorum omnium vulgata fama fuit filius Agenoris. . . . Hic tamen, ut scribit Ovidius (*Metamorph.* iii, 3–13) cum rapuisset iuppiter europam, ad ipsius perquisitionem ab agenore patre missus est, hac ei indicta lege ne absque eam reverteretur in patriam. Qui sumptus sociis cum quorsum quæreret ignoraret, novas sibi exquirere sedes statuit. Et cum haud longe a parnasso applicuisset, oraculum consuluit, et habito responso ut bovem sequeretur indomitam et ibidem ubi consisteret sedes assumeret; qui in destinatum sibi locum ductus acquievit, et regione a bove vocata bœtia civitatis fundamenta iecit, eamque ab antiquis thebis ægyptiis ex quibus prædecessores eius advenerant thebas appellavit."

Lydgate has confounded Ovidius' fable about the ox that guided Cadmus to the site of future Thebes (as retold by Boccaccio) with the story of the artful Dido who bought of king Jarbas as much ground as could be compassed by an oxhide.

293–96. Cf. *C. T.* A 1545–1549 (*The Knightes Tale*):

> " Allas ! y-broght is to confusioun
> The blood royal of Cadme and Amphioun;
> Of Cadmus, which that was the firste man
> That Thebes bulte, or first the toun bigan,
> And of the citee first was crouned king."

See also *RE* A ii back : " Le roy Cadamus qui premierement fonda Thebes eut deux filz qui apres luy tindrent la cite; dont lung eut nom Arthamas et lautre Pentras. Et apres ceulx regna Layus, qui estoit de leur lignee."

307. " Story " is here exceptionally Boccaccio's *Genalogia Deorum*; see 199 ff. note (in two places).

319. " clerkes " refers to Boccaccio; see Notes 199, 293.

332. þe stok of Amphyoun] Lydgate here, leaving Boccaccio, follows *RE*; see the last line in the note to 293–96. According to *G. D.* lib. ii, cap. 68, 69, Laius did not belong to "þe stok of Amphyoun" " be lyneal discent," but was the son of Labdacus, a younger brother of Cadmus. Labdacus was recalled to Thebes after Amphion had committed suicide.

335. " bookes " and 341. " story " both refer to *RE*, Lydgate's principal source, from which he has now begun to draw his tale. See fol. A i back : " Cy commence le liure de Edipus. Ung Roy estoit adoncques assez riche et puissant Layus fut nomme lequel auoit femme moult belle de son lignaige qui Iocaste fut appellee."

341. Ful wommanly, the story seith certeyn] *RE* says only "moult belle."

342–57. There is nothing said in *RE* about king Laius' wish to have an heir and his supplications to gods and goddesses for that purpose.

353. That he be not defrauded of His bone] Cf. 2706–7, Lest of his puple . . . He be defrauded. The verb " defraude " is not found in Chaucer's works. In Lydgate's usage, the notion of " fraudulently depriving or cheating " implied in the verb is thrown into the background, so that there remains essentially the simple sense of " disappointing or depriving."

358. Which whan] Latin construction (quod quum).

359–99. In *RE* A i back we find only this short account of the measures taken by Laius to ascertain the future doings of his new-born son: "Quant le roy Layus qui moult auoit veu aduenir dauentures, vit que il eut vng beau filz, il alla a ses dieux pour scauoir et pour entendre que celuy filz pourroit estre: et comment il se maintiendroit: et a quelles prouesses il viendroit en sa vie. Et luy fut dit que celuy filz feroit merueilles, et quil occiroit son pere." Boccaccio says briefly, *G. D.* lib. ii, cap. 69: "consuluit de futura prole oraculum," and *De casibus*, fol. iiii back: "consuluit de nascitura prole Laius apollinem." The rest is Lydgate's free invention: the calling in of diviners and philosophers and the detailed astrological calculations and observations made by these learned men, leading to the tragic prophecy of 398.

380. See Chaucer's *Astrolabe*, ii, 44: "consider wel that fro 1 to 20 ben *anni expansi*, and fro 20 to 3000 ben *anni collecti*." Cf. *C. T.* F 1273 ff. (*The Frankeleyns Tale*):

> "His tables Toletanes forth he broght,
> Ful wel corrected, ne ther lakked noght,
> Neither his collect ne his expans yeres,
> Ne his rotes ne his othere geres."

395–98. Omission of the predicate (was) in the consecutive sentence and inversion in the noun clause (397–98): the final judgement was that his father, by an inevitable fatal destiny, should be killed by his son.

400–19. *RE* A i back: "Quant le roy Layus entendit ceste chose il sen esmerueilla moult et ne sceut que faire aincoys fut dolent en son cueur. Lors commanda a la royne sa femme que celuy enfant feist occire et destruire. Et quant la Royne ouyt ainsi parler le roy, si en fut moult dolente, et en la parfin ne losa refuser, aincoys print lenfant et le fist porter hors dauec elle, et commanda quil fust porte en la forest et quil fust occis."

420–33. *RE* A i back: "Les sergens qui emporterent lenfant le veirent si beau et de si belle forme que ilz se pourpenserent que ia ilz ne locciroient, aincoys le pendroyent emmy la forest par les piedz a vng arbre pource que les bestes sauluaiges ne le deuorassent. Et ainsi le laisseroient si en conuenist bien aux dieux de sa mort ou de sa vie." A ii front: "Et lors pendirent lenfant a vng arbre parmy la plante des piedz que ilz luy percerent, et ainsi le laisserent. Et puis sen retournerent."

452–54. *RE* A ii front: "mais le roy Polipus Darcade luy mist nom Edipus pource quil eut les plantes des piedz percees."

468–74. *RE* A ii back: "Edipus deuint orgueilleux et moult cointe comme celuy qui cuidoit estre filz de Polipus, moult deuint felon et malicieux a ses compaignons car il ne pensoit neant leurs affaires, et si vouloit estre seigneur et damoysel sur tous les aultres."

507. and not spare] These words are put in parenthetically, and should in the text be enclosed within commas.

523. of hap or of fortune] causal adjuncts of the verb "lere."

533–44. *RE* A iii back: "Edipus cest mis en la voye du temple ou ceulx de la contree adoroient et erra tant que il vint la et auoit a nom celuy dieu Appollo: Cestoit le conseil quilz adoroient et auoient faicte vne ymaige dor moult grant qui seoit sur vng chariot a quatre roues qui estoit de moult riche semblance. Le dyable habitoit en celuy ymaige qui parloit et donnoit responces a ceulx qui a luy venoient et ladoroient."

The sequel is omitted by Lydgate: "Et scauez vous pourquoy lymaige estoit sus le chariot pource que le soleil en qui signifiance il estoit faict tournoye sans seiour."

537. boornyd bright and shene] qualifies " char of golde " and especially " golde "; cf. *Fall,* IV, 528 f.:

> " Withyne a chaar, ful richeli beseyn
> He shal be set, of gold bornid briht."

551–57. *RE* A iiii front: " Adoncques commenca le dyable a coniurer qui estoit en celuy ymaige. Et adoncques en yssit vne voix moult horrible qui luy dist quil sen allast a Thebes et la en orroit il certaines nouuelles."

560–61. *RE* A iiii front: " et cheuaucha tant que il vint a vng chastel qui auoit nom Pliote."[1] *HT* has: " vng chasteau nomme poliodes ou pleodes."

563–81. In Lydgate's *Fall* there is a different version of Layus' death by the hand of his son.

574. Al be that some founde ful vnsoote] There is no doubt but that the reading of Ar. G. Bo. T_1. Du. Lb. E_1. L_2. is correct. Cf. 2191 and **3673**; also *Fall,* Book I, 1627 f.: (This flood) . . .

> " Causid also scarsete off vetaile,
> That many a man felte ful vnsoote."

The phrase is one of the characteristics of Lydgate's language. The verbs " find " and " feel " are used intransitively (reflexively). The objective " it " in the majority of the MSS. is a later addition. Cf. *Oxf. Dict.* Find, 3 b, with *inf.* as *obj. Obs. rare.* 1375 *Cantic. de Creatione* 851 in *Anglia* I, " þat y may fynden glad to be in al my lyf tyme ones."

578–87. *RE* A iiii front: " Quant ilz yssirent hors de la porte le roy Layus de Thebes y venoit a moult grant compaignie pour veoir les ieux. Et quant ilz vindrent a la porte, ilz entendirent que au chastel auoit grant meslee. Si voulurent entrer dedans: mais ilz ne peurent pour la bataille et pour la presse. Et lors commenca la meslee. Entre les aultres Edipus occist la nuict le roy qui son pere estoit, et ainsi fut mort le roy de Thebes; mais nul ne sceut qui lui auoit donne le coup dont il fut mort. Et Edipus se mist entre les aultres." In *HT* and *RT* different accounts are given. According to *RT* Edipus kills the king and cuts off his head. According to *HT* Edipus in the turmoil was hit with a stone, and getting angry at this threw back another, which happened to hit Layus so as to kill him.

593–602. *RE* A iiii back: " Ilz prindrent le corps et lemporterent a Thebes a la royne Iocasta sa femme qui moult grant dueil en mena. Apres print on le corps si lardit lon et en feist on cendre et le mist on au temple des dieux en vne moult riche sepulture, car la coustume du pays estoit telle."

613–14 (in story as I fynde 614)] This is not in *RE* (nor in *HT*). With regard to 609–23, see *RE* A iiii back: " Il ne alla mye le droit chemin aincois sen alla par deuant la mer delez vne montaigne en laquelle il habitoit vng monstre de moult merueilleuse facon et si vous diray ce que les anciens dient. Celuy monstre auoit le corps de lyon et les piedz et les ongles des le corps en mont auoit il corps et visaige de damoyselle merueilleux et cruel. Ceste beste auoit la contree si effrayee par sa cruaulte et toute la terre selon la marine que il ny osoit aller ne venir nulle creature."

624. *RE* l.c. Ceulx de la contree lappelloient Spin; in *HT* Spinx.

639. of mercy] adverbial adjunct (not " graunte of mercy ").

651. Set at a fyn sothly be daies olde] *i.e.* this adventure which has been put at a fine, made liable to a penalty in (since) old days. There is nothing exactly corresponding in the French original; but see the last words of the description of the Sphinx's first meeting with Edipus, *RE*

B i front: "se arresta emmy la voye, et si luy demanda sil ne daignoit ou vouloit respondre a sa deuinaille il le feroit mourir; et se celluy scauoit exposer sa deuinaille il pouoit la beste occire; car ainsi estoit la loy assise." Cf. *Thebes*, 738: "To the lawe that thow most nedes stonde."

663. thogh he hadde it sworn] The phrase indicates an absolute impossibility. Cf. *C. T.* G 681: "We mowen nat, al-though we hadde it sworn, It overtake."

669. An addition of Lydgate's: of different bearing and wonderful (beautiful) countenance, *i.e.* in comparison with his earlier appearance.

680. Repeated l. 2175.

688–98. In the original Edipus treats the monster with ironical courtesy. *RE* B i back: "Edipus luy dist tantost Belle creature de moy mesmes as tu faict ta decepuance, or entens et ie le te diray."

690. Thow foule Monstre] The reading "foule" has been adopted from Bo. and the majority of the MSS. (Bo. Du. L_1. Lb. M. Di. Ad_1. Ad_2. I. Ra. Ba. E_1. S. T_2. P. E_2.; gap in T_1. Ro. C.). Also the rubric in Ar. (see l. 618, p. 28) has "the descripcioun of the foule Monstre." In Lydgate's *St. Giles* (ed. Horstmann) "ful" is used in a somewhat similar connection, l. 346: "The flessh, the world, the dreedful ful serpent."

For all that the "vyle" of Ar. G. L_2. Ap. ought perhaps to have been left undisturbed. Vile adj. had been adopted into English more than a hundred years before Lydgate wrote *Thebes*, the earliest reference in *Oxf. Dict.* dating from 1290. In *Oxf. Dict.* s.v. Conversant 6, the following quotation from Lydgate is given: "The vile serpent the Leuiathan" (*Chron. Troy*, II. xvii). Spenser, *Faërie Queene*, I. i. xiii, has: "A monster vile, whom God and man does hate."

726, 731, 733. Anacoluthon.

734. Autropos] In *Temple of Glas*, 782, Lydgate uses the form "Antropos," also in *Troy Book*, II, 142, and *Reson and Sensuallyte*, 1254. Chaucer *Troil.* has "Attropos."

740. *i.e.* unless you can state any reasonable objection.

741–46. *RE* says briefly, B i back: "Tantost tira Edipus son espee et luy coupa la teste: et ainsi fut de luy la contree deliuree." In *HT* we find (fol. 72 front, col. 1): "Adonc fut le monstre bien esbahy et ne sceut que contredire que edipus ne le tuast." *LT* here agrees more nearly with *HT*.

761. For heire was non, as bookes specifie] *RE* B ii front: "Lors vindrent tous les haulx hommes de la cite de Thebes a la royne Iocaste . . . et luy dirent que en la grant douleur demener ne pouoit elle riens gaigner, aincois regardast elle quelle feroit, car elle nauoit ne filz ne fille qui apres luy tenist son heritaige."

786–874. An addition of Lydgate's based partly upon his own resources, partly on St. Luke, partly on Martianus.

794–801. Cf. *St. Luke* iii, 19–20.

831–42. Martianus Capella, a Latin writer of the first half of the fifth century, author of a work, part in verse, part in prose, in nine books, the two first being allegorical, "*De nuptiis Philologiæ et Mercurii*," the seven following treating of the seven liberal arts. This work was much studied during the Middle Ages. Lydgate alludes several times to the wedding of Philology and Mercury, *e.g.* in his *Temple of Glas*, 129–36 (see Schick's Note). For other references in Lydgate, Chaucer, Bennet Burgh, see Schick, *l.c.*, and Skeat's Notes to *HF* 985, *C. T.* E 1732.

839–42. *i.e.* the poet demonstrating there that in this marriage this lady was wedded, etc.

855–66. Lydgate has taken from Boccaccio's *G. D.*, where we read (in the Index), fol. 1 front, col. 2: "De Herebo nono Demogorgonis filio cui fuerunt filii xxi. Quorum primus Amor. Secunda Gratia. Tertius Labor. Quarta Inuidentia. Quintus Metus. Sextus Dolus. Septimus (sic) Fraus. Octava Pertinacia. Nona Egestas. Decima Miseria. Vndecima Fames. Duodecima Querela. Decimustertius Morbus. Decimusquartus Senectus. Decimusquintus Pallor. Decimasexta Tenebra. Decimusseptimus Somnus. Decimaoctava Mors. Decimusnonus Charon. Vigesimus Dies. Vigesimusprimus æther." These are treated at large, lib. i, cap. 14–34. Lydgate has introduced half of them into his poem (ll. 860–66) in the following order: 3. 4. 5. 7. 6. 9. 11. 18. 10. 12. 15. 16. 14.; three of these he has doubled. The wife of Herebus "with her browes blake" is Nox; the three Furies were her daughters, see e.g. *G. D.* lib. iii. cap. 6. "De furiis filiabus Acherontis in generali. . . . Primo igitur eas dicunt acherontis fuisse filias atque noctis."

874. As the story after shal declare] Cf. *RE* B ii back: "La feste fut moult grande et noble en la cite de Thebes de cestuy mariage, mais puis en fut moult grant douleur si comme vous orrez ains que lhistoire faille."

877–84. And as myn autour writ in wordys pleyn etc.] *RE* B ii back: "Le roy Edipus eut deux filz et deux filles de la royne sa mere, dont le premier eut nom Ethiocles, et lautre Policenes, et la premiere fille eut nom Cogne, et lautre y eut nom ymenee."

The reference in l. 880 to "sondry clerkes" is made only for ornamental purposes.

895. For whan this kyng passyng of gret myght] Cf. *Temple of Glas*, 270: "So femynyn or passing of beaute." One might think of altering the sequence of words to "passyng gret of myght"; cf. *Thebes*, 469, "was in his port passyng ful of pride." But as all the MSS. agree in the reading given, it had much better be left as it stands. Lydgate's *St. Edmund*, II, 653 has:

"With men of armys passyng a gret route."

902. Turnyng her face brast out forto wepe] A good line of Lydgate's independent composition. *RE* B ii back: "De ceste chose fut la royne moult esbahye, mais elle nen fist point semblant pource quelle ne fust apperceue, aincois demoura la chose iusques a la nuict que tous furent couchez. Et quant ilz furent tous appaisez la dame getta vng moult grant souspir comme celle qui estoit en grant pensee."

927–28. See Introduction, Chap. VI, § 23.

940. Which lad hym forth] "Lad" has the sense (now dialectal) of "convey, carry"; see *Oxf. Dict.* s.v. Lead 1. b. Cf. *Fall*, Book I, 3213 ff.:

"Lik his biddyng the mynystres wrouhte in deede,
Takyng the child, tendre and yong off age;
And in-tafforest with hem thei gan it leede."

948. kyng Layus slayen was but late] Edipus and Jocasta had now a family of two sons and two daughters. The preposterous remark is altogether Lydgate's own invention. In *RE* B iii back Jocasta says: "quant vous venistes premierement en ceste ville lors estoit mort le roy Layus mon seigneur."

The form *slayēn* has been put in instead of *slayn*(*e*) for metrical reasons; cf. 3873, 3877. *Slawe* is also a possible emendation.

961–67. *RE* B iii back: "Et quant la royne louyt si requist et tant coniura le roy Edipus par ses dieux que il ne luy celast point qui il estoit et par quelle aduenture il vint a la cite de Thebes."

994–1001. "a Tragedye of Moral Senyk," see Rubric. Seneca's *Œdipus* is, of course, meant.

1002. And bookes seyn his eyen out he wepe] *RE* B iiii back: "Le roy Edipus plora tant que il en perdit la veue."

1003–9. And as myn auctour liketh to devise etc.] *RE* B iiii back: "Vng iour aduint que ses deux filz furent deuant luy, si luy dirent moult de villenies et villaines paroles. Si se ayra tant que en leur despit il se creua les deux yeulx du chief et les iecta deuant ses deux filz, et ilz monterent dessus a deux piedz et les deffoullerent."

1010–12. In Lydgate's original, Edipus is thrown by his sons alive into a pit. *RE* B iiii back: "Et saichez que ses filz le mirent et auallerent en vne fosse ou il mourut a moult grant douleur et a moult grant chetiuete." The same story is found in *HT*. Lydgate has somewhat toned down this revolting version.

1023. of what estat thei be] "they" in 1024 refers to "man and child" in 1019, "thei" in 1023 refers to "fader and moder" in the same line.

1032–38. These lines are full of anacolouthons: He shall be infortunat; Fortune [will be] froward to hym; [there will be] Waast of his good; and [he will] pleynly appaire, [and] Fynde plentè of contek; [he will be] gracelees, [and he will find] Hatrede of god and man.

1044–47. West of Canterbury is a piece of elevated land, the highest point of which (at Dunkirk) reaches 390 feet. From there the ground falls away steeply to Boughton under Blean. This is "the hil" in l. 1044. Just west of Boughton the level is only 50 feet, but the ground soon rises somewhat. This is "the lowe vale" in l. 1045. "Bowtoun on þe ble" is an unusual form of the name; the more common one is "B. under [the] Blee" (Blean), that found in L_1. Ad_2. I. Chaucer, *C. T.* G 556, has "Boghton under Blee." Blean is the name of an old forest district; cf. "to blean ðem wiada" in Sweet's *Oldest English Texts*, p. 438 (A.D. 858).

Boughton is six miles from Canterbury. It is now nine o'clock and the pilgrims will easily reach Ospringe in time for dinner. In l. 324 the poet had informed his fellow-pilgrims that his tale will last "the space, as I suppose, of vii. myle." At Boughton, however, he had only told Prima Pars, not the fourth part of the whole.

1051–53. Cf. *Reson and Sensuallyte*, 450 ff.:

> "Whan Phebus with his bemys bryght
> Ys reysed vp so hygh alofte,
> And on the herbes tendre and softe
> The bawmy dropes siluer fair
> Vapoured hath vp in the ayr."

1054. Cf. *C. T.*, Prol. 5: "Whan Zephirus eek with his swete breeth."

1083. Cf. l. 1107.

1119–21. *RE* C i front: "Et endementiers que lung regneroit lautre sen yroit en estranges terres pour pris et honneur conquerre."

1138. be oth of sacrament] See Glossary, s.v. Sacrament. Lydgate overlooks the incongruity of such a ceremony being performed by heathens.

1150–52. armed briȝt in stele . . . on a Ryal stede] *RE* C i back: "Donc se mist Policenes a la voye tout arme de toutes armeures et fut monte sur vng moult riche cheual sans plus de compaignie."

1157. pursued] *RE* C i back: "Et alla vers vne grant forest moult grant alleure, car il doubtoit moult la malice de son frere que ne le suyuist pour loccire pour la conuoitise de tenir tout le royaulme en paix."

1177–82. *RE* C i back: "Et les bestes sauluaiges ours et lyons estoient si esbahis parmy la forest quelles ne scauoient quelle part fuyr." Lydgate has added tigers and boars and made the roaring of the frightened wild beasts accompany the uproar of the elements and heighten the terror of the scene.

1186–91. *RE* C i back: "Et quant ce vint vers mynuict que le vent et la pluye sacoyserent vng petit et lair fust esclarcy, Policenes choisit vng petit les (sic) salles au roy darges."

1192–1205. *RE* C ii front: "Lors en celle cite auoit vng roy qui auoit nom Adrascus moult preudhomme et moult saige et nestoit point de la lignee ne de la value des aultres roys qui deuant luy regnerent aincoys fut nay de lisle de Sicione filz du roy Chaloy. Et pour le grant sens que Adrascus auoit en sa ieunesse leslirent ceulx darges a roy et en feirent roy de toute Grece. Celuy roy estoit moult preux et tint bien iustice."

1206–16. *RE* C ii front: "et si eut deux belles filles qui plus belles ne furent veues ne trouuees. Lune eut nom Argila et laultre Deiphile. Le roy nauoit nul hoir masle, dont il auoit moult grant dueil: mais il pensoit que par ses filles pourroit il auoir lignee."

1222–32. *RE* C ii front: "Et non pourtant ce luy troubloit son couraige que il auoit veue vne aduision en dormant que vng sanglier et vng lyon seroient ses gendres. . . . De ceste chose se merueilloit moult le roy Adrascus moult durement et en estoit en moult grant effroy."

1244–60. With the exception that *HT* mentions "lentree du pallays du roy" (cf. the paleys 1244), whereas *RE* speaks of "la salle du roy," a difference of little consequence, Lydgate's poem agrees more closely with *RE*. Conclusive on this point are the following particulars in *RE* C ii back: "Si descendit de dessus son cheual. . . . Si commenca moult fort a sommeiller, car il estoit moult las et tenoit tousiours son cheual par la resne quil auoit mis en son bras pour ce quil ne se meust." Cf. *HT*: "la sendormit son cheual empres soy en attendant que le iour venist."

1263–69. *RE* C ii back: "Vng aultre cheualier vint illec par telle aduanture quil auoit a force deguerpie sa contree. Le cheualier auoit nom Thideus qui moult estoit preux hardi et courtois et saige et estoit filz au roy de Calcidoyne."

1270–81. With respect to the particulars of the homicide committed by Tydeus, Lydgate quotes (1272) Statius as his authority. But these particulars are not to be found in the *Thebais*, which has only (I, 401–404)

> "Ecce autem antiquam fato Calydona relinquens
> Olenius Tydeus (fraterni sanguinis illum
> Conscius horror agit) eadem sub nocte sopora
> Lustra terit." (See Koeppel, *op. cit.*, p. 19.)

Nor has Lydgate drawn here from his usual source. For *RE* has a quite different version. C ii back (in continuation of the preceding note): "Celuy Thideus auoit deux filz dont lung eut nom Menalipus et laultre Melages dont il occist ne scay lequel. Et les aultres dyent que ce fut vng sien oncle; par ceste aduenture auoit Thideus vuyde la contree a (*sic*) son Royaulme et alloit comme exille en diuerses contrees." Neither is *HT*, though here agreeing much more closely with Lydgate than *RE*, the poet's authority. *HT* says that the king of Calidoine had three sons "lesquelz auoient semblable discort entre eulx (referring to the hatred and envy prevailing between king Edippus' sons Ethiocles and Polymyte) si que Thideus fist vng meurtre, les vngs disent quil tua vng de ses freres . . ., les autres disent que ce fut vng de ses oncles," etc. But

Lydgate could not possibly think of or represent Tydeus, his chevalier sans peur et sans reproche, as a deliberate fratricide.

It is from Boccaccio's *G. D.* that Lydgate has taken his information, lib. ix, cap. 21: "Dicit . . . Lactantius eum e calydonia discessisse quia Menalippum fratrem suum in venatione minus advertenter occiderat."

1281. *i.e.* as the law strictly fixed its ordinance (its decree as to the punishment of such a crime, however unintentional).

1300. entred the porche] "entred" is to be pronounced as a trisyllable, *i.e.* "entërëd."

1303. as I rede] *RE* C iii front: "Le destrier de Policenes qui sentit leffroy de laultre cheual (cf. 1296), tira a luy son frain et grata et hennyt si durement que Policenes en fut tout effroye, tantost saillit sus Policenes qui veit le cheual et le cheualier arme de toutes armes."

1309. tydinges] The reading of Ar. Ad_1. Ra. and others was kept in the text because it seemed much more likely that the scribes would alter "tydinges" into "tydeus" than "tydeus" into "tydinges." The reading "Tydeus," however, agrees better with the Old French original. *RE* C iii front: "Si monta tantost dessus son cheual affin qui ne fust deceu: et tantost demanda a Thideus et dist, Sire cheualier qui estes vous et que querez vous?" "Tydeus" is supported not only by Bo. but by L_2. Ro. Ap. and others.

1329–38. *RE* C iii front: "Thideus luy respondit que il luy disoit moult grant vilennie et qui (sic) luy sembleroit quil neust point de heritaige, ne ne se humilioit mye."

1349. pompous and ellat] A favourite combination of Lydgate's. See e.g. *Thebes*, 3530, *St. Giles*, 172, "Meek of thy poort, nat pompous nor elat," *Troy Book*, I, 3110, "ful pompus and elate."

1357–8. The common original of all the MSS. had shifted "And" from 1357 to 1358. Then five MSS. have amended the syntax of the corrupt passage by omitting the conjunction "that" in 1357. Cf. 927 f. and see *Notes* to the lines.

1369–73. *RE* C iii back: "Le roy Adrascus aualla lez degrez pour scauoir qui cestoit, et auecques plusieurs de sa mesgnie qui portoyent fallotz ardans."

1374–86. The description of king Adrastus' intervention in the fight has been drawn, partly from *RE*, partly from Chaucer. *RE* C iii back: "Lors parla le roy a eulx et leur dist quilz cessassent de combatre et quilz dissent quelle aduenture les auoit amenez pour combatre a celle heure . . . print tantost les espees pource que plus ne feissent mal." As to 1377–86, cf. the intervention of duke Theseus between Arcite and Palamon, as told by Chaucer in the *Knightes Tale* (*C. T.* A 1704–13). The nightly scene is not badly painted in Lydgate's poem.

1404. In *RE* Tydeus mentions the name of the king his father ("qui Omites fut appelle,") which Lydgate wisely left out as irrelevant.

1413–20. *RE* C iiii front: "mais il eut honte et vergongne de nommer son pere pource que le roy Edipus estoit son pere et son frere. Le roy Adrascus scauoit bien ceste affaire . . . et dist que de son lignage ne debuoit il point auoir honte."

1430–45. Lydgate's original says briefly (*RE* C iiii front): "tantost les fist desarmer et fist penser les cheuaulx, et puis les enuoya en ses salles et leur fist apporter deux manteaulx." No mention of "manteaulx" is made in *HT*.

1440. Frett with peerle and riche stonys] Cf. *Fall* (MS. Harl. 1766 fol. xxxiii a), "Golde vpon golde with perle & stones wroght." See Glossary.

1446–52. *RE* C iiii front: "Ilz mengerent et beurent ensemble, car il sestoient ia accordez par la priere Adrascus, et puis fut entre eulx deux si grant la compaignie que vous pourreȝ ouyr cy apres."

1456–1505. *RE* C iiii back: "Les napes furent ostees et le roy manda ses deux filles pour veoir les deux cheualiers estranges. Les damoyselles firent le commandement de leur pere et vindrent es chambres au Roy plus blanches que noif. Les cheualiers se leuerent encontre les damoyselles qui les cheualiers ne cognoissoient en rougirent; ainsi en doubla leur beaulte. Et tandis quilz sentreregardoyent et parloient ainsi ensemble, le roy commanda les lictz a faire, et puis les fist aller coucher pour la grant peine quilz auoyent eue. Lors se partirent les damoyselles, et le roy mesmes se coucha."

In *RE* the king on the very night of the arrival of the knights calls in his daughters to make the acquaintance of the strangers. Lydgate shows his good taste in not copying this particular; he puts off the meeting till the following day. On the other hand, he passes in silence the modest blushes of the two princesses (cf. Introduction, Chap. II, § 1). As if to compensate for this omission Lydgate introduces a characteristic custom (not alluded to in *RE*) prevalent in several countries not only in his time but even much later, viz. that of offering one's guests a cup (glass) of spiced wine or some other strong drink (a "nightcap") just before going to bed (see 1499–1501).

1506. But as I fynde, 1507. the story specifies] *RE* (in continuation of the preceding note): "et ne sendormit pas tantost, ains pensa et repensa comme preudhomme et saige quil estoit, que a ses (*sic*) deux barons donneroit ses deux filles en mariage, car bien luy sembloyent vaillans et preux. En ceste pensee sendormit le roy iusques a lendemain au matin, et lors vint ceste aduision que vous auez ouye arriere" (see note to 1222–32). To judge by the words of *RE* "et lors vint ceste aduision" Adrastus had his portentous dream in the same night that the two knights arrived at Arge, whereas in fact it had happened some time before. Lydgate puts the matter right by speaking (1519) of "the remembrance of his avisioun."

1515. Cf. Lydgate's *St. Edmund,* III, 477: "Thus atween tweyne hangyng in ballance."

1528. on his book] *i.e.* in his Prayer-book. A custom foreign to Greek heathendom.

1530–51. In *RE* Lydgate found C iiii back: "Et ilz (*i.e.* ses dieux) dirent que il regardast es deux escus sil y verroit les deux bestes que laduision luy auoit demonstree. Et quant le roy Adrascus fut seur de ceste chose ou il auoit creance si en eut moult grant ioye." The description of the outer garments of the two knights (1541–46) is taken from Boccaccio (*G. D.* lib. ii, cap. 41): "Et cum vidisset (*i.e.* Adrastus) alterum pelle leonis tectum, Pollynicem scilicet, qui regius iuvenis insigne illud in testimonium virtutis thebani Herculis ferebat, et alterum cute apri qui ob occisum a meleagro patruo aprum in decus prolis ea tectus incedebat; responsi ambiguitate intellecta cognovit hos sibi generos esse transmissos." The next three lines (1547–49), in spite of his words "as the story lerys," are a free invention of Lydgate's. Thus in our poem the lion and the boar are represented thrice, first in the shields (1539 = *RE*), secondly in the garments (1542–6 = *G. D.*), thirdly in the banners (1548 Lydgate's invention). A banner of this kind is described in *C. T.* A 975–977. But, of course, Lydgate had seen with his own eyes many banners with different devices.

1540. The beestes rage with her mortal lokys] With regard to the necessary correction of the rhyme-word the preponderance of the MSS. (Bo. M. etc. against Lb. Ra. etc.) is on the side of "crokes." The reading "lokes" has been preferred because (1) a boar cannot be said to have claws, (2) "mortal lokes" fits in well with the rest of the description.

1555–65. *RE* D i front: "Et quant ilz eurent adore selon leur coustume ilz sen yssirent du temple et sen vindrent auecques le roy en ses salles ou les tables furent mises pour menger."

1562–65. Cf. *C. T.* F. 65–68 (*The Squieres Tale*):

"And eek it nedeth nat for to devyse
At every cours the ordre of hir servyse.
I wol nat tellen of hir strange sewes,
Ne of hir swannes, ne of hir heronsewes."

1594. Inversion, *i.e.* I despair of having an heir to succeed me.

1618–21. *RE* D i front: "et il se pourroit deduire en bois et en riuiere, car il ne vouloit mais aultre chose faire." There is nothing of the kind in *HT*.

1631. Trisyllabic "thankëdë" is necessary for the metre, and it has been so marked, although such a form is, perhaps, quite exceptional in Lydgate's verse. See ten Brink, *Chaucer's Sprache,* § 194 and 256; Morsbach, *Mittelengl. Gr.*, § 48 and 71; Sieper, *Reson and Sensuallyte*, l. 946. In any case the line has to be corrected, unless we are to regard Lydgate as guilty of great carelessness. On the supposition that one word has been missed by the first copyist, two ways of correction offer themselves; either "than" or "vnto" (cf. 2417) may be re-inserted after "thanked." What makes it rather probable that the fault is to be ascribed to the inattention of the first copyist, is the fact that 1635 is another instance of a four-beat line; here also "than" may be inserted after "euer." Later on Lydgate became more careless in his versification. His poem in praise of St. Edmund, written in great haste in order to be presented to the young king Henry VI on the occasion of his celebrating the Christmas of 1433 in Lydgate's convent at Bury St. Edmunds, offers many signal proofs of this, *e.g.* II, 11, "to stuffe ther shippis with gret meyne," but it is not to be placed on a level with his *Thebes*, which was a work of his mature manhood and a labour of love.[1]

1635. To all that euer the kyng haþ sayd] A four-beat line. See preceding note.

1637. In the story as it is conprehendid] *RE* D i front: "Thideus . . . dist Sire ce ne refuse ie mye que ie orendroit de moy lune ne preigne, et mon compaignon sil luy plaist preigne laultre, et preigne a sa deuise celle que mieulx il aymera. Et Policenes dist que moult bien ceste chose luy aggree, et dist quil prendroit Argila laisnee."

1650–73. *RE* D i front and back says briefly: "Quant le roy Adrascus sceut la volunte de ses (*sic*) deux barons il manda tous les princes de son royaulme pource que ilz fussent a celle assemblee. Et quant ilz furent venus il donna aux deux barons ses deux filles deuant tout le bernaige." The two lines 1655–56 are a characteristic addition of Lydgate's. The following lines 1657–73 are also added by Lydgate in spite of his "þe Story seith," 1660.

1670–72. This simile is often used by Lydgate. Cf. *e.g.* Glauning, *The two nightingale poems*, i, 44: "The fende (*i.e.* the devil) . . . Goth fast

[1] It does not seem impossible that "thankede" is a phonetic spelling for "thanked (h)e."—E. E.

a-boute . . . Leying hys lynes and with mony a bayte Wsynge his hokes, on theym you to receyue;" also his Note, pp. 48–49.

1679. Myn auctour writ] *RE* D i back: "La nouuelle fut tantost espandue parmy toute la contree que le roy Adrascus auoit mariees ses deux filles et donnees a deux haulx barons de moult grant lignaige. Iusques a Thebes en est la nouuelle allee a Ethiocles le frere de Policenes, a qui elle ne fut pas belle."

1695. by bond of oth I-sworn] *i.e.* by the bond of (his) sworn (pledged) oath. Parallel with and equivalent in meaning to 1696, "Be couenauntes assured her to-forn." Cf. 1938 f., "ȝe ar sworn ȝour oth to kepe."

1702–14 agree much better with the four lines of *RE* D i back ("Et pour ceste chose il manda tous les barons de son royaulme pour querre conseil comment il pourroit cheuir de cest affaire. Les barons entendirent bien que le roy nauoit talent de tenir sa conuenance qui estoit diuisee entre luy et son frere") than with the thirty-line speech in *HT*, which begins: "Seigneurs barons, cheualiers, bourgeois et citoyens de cet royaulme de Thebes."

1716. I fynde writ] In ll. 1715–20 Lydgate seems to follow *HT* rather than *RE*, but this is due to the fact that the text of *RE* is faulty. *RE* D ii front has: "Il y eust deux qui le blasmoient moult de ceste besongne et de ceste parolle, et telz en y eut qui le louoient, car ilz veoient que la fin de ceste trahyson viendroit a malle aduenture." The causal clause is misplaced. The printer of *RE* omitted a third sentence, which is found in all the MSS. MS. BN fr. 301, from which *RE* was printed according to Constans, *Légende d'Œdipe*, 339, reads as follows: "Il y ot telz qui le blasmoient de ceste besoingne et de ceste parole et telz qui le louoient *et telz y ot qui s'en fouirent*, car ilz ne savoient la fin de ceste raison ne de si grant male aventure." Other MSS. have different readings. Some, *e.g.* BN 24396, BN 22554, have "se faignirent," "se faingnoient" or the like instead of "s'en fouirent," others, *e.g.* BN 12586, BN 687, have "se teurent," "s'en teurent" or the like. Lydgate evidently followed a MS. of the type that had "se faignoient" or the like.[1] *HT* has "les autres sen taisoient."

1721–91. Essentially a long addition of Lydgate's.

1724. as a Centre stable] Cf. *C. T.* F 21, 22 (*The Squieres Tale*):

> "Sooth of his word, benigne and honurable,
> Of his corage as any centre stable."

Also *Secrees of old Philisoffres*, 1163–5:

> "A kynges promys/shulde be Iust & stable,
> As a Centre/stonde in O degre,
> Not Chaunge lightly/nor be varyable."

1728–41. These lines refer to what is told in the first and second chapters of the Book of Nehemiah, which is described by Lydgate as "of Esdre the book." The Book of Nehemiah was sometimes joined into one with the Book of Ezra under the latter title, sometimes called the Second Book of Ezra.

Nehemiah, the Jewish cupbearer of Artaxerxes king of Persia, on hearing

[1] The information on the readings of the French MSS. has been kindly supplied by Dr. Gunnar Tilander of Lund University, who was good enough to examine the MSS. in December 1927. Professor Erdmann, who was not aware of the readings of the MSS., had already conjectured that the printed text had a gap in this place. The note to this passage has been rewritten in accordance with the new information obtained.—E. E.

bad news concerning the condition of Jerusalem and the Jews returned there, beseeches God to remember his word to Moses. A short time afterwards, as he is "taking up the wine and giving it unto the king," the king asks the cause of his unusual sadness, and at his prayer graciously, in the presence of the queen, gives him leave to go to Judah and to rebuild Jerusalem.

The form of the names, "Esdre" and "Neemye," point to a French version of the Old Testament as the source of Lydgate's reference. The syntax of the passage is, in parts, rather loose; "ben ek set asyde" in 1732 is the predicate of "kings, wine and women," but "ek" belongs only to the last two. See on l. 1732, also Chap. VI, § 2, *d*.

Cf. *C. T.* B 3832–5 (*The Monkes Tale*):

> "He (*i.e.* Alexander) was of knighthode and of fredom flour;
> Fortune him made the heir of hir honour;
> Save wyn and wommen, no-thing mighte aswage
> His hye entente in armes and labour."

See also Gower, *Confessio Amantis* (Macaulay's ed.), Introduction, p. lxxxi. King, Wine, Woman and Truth, and Book vii, 1950–56:

> "Lo, thus Zorobabel hath told
> The tale of his opinion:
> Bot for final conclusion,
> What strengest is of erthli thinges,
> The wyn, the wommen or the kinges,
> He seith that trouthe above hem alle
> Is myhtiest, hou evere it falle."

1738. The reading has been altered against all the MSS. The clause cannot have two such subjects as "the influence" and "Neemye." As "Neemye" must be taken as the subject of "gat hym licence," "the influence" in l. 1738 must be an adverbial adjunct, and a preposition—most probably "Be," because most easily skipped before "the"—has to be supplied at the beginning of the line. The fault must have been in the common original of the MSS.

1743. For Salamon writ] *Proverbs* xx, 28: "Mercy and truth preserve the king: and his throne is upholden by mercy." Hoccleve in his *Regement of Princes*, 3417–18, refers to the same verse:

> "Salomon in his prouerbis expressith,
> Mercy and trouthe, wardeynes ben of kynges."

1753. Of kyngges redeth the story doune be rowe] Lydgate probably refers—at least principally—to the Books of the Kings in the Old Testament. He may, however, have thought also of Boccaccio's *De casibus virorum illustrium*.

1755. Cf. 890 "(Tyl fortune . . .) From her wheel she plonged hym a-doun." Also Chaucer, *Troil.* IV. 6: "And whan a wight is from hir wheel y-throwe." In Brit. Mus. MS. Royal 18. D. II there is a miniature illustrating the process.

1769. Cf. 269.

1790. blowen in an horn] Cf. Chaucer, *C. T.* A 3387 (*The Milleres Tale*):

> "That Absolon may blowe the bukkes horn;
> He ne hadde for his labour but a scorn."

1791. pypen in a red] Cf. Chaucer, *Troil.* V, 1432 f.

> "But Troilus, thou mayst now, est or west,
> Pype in an ivy leef, if that thee lest."

Also *C. T.* A 1837 f.:

> "That oon of yow, al be him looth or leef,
> He moot go pypen in an ivy-leef."

1807–10. *LT* closely resembles *HT*: "la fin de lan approchoit quil deuoit aller prendre la pocession de son royaulme; par quoy vng iour vint deuant le roy adrascus." . . . *RE* D ii front: "Policenes . . . desiroit moult le terme que il fust en lhonneur et en la seigneurie ainsi comme auoit este son frere, et pour ce quist conseil au roy Adrascus."

1817–23. In *RE* Polymytes when asking advice of Adrastus declares from the first his resolution of going himself to Thebes to claim the honour due to him. *RE* D ii front: "et luy dist que il yroit a Thebes pour son honneur requerre a son frere." Lydgate makes him set forth a twofold (seemingly a threefold) dilemma; either "to gon" or "to abyde" or "to ryde hym-silf." But the statement is confused: "to gon" is really the same thing as "to ryde hym-silf." Instead of "to gon," he should have mentioned the third alternative "to send" (a messenger, make a message), "to abyde" being then understood to mean "stay quietly at Arge, leaving the matter alone."

1839. outward be some signe] *RE* D ii front: "car il ne pourroit estre que se Ethiocles pensoit mal ne vilennie quil nen fist au messagier demonstrance." There is nothing corresponding in *HT*.

1856. so wel a preued knyght] *i.e.* a so wel preued knyght (so well-proved a knight). Such a position of the words, though not usual, is perfectly admissible; cf. 2456, "That, in space of a daies fewe" and the reading of several MSS. in 3098 ("to right a faire welle") and 3742 ("with right a glad chere"). See also examples from Mandeville ("riȝt a faire,") Caxton ("ryght a noble,") etc. in *Oxf. Dict.* s.v. Right adv. 11.

1874. the story telleth vs] *RE* D iii front: "Thideus le courtoys erra tant quil vint a Thebes. Il descendit dehors la ville en vng pre. . . . (D iii back:) Thideus qui fut entre dedans la ville cheuaucha toute la maistresse rue: et veit cheualiers ester deuant vng temple, et leur demanda ou le roy Ethiocles estoit. Et ilz lui dirent que il estoit en ses salles."

1889. Wher as the kyng] The predicate "was" or "sat" is omitted.

1901. No MS. has "Sir" or "Sire" except P. and Ro., in which "Sir" has certainly been re-inserted by the scribes. Without "Sir" the line is metrically imperfect. The original of the MSS. had omitted the word "Sir," leaving an open space for the illumination, as is indicated by the Q in Ar. being a two-line capital.

In the Old French original the term of address is "Roy." See *RE* D iiii front: "Roy faict Thideus entens a moy, et toy et ta mesgnie et saiches que ce que ie te diray ne te doit desplaire, se tu veulx raison entendre." In *RE* E i back Tydeus, in his address to the barons present at his interview with Ethiocles, designs this king as "vostre sire le roy" (see 2084, note).

1983. Supposing pleynly euermor] One of the head- and waistless lines.

1991. To interrupte my possessioun Of this . . . Regioun] This is the reading of Ar. G. Ad_1. Ad_2. I. C. T_2. P. E_2. L_2. (gap in Ro) Ap.

It is confirmed by other passages in Lydgate's poems, e.g. *Fall*, Book I, 6131 f. :

> "That she may haue no iurediccioun
> To interrupte thi possessioun."

Cf. also *Secrees of old Philisoffres*, 1117.

Lydgate has wisely left out the closing words of Ethiocles' answer, in which he pretends to believe that Polymytes' wife Deiphile, being nourished in luxury, would not be able to put up with the poverty of the Theban kingdom, and gives vent to his fear that she should quarrel with his mother and sisters.

1995. the story can ȝou teche] *RE* E i front and back : "De ce eut Ethiocles moult grant ire, et respondit moult fierement au messagier, Cheualier tu as parle follement, ie ne te tiens mye a saige (cf. 2016). Jentens bien a tes parolles que celuy qui ta icy enuoye ne vouloit gueres exploicter de sa besongne par toy ny par aultre, mais dis luy de par moy que en ce que iay nait il nulle fiance, ne iamais nul ne me parle de conuenance de par luy que iamais en sa vie ne tiendra plein pied de ma terre (cf. 2006) tant comme iaye pouuoir de me deffendre, Ains verray qui sur moi viendra et qui mes murs abatra."

2026. Ageynes me to seke occasioun] Cf. Wyclif 2 *Kings*, v. 7 : "Takith heed and seeth, that occasiouns (*Vulg.* occasiones) he sechith aȝeyns me." Authorised Version : "wherefore consider, I pray you, and see how he seeketh a quarrel against me."

2038. Conceyuyng eke the grete felonye] As is proved by 2039, "In his apport, lik as he wer wood," "felonye" is here used by Lydgate in the sense of "anger, fury" usual in Old French and no doubt familiar to our poet. But as a matter of fact the word in the corresponding passage of *RE* means "treachery, perfidy" (as in 2150). *RE* D iiii back : "Et quant Thideus ouyt ainsi parler Ethiocles il entendit bien sa felonnie et sa decepuance, et tantost respondit et dit Roy tu es mal conseille de ceste affaire." (E i front :) "Saiches bien que. . . . Et si te debuera moult greuer quant tu verras que le roy Adrascus se meslera de cest affaire (cf. 2060) qui tous les barons de Grece emmenera sur toy et en ta terre."

2045. I dar it seyn and vowen at the best] "atte best, at the best, att best, at the beste" is the reading of Bo. T_1. Du. Lb. M. Di. C. T_2. P. E_2. L_2. (gap in Ro.). This reading is to be preferred to that of Ar. and others, "at the lest, at the leste, atte leste, att leste." This "at the lest," does not fit in with the general tenor of the passage, as Tydeus gives expression to the severest possible accusation, viz. that of perjury. On the contrary, "at the best" in the sense of "in amplissima forma, downright" is in conformity with Tydeus' bold and open manner. Cf. Lydgate, *Pilgrimage*, 14968, "ffor they ha leyser at the beste" (*i.e.* completely, quite).

2060. medle in this matere] "in" is the reading of the vast majority of the MSS. However, the "of" of Ar. L_2. Ap. might just as well have been kept. Cf. Old French "s'en meller" and *Romaunt of the Rose*, Fragm. B (written by Lydgate) 4545 :

> "To medle of love, that has me shent."

See also *Oxf. Dict.* Meddle 8.

2069. Of thy promys atteynt and ek outrayed] *i.e.* with regard to your promise you are convicted (viz. of dishonesty) and you have broken away from it, trespassed against it.

2078. Ar. Ad_1. Ra. L_2. and others have lost " in feeld," which is essential to the force of the phrase. Falseness will not be able to fight against truth in open battle, though it may for some time be victorious through underhand means. Cf. 2237, 2244.

2081. As I that am next of his alye] The reading of Ar. Bo. and all the other MSS., except Ra. Ba., though unexceptionable with regard to syntax and meaning (cf. 2735, 2754), leaves the line metrically imperfect, making it one of four beats only. On this account it seems almost certain that the rarer construction " next of his alye," shown by Ra. Ba., is that of the original poem. As to this sense and construction of the substantive, see *Oxf. Dict.* Ally sb., where three examples (*c.* 1400, 1494, 1592) are cited. Cf. also Lydgate's *Troy Book*, I, 2882, and his *Ballad in honour of Duke Humphrey and Jacqueline of Holland* (written in 1422), stanza 26:

" And ymeneus / þow fortune þis matere
Thorough helpe of Iuvo (*sic*) / nexst of þyne allye."

2082. *RE* E i back: " Roy ie te deffie de par ton frere, que lon ne die mye que ie mespargne de mon messaige."

2084. *ibid.*: " Lors ne dist plus mot au roy ains se tourna deuant les barons qui es bans se seoient (2097). . . . Seigneurs faict Thideus aux barons or pouez entendre comment vostre sire le roy se pariure plainement."

Confusion between ȝe (ye) and þe is easily intelligible; " ȝow " in 2085 makes the correction necessary.

2111. Lydgate has omitted the remark, found in *RE* E ii front, that none of the Theban barons addressed by Tydeus answered a word and that Tydeus wondered at this; also the remark that after his departure the Theban barons " parlerent entre eulx " and agreed among themselves that Policenes had had a good and bold and well-spoken messenger.

2137. with al the worthy Choys of his housholde] " choys, choyse " etc. is the reading of Bo. T_1. Du. L_1. Lb. M. Di. Ad_1. Ad_2. I. (Ra.) Ba. S. T_2. P. E_2. Ap.; Ar. has " Chooce," and so have G. E_1. C. (see footnotes); L_2. has " chosyn "; gap in Ro.

" Choys " as well as " Chooce (chose) " is in M.E. both adjective, " select, picked," and substantive, " pick, flower, *élite* " (see *Oxf. Dict.*); in either case the word gives good sense here. Lydgate has " choys," choice, election, *Thebes*, 4390. The earliest example adduced in *Oxf. Dict.* of the meaning " pick, *élite* " is from Fabyan 1494; but this use may quite well have been earlier. Probably Lydgate here meant the word to be an adjective in the plural, " the select, picked men of his (military) household." This will appear more clearly if the attribute " worthy " be left out for the nonce.

In spite of the strong preponderance of the MSS. in favour of " choys," there remains a certain probability of " chooce (chose) " being Lydgate's form here. Lydgate uses " chose " often enough as an adjective, " select, picked." See *St. Edmund*, I, 422, " With othre martirs, most parfit, chose and good," and *ibid.* III, 499, " Off chose personys in this ambassiat"; *Troy Book*, I, 3874, " Of knyȝtis chose piken out a fewe "; *St. Edmund*, I, 709, " This chose off god ful meekly doun knelyng." *RE* affords no clue; 2137 is one of Lydgate's additions. *RE* E ii back: " Or tost dist il a son connestable suyuez le tost et menez tant de ma mesgnie des plus hardis auec vous quil ne vous eschappe mye et gardez que vous ne le ramenez mye, ains luy tollez la vie, mais par les dieux en qui ie croy iamais ne aurez fiance en moy ne retour."

2141. Cf. *C.T.* A 1707 (*The Knightes Tale*):

"Namore, up peyne of lesing of your heed."

2144. Myn autour seith] *RE* E ii back: "Quant ilz furent montez et armez ilz sen yssirent par vne poterne de la ville et furent cinquante tous ensemble."

"Encombre" in the sense of "overpowering by physical force" is common in Lydgate's poems. Cf. *St. Edmund*, III, 608–609:

("lord . . . Which . . .):
Made foure and twenty, but a fewe in noumbre,
Fourty thowsand Danys to encoumbre."

2148. By a geynpath that ley oute a-side] The word "geynpath" has been kept, although neither *Oxf. Dict.* nor Wright's *English Dialect Dictionary* ("a gain way") registers such a compound. Bo. writes "a geyn path," and *Reson and Sensuallyte*, 2725, has "For other geyn path was ther noon." Swedish has the compound "genväg" (short cut) as well as "genaste vägen" ("the gainest way," see *Oxf. Dict.*).

2154. couartly (couertly): cowardly] Lying in ambush could not, in general, be said to be cowardly. In the present case, there being fifty against one, it certainly was cowardly not to attack in the open road. Still the reading of Ar. L_2. Ap. seems preferable here.

2158. At thylke mount wher that Spynx was slawe] *RE* E ii back: "ilz furent a lencontre de la forest selon la montaigne ou la malle feste souloit estre. La auoit vng trespas moult fort qui ne pouoit estre escheue." . . . ; and E iii front, bottom of the page: "En ce lieu ou Thideus monta souloit habiter la mauluaise beste quon appelloit Spin."

2175. But wel assured in his manly herte] Taken almost literally from *RE* E iii front: "Lors sasseura Thideus en son gentil cueur."

2177. Lydgate has omitted the not unimportant detail of this chivalrous adventure mentioned in *RE* E iii front: "leur demanda quelz gens cestoient qui a celle heure aguetoient illec, si ne luy respondit nul mot ains lenuironnent et luy courent sus de toutes pars."

2181. *RE* E iii front: "Et Thideus en frappa vng qui leur estoit maistre (see 2135) si lourdement qui (*sic* for que) luy bouta fer et fust dedans le corps et labatit du cheual mort a terre."

2184–91. *RE* E iii front: "le gentil cheualier qui auoit en luy proesse et hardement apres lespie tira lespee et se deffendit durement, et de lespee les fiert telz coups et telles collees que cestoit grant merueilles a veoir." There is nothing corresponding to this in *HT*.

2197–200. Cf. *C.T.* A 1655–1658 (*The Knightes Tale*):

"Thou mightest wene that this Palamoun
In his fighting were a wood leoun,
And as a cruel tygre was Arcite:
As wilde bores gonne they to smyte."

2211. An huge ston large rounde and squar] The stone was square, four-cornered, but the corners were rounded, and so it could be rolled more easily.

2220. That non but on was left of hem aluye] Lydgate probably wrote "was left." The predicate was then omitted by the scribe of the common original of all the MSS. Line 2220 is a waistless one, thus not only admitting the insertion of "was," but being bettered by it. It is not to be supposed that Lydgate went out of his way in order to compose a line halting in syntax and metre. Cf. the different case of 2227, in which there is also omission of the predicate "was."

2228–34. Cf. 2251–53.

2232. Euerich of hem his lyf left for a wed] "Every one of them left his life as a pledge," *i.e.* lost his life. Cf. 4206, "And who cam nexte leid his lyf to wedde," put his life in pledge, *i.e.* lost it. Also *St. Edmund*, III, 54, "Blissid Blasy his hed to wedde he leith." Chaucer does not use either of the two phrases, nor does "wed" in his language enter into any combination that has developed the sense of "losing" (instead of "risking"). He has "lye to wedde" (to be in pledge, at stake) and "have to wedde" (to hold in pledge).

2244. Arn to feble to holden Chanpartye Ageynes trouthe] *i.e.* are too weak to hold the field against, to resist truth successfully. In *Oxf. Dict.* s.v. Champerty it is shown that this use of the phrase—which is peculiar to Lydgate and common in his works (see *Oxf. Dict.* and Schick, *Temple of Glas*, l. 1164 and Notes)—is based on a false conception of the signification of the noun.

2257. But as he myght hym-silue tho sustene] *RE* E iiii front: "si monta dessus tout au mieulx comme il peult comme celuy qui estoit moult las et vain."

2261. Lydgate's scant interest in the tender feelings of the human heart shows itself here by his omission of any reference to what *RE* says of his wounded and exhausted hero, E iiii front: "Si regrettoit (*i.e.* Tydeus) Deiphile sa femme et son compaignon Policenes, et son pere le roy Adrascus quil aymoit moult; si les alloit accomptant lung apres laultre." On the contrary, he delights in nature-painting, and 2287–90, 2294–2304 and 2310–12 are his own additions.

2263. But anguysshous and ful of bysy peyne] *RE* E iiii front: "Ainsi cheuaucha Thideus moult angoisseux les destrois de la montaigne, car la paour quil auoit de la trahison du roy Ethiocles le faisoit haster."

2273. crestes marcyal] Cf. 4145. Also Lydgate, *Troy Book*, II, 501 f., "To reise a wal, With bataillyng and crestis marcial" (see *Oxf. Dict.* Crest).

2274–75. With regard to the situation described, cf. Chaucer, *C. T.* A 1060 (*The Knightes Tale*):

> ("The grete tour . . .)
> Was evene joynant to the gardin-wal."

2301. The syluer dewe vpon the herbes rounde] "rounde" is adverb; cf. 2305. "The syluer dewe" is co-ordinated with "the heghe hylles," both being objects of "Phebus gilte."

2305. that the soyl was depeynt] "was" had better be struck out again. Lydgate not rarely omits the auxiliary verb; see Introduction, Chap. II, § 3, 7. "Round about" is an adjunct of "depeynt" not of "rynne."

2309–10. Inversion. Every morning Lygurgus' daughter used to come among the fresh many-coloured flowers in this garden.

2317. the herbes colde] The grass is "cold" because the night has been cool enough to make the dew fall plentifully (see 2301).

2322. The cæsura in this line is incorrectly marked by the scribe of Ar.; the stroke should be after "aboute," which is here put after its noun instead of before it. "Sprad aboute al the grene ther (= where) she stood."

2330. *RE* E iiii back: "Adonc saprocha tant quelle le crolla vng petit pour scauoir sen luy auoit point de vie." In *HT* the princess dares not go up to the sleeping knight.

2333. **lich as a man adawed in a swogh]** The pp. "adawed" is here to be referred to the intransitive "adawen" (see in *Oxf. Dict.* the examples from Chaucer and Lydgate). The verb "adawen" is generally construed with "of," also by Lydgate; but as in our passage not only Ar. L_2. Ap., but also Bo. M. Ra. C. and others have "in," against Lb. Ad_1. Ad_2. I. "of," it may be safely concluded that Lydgate wrote "in" here. Possibly he felt a difference of meaning between "of" and "in," and was influenced by it in forming his phrase: "adawed of a swogh" means "come out of a swoon by awaking," "adawed in a swogh" seems to imply that the person, though awaked from his swoon, is still partly in it, only half awake.

2343–45. Tydeus explains that his apparent recklessness in drawing his sword against the young lady was due to his fear of being surprised by Thebans; he now humbly promises to keep the peace, and says that he is sorry to have trespassed in entering the garden.

2374. And at the hil of the woode Rage] "of the woode Rage" is co-ordinate with "touching his massage." The inverted order of words in this line, used by Lydgate for the sake of the rhyme, has been an early cause of misapprehension. The fault must have occurred in the common original of the MSS. Perhaps the "at" or "atte" was mistaken for "aꝉꝉ." A few scribes have seen and corrected the error (at the hylle L_2); G.'s "atte" against "al" Ar. is especially to be observed. *RE* has F i front: "Et lors compta a la damoyselle le commencement et la fin comment il estoit alle au roy de Thebes, et comment il lauoit faict guetter a cinquante cheualiers ou destroit de la montaigne et comment il en estoit deliure par layde des dieux qui luy auoient secouru: mais il estoit naure tant quil ne pouoit cheuaucher en nulle maniere et nen cuydoit mye guerir."

2402–4. *RE* F i back: "Et lors le fist vng peu menger de telle viande qui est necessaire a auoir." Lydgate's expressions come nearer to *HT* fol. 82 back, col. 2: "et (le) firent repaistre de bonnes et delicatiues viandes au mieulx quilz peurent."

2421–23. Beheestyng hir. . . . He wolde be hir seruaunt . . . of what she wold hym charge] The passages 2405–8 and 2417–23 are additions of Lydgate's. With the last two lines cf. 3150–52, also 3143–45.

2432–34. These three lines when put side by side with the terms used by *RE* afford another instance of Lydgate's comparative indifference to scenes of a sentimental character (see 2261, *Notes*). *RE* F ii back: "Thideus compta au roy . . . toute laduenture . . . , mais il neust mye bien tout compte quant Deiphile sa femme qui estoit en ses chambres en ouyt les nouuelles. Lors sen vint en la salle toute escheuelee vestue dung blanc drap de soye si belle que selle ne fust esmayee ne conuiendroit au monde querre plus belle creature. Quant elle vit Thideus qui contre elle se leua elle commenca a plorer, mais il la moult bien reconfortee, car il lassist au coste de luy."

2438. his soorys ek vnsounded] *RE* F ii front: "Et quant il (Adrascus) vit les plaies qui nestoient pas encores closes il parla et dist" etc. But Lydgate has forgotten what he says 2393.

2494. Nay, quod this knyght, it is no-thing so] This line, in the majority of the MSS. (gap in Ba.), has only four beats. "no thing" is the reading not only in C. P. E_2. (gap in T_2), but in L_2. Ro. Ap.

2509. both at eue and morowe] *i.e.* the whole day, always.

2523. of the woode rage] Bo. T_1. Du. Lb. M. Di. C. (gap in T_2.) P. E_2. have "of," against "and" in the other MSS.; "the woode rage" refers to the fierce combat at the hill (cf. 2374), not to the suicide of the messenger-knight.

2531. Ful busy wern this Rumour to dysesse] This verb "dysesse," which in *Thebes* is found only here (rhyming with "appese"), is the same word as N.E. disseise (disseize). It is not used by Chaucer. But we find it in *Rom. of the Rose,* fragment B 2076, in its usual sense "dispossess, deprive." In this passage of *Thebes* "dysesse" has the rarer signification "to oust, expel, dispel (stop, put a stop to)," which is duly registered in *Oxf. Dict.* 2. b.

2544–52. Lydgate's addition.

2553 ff. O Cruel Mars . . . what was cause that thow were so wroth with hem of Thebes? thorgh whoos feruent Ire the Citè . . . was sette a-fyre] In writing this apostrophe to Mars Lydgate seems to have had in his mind Chaucer's *Anelida and Arcite,* 50 ff.:

"Mars, which that through his furious course of yre,
The olde wrath of Juno to fulfille,
Hath set the peples hertes bothe on fyre
Of Thebes and Grece, everich other to kille."

2554. combust] This adjective is used by Chaucer and others in an astrological sense, to denote the condition of a planet when in or near conjunction with the sun. See *Oxf. Dict.* s.v. But Lydgate here has "combust" in the general sense of "burnt," without any reference to the temporary position of Mars in relation to the sun. Mars is said to be by nature (of thy kynde) hot, burnt, and dry, such a condition of the planet being indicated by the redness of its light.

2563. the story maketh mynde] The whole passage (2553–67) is an addition of Lydgate's. There is, of course, nothing of the kind in the "story," *i.e.* in his French original.

2565. Bynfeccioun called Orygynal] The primary cause of the mutual hatred of the Theban brothers Lydgate finds in the original sin, *i.e.* the innate depravity of man's nature inherited from Adam in consequence of the Fall.

2577. as maad is mencioun] *RE* F iiii front: "Le roy Adrascus manda par toute sa region ses cheualiers et ses barons."

2590. To stuffen hem and taken vp meynè] Cf. *St. Edmund,* II, 11, "To stuffe ther shippis with gret meyne." "stuffen hem" may here refer to "meynè," the reflexive verb (*intell.* with) being synonymous with "taken vp"; such a parallelism of expression is a frequent feature of Lydgate's style. But more probably Lydgate has here used "stuffen hem" in a more general sense, meaning "furnish themselves with the necessaries of war, arms and provisions as well as men."

2597. And as I rede, 2603. And as I fynde, 2608. the story telleth vs, 2612. Myn Autour seiþ] *RE* F iiii back: "La vint Parthonolopeus qui estoit filz du roy Archade et cil de Michenes et le Roy ypomedon, le roy Capaneus, le roy Melagus, le roy de Crete, le roy Agenor, le roy Lacres prays tortholomus Palemon, et encores plusieurs aultres auec moult grant cheualerie sassemblerent dessoubz Arges."

2615. renomed] A hybrid word, being in form an English passive participle, but with the accent kept on the last syllable as in Old French "renomé." In 4130 "renomed" stands at the end of the line, rhyming to "tak hed."

2633. And they obeye ful lowly his biddyng] The reading "ful" of L_2. Ro. Ap. together with C. (gap in T_2.) P. E_2. Lb., is clearly the original one, which has been variously altered in the other MSS. The change of tenses, from the present "obeye" to the preterite "made," is common in Lydgate.

2653–55. With "the floure of Chyvalrye" 2654 cf. *RE* G 1 front: "car la estoit toute la fleur de Grece des cheualiers qui adonc y estoyent."

2661–63. Cf. *C.T.* A 2118–27, 2496–512 (*The Knightes Tale*) and see Introduction, Chap. III, § 2 : Lydgate's Vocabulary.

2699. Nor hem coarten from her lybertè] "coarten" is Lydgate's form. Cf. 3666 "coarte" (: Marte). Also *St. Edmund*, I, 893 :

"He koude the reynes coarten and restreyne
Of such as lyued by fals robberye."

In *Oxf. Dict.* Coarct v. are two instances of the verb from Lydgate (*Bochas* and *Chron. Troy*), the first of them showing "coarte" as rhyme-word. The simple "arte" is used by Lydgate in *St. Edmund*, II, 693 :

"In Cristes feith to arte my conscience."

2688–736. Lydgate's addition.

2701 ff. There is, in *Secrees of old Philisoffres*, a parallel passage which deserves to be quoted (Steele's ed., E.E.T.S.) ll. 785–91 :

"To alle suych / A prynce of hihe noblesse
Shal nat spare / his gold / nor his tresour
To parte with hem / Stuff of his Rychesse,
Thing Apropryd / to euery Conquerour.
But yif ffredam / Conduite his labour,
That liberallyte / his Conquest doo provide,
At his moost nede / his men wyl nat abyde."

2705. Be on accord that they his brydel lede] Inversion, and repetition of the conjunction "that" from 2704. "Be" is the preposition; in most of the MSS. it is spelt "By," *e.g.* "By oon accord" L_2.

2720. Stondeth in loue abouen alle thyng] *i.e.* a king's treasure consists, above all, in the love of his people (see *Oxf. Dict.* s.v. Stand v., 72. i.). The correction "abouen" seems necessary with regard to the metrical accentuation of the preposition. Lydgate having the free choice between "aboue" and "abouen" ought not to be charged with choosing the former.

2737–45. *RE* G i front : "Ethiocles sceut par ses espies ou par ses messaigiers la grant assemblee des Grecz. . . . G i back : si en fut moult dolent et triste et ne sceut que faire; mais par le conseil de ses barons manda tous les barons" etc.

2757–60. *RE* G i back : "Et tantost fist les murs de la cite haulcer et enforcir les haultes tours de pierres pour auoir meilleures deffences."

Lydgate's anachronism in placing guns, small and great, on the walls of ancient Thebes (see also 4315), has a counterpart in Chaucer's description of the battle of Actium; see his *Legend of Cleopatra*, l. 637 : "With grisly soun out goth the grete gonne."

2764. "ouermore" or "ouermor" (Ar. M. Ad_1. and three other MSS.; see *vv. ll.*) is evidently the right word (moreover, furthermore) here, not the reading "euermore" (always) found in the rest of the MSS. (euer more Bo. Du. L_1. Lb. P. euermore Di. Ba. E_1. E_2. Ro. Ap.). The pause-bar between "ouermore," and "to" represents also a comma. "Ouermore" is not unusual in Lydgate's poems. Cf. *St. Edmund*, III, 104 f. :

"And ouermor, myn auctour seith the same,
Prophesied what sholde be his name."

And 197 : "And ouermor in pleyn language he seith."

The adverb is found also in Gower, but not in Chaucer, who uses "forthermore" and "forther-over"; see *Oxf. Dict.* and Skeat's Glossary.

2767. as I rede] *RE* G i back: "et leur manda moult et pria par ses messaigiers que leurs parens at amys amenassent auec eulx et il leur donroit or argent et bonne cheuance de pris de draps de soye."

2778–85. *RE* G i back: "et iura luy mesmes les dieux quil auoit creancez que a son frere Policenes ne au roy Adrascus ne rendroit il pas la cite pour nulle doubtance, ains leur vouldra vendre moult cherement ainz quilz layent en nulle maniere." Lydgate's version is decidedly superior to his French original.

2794–831 (as bookes specifye 2809)] *RE* G ii front: "Adonc auoit en la cite le roy Adrascus vng saige homme qui estoit maistre de leur loy, et estoit appelle Amphoras; celuy estoit regnomme de science sur tous aultres du royaulme. Celuy Amphoras auoit parle a leur ymaige quilz aouroient ou le dyable donnoit responce qui la demandoit, et luy auoit demande de lhost des Grecz et de la bataille, et il auoit respondu que sil alloit auec le roy a Thebes quil nen retourneroit mye, ains ouureroit la terre soubz luy, et fonderoit et cherroit en abisme tout vif."

2810–18. Much amplified by Lydgate on the basis of the single word "science" in *RE*.

2839–46 and 2850–63 are Lydgate's additions.

2847–86. *RE* G ii back: "Ceulx que le roy y enuoya le quirent assez, mais ilz ne le trouuerent mye, mais en la fin lenseigna sa femme voulsist ou non, et luy conuint aller en lhost dont il fut moult dolent. Et quant il fut venu en lhost moult y eut grant ioye, car par luy se asseuroient les Grecz."

2865–86. Lydgate's addition.

2887 (And as the story fully hath devised)—2921] *RE* G ii back: "Le roy luy pria moult quil dist la fin de la bataille ainsi comme il auoit enquis, et il luy dist que se il alloit petit en reuiendroit de sa gent et de sa cheualerie, ains seroient tous mors et occis de ce ne doubtoit mye. Et saichez bien roy Adrascus que se ie vois en la bataille ie seray destruict et mort et mengloutira la terre, car ainsi le mont dit les dieux: et quant tu voirras ce aduenir tu scauras bien que ie nay pas dict mensonge." *RE* has been amplified and improved by Lydgate.

2904–5. Inversion: The hegh noblesse of Grekes blood shal drawe to declyne.

2912–21 and 2926–97 are Lydgate's additions or extensive enlargements.

2951. Broseth hym-silf vnwarly and parbraketh] The MSS. have "parbraketh" G. Du. Ad_2. E_1., "parbrakethe" Ro., "parbrakith" T_1. M. Di. Ad_1. I. Ra. Ba. S., "ꝑbraketh" Ar. Bo. Lb. P., "ꝑbrakith" C. T_2., "ꝑbrakyth" L_1. L_2. (in Ap. the last word of l. 2951 is burnt), "perbraketh" E_2.; ꝑ in Ar. may be *par*, as in ꝑcel 2504, ꝑlement 2096, Iupte 1826, or *per*, as ꝑaunter 1248, Bexꝑience 1504, chambleynes 1359. As to the signification of the word, it is quite clear from the context that "parbraketh" (hym-silf) here means "breaks (himself) thoroughly, is crushed, shattered" (= broseth hym-silf). This signification is not given in *Oxf. Dict.* sub Parbreak, Parbrake, but see Perbreak v., Brake v^1.

In l. 2949 "set" may be either past part. or pres. ind. 3. sing. The latter interpretation has been preferred, and so no comma has been put at the end of 2950. However, the pronoun "hym-silf" of 2951 can be referred also to "ȝouth" (cf. 2944, 2948, 2953, 2962), and it is possible, with Lydgate's looseness of grammatical construction, that he may have meant 2951 to refer to 2949 ("set" pp.) as well as to 2950.

2971–75. In these lines Lydgate makes the most of his opportunity to impress his readers with the wide scope of his learning by quoting no less than seven Greek, Roman and Moorish authorities. There is, of course, nothing of this in *RE*, and, indeed, the whole outburst must be allowed to be strangely incongruous with Lydgate's leading idea of representing himself as telling his tale to the Host and the other pilgrims during their return journey from Canterbury.

2973. Albumasar and prudent Tholomee] Albumasar is the Arabian astronomer Abu-Maaschar, who lived in the ninth century (in Khorasan, Persia). Tholomee is, of course, Ptolemy, the famous astronomer and geographer (born *c.* 100). Albumasar and Ptholomy are mentioned together by Skelton, *Philip Sparrow*. See also Koeppel, *op. cit.* p. 73, foot-note 1.

3005. But ful gret drouht, as mad is mencioun] *RE* G iii front: "ilz vindrent en la terre du roy Ligurge ou ilz trouuerent grant faulte deaue, car bien auoit trois moys quil ny auoit pleu." Lydgate has somewhat magnified the three months of his original.

3015. And sperys hedes, in story as is told] *RE* G iii front: "et mettoient les fers de leurs lances en leurs bouches pour refroider."

3034. Called ligurgus, in story as I rede] *RE* G iii front: "il regarda soubz vng laurier et veit la seoir vne damoiselle qui tenoit vng petit enfant au serain, lenfant estoit au roy Ligurge qui nauoit plus denfans si laymoit moult sur toute creature."

3030–37. This Ligurgus seems to be another person than the king of the same name mentioned 2308, 2353, and the country as well as the garden are apparently quite unfamiliar to Tydeus. In the second part of the poem Tydeus had been found, a severely wounded knight, in the garden of King Lygurgus by the king's daughter, who was a full-grown maiden (2307 ff.). Here he sees a young lady holding in her arms the only son (child) of King Ligurgus, a baby of very tender age. See 3520–21, "And the kyngdam . . . of lygurgus was ycalled Trace." The difficulty cannot be laid to Lydgate's charge, as he only copied his Old French original. It may be, however, that *RE* as well as Lydgate in both passages have the same king and the same kingdom in view.

3043. The familiar and reassuring address "sustir" our poet found in *RE* G iii back: "Thideus . . . luy dist, Belle seur nayez nulle paour." But the endearing expression at the end of Tydeus' speech (3068) "myn owne suster dere" is Lydgate's own contribution to the scene.

3131–53 (the story maketh mynde 3146)] *RE* G iiii front: "Lors admena Thideus la damoyselle au roy Adrascus qui leaue auoit enseignee. Le roy len remercia haultement et luy dist que selle auoit mestier de luy il luy seroit en ayde."

3154–204 (together with the concluding lines 3510–19, on which see below) are drawn from several sources, being a combination of *RE* (myn autour 3154) with Boccaccio's *Genealogia Deorum*, lib. v, cap. 29, his *De claris mulieribus*, cap. 15, and Chaucer's *Legend of Hypsipyle*. 3155–87 (except 3180 and 3182–83) are all given in *RE* (see 3154, "And her myn autour makeþ rehersaille," 3157, "as ȝe may rede"). *RE* G iiii front and back: (la damoyselle) "respondit au roy et luy dist, Sire ie suis vne essillee et chassee de ma contree, si fus nee et nourrie en lisle de Uiones (or Viones) et suis fille au roy qui en tint la terre, ie ne scay se vous ouystes oncques parler de la trahison que les dames de la contree firent et pourpenserent . . . . que leurs marys occiroyent et leurs filz et leurs filles et leurs nepueulx et tiendroyent leurs honneurs et les seigneuries et ne seroyent a nulz subjectes (cf. 3174–76); . . . elles me prindrent et dirent que a leur

conseil me tenisse et mon pere tuasse, mais ie ne me vouluz oncques accorder comme de si grant mal faire comme de mon pere occire; elles ne se tarderent mye . . . et a tout (*sic*) couteaulx la nuict occirent leurs maris en dormant, leurs filz et leurs filles, et mon pere mesmes destrenchererent. Et se ie ne me fusse errament emblee et fouye elles me eussent tuee. . . . Deslors men vins au roy Ligurge qui ma honnoree et gardee tant quil ma baille son enfant petit a garder."

Lydgate has followed this relation, with the exception of three particulars. In *RE* (1) Isyphile does not succeed in rescuing her father's life, the other Lemnian women trucidating him against her will (cf. 3180); (2) there is no mention of Isyphile being captured by pirates and brought to Lygurgus by them (cf. 3182); (3) the name of the young lady, Isyphile, is nowhere mentioned, she being designated as " la damoyselle," " la dame," " la meschine." These particulars Lydgate has taken from Boccaccio, whom he quotes (3171, "as bochas telle can ") as his authority for 3171 ff. Lydgate has read and used both the works named above (see especially 3182 and 3518).

3188. " some bookis telle " refers to Boccaccio's *De claris mulieribus* (see 3201) and—principally—to Chaucer's *Legend of Hypsipyle*. It is only in Chaucer's poem that Hercules is specially mentioned as Jason's companion; see 1512 ff.:

" She knew, by folk that in his shippes be,
That hit was Jasoun, ful of renomee,
And Ercules, that had the grete los,
That soghten the aventures of Colcos " (cf. *Thebes*, 3190–92);

and 1559 ff.:

" The somme is this, that Jasoun wedded was
Unto this quene, and took of her substance
What-so him liste, unto his purveyaunce;
And upon her begat he children two,
And drow his sail, and saw her never-mo " (cf. *Thebes*, 3188–89).

3193–207. Lydgate—very inappropriately with regard to the pilgrims who are supposed to be listening to his tale—refers readers interested in learning the complete story of Isyphile to " the book that Iohn Bochas made whilom of wommen," Here, as well as in *Geneal. Deorum* and in Chaucer's legend (l. 1468), her father's name, Thoas, is given. Thus Lydgate, 3195, " Hir fadres name of which also I wante," can only mean to imply that he wanted sure information on the subject as " some bokes vermes ek hym calle " (cf. *vv. ll.* to 3197). The explanation of this name Vermes is doubtful. Koeppel, *op. cit.* p. 62^3, has tried to explain it as a perversion of Lemnos. Constans, *Roman de Thebes*, ii, p. clxiii, foot-note 3, thinks it is rather a corruption of the name of one of the sons that Hypsipyle had with Jason. The point is unimportant in itself, but Lydgate's notice is characteristic of his poetic taste.

3194. The story of Isyphile, abruptly broken off by 3195–97, is resumed 3198.

3206. The two " her " refer to Isyphile, the " her " of 3207 to the queen Iane.

3211. To the gardyne til she is repeyred] Ar. G. Lb. Ba. have "Til the g." This use of the prep. til is characteristically Northern in reference to place or purpose, though in M.E. occasionally Midland and Southern, *Oxf. Dict.* s.v. p. 28^3. See also Morsbach, *Schriftsprache*, p. 162; Skeat,

Works of Chaucer, Glossary, p. 265. Ar. G. have "to s.i.r." This use of "to" (= till, until) is also Northern and rare, see *Oxf. Dict.* s.v. p. 90[2].

3212. But now, allas! my mater disespeyred] The reading of Ar., with the predicate "is" omitted, has been kept as being confirmed not only by L_2 and Ap., but also by Bo. and the majority of the good MSS. The verb "disespeyre," not found in Chaucer's works, is often used by Lydgate, e.g. *Minor Poems* (Percy Soc.), p. 236: "Jhesu, to putte a verray preef Of his mercy, that no man disespeyre, Upon the cros gafe graunt unto the theef"; *ibid.* p. 179: "Graunt us, Jhesu, . . . indulgence, . . . Disespeyred of our owne offence."

3224–59. This passage has been much amplified by Lydgate. *RE* has H i front: "Lasse, faict elle, que pourray ie deuenir, et que pourray ie faire, car par droicte raison ie dois estre liuree a mort; car quant le roy scaura cest affaire, moult sera grant merueille sil demeure longuement en son sens, et especiallement madame la royne aussi."

3246. to fallen] has been kept because it makes the sentence stress more natural. The circumstance of L_2. and Ro. going with Bo. and others against Ar. Ap. and others is of no consequence on such a point.

3260–72. Lydgate has improved and partly altered (cf. 3271) the account of *RE* H i front: "Tantost apres demena la dame grant douleur et plouroit et ne sceut que faire. Ains Iaissa lenfant et courut a la riuiere ou elle auoit laisse lhost, et vint a Thideus et luy dist tout en plourant que mort auoit trouue lenfant quelle gardoit, et ne scauoit par quelle aduenture. Beau sire cheualier faict la damoyselle par vous mest aduenu ce dommaige; ne iamais noseray retourner au roy Ligurge qui tant aymoit lenfant que pour luy me feroit occire, et sil aduenoit faict la damoiselle que le roy ne me demandast la mort de son filz si me feroit la royne occire et desmembrer."

3316. ȝe be welcome to ȝoure owne place] *i.e.* I (Lygurgus) place my palace at your disposal to use as if it were your own. This expression of exquisite courtesy is inserted by Lydgate. It is not in *RE*: see next note.

3313–39. *RE* H i back: "Le roy Ligurge luy fist moult grant feste et moult grant ioye et luy dist que oncques ne fut si ioyeulx en sa vie comme de ce quil estoit venu en sa cite; si luy dist: Sire vous hebergerez huy mais ceans et vostre compaignie, et ceulx qui ne pourront entrer ceans se hebergeront la hors et prendront viande ceans dont il y a grant plante."

3340–50. *RE* H ii front: "mais il estoit a luy venu pour vng don requerre qui luy donnast et octroyast se oncques lauoit ayme en nul iour."

3346. Of our request ȝif that ȝe nat ne faille] That was probably the original reading of the line. Many copyists, being struck by the contraposition of "our" and "ȝe," altered it into "our," "we," or "ȝour," "ȝe." They were the more inclined to do so because the use and construction of the verb "faille" in 3346 are rather unusual. The reading "Of our request ȝif that we nat ne faille," besides making very good sense, is quite in accordance with a common use of the verb (cf. 609), and it is that of the group L_2. Ro. Ap. (and other MSS.), which is, in general, a good authority in this part of the poem. Only, if this reading were the original one, the difficulty consists in explaining why there arose any confusion at all. The reading "ȝour," "ȝe," although it is that of Ar. Bo. M. Ad_1. and others, bears no meaning, and is due to sheer thoughtlessness. But while "ȝe" is supported by these excellent MSS., "our" is confirmed by L_2. Ro. Ap. and other groups. And, as pointed out above, it seems easier to explain how "ȝe" came to be altered to "we" than "we" to "ȝe." The construction of "faille" in 3346, as it stands in the text, is borne out by good analogies, the intransitive verb being often followed by "of"; in signification "faille" comes very near to "faileth" in 2717 (see Glossary). It is not necessary to explain the phrase by taking " faille " to be logically transitive, so that " us " would have to be understood. This is the way in which the passage has been interpreted by Stowe. The line means: if you do not fail (*i.e.* if you do not disappoint us) with regard to our request.

3375–407. Lydgate's description of the passionate grief displayed by the king and the queen is throughout much enlarged by his own additions.

3376. hent hym by the herte] *i.e.* seized him by his heart; " hent " is preferable to " rent," because with " rent " one should expect the construction to be: " rent his herte."

3378. *i.e.* he felt as if every nerve in his body were cut all through. A description of that keen nervous pain that will sometimes shoot through the body, especially of an old person, when he is suddenly subjected to a violent mental shock. Lydgate may have written from his own personal experience. His French original, *RE* H ii front, says: " Quant le roy ouyt ces nouuelles, il fut si courrouce (*i.e.* sorrowful) si dolent et si triste que a peu quil ne sest pasme deuant le roy."

3379. The rage gan myne in hym so depe] Cf. *Troil.* II, 676 f.:

> " And after that, his manhod and his pyne
> Made love with-inne hir for to myne."

3381–88. *RE* H ii front: " Tantost quelle entendit la nouuelle de son filz qui estoit mort, elle cheut sur le pauement. Et quant elle fut releuee de pasmoison elle batit ses paulmes et si feist grant dueil que tous ceulx qui la ouyrent y coururent pour veoir la merueille."

3384. Almost identical with *Troil.* V, 726: " Hir nedede no teres for to borwe."

3389–400. *RE* H ii back: " Et quant le roy veit lenfant mort et enfle du venin, moult en eut grant dueil et grant pesance. La royne demenoit si grant dueil et si grant pleur sur le corps de son enfant quelle faisoit le roy Adrascus plorer et toute la cheualerie."

3398. Cf. *Knightes Tale*, 903: " For pitee renneth sone in gentil herte."

3401. There is a curious discrepancy between " al a day " of this line and " in the space almost of an hour " of 3405.

3414–51. Lydgate's addition. The exhortations and admonitions are mostly commonplaces. Lydgate, probably, in the course of his life had occasion more than once to act as mediator, as would indeed accord well both with his calling as a priest and with the natural kindness of his heart.

3414. " thouht " in the emphatic meaning " heavy thought," " sorrowful meditation "; see Schick, *Temple of Glas*, l. 1, Notes.

3415. *i.e.* since no one can recover loss (suffered) by death.

3421–23. Comparisons between the flood and ebb of the sea and the vicissitudes of human life must at all times come naturally to the poets of sea-girt England. Cf. *C.T.* B 1133–34 (*The Tale of the Man of Lawe*):

> " Joye of this world, for tyme wol nat abyde,
> Fro day to night it changeth as the tyde."

3424. " whos " refers to " an exile and a pilgrymage " of 3419. The context has been interrupted by the simile of 3421–23.

3427–28. Alliteration: manace. marke. man. mortal. mace. Cf. 3426 shroude. shour.

3432. Sauffecondit] When speaking of the uselessness of a safe-conduct in warding off death, Lydgate may well have had in view the treacherous murder of John Duke of Burgundy on Sept. 10, 1419, at his appointed meeting with King Charles VI of France, a deed that caused the greatest sensation and had important political consequences. Cf. also *Troy Book*, V, 3553–56:

> " Vnwar slauȝter compassed of envie,
> Mordre execut by conspirasie,
> Awaite liggyng falshede and tresoun,
> And of kyngdammys sodeyn euersioun."

Supersedyas] Cf. *Piers Plowman*, C. Passus v. 190: " Ne sende *supersedeas* bote ich asente, quath reson."

3441. which seeld or neuere stont in Suertè] refers to " this present lyff " in 3439.

3443–44. Cf. Langland's *Richard the Redeles*, Prol. 35 (E. E. T. S.):

> " And not to grucchen a grott aȝeine godis sonde,
> But mekely to suffre what so him sente were."

It is more probable that plur. " goddis " was altered by scribes into " god " than *vice versâ* (cf. 2914, 2778).

3452–53. *i.e.* Til that he fond a tyme conuenyent forto preye for ysyphilee.

3456–67. Lydgate's addition.

3473–74. That the serpent . . . lay his hed to borowe] *i.e.* " that the serpent put its head in pledge and lose it," " that the serpent lose its head (life)." Chaucer uses the phrase " lay to borwe " several times in the sense of " putting in pledge, pawning," e.g. *Troil.* II, 963, " And also hath she leyd hir feyth to borwe "; also *Troil.* V, 1664, *Knightes Tale*, 764 (see Skeat's Gloss. Index, and *Oxf. Dict.* s.v. Borrow s.). *Compleynt of Mars*, 205, " They mighten lightly leye hir heed to borowe," offers the same expression as in our line and is interpreted by Skeat (*Works of Chaucer*, Vol. I, Notes, p. 503): They might readily leave their head as a pledge, *i.e.* might devote themselves to death. Cf. above 2232, Notes.

3496. Hent out a swerde] Thirteen MSS., among them Ad_1. M. Ra., have " Hent." The very phrase is found *c.* 1450 in *Merlin* (*Oxf. Dict.* s.v.). As to " Rent " (pret. of Rend) in this combination, *Oxf. Dict.* offers no exact parallel, but its ordinary sense " to tear out " comes pretty near; there is, however, a marked difference between rending a leaf out of a book, or rending off one's clothes (see *Oxf. Dict.*), viz. the important notion of tearing to pieces, and rending out a sword in order to use it. There would be no doubt in the case, if the following line did not offer a second " hent." But this repetition may be due to Lydgate's need of a word to rhyme with " present." As to the third alternative, " rent " pret. of " rennen," it need not be discussed here (see Björkman, *Scandinavian Loan-words in Middle English*, p. 185, and dictionaries).

3506–9. This is founded on the short statement of *RE* H ii back: " Ainsi fut la damoyselle accordee au roy et a la Royne."

3510–19. Boccaccio says in his *G. D.*: " ab Adrasto reliquisque regibus et a filiis suis seruata est. Quid tandem ex ea contigerit nusquam legisse memini."

3520–21. but ȝif bookes lye] Boccaccio in *G. D.* (see l. 3538) lib. xi, cap. 22, quotes Lactantius respecting Lycurgus' kingdom, (" Lactantius autem eum Thracum dicit regem et in mare precipitatum "; cf. 3535), Homer, Servius and Lactantius with regard to his offences against Bacchus and his punishment (cf. 3528–35).

3522–27. as I rede in an other place] See Chaucer *C.T.* A 2128–48 (*The Knightes Tale*), beginning:

> " Ther maistow seen coming with Palamoun
> Ligurge him-self, the grete king of Trace."

3548. Of ligurgus with his browes blake] Cf. Chaucer, *ibid.* 2134 :

> " With kempe heres on his browes stoute,"

and 2143 f.

> " His longe heer was kembd bihinde his bak,
> As any ravenes fether it shoon for-blak."

3537–43. Lydgate quotes Boccaccio's *Genealogia Deorum* in twelve books (" i-braunched out vpon twelue trees "), and says that among poets of Italy he certainly ranks next to Petrarch.

3563–64. And pight her tentys proudly, as I rede] *RE* H iii front : " Quant le roy Adrascus eut prins congie au roy et a la royne, ilz errerent tant quilz furent dessoubz Thebes en la prayerie."

3581–600. Very much enlarged and filled with particulars by Lydgate. Cf. the short statement of *RE* H iii front : " Lors se logerent les Grecz, et les fourriers sespandirent par la contree quilz ardirent et gasterent."

3601–9. Lydgate's addition.

3603. Mynistring hem occisiones felle] All the MSS. have " occasions (occasiouns) " here. In 4204 the great majority of the MSS. have " occasion " against " occisioun " in five (mostly inferior) MSS. There can be no doubt that in both these lines the word is owing to a mistake, or to a deliberate alteration, made by the man who wrote out the copy which is the ultimate original of all our MSS. He may not have known the word " occision." But " occasion " in the sense demanded here by the context is not to be found either in Middle English or in Old or Middle French (see 2026, *Notes*). On the other hand, " occision " (killing, slaughter) is a well-known word in both these languages (see Littré and *Oxf. Dict.*). The passage quoted in *Oxf. Dict.* from Barbour's *Bruce* is especially in point :

> " The . . . Erll . . . Maid sic a slauchtir in the toune,
> And swa felloune occisioune."

Compare with this 3603, " occisiones felle " and 4204, " So gret slaughter and occisioun." Moreover, the word " occision " occurs in Lydgate's French original, although it is not used in the present passage; cf. *RE* K ii front : " La y eut grant occision de ceulx de dedans et daultre menue gent." Lydgate himself uses the word in *Pilgrimage of the Life of Man* (ed. Furnivall), 14840 : " By slauhtre and gret occisioun."

3614–20. *RE* H iii front : " Mais de ses hommes doubtoit il quil ne fust trahy, car bien scauoit que les plusieurs aymoyent mieulx son frere, encores fussent ilz dedans la ville."

3619 list . . . that] " list " for " lest " is common in Lydgate's works : see e.g. *St. Edmund*, III, 6, 469; *Troy Book*, I, 1009, 3134, 3151.

3621, 3623, 3625, 3626. These four lines begin with the causal conjunction " for."

3628. Evidently this line was omitted in the immediate original of L_2. and Ro.; the copyists, observing the gap, composed a supplementary line, each in his own clumsy manner.

3648–708. Lydgate has much enlarged this passage. *RE* H iii back : " La royne detrahit son filz a vne part et luy dist : croy les haulx hommes et tu feras que saige. Tu ne sces mie les couraiges de tous les haulx barons, et se tu les crois tu y pourras bien perdre : pourquoy veulx tu ton frere desheriter et luy tollir sa terre quil doibt auoir en heritaige."

3655–73. These lines, which are the poet's own addition, may have a double address. As in ancient Thebes, public opinion in England, at the time when Lydgate was writing his poem, was no doubt divided on the question of war or peace. There were a great many people discontented with the long war with France and heartily wishing for peace. Lydgate's effusion may be an echo of their feelings and reasonings. On the other hand, not only King Henry V, but numbers of the subjects, especially many knights and lords, were eager for conquest and honour. In ll. 4134–44, a passage also enlarged by Lydgate, he may give utterance to the opposite opinion. Thus he may have been a mouthpiece for conflicting opinions, certainly with a strong leaning towards the party of peace.

3665. And ȝif we put our mater hool in Marte] *i.e.* if we leave our dispute to be decided by the fortune of war. Cf. 3662, " To putte a strif in martys Iugement."

3687. And thow art dryve so narowe to þe stake] A figurative use of terms taken from the sport of jousting. Cf. *C. T.* A 2552, 2642, 2648 (*The Knightes Tale*).

3709–25. *RE* H iii back: " Quant Ethiocles ouyt ainsi parler sa mere si en eut grant ire quil ne sceut que dire, . . . Ethiocles octroya la paix moult enuis . . . et dist en la fin quil nen feroit riens sil nauoit la seigneurie et que son frere tenist de luy."

3734. Vpon the houre whan it droh to pryme] The time of day is here either at sunrise or 9 a.m. Cf. 124. See *Oxf. Dict.* s.v. Prime, 2: " The first hour of the day, beginning either at six o'clock throughout the year, or at the varying time of sunrise; also sometimes . . . about nine o'clock."

3757–63. There is nothing corresponding in *RE*. *HT* says: " quil se condescent a faire appoinctement par ainsi quil rendra la seigneurie a son frere pourveu que le droict et domination principalle luy en demeurera, et la tiendra polimites comme soubz luy." But Lydgate may have repeated Ethiocles' offer from 3714–18.

3799. And to this fyn/Iustly hold vs to] The full-stop at the end of 3798 should be exchanged for a comma. 3799 is co-ordinated with 3797, both infinitives (" delyuer " and " hold vs ") being governed by " assure " in 3794: The Greeks will engage to give up possession again and to hold faithfully to this agreement. As to the change from *oratio obliqua* in 3794 (" Grekys shal ") to *oratio recta* in 3799 (" hold vs," *i.e.* hold ourselves), cf. 3796 (" in our beste wise "). The reflexive form of " hold " (" hold vs to ") has in modern English been replaced by the intransitive one. The preposition " to " is put twice (" to this fyn " and " hold vs to "). With regard to " fyn " *s.* with the meaning of agreement (see *Oxf. Dict.*), cf. ende *s.* 3724, 3732 and see *Oxf. Dict.*, s.v. End *s.*

3805. Fro which apoynt we cast vs not to varye] Six MSS., Bo. at their head, have " a poynt (.o. point, oon poynt, on poynt)," some scribes having divided " apoynt " into " a poynt," others improving on this correction by substituting the numeral for the indefinite article. It is doubtful if " which a, which oon " is used as a relative pronoun by Lydgate or Chaucer. The verb " apoint " occurs in *Thebes* 2793 with the sense of " settle, decide." Though the examples of " apoint " *s.* given in *Oxf. Dict.* are more than a hundred years later than *Thebes*, there can be no objection to our dating the substantive as early as Lydgate. The meaning of the word here is " decision, resolution " (cf. *Oxf. Dict.* Appoint *v.* 5, 6) or " settlement, agreement " (as in the earliest example, 1555, of *Oxf. Dict.*).

3831. the whiche beest] See Glossary, s.v. " which," 1173, 4668.

3831. "by record of scripture" and 3835. "as Clerkys make mencioun" refer to *RE*. See next note.

3832–34. *RE* H iiii back: "et si estoit forte et legiere autant comme vne aultre beste sauluaige . . . De sa cruaulte nest nulle beste quant elle est courroucee."

3836–37. *RE* ibid.: "Et auoit piedz et iambes et queue de lyon, mais la teste auoit gente et belle, et long museau ainsi comme vng leurier."

3838 is an addition of Lydgate's. *RE* says nothing about the tiger's eyes. As to the readings "fyret (feret)" or "fyre," the metre, which requires a disyllabic word here, proves that the reading of Ar. L_2. Ro. is the correct one. "Fyre" is a monosyllable. Besides, the tiger is throughout compared with other animals. It was and is usual enough to compare red or fierce eyes with those of a ferret (see *Oxf. Dict.*).

3839–46. Ek of his Skyn, wryten as I fynde] *RE* says *l.c.*: "elle auoit le poil luysant par nature ainsi comme selle fust doree." There is no mention of a panther in *RE*. Lydgate drew his description (3840–41) of the skin, as well as the information about the method used for capturing tigers, from his various reading. Cf. *Reson and Sensuallyte*, 6975 ff.

> "A Tigre, which that ys so rage,
>
> . . . . .
>
> He ys deceyved by merours
> Which the hountys for socours
> Caste in the waye for a treyne;"

and see Sieper's note, Part II, p. 132.

3848–61. myn autour writ the same] *RE* H iiii back: "auoit si perdue sa nature que en elle nauoit ireur nomplus quen vng aigneau; ains alloit par la salle comme vng leurier, ne ia ne luy fist on tant de villennie quelle montrast point direur, moult estoit la tigre en la cite aymee, et qui en eust voulu donner au roy Ethiocles cent marcs dargent il ne les en eust pas prins."

3862. the story doth expresse] The following passage, 3863–915, agrees with the description of the first fight, given in *RE* I i front, but this description has been much enlarged and improved by Lydgate.

3893–915. *RE* I i front: "Thideus assembla tout premier a ceulx de la ville et Ethiocles et le tremos a ceulx du dehors qui ne les espargnerent mye: et icy y eut moult grant bataille; pour ceste chose moult en y eut de mors dune part et daultre a ceste premiere assemblee, mais ceulx de la ville en eurent le pire."

3897. That made Grekes to forsak her place] Cf. 4218, "And mortally made hem lese her place."

3920. cessen her bataylle, and 3924. Grekes made hom ageyn resorte] *RE* I i front: "la royne Iocaste qui manda a son filz Policenes quil fist cesser la bataille et sa gent ressortir arriere."

3926–27. And they of Thebes . . . Ful trist and hevy] *RE* I i back: "Et ceulx de la ville retournerent dedans les portes dolens et tristes."

3940. avisè] A hybrid word, the Old French form with English accentuation: cf. "avised" (Glossary) and "renomed" 4130.

3945–63. *RE* I i back: "A tant print congie et se departit de lhost et ses deux filles. Si la conuoya vers la cite Policenes et Thideus et Parthonolopeus le noble roy Darcade qui moult ayma ymene pour sa grant beaulte."

3956. her fresshly face] The adjective "fresshly" seems to belong exclusively to Lydgate's language, generally used in connection with "face." We find it in *Temple of Glas*, 273, "The goodlihed eke of hir fresshli face"; and in *Troy Book*, from which Schick quotes (*Temple of Glas*, p. 90), a line almost identical with the one last quoted. See also *Thebes*, 3307. In l. 1975 "fresshly" is better explained as an adverb. *Oxf. Dict.* does not register "freshly" as an adjective.

3971–77. *RE* I i back and ii front: "Et dirent plusieurs que Policenes et Thideus et Parthonolopeus entrerent dedans Thebes auec la royne . . ., mais ie ne le croy pas certainement, car Thideus nestoit pas si fol quil sembatist sur ses ennemis desarmes."

3975. The close connection of 3975 with "Ne wold" is somewhat obscured, 3975 being seemingly co-ordinated with "of hegh discrecioun." The faulty construction of the sentence might have been avoided by Lydgate making 3976 precede 3975.

3980. Lich as it is put in remembrance] Notwithstanding this reference to some literary source, the whole passage, 3978–87, is an invention of Lydgate's. There is nothing of the kind in *RE*.

3983. Polymytes besought the queen not to cease that night in her endeavours to persuade Ethiocles to keep the agreement. "Bysouhte" is construed with a pure infinitive "not fyne."

3992–93. This is a feature of natural scenery pictured by Lydgate in his poem that has certainly been drawn from his own observation. The description of fields and gardens with their abundance of many-coloured flowers (*e.g.* 13–17, 2309–13) was one of the conventionalities of the poetry of his time. But the moonlight shining on castles or other grand buildings Lydgate has seen many a night with his own eyes and been impressed with the magic charm of the scenery. See also 2268–73.

4000. (the conuencioun, Of old engrocyd . . .) which is enrollyd and put in remembrance] Cf. 2099 "(By Iust accord . . . Engrosed vp, as it is wel knowe,) And enrolled, only for witnesse, In ȝoure regestres."

4022. And richely I-armyd in his char] "I-armyd" against all the MSS. The cæsura logically falling before "in," the metre requires the trisyllabic form "I-armyd."

4022–46. *RE* I ii front: "Et en celle bataille fut Amphoras arme sur vng riche destrier pour ayder a ceulx de Grece. La ou il estoit entre en la grant presse ouurit la terre si que Amphoras cheut dedens et le cheual qui le portoit, et de ceulx qui auecques luy estoient. Apres se reuint la terre ensemble comme deuant, . . . Et Amphoras fut tresbusche en enfer tout vif: ce fut pour la grant desloyaulte quil auoit menee, car tous les iours de sa vie cuidoit les diables seruir sans auoir sa desserte." Lydgate's French redaction evidently had the same reading as *HT*: "estoit en ceste bataille amphorus leuesque darges . . . Sur vng grant chariot a quatre roes estoit il monte . . . et fut transglouty amphorus auec son chariot et aucuns qui estoient pres de luy."

4078. To serche and seke thorgh-out al the host] An abbreviated concessive clause, viz. even though one should search through the whole army for his equal.

4088–97. *RE* I ii back: "En la cite auoient grant ioye, . . . Tantost les guettes crierent la nuict sur les murs: et cryoyent aux Grecs quilz sen allassent, car ilz auoient trop perdu quant perdu auoient leur deuineur en qui auoient leur fiance." Lydgate's narrative has more life and colour. The following lines 4098–103 are an addition of his.

4116. contune] pres. ind. 3 plur., with change of tense from the preceding line ("made") for the sake of the rhyme.

4104–61: *RE* I iii front: "le roy Adrascus manda ses barons pour querre conseil de laduenture qui estoit si perilleuse et leur dist, seigneurs ie ne scay que faire, car ie suis en grant doubtance; se nous leuons le siege deuant que ceste cite soit prinse, moult en aurons grant honte. Et daultre part nous sommes en peril que la terre ne nous engloutisse. Or ie vous prie que vous me dictes ce quil vous en semble, car ie ne vouldroye en nulle maniere que nous feissons chose pourquoy lhonneur de Grece fust abaisse, ne que les hoirs de tant haulx barons fussent reprochez. A ce conseil y eut moult parle, mais en la fin saccorderent ilz quilz ne sen partiroient mye, ou ilz mourroient ou prendroient la cite."

4128–40. In *RE* Adrascus, in his opening address to his barons, lays most stress on their duty of not dishonouring their descendants (hoirs) by weakly abandoning a dangerous enterprise. In Lydgate, on the contrary, Adrastus reminds the council of the example of their "progenitours" who had proved "so manly conquerours" (Edward III and his son "the Black Prince"). Lydgate's own sentiments are probably revealed most sincerely in Iocasta's admonitions to her son Ethiocles (see above, 3655–73, with note).

4130. See 2615, note.

4135. wher as they han passyd] "they" *i.e.* the Greeks (indicated by "whoes" 4134).

4136–38. The beams of their renown have not yet been dimmed by any rumour that they should have given up any enterprise, by sea or by land, that they have begun.

4184–85. Cf. 4164–65.

4193–98. in story as is told] *RE* I iii front: "Ainsi furent les Grecz rasseurez a qui il voulsist mieulx quilz sen fussent allez, car moult souffroient de peine et de trauaulx, et de chault et de froit et dehors et dedens sentreoccirent comme gens qui de eulx nauoient conte ne cure."

4199–239. Lydgate's addition. In *RE* and *HT* Tydeus' death is told in a few words; in *G. D.* with much more detail. Lydgate enlarged the passage, feeling the poetical necessity of treating the death of the foremost hero of the poem more at length. He has left out the coarse features of the case as told by Boccaccio, which would have been in sharpest contrast to the humanity and chivalry of Tydeus.

RE I iii back says only: "Au commencement fut mort Thideus le bon cheualier qui tant fut preux que encores en parle lescripture." *HT* fol. 92 back has: "Premier le notable cheualiers Thideus qui de auidite et grant desir quil eut de trouuer Ethiocles en son chemin se mist et habandonna si auant quil fut subcombe de ses ennemis et mis a mort." *G. D.* lib. ix. cap. 21: "Tandem cum Adrasto et Polynice, iam uno ex Deiphile suscepto filio Dyomede ad obsidionem venit thebarum convocatis amicis. Ibi autem cum tanquam rem suam ageret acriter sæpe pugnans die una a quodam Menalippo in mortem vulneratus est. Quod cum impatienter ferret seque acerbitate vulneris in mortem trahi cerneret, fere in rabiem versus sotiis eius qui eum vulneraverat postulavit caput. Qui postquam illud multo sanguine fuso obtinuerunt eique detulerunt, ipse non aliter quam canis iam deficiens cervici dentem infixit et illam dum bestiali ritu devoraret, occubuit."

4227–28. Cf. 3235–36.

4240–51 (as mad is mencioun 4246)] *RE* I iii back: "Apres mourut Parthonolopeus, et ypomedon fut noye en leaue ou il se combatoit apres ses ennemys par sa grant prouesse."

4252–54 (Mor to declare than myn Autour doth 4254)] *RE* I iii back: "Et saichez que ie ne me veulx entremettre de racompter le iugement ne de dire les noms par qui la cite deust estre perie, car trop en seroit grant parolle, et lairrons ester maintes choses a retraire."

4253. The comma at the end of this line had better be struck out and "slaughter" taken as the direct object of "declare," this infinitive being co-ordinate with the finite tense of 4252. Such an anacolouthon is quite within the range of grammatical licences allowed in Lydgate's poetical style.

4255–95 (4255. I fynde as ȝe may sen)] Cf. *l.c.* "Apres sentrerencontrerent les deux freres, cestassauoir Ethiocles et Policenes. Et vous diray comment Policenes abatit a iouste son frere Ethiocles, et le ferit dung glaiue parmy le corps tant quil fut naure. Quant Policenes veit yssir le sang de son frere il en eut pitie et descendit a terre de dessus son cheual et trait hors sa lance . . . car entre deux que Policenes le baisoit en plourant Ethiocles le ferit dung cousteau " . . . The description of the combat is much enlarged in Lydgate's poem.

4298–99. And in Thebes, loud as eny shalle, The Cry aroos] *RE* I iiii front : " Quant ilz se apperceurent que les deux freres furent entreoccis il y eut grant cry et grant huee."

4309–48. A vivid description of the last act of the fight, much amplified and improved by the poet. *RE* says briefly : " Si trayt le roy Adrascus arriere qui auoit perdu tous ses ducz et ses princes en la bataille et es assaulx, fors que seul Capaneus." See also 4312, note.

4312. And betyn of with grete rounde ballys] *RE* I iiii front : " Et ceulx de la ville qui aux carneaux estoyent gectoient pierres aux Gregois qui les portes enuahyssoyent et les occioient."

4358–71. *RE* I iiii front says only : " Et lors ensepuelirent le roy Ethiocles et y eut mainte larme plouree de la royne et de ses seurs et daultres dames."

4364. Cf. *The Knightes Tale*, 978 ff. :

" And by his (*i.e.* Theseus') baner born is his penoun
Of gold ful riche, in which ther was y-bete
The Minotaur, which that he slough in Crete."

4372–99 (lik as it is founde 4391)] *RE* I iiii front : " Apres dirent les barons que il leur conuenoit faire roy a qui ilz eussent aliance. Et esleurent Creon qui estoit ancien cheualier et preux. Le roy fist venir deuant luy tous ceulx de la ville, et leur mist habandon or et argent et draps pour ce que ilz aydassent a tenir et a deffendre a leur pouoir ladicte cite contre leurs ennemys, si sen hardirent et dirent que si feroyent ilz. Et si firent ilz tant comme ilz vesquirent."

4400–36 (4417. lik as I rede; 4426. And as myn Autour doth clerly certifie)] *RE* I iiii front : " Et le roy Adrascus enuoya vng cheualier qui estoit naure dune lance et luy dist quil allast a Arges, et fist noncer par toute Grece la grant douleur et la grant meschance. I iiii back : Le messagier qui vint a Arges compta aux dames de la cite les nouuelles douloureuses qui furent espandues par toute la contree : et les filles du roy Adrascus, Argila et Deiphile, firent si grant dueil de leurs maris et de leur pere quil ny auoit nul reconfort, et tant parlerent que elles dirent quelles yroient en la fin a Thebes, et recognoistroient leurs amys et les ensepueliroient et mettroient en terre selon leur estat. A ce conseil saccorderent les filles du roy Adrascus et disoyent que auec les aultres yroient."

4412–14. See *The Knightes Tale*, 922–23. Here the spokeswoman of the ladies says to Theseus :

" For certes, lord, ther nis noon of us alle,
That she nath been a duchesse or a quene."

4437–62 (And as the story liketh to declare 4437)] *RE* says shortly I iiii back : " Quant celles furent appareillees si sen allerent tous nudz piedz (4438, 4445, 4469) et a grant destresse vers Thebes."

4448. And as I fynde, they weryn alle trwe. 4452. And feithful alle, bookys can not lye] *RE* has nothing about the faithfulness of the ladies. The idea of this eulogy on womanly faith may have occurred to the poet from the particular mentioned in *RE*, that the ladies performed their sad pilgrimage barefoot. Nevertheless there is scarcely any doubt but that the eulogy has a tinge of satire.

4463–90 (wrytyn as I fynde 4465)] *RE* I iiii back : " Tant allerent par leurs iournees quelles apperceurent ceulx de Thebes et les tentes des Grecz qui estoient toutes vuydees. Le roy Adrascus . . . et le roy Capaneus . . . sadresserent encontre elles. . . . Lors commenca grant le cry delles et des aultres. Et quant le roy Adrascus les eust cognues il eut si grant douleur au cueur quil se fust feru dune espee parmy le corps se ne fut Capaneus qui luy tollit." Lydgate has modified this attempt at suicide into the king's wish (4490) that his heart " parted wer on tweyne."

4463–540. This part of the poem is principally based on Chaucer's *The Knightes Tale* (see 4501, And as my mayster Chaucer list endite). Lydgate follows Chaucer closely, many lines being copied almost word for word; see *e.g.* 4529–30, which prove that Lydgate had now a MS. of *C. T.* or a copy of *The Knightes Tale* (cf. 957–68) before him. However, " myn autour " is not forgotten. The two sources are intimately combined. In *RE* and in our poem Theseus arrives at Thebes on the morning of the day after the arrival of the ladies and is met by Adrastus, who implores his help. In *The Knightes Tale* the ladies have been waiting a fortnight in the temple of " Clemence " for the coming of Theseus and his army (= *Thebes*, 4502–11). In *RE* and in our poem it is Adrastus that introduces the mourning ladies to Theseus. In *The Knightes Tale* (892–98) Theseus meets the procession of the ladies in the road near Thebes and listens to their prayers for assistance against Creon, spoken by " the eldest lady of hem alle." Chaucer does not mention Adrastus at all. In Lydgate's poem Adrastus has played throughout a leading rôle (from 1192) and, of course, remains an important actor to the end.

4469. Clad all in blak] This particular is taken from *The Knightes Tale*, 899 : " Ech after other, clad in clothes blake "; and 911 : " And why that ye ben clothed thus in blak."

4491–500. *The Knightes Tale*, 941–47. *RE* K i back : " Lors enuoya (viz. Theseus) deux messagiers au roy de Thebes, et luy demanda quil luy rendist les corps qui deuant sa cite gisoyent mors et destrenchez. Le roy Creon respondit moult laidement aux messagiers et leur dist que pour luy nen feroit riens."

4514–16. This is in accordance with the statement of *RE* K i front : " et quant vint la matinee le roy Adrascus regarda entour la montaigne. Si apperceut cheualiers et sergens venir a si grans compaignies . . . il monta sur son cheual et alla vers eulx grant alleure. . . . Et ilz dirent que cestoit le duc dathenes qui passoit par illec. . . . Lors vint au duc . . . et luy pria a ioinctes mains que par sa pitie luy fist secours et ayde."

4520–24. Here Lydgate endeavours, in the most effective way, to make his readers realise that he is telling his tale just to Chaucer's pilgrims. Depforth is Deptford (in south London). In *C. T.* " Depeford " is mentioned in the Prologue to the *Reves Tale* (A 3906), not in connection with *The Knightes Tale*.

4541–61. as some auctours make mencioun (see also 4545)] *RE* K ii front : " Endementiers . . . les dames enfondrerent les murs a pieux et a marteaulx. . . . Le roy Capaneus veit bien que ceulx de dedans ne pourroient durer. Si commenca a monter dessus vne eschelle que ceulx de dehors luy auoyent dressee a force : la luy cheut vne pierre sur le chapel et luy assomma toute la teste. . . . Le duc fist par toute la ville le feu bouter. . . . Lors feist le duc la royne Iocaste et ses deux filles prendre a ses dames et damoyselles et aultres prisonniers."

4562–87. The short description of the funerals in *RE* K ii front and back (" Quant ce fut faict grant douleur reprenoyent aux corps des Grecz mettre en cendre et en sepulture faire, nul ne pourroit dire la grant douleur que les dames demenoient et faisoient. Ie ne vueil mye de chascun compter la sepulture, car ie ne pourroye ne ne scauroye ") has been considerably amplified by Lydgate, partly by particulars borrowed from *The Knightes Tale*. But the poet has chosen to omit that striking feature of the legend which is told by *RE* l.c.: " Mais a la fin print on les deux corps des deux freres, et par le commandement du roy Adrascus on les brusla ensemble. Et sachez que la flambe des corps sailloit et se partissoit elle, et seleuoient lune au dessus de laultre, et ne se approchoient ne tant que quant."

4562–64 are borrowed almost verbally from *The Knightes Tale*, 991–92. It would seem, with regard to the following description of the funerals, that " bones " should be replaced by " bodies " (MSS. Lb. M. and others). But the almost identical lines in *The Knightes Tale* prove conclusively that " bones " is the right word here.

4567–68 with the rhyme-words " devise : Guyse " correspond to *The Knightes Tale*, 993–94, with their rhyme-words " gyse : devyse."

4571–72. of relees] The explanation given in *Promptorium Parvulorum*, p. 429 (" Reles, tast or odowre ") can hardly be right. The compiler's translation of the word " relees " is certainly a mere guess founded only on this line, which he has misunderstood.[1] There should be a comma after " swetter " and " of relees " means " for relief," *i.e.* to relieve the discomfort of smelling the disagreeable odour of the corpses that were burnt. In authors of the fourteenth and fifteenth centuries such an idea—borrowed by Lydgate from Chaucer; see *The Knightes Tale*, 2938—with regard to the supposed custom of the ancients to put incense, myrrh and other fragrant things into the funeral fires, is easily intelligible. For the structure of 4571 and the mark of cæsura, cf. Prologue 88.

4573–86 are, like the last-mentioned two lines, mostly borrowed from Chaucer's description of Arcite's funeral.

4573–74. Cf. *The Knightes Tale*, 2949–50; 4576 *ib.* 2957; 4584–86 *ib.* 2958–61.

4592–98. Also these lines are more or less literally copied from Chaucer. Cf. ll. 4592–94 with *The Knightes Tale* 997–99; ll. 4595–98 with *The Knightes Tale* 1026–27. 4599 is added by Lydgate.

4611–27 (4611. as myn auctour liketh to compyle; 4622. in bookys ȝe may Se; 4623. as mad is mencioun)] *RE* K iii front: " Ainsi retourna le roy Adrascus en sa contree : il ne vesquit gueres ains mourut moult tost, car il auoit grant douleur au cueur. Ainsi comme vous auez ouy fut Thebes arse et destruicte quatre cens ans deuant que Romme fust fondee."

4628–4716. This epilogue is Lydgate's own composition.

4660–67. And as the byble trewly kan devyse. 4665–66. Michael . . . with his Feerys] Cf. *Isa.* xiv, 12 : " How art thou fallen from heaven, O Lucifer, son of the morning," and xxvii, 1 : " In that day the Lord with his sore and great and strong sword shall punish leviathan the piercing serpent, even leviathan that crooked serpent; and he shall slay the dragon that is in the sea." Also *Revel.* xx, 1–3 : " And I saw an angel come down from heaven. . . . And he laid hold on the dragon, that old serpent, which is the Devil, and Satan, and bound him in a thousand years, And cast him

[1] Cf., however, *Oxf. Dict.* s.v. *reles*.—E. E.

into the bottomless pit, and shut him up." Finally *Revel.* xii, 7: "And there was war in heaven: Michael and his angels fought against the dragon; and the dragon fought and his angels"; xii, 9: "And the great dragon was cast out, that old serpent, called the Devil, and Satan, which deceiveth the whole world."

Cf. Lydgate, *St. Edmund* III, 379, "The olde serpent hadde at hym enuye"; and *St. Margaret*, 286, "The olde serpent, whiche called is Sathan."

4663. The olde Serpent, he levyathan, was the first that etc.] Cf. *e.g.* *C. T.* B 4584–85 (*The Nonne Preestes Tale*), "Certes, he Jakke Straw, and his meynee, Ne made never shoutes half so shrille"; Lydgate, *Temple of Glas*, 81, "Wiþ þilk[e] swerd of him Piramus"; *Troy Book*, II, 5861, "þe olde serpent, þat is so lowe falle," and 5865, "þe vile serpent, he, Leuyathan."

4668. "Cockle" occurs only once in the Bible, viz. *Job* xxxi, 40; its use here has no application to this passage of *Thebes*.

4679. The reading of the four MSS. L_2. G. C. P. against those fifteen (Ar. Bo. Ad_1. M., etc.) in which there is no gap, is evidently right, as proved by the rubric and by *Luke* xxi, 10, "Then said he unto them, Nation shall rise against nation, and kingdom against kingdom."

4690–703 refer to the joyful news, received in England in the spring of 1420, of the treaty of peace concluded between France and England May 1420.

4698–703 are framed in conformity with the terms of the 24th paragraph of the said treaty; cf. Introduction, Chap. I, § 5, also Temporary Preface, p. vii.

4703. Pees and quyet, concord and vnytè] These expressions, translated from the French text of the treaty, are effectively contrasted with 4691, "Of strif, of werre, of contek, and debat."

The colophon: "Here endeth the destruccioun of Thebes." Cf. 4604–7.

RHYME-LISTS

-able.
variable, *adj.*: stable, *adj.* 1723/4, 3629/30.
vnstable, *adj.*: fauorable, *adj.* 3619/20.
-ace.
embrace, *inf.*: face, *s.* 3392/1.
enbrace, *inf.*: place, *s.* 3315/16, 3746/5.
enchace, *inf.*: place, *s.* 3872/1, 3898/7, 4217/18.
face, *s.*: manace, *inf.* 621/2.
face, *s.*: passe, *inf.* 3956/5.
face, *s.*: place, *s.* 3/4, 1867/8, 2863/4, 3217/18.
face, *s.*: vnbrace, *inf.* 4283/4.
grace, *s.*: manace, *pres. conj.* 806/5.
grace, *s.*: place, *s.* 1738/7, 3046/5, 4518/17.
grace, *s.*: purchace, *inf.* 3302/1, 3935/6.
grace, *s.*: space, *s.* 3466/5.
grace, *s.*: trespace, *s.* 2337/8.
mace, *s.*: manace, *inf.* 3428/7.
manace, *inf.*: place, *s.* 4694/3.
manace, *inf.*: space, *s.* 3586/5.
place, *s.*: race, *inf.* 1005/6.
place, *s.*: purchace, *inf.* 4168/7.
place, *s.*: space, *s.* 302/1, 504/3, 1475/6, 1808/7, 1922/1.
place, *s.*: Trace, *n. pr.* 3522/1.
-acid.
passyd, *pp.*: diffacyd, *pp.* 4135/6.
-acis.
facys, *s. plur.*: placys, *s. plur.* 4477/8.
-ăd.
bad, *pret.*: lad, *pp.* 977/8, 1493/4.
glad, *adj. sing.*: sad, *adj. sing.* 1551/2.
rad, *pp.*: sad, *adj. sing.* 1407/8.
sad, *adj. sing.*: shad, *pp.* 3940/39.
-adde.
adrad, *pp. plur.*: mad, *adj. plur.* 1177/8.
hadde, *pret.*: ladde, *pret.* 1553/4.
-āde.
glade, *adj. plur.*: made, *pret.* 2432/1, 3202/1.
made, *pret. sing.*: ouerlade, *pp.* 4548/7.
-age.
age, *s.*: auauntage, *s.* 1143/4.
age, *s.*: damage, *s.* 3853/4.
age, *s.*: dotage, *s.* 997/8.
age, *s.*: heritage, *s.* 1090/89.
age, *s.*: lynage, *s.* 1399/1400.
age, *s.*: passage, *s.* 665/6.
age, *s.*: pilgrimage, *s.* 93/4.
age, *s.*: rage, *s.* 866/5, 914/13.
age, *s.*: sage, *adj.* 1194/3.
age, *s.*: sauage, *adj.* 3869/70.
age, *s.*: visage, *s.* 3032/1.
aswage, *inf.*: corage, *s.* 3499/500.
auauntage, *s.*: forage, *s.* 3599/600
auauntage, *s.*: herytage, *s.* 3791/2.
auauntage, *s.*: passage, *s.* 2156/5.
baronage, *s.*: mariage, *s.* 1651/2.
corage, *s.*: mariage, *s.* 1222/1.
corage, *s.*: massage, *s.* 1891/2.
corage, *s.*: passage, *s.* 646/5.
corage, *s.*: rage, *s.* 3245/6.
damage, *s.*: fage, *s.* 2052/1, 2822/1.
damage, *s.*: mariage, *s.* 1686/5.
damage, *s.*: outrage, *s.* 1322/1.
damage, *s.*: passage, *s.* 1287/8.
damage, *s.*: rage, *s.* 4656/5.
damage, *s.*: surplusage, *s.* 3988/7.
damage, *s.*: viage, *s.* 2358/7.
herbygage, *s.*: rage, *s.* 1301/2.
heritage, *s.*: massage, *s.* 1824/3.
heritage, *s.*: rage, *s.* 1333/4.
heritage, *s.*: sage, *adj.* 3706/5.
language, *s.*: pilgrimage, *s.* 47/8.
lynage, *s.*: rage, *s.* 2524/3.
lynage, *s.*: viage, *s.* 556/5.
mariage, *s.*: passage, *s.* 1676/5.
mariage, *s.*: rage, *s.* 1230/29.
mariage, *s.*: sage, *adj.* 768/7, 839/40.
massage, *s.*: rage, *s.* 2018/17, 2373/4.

passage, *s.*: rage, *s.* 617/18, 2198/7, 3437/8.
passage, *s.*: rage, *adj.* 1167/8.
phage, *s.*: langage, *s.* 453/4.
pilgrymage, *s.*: rage, *s.* 3419/20.
pilgrimage, *s.*: stage, *s.* 20/19.
pylgrymage, *s.*: visage, *s.* 4439/40.
rage, *s.*: sauage, *adj.* 3593/4, 3834/3.
rage, *adj.*: viage, *s.* 431/2.

-ages.
vilages, *s. plur.*: pillages, *s. plur.* 3589/90.
outrages, *s. plur.*: wages, *s. plur.* 4039/40.

-aid.
affrayd, *pp.*: dismayd, *pp.* 2350/49.
apayd, *pp.*: said, *pp.* 2127/8.
apayd, *pp.*: sayd, *pp.* 1636/5, 3697/8.
laide, *pp.*: saide, *pp.* 2112/11.

-aide.
abrayde, *inf.*: saide, *pret.* 479/80.
apeyde, *pp. plur.*: leyde, *pp. plur.* 4498/7.

-ail.
avail, *s.*: counsail, *s.* 3707/8.

-aile.
apparaylle, *s.*: mervaille, *inf.* 3612/11.
assaylle, *inf.*: bataylle, *s.* 3919/20.
assaylle, *inf.*: gouernaylle, *s.* 3882/1.
assaylle, *pres. plur.*: maylle, *s.* 4309/10.
assaylle, *pres. plur.*: raylle, *inf.* 2201/2.
availe, *inf.*: batayle, *s.* 2077/8.
availle, *inf.*: dyvynaylle, *s.* 4169/70.
avaylle, *inf.*: entaille, *s.* 244/3.
availle, *inf.*: faille, *pres. conj.* 3345/6.
availe, *inf.*: gouernaile, *s.* 1111/12.
avaylle, *inf.*: gouernaylle, *s.* 2001/2, 4382/1.
availle, *inf.*: maylle, *s.* 4075/6.
availle, *inf.*: (for no) travaylle, *s.* 3294/3.
bataylle, *s.*: faille, *inf.* 3659/60.
bestaylle, *s.*: vitaille, *s.* 3592/1.
dyvynaile, *s.*: fayle, *inf.* 630/29.
faille, *inf.*: rehersaille, *s.* 3153/4.
faylle, *pres. conj.*: vitaylle, *s.* 2678/7.
maile, *s.*: mervaile, *s.* 1365/6.
porayle, *s.*: sowpowayle, *s.* 268/7.

-ailed.
apparayled, *pp.*: yrayled, *pp.* 2385/6.
batailled, *pp.*: apparaylled, *pp.* 4145/6.

-ailles.
maylles, *s. plur.*: aventaylles, *s. plur.* 4327/8.

-ain.
agayn, *adv.*: slayn, *pp. plur.* 4564/3.
sayn, *pres. plur.*: slayn, *pp. sing.* 4545/6.

-air.
ayr, *s.* (air): fayr, *adj.* 2297/8, 3027/8.
eir, *s.* (air): feir, *adj.* 1056/5.
eyre, *s.* (air): repeyr, *s.* 2307/8.
dispeir, *s.*: heyre, *s.* (heir) 516/15, 1593/4.
fair, *adj.*: hair, *s.* (heir) 917/18, 2626/5, 3365/6.
fair, *adj.*: hayr, *s.* (heir) 461/2.
faire, *adj. plur.*: repaire, *s.* 3749/50.
hair, *s.* (heir): repair, *s.* 1126/5.

-aire.
appaire, *inf.*: contrayre, *adj.* 1034/3.
contrayre, *adj.*: debonayre, *adj.* 1960/59, 3178/7.
contrayre, *adj.*: faire, *adv.* 1340/39.
debonayr, *adj.*: fair, *adv.* 1025/6.
debonayre, *adj.*: fayre, *adv.* 248/7.
debonayre, *adj.*: (the) faire, *adj.* 3200/199.
dispeire, *inf.*: repeyre, *inf.* 4085/6.
fayre, *adv.*: repayre, *inf.* 3917/18.
repaire, *inf.*: staire, *s.* 1496/5.

-ăk.
a-bak, *adv.*: wrak, *s.* 2216/15.
bak, *s.*: wrak, *s.* 4307/8.
horsbak, *s.*: brak, *pret.* 1351/2.
brak, *pret.*: spak, *pret.* 1963/4.
lak, *s.*: spak, *pret.* 2482/1.

-āke.
awake, *inf.*: shake, *inf.* 4698/7.
blake, *adj. plur.*: make, *inf.* 857/8.
blake, *adj. plur.*: make, *pres. plur.* 4417/18.
blake, *adj. plur.*: take, *pp.* 3548/7.
brake, *s.*: sake, *s.* 4224/3.
forsake, *inf.*: vndirtake, *pp.* 4120/19.
mak(e), *inf.*: sak(e), *s.* 1692/1, 2569/70, 3267/8, 3677/8, 3724/3.
make, *inf.*: stake, *s.* 3688/7.
make, *inf.*: take, *pp.* 971/2, 2588/7.
make, *inf.*: ytake, *pp.* 3846/5.
make, *inf.*: i-take, *pp.* 3555/6, 4015/16.
make, *inf.*: take, *inf.* 1809/10, 1905/6, 2723/4.
sake, *s.*: take, *pres. plur.* 1491/2.
sake, *s.*: take, *pp.* 2871/2, 3207/8.
sake, *s.*: vndertake, *inf.* 1847/8.

shake, *inf.*: take, *pp.* 4587/8.
take, *pp.*: shape, *pp.* 1247/8.
-aketh.
parbraketh, *pres. sing.*: vndertaketh, *pres. sing.* 2951/2.
-al.
al, *adj.*: historial, *adj.* 49/50.
al, *adj.*: royal, *adj.* 316/15.
al, *adj.*: smal, *adj.* 2278/7.
al, *adj.*: special, *adj.* 3770/69.
alle, *adj. sing.*: special, *adj.* 1094/3.
bal, *s.*: metal, *s.* 597/8.
celestial, *adj.*: especial, *adj.* 1470/69.
especial, *adj.*: royal, *adj.* 2823/4.
fal, *s.*: shal, *pres. plur.* 1132/1.
funeral, *adj.*: royal, *adj. plur.* 594/3.
fynal, *adj.*: special, *adj.* 395/6.
lyberal, *adj.*: royal, *adj.* 1559/60.
marcyal, *adj.*: royal, *adj.* 1121/2.
marcyal, *adj.*: wal, *s.* 2273/4.
mortal, *adj.*: orygynal, *adj.* 2566/5.
principal, *adj.*: wal, *s.* 1244/3.
royal, *adj.*: wal, *s.* 4342/1.
-alle.
alle, *adj. plur.*: apalle, *pres. conj.* 4160/59.
all(e), *adj. plur.*: befall(e), *pp.* 2472/1, 2487/8.
all(e), *adj.* plur.: call(e), *inf.* 67/8, 1360/59, 2011/12.
alle, *adj. plur.*: calle, *pres. plur.* 3198/7.
alle, *adj. plur.*: falle, *inf.* 518/7.
all, *adj. plur.*: falle, *pres. plur.* 2181/2.
alle, *adj. plur.*: falle, *pres. conj.* 3725/6.
alle, *adj. plur.*: falle, *pp.* 773/4, 937/8, 2797/8, 3459/60, 4406/5.
alle, *adj. plur.*: shalle, *s.* 4297/8.
befalle, *pres. conj.*: calle, *inf.* 2133/4.
calle, *inf.*: falle, *pp.* 4066/5.
calle, *inf.*: halle, *s.* 456/5.
falle, *inf.*: (in his) stalle, *s.* 4185/6.
-āle.
avale, *inf.*: pale, *adj.* 8/7.
male, *s.* (bag): sale, *s.* 76/5.
pale, *adj.*: smale, *adj. plur.* 2332/1.
pale, *adj.*: tale, *s.* 496/5, 1956/5, 2439/40, 4423/4.
smale, *adj. plur.*: tale, *s.* 429/30.
tale, *s.*: vale, *s.* 1046/5, 2910/09, 4524/3.
-alled.
called, *pp.*: stalled, *pp.* 3541/2.
i-callyd, *pp.*: ystallyd, *pp.* 4044/3.
ycalled, *pp.* : walled, *pp.* 561/2.

-allys.
ballys, *s. plur.*: wallys, *s. plur.* 4312/11.
mallys, *s. plur.*: wallys, *s. plur.* 4543/4.
-alys.
valys, *s. plur.*: talys, *s. plur.* 17/18.
-ăm.
cam, *pret. sing.*: ram, *s.* 2/1, 3191/2.
-āme.
blame, *s.*: fame, *s.* 4132/1.
blame, *s.*: shame, *s.* 1419/20, 4155/6.
fame, *s.*: name, *s.* 2606/5, 2764/3, 2800/799.
game, *s.*: lame, *adj.* 4336/5.
game, *s.*: name, *s.* 159/60.
lame, *adj.*: name, *s.* 2079/80.
name, *s.*: shame, *s.* 96/5, 2498/7, 4122/1.
same, *adj.*: tame, *adj.* 3848/7.
-an.
can, *pres.*: man, *s.* 63/4, 1944/3, 3171/2, 3959/60, 4232/1.
can (kan), *pres. plur.*: man, *s.* 2389/90, 2638/7, 3554/3.
can, *pres. sing.*: ran, *pret. sing.* 1673/4, 3261/2.
gan, *pret.*: levyathan, *n. pr.* 4664/3.
gan, *pret.*: man, *s.* 1568/7.
gan, *pret.*: ran, *pret.* 4613/4.
began, *pret.*: man, *s.* 296/5, 2657/8.
began, *pret.*: ran, *pret.* 329/30, 2568/7.
geseran, *s.*: ran, *pret.* 4329/30.
man, *s.*: ran, *pret.* 3865/6.
ran, *pret. plur.*: Theban, *s.* 4302/1.
-and.
land, *s.*: hand, *s.* 1689/90, 3050/49.
-ante.
wante, *pres. sing.* 1.: Thoante, *n. pr.* 3195/6.
-āpe.
eskape, *inf.*: gape, *pres. plur.* 2226/5.
eskape, *inf.*: iape, *s.* 166/5, 633/4.
eskape, *inf.*: shape, *pp.* 1234/3, 3233/4.
-appe.
lappe, *s.* : wrappe, *inf.* 3089/90.
-ar.
char, *s.*: war, *adj.* 2868/7, 4022/1, 4649/50.
dar, *pres. sing.*: war, *adj. plur.* 1773/4.
-āre.
bare, *adj. sing.*: care, *s.* 4561/2.

bare, *adj. plur.*: declare, *inf.* 631/2, 4438/7.
bare, *adj. sing.*: declare, *inf.* 873/4.
care, *s.*: declare, *inf.* 3065/6.
declare, *inf.*: fare, *s.* 941/2, 2469/70, 4403/4.
declare, *inf.*: spare, *inf.* 508/7, 2372/1.
squar, *adj.*: war, *adj. plur.* 2211/12.

-arge.
Arge, *n. pr.*: charge, *inf.* 1683/4, 1971/2, 2424/3.
Arge, *n. pr.*: charge, *s.* 1282/1, 2632/1, 4601/2.
Arge, *n. pr.*: large, *adj.* 1190/89, 2414/13, 4626/5.
charge, *s.*: large, *adj.* 929/30, 2122/1, 2698/7, 3075/6.

-arpe.
sharpe, *adj. plur.*: harpe, *s.* 205/6, 274/3.

-arte.
coarte, *inf.*: Marte, *n. pr.* 3666/5.
departe, *pres. plur.*: Marte, *n. pr.* 4600/599.
departe, *inf.*: iuparte, *inf.* 1382/1, 3085/6, 3967/8.

-artes.
quartes, *s. plur.*: caartes, *s. plur.* 375/6.

-arie, -arye.
carye, *pres. plur.*: tarye, *inf.* 2994/3.
contrarye, *adj.*: varye, *inf.* 3806/5.
tarye, *inf.*: varye, *inf.* 1140/39, 1700/699.

-as.
allas, *interj.*: cas, *s.* 3229/30.
Bochas, *n. pr.*: was, *pret.* 1541/2.
caas, *s.*: supersedyas, *s.* 3431/2.
cas, *s.*: fallas, *s.* 1831/2.
cas, *s.*: pas, *s.* 3280/79.
chas, *s.*: pas, *s.* 3925/6.
cas, *s.*: was, *pret.* 3160/59, 4619/20.
gras, *s.*: was, *pret.* 2288/7.

-aste.
faste, *s.*: paste, *pp. plur.* 155/6.
faste, *adv.*: laste, *inf.* 4351/2.

-āt.
amaat, *adj.*: dysconsolat, *adj.* 741/2.
ambassyat, *s.*: estat, *s.* 3728/7.
astat, *s.*: infortunat, *adj.* 1029/30.
debat, *s.*: desolat, *adj. plur.* 4628/7, 4691/2.
debat, *s.*: ellat, *adj.* 1350/49, 3529/30.
debat, *s.*: estat, *s.* 732/1, 1398/7, 1431/2, 1928/7, 4669/70.
debat, *s.*: infortunat, *adj. plur.* 385/6.
disconsolat, *adj. plur.*: estat, *s.* 4430/29.
enbassyat, *s.*: infortunat, *adj.* 1849/50.
estat, *s.*: fortunat, *adj.* 271/2, 2805/6.
estat, *s.*: infortunat, *adj.* 3057/8.
indurat, *adj.*: obstynat, *adj.* 4007/8.

-āte.
date, *s.*: late, *adv.* 947/8.
debat, *inf.*: gate, *s.* 577/8.
debate, *inf.*: hate, *s.* 475/6, 1064/3.
faate, *s.*: late, *adv.* 1235/6.
gate, *s.*: hate, *s.* 3910/09, 4211/12.
gate, *s.*: late, *adj.*, *adv.* 981/2, 1250/49, 2772/1, 3572/1.
late, *adv.*: Lydgate, *n. pr.* 91/2.

-ātis.
estates, *s. plur.*: platis, *s. plur.* 1435/6, 1863/4.
gatys, *s. plur.*: platys, *s. plur.* 4243/4.

-aught.
draught, *s.*: faught, *pret.* 4248/7.
draught, *s.*: rauht, *pp.* 157/8.

-aunce.
affiaunce, *s.*: chaunce, *s.* 4083/4.
affiaunce, *s.*: gouernaunce, *s.* 1703/4.
affiaunce, *s.*: meschaunce, *s.* 4056/5.
affiaunce, *s.*: variaunce, *s.* 893/4.
aliaunce, *s.*: balaunce, *s.* 1516/5.
alliaunce, *s.*: distaunce, *s.* 1071/2.
aliaunce, *s.*: purueaunce, *s.* 844/3.
allyaunce, *s.*: variance, *s.* 1590/89.
assuraunce, *s.*: lygeaunce, *s.* 2645/6.
attendaunce, *s.*: plesaunce, *s.* 1620/19.
avaunce, *inf.*: contenaunce, *s.* 278/7.
balaunce, *s.*: chaunce, *s.* 3682/1.
chaunce, *s.*: ignoraunce, *s.* 810/9.
chaunce, *s.*: remembraunce, *s.* 2512/11.
chevysaunce, *s.*: perturbaunce, *s.* 4106/5.
circumstaunce, *s.*: remembraunce, *s.* 37/8.
contenance, *s.*: gouernance, *s.* 1389/90.
contenaunce, *s.*: obseruaunce, *s.* 1473/4.
contena(u)nce, *s.*: remembra(u)nce, *s.* 497/8, 3979/80.
daliaunce, *s.*: remembraunce, *s.* 1478/7.

diffiaunce, *s.*: remembraunce, *s.* 2130/29.
gouernaunce, *s.*: plesaunce, *s.* 148/7.
gouernaunce, *s.*: purueaunce, *s.* 2959/60.
greuaunce, *s.*: plesaunce, *s.* 3857/8.
greuaunce, *s.*: purvyance, *s.* 2839/40.
greuaunce, *s.*: substaunce, *s.* 3270/69.
habundaunce, *s.*: plesaunce, *s.* 2676/5.
habundance, *s.*: suffisaunce, *s.* 1969/70.
launce, *s.*: remembraunce, *s.* 1487/8.
lygaunce, *s.*: variaunce, *s.* 2090/89.
meschaunce, *s.*: outraunce, *s.* 2217/8.
meschaunce, *s.*: traunce, *s.* 3387/8.
meschaunce, *s.*: variance, *s.* 3622/1.
meschaunce, *s.*: vengeaunce, *s.* 791/2.
obseruaunce, *s.*: remembraunce, *s.* 4582/1.
ordynaunce, *s.*: purveaunce, *s.* 1571/2, 2741/2.
purvyance, *s.*: remembrance, *s.* 3999/4000.
purvyaunce, *s.*: vengeaunce, *s.* 3462/1.
substaunce, *s.*: variance, *s.* 53/4.

-aunces.
circumstances, *s. plur.*: daunces *s. plur.* 1663/4.
circumstancys, *s. plur.*: gouernancys, *s. plur.* 1579/80.
circumstaunces, *s. plur.*: obseruaunces, *s. plur.* 1555/6.

-aunt.
graunte, *s.*: ignoraunte, *adj. sing.* 639/40.

-ave.
caue, *s.*: saue, *inf.* 1182/1, 4073/4.
graue, *pp.*: haue, *inf.* 1061/2, 1599/600.
haue, *inf.*: saue, *inf.* 3105/6.
haue, *pres. sing.* 1.: saue, *inf.* 3338/7.

-aves.
caues, *s. plur.*: gravis, *s. plur.* 3483/4.

-awe.
dawe, *inf.*: lawe, *s.* 129/30.
drawe, *inf.*: felawe, *s.* 1162/1.
drawe, *inf.*: slawe, *pp.* 750/49, 2157/8.
drawe, *inf.*: wawe, *s.* 4257/8.
withdrawe, *inf.*: mawe, *s.* 133/4.
withdrawe, *inf.*: slawe, *pp.* 586/5,
withdrawe, *pp.*: slawe, *pp.* 397/8, 2825/6, 3180/79.
lawe, *s.*: slawe, *pp.* 786/5.

-awes.
dawes, *s. plur.*: lawes, *s. plur.* 543/4.

-ay, -aye.
affray, *s.*: day, *s.* 1232/1, 3372/1.
affray, *s.*: delay, *s.* 963/4, 4114/13.
affray, *s.*: lay, *pret.* 1296/5.
aray, *s.*: may, *pres. plur.* 2594/3.
array, *s.*: way, *s.* 3312/11.
away, *adv.*: day, *s.* 191/2, 1489/90.
day, *s.*: lay, *pret. plur.* 3132/1.
day, *s.*: may, *pres.* 434/3, 605/6, 2003/4, 4251/2.
day, *s.*: nay, *adv.* 128/7, 778/7, 1597/8.
day, *s.*: pay, *s.* 2683/4.
day, *s.*: way, *s.* 1153/4, 2151/2, 2415/16.
play, *s.*: way, *s.* 161/2.
forraye, *inf.*: laye, *pret. plur.* 3588/7.

-ayed.
affrayed, *pp.*: dismayed, *pp.* 3044/3.
delayed, *pp.*: outrayed, *pp.* 2070/69.

-ayes.
allayes, *s. plur.*: assayes, *s. plur.* 4461/2.
daies, *s. plur.*: delayes, *s. plur.* 1876/5, 4230/29, 4615/16.

-ẹ̄.
aduersitè, *s.*: degrè, *s.* 1746/5, 2544/3.
aduersitè, *s.*: iournè, *s.* 2885/6.
adversitè, *s.*: me, *pron.* 2365/6.
adversitè, *s.*: necessitè, *s.* 1318/17.
aduersitè, *s.*: solempnytè, *s.* 847/8.
aduersitè, *s.*: voluntè, *s.* 3658/7.
Antigonè, *n. pr.*: bewtè, *s.* 3747/8.
Antigonè, *n. pr.*: Prothonolopè, *n. pr.* 3949/50.
Antygone, *n. pr.*: se, *inf.* 882/1, 3850/49, 4369/70.
antiquytè, *s.*: auctoritè, *s.* 2803/4.
antiquytè, *s.*: be, *pres. conj.* 4128/7.
antiquitè, *s.*: Iosuè, *n. pr.* 187/8.
antiquitè, *s.*: meynè, *s.* 4024/3.
auctoritè, *s.*: citè, *s.* 3335/6.
be, *inf.*: citè, *s.* 2528/7, 3945/6.
be, *pres.*: contrè, *s.* 88/7.
be, *inf.*: degrè, *s.* 3328/7.
be, *inf.*: destanyè, *s.* 922/1.
be, *inf.*: flee, *inf.* 683/4.
be, *inf.*: Ysiphilè, *n. pr.* 3304/3.
be, *inf.*: iournè, *s.* 4464/3.
be, *inf.*: libertè, *s.* 3176/5.
be, *inf.*: natiuitè, *s.* 218/17.
be, *inf.*: pytè, *s.* 406/5, 3254/3.

be, *inf.*: se, *inf.* 1362/1, 4680/79.
be, *inf.*: see, *s.* (see) 1147/8, 2132/1.
be, *inf.*: the, *inf.* 1023/4.
be, *inf.*: thre(e), *numer.* 349/50, 672/1, 712/11, 3351/2.
be, *inf.*: tretè, *s.* 3732/1.
beautè, *s.*: pytè, *s.* 421/2.
Ble, *n. pr.*: se, *inf.* 1047/8.
bountè, *s.*: Ysiphylè, *n. pr.* 3206/5.
Calyope, *n. pr.*: thre, *numer.* 831/2.
charitè, *s.*: degrè, *s.* 4671/2.
cytè, *s.*: contrè, *s.* 238/7, 564/3, 950/49, 1410/09, 4401/2.
citè, *s.*: crueltè, *s.* 3908/7, 4210/09, 4319/20.
cytè, *s.*: degrè, *s.* 2674/3, 4416/15.
citè, *s.*: dignytè, *s.* 1128/7.
citè, *s.*: iournè, *s.* 2636/5.
cytè, *s.*: me, *pron.* 4609/10.
cytè, *s.*: Parthanolopè, *n. pr.* 4241/2.
citè, *s.*: pouertè, *s.* 1097/8.
cytè, *s.*: ryaltè, *s.* 1947/8.
citè, *s.*: se, *inf.* 1878/7, 4632/1.
citè, *s.* souereyntè, *s.* 3718/17.
commoditè, *s.*: degrè, *s.* 3126/5.
contrè, *s.*: Deyphylee, *n. pr.* 4410/09.
contrè, *s.*: enmytè, *s.* 4094/3.
contrè, *s.*: he, *pron.* 966/5.
contrè, *s.*: Ysyphylee, *n. pr.* 3482/1.
contrè (cuntrè), *s.*: se(e), *inf.* 2619/20, 3021/2, 4450/49.
contrè, *s.*: tre, *s.* 931/2.
contrarionstè, *s.*: crueltè, *s.* 2897/8.
crueltè, *s.*: thre, *numer.* 2206/5.
degrè, *s.*: humanytè, *s.* 3743/4.
degrè, *s.*: meynè, *s.* 2589/90.
degrè, *s.*: moralitè, *s.* 21/2.
degrè, *s.*: natyvytè, *s.* 371/2.
degrè, *s.*: Protonolope, *n. pr.* 2597/8.
degrè, *s.*: se(e), *s.* (see) 1239/40, 4190/89.
degrè, *s.*: three, *numer.* 3055/6.
Deyphylè, *n. pr.*: iournè, *s.* 1866/5.
Deyphylee, *n. pr.*: se, *inf.* 1648/7, 4485/6.
diuersytè, *s.*: se, *inf.* 2942/1.
fre, *adj.*: lybertè, *s.* 2700/699, 3507/8.
iniquytè, *s.*: prosperitè, *s.* 887/8.
Isyphilee, *n. pr.*: Parthonolopè, *n. pr.* 3502/1.
Ysyphilee, *n. pr.*: pitè, *s.* 3453/4.
Isyphilè, *n. pr.*: se, *inf.* 3156/5, 3194/3.
kne, *s.*: se, *inf.* 505/6, 2235/6.
me, *pron.*: suretè, *s.* 1999/2000.
me, *pron.*: suertè, *s.* 3442/1.
mutabilitè, *s.*: vnstabiletè, *s.* 1749/50.
natiuytè, *s.*: se, *inf.* 660/59.
Parthonolopè, *n. pr.*: se, *inf.* 3487/8.
pytè, *s.*: see, *inf.* 450/49, 3059/60.
prolixitè, *s.*: superfluytè, *s.* 1907/8.
prosperitè, *s.*: se, *inf.* 1772/1.
pryvetè, *s.*: secrè, *adj.* 2808/7.
ryaltè, *s.*: solempnytè, *s.* 1661/2.
se, *inf.*: solempnytè, *s.* 4622/1.
see, *inf.*: Thesiphonee, *n. pr.* 859/60.
se, *inf.*: tre, *s.* 426/5, 444/3.
she, *pron.*: tre, *s.* 3030/29.
souereyntè, *s.*: Tholomee, *n. pr.* 2974/3.
thre, *numer.*: vnytè, *s.* 4704/3.

-ē: O.E. ǣ[1].
contrè, *s.*: see, *s.* (sea) 611/12, 1164/3, 3181/2.
me, *pron.*: see, *s.* (sea) 3536/5.

-ēche.
leche, *s.* (leech): seche, *inf.* 2450/49.
speche, *s.*: teche, *inf.* 226/5, 1996/5.
spech, *s.*: tech, *inf.* 3411/12, 3816/15.

-ĕd.
sped, *pp.*: wed, *s.* 2231/2.

-edde.
fledde, *pret. plur.*: (to) wedde, *s.* 4205/6.

-ēd, -ēde.
-ẹ̄: ẹ̄.
blede, *inf.*: possede, *pres.* 2783/4.
hede, *s.*: nede, *s.* 265/6, 2419/20, 2682/1, 2979/80.
hede, *s.* (heed): spede, *s.* 1835/6.
hede, *s.*: spede, *inf.* 2245/6.
hede, *s.* (heed): succede, *inf.* 463/4.
possede, *inf.*: succede, *inf.* 1066/5.
spede, *inf.*: stede, *s.* (steed) 1347/8, 2120/19.
hed, *s.* (heed): renomed, *pp.* 4129/30 (Fr. -é > M.E. -ed).

O.E. ǣ[2]: ǣ[2].
drede, *s.*: rede, *s.* 2743/4.
mede, *s.* (meadow): rede, *pres.* (read) 3564/3.

O.E. ǣ[2]: O.E. ē(o), Fr. ē.
dede, *s.*: mede, *s.* (meed) 2071/2.
dede, *s.*: nede, *s.* 3048/7, 3653/4.
dede, *s.*: possede, *inf.* 3772/1.
dede, *s.*: procede, *v.* 1060/59, 1639/40, 3810/09.
dede, *s.*: spede, *inf.* 418/17, 3646/5.
drede, *s.*: mede, *s.* (meed) 3260/59.

drede, *s.*: nede, *s.* 1027/8, 1980/79, 3463/4.
mede, *s.* (meadow): mede, *s.* (meed) 3886/5.
rede, *s.*: hede, *s.* (heed) 2932/1.
rede, *pres.*: nede, *s.* 2767/8.
reed, *s.*: red, *s.* (reed) 1792/1.
rede, *pres.* (read): blede, *inf.* 452/1.
rede, *v.*: hede, *s.* (heed) 1019/20.
rede, *v.*: procede, *inf.* 327/8, 1844/3.
rede, *pres.*: stede, *s.* (steed) 1151/2, 1303/4.
rede, *pres.*: succede, *inf.* 335/6, 3034/3.
wede, *s.* (weeds): glede, *s.* 1668/7.
wede, *s.*: nede, *s.* 864/3.
wede, *s.*: stede, *s.* (steed) 1869/70.

O.E. ǣ²: O.E. ǣ¹.
dede, *s.*: broþerhede, *s.* 1451/2.
drede, *s.*: wommanhede, *s.* 2340/39, 2841/2, 3183/4.
rede, *inf.*: kynrede, *s.* 3157/8.

O.E. ǣ²: O.E. ēa.
dred(e), *s.*: ded(e), *adj. sing.* 1009/10, 1099/1100, 1709/10, 2325/6, 3053/4, 3511/12.
drede, *s.*: rede, *adj. plur.* 3094/3.
red(e), *s.*: ded(e), *adj.* 685/6, 3235/6, 4227/8.
rede, *s.*: hede, *s.* (head) 953/4.
sede, *s.* (seed): rede, *adj.* 118/17.

O.E. ǣ¹: ǣ¹.
brede, *s.* (breadth): sprede, *inf.* 4699/700.
brede, *s.*: wommanhede, *s.* 2387/8.
brotherhede, *s.*: hatrede, *s.* 1989/90.
hatrede, *s.*: kynrede, *s.* 855/6.
kynrede, *s.*: lede, *inf.* 1429/30.

O.E. ǣ¹: O.E. ēa.
wommanhede, *s.*: dede, *adj. plur.* 4435/6.

O.E. ǣ¹: O.E. ē, O.Fr. ē.
hatrede, *s.*: succede, *inf.* 1917/18.
kynrede, *s.*: hede, *s.* (heed) 490/89.
kynrede, *s.*: spede, *inf.* 984/3.
lede, *inf.*: nede, *s.* 2705/6.
manlihede, *s.*: stede, *s.* (steed) 3308/7.
sprede, *inf.*: hede, *s.* (heed) 2312/11.
wommanhede, *s.*: hede, *s.* (heed) 3287/8.

O.E. ēa: O.E. ēa.
ded, *adj.*: hed, *s.* (head) 743/4, 4235/6, 4299/300.
dede, *adj.*: hede, *s.* (head) 2142/1.
dede, *adj.*: rede, *adj.* 2204/3, 3364/3.
hed, *s.* (head): red, *adj.* 10/9, 3837/8.
led, *s.*: red, *adj.* 2289/90.

O.E. ēa: O.E. ē.
dede, *adj.*: hede, *s.* (heed) 1914/13.
ded, *adj.*: sped, *s.* 4162/1.
hed(e), *s.* (head): hed(e), *s.* (heed) 801/2, 2165/6, 2285/6, 4378/7.

-edis.
weedys, *s. plur.* (clothes): stedys, *s. plur.* (steeds) 4441/2.

-ēf, -ief.
chief, *adj.*: prief, *s.* 2327/8.
repreef, *s.*: mescheef, *s.* 2689/90.

-ein.
ageyn, *adv.*: disdeyn, *s.* 1092/1.
ageyn, *adv.*: beseyn, *pp.* 1557/8.
ageyn, *adv.*: certeyn, *adj.* 935/6, 3544/3.
ageyn, *adv.*: pleyn, *adj.* 674/3, 1626/5, (pleyn, *s.*) 4067/8.
ageyn, *adv.*: seyn, *inf.* 604/3, 1954/3, 2042/1.
ageyn, *adv.*: seyn, *pp.* 2335/6.
ageyn, *adv.*: seyn, *pres. plur.* 3972/1.
ageyn, *adv.*: veyn, *adj.* 1799/1800, 3721/2.
ageyn, *adv.*: withseyn, *inf.* 717/8.
bareyn, *adj.*: certeyn, *adv.* 342/1.
beseyn, *pp.*: reyn, *s.* 1285/6.
certeyn, *adj.*: geyn, *s.* 2831/2.
certeyn, *adj.*: mounteyn, *s.* 980/79.
certeyn, *adv.*: seyne, *pp.* 4031/2.
certeyn, *adv.*: seyn, *inf.* 4554/3.
desdayne, *s.*: slayne, *pp. sing.* 3883/4.
disdeyn, *s.*: soleyn, *adj.* 250/49.
disdeyn̄, *s.*: with-seyn, *inf.* 473/4.
greyn, *s.*: seyn, *inf.* 56/5.
pleyn, *s.*: seyn, *pp.* 2596/5, 3560/59.
pleyn, *adv.*: seyn, *pp.* 4148/7.

-eine.
atteyn, *inf.*: compleyn, *inf.* 3331/2.
atteyn, *inf.*: feyne, *inf.* 1582/1.
atteyne, *inf.*: peyne, *s.* 2264/3.
atteyn(e), *inf.*: tweyn(e), *numer.* 714/13, 4173/4.
Breteyne, *n. pr.*: feyne, *inf.* 40/39.
cheyne, *s.*: tweyne, *numer.* 1744/3.
compleyn, *inf.*: restreyn, *inf.* 2686/5.
compleyn(e), *inf.*: tweyn(e), *numer.* 3225/6, 3671/2, 4367/8, 4489/90, 4633/4.
constreyne, *inf.*: pleyn̄, *inf.* 962/1.
constreyne, *inf.*: reyne, *s.* (rein) 2695/6.
constreyn, *inf.*: tweyn, *numer.* 1518/17.
dareyn, *inf.*: tweyn, *numer.* 656/5.
feyne, *inf.*: peyne, *s.* 514/13.
feyn(e), *inf.*: tweyn(e), *numer.* 667/8, 1415/16, 1720/19, 4345/6, 4456/5.

Ymeyne, *n. pr.*: peyne, *s.* 3952/1.
Ymeyne, *n. pr.*: tweyne, *numer.* 3736/5.
ordeyne, *inf.*: tweyn, *numer.* 3938/7.
peyn(e), *s.*: tweyn(e), *numer.* 1220/19, 1425/6, 1486/5, 3129/30, 4549/50.
peyne, *s.*: veyne, *s.* 3377/8.
pleyn, *adj. plur.*: tweyn, *numer.* 877/8.
reffreyn, *inf.*: reyne, *s.* (rein) 2948/7.
refreyne, *inf.*: tweyne, *numer.* 1997/8.
reyn, *inf.*: restreyn, *inf.* 3400/399.
restreyne, *inf.*: tweyne, *numer.* 3683/4.

-eine: -ein.
Ymeyne, *n. pr.*: souereyn, *adj.* 883/4.
ordeyne, *inf.*: sodeyne, *adj. sing.* 4027/8.

-eined.
atteyned, *pp.*: be-reyned, *pp.* 1238/7.
atteyned, *pp.*: constreyned, *pp.* 560/59.
atteyned, *pp.*: yfeyned, *pp.* 1678/7.
bereynyd, *pp.*: disteyned, *pp.* 3264/3.
feyned, *pp.*: refreyned, *pp.* 1958/7.
ordeyned, *pp.*: restreyned, *pp.* 4658/7.

-eins.
foreyns, *s. plur.*: citezeyns, *s. plur.* 1079/80.
mounteyns, *s. plur.*: playns, *s. plur.* 1165/6, 2428/7.

-eines, -eynys.
pleynys, *s. plur.*: reynys, *s. plur.* (rains) 3003/4.

-eint.
atteynt, *pp. plur.*: feynt, *adj. sing.* 2253/4.
depeynt, *pp.*: meynt, *pp.* 2305/6.
depeynt, *pp.*: ymeynt, *pp.* 16/15.

-eired.
apeyryd, *pp.*: disespeyryd, *pp.* 4097/8.
dispeyred, *pret.*: repeyred, *pret.* 3017/18.
disespeyred, *pp.*: repeyred, *pp.* 3212/11.

-eised.
preised, *pp.*: reised, *pp.* 193/4.

-eit.
disceyte, *s.*: a-weyte, *s.* 1763/4.

-eive.
conceyve, *pres. sing.*: deceyue, *inf.* 691/2.

-eived.
conceyued, *pp.*: perceyued, *pp.* 357/8.
conceyued, *pp.*: receyued, *pp.* 2649/50.

-ĕk (-ekke).
bekke, *s.*: effecte, *s.* 169/70.
nekke, *s.*: rekke, *pres. conj.* 2485/6.

-ēk.
Grek, *n. pr.*: ek, *adv.* 3149/50, 4316/15.

-eke.
speke, *inf.*: breke, *inf.* 4525/6.

-ēl.
(euery) del, *s.*: (neuere a) del, *s.* 2377/8.
(euery) del(l), *s.*: wel, *adv.* 1421/2, 4531/2.
(neuer a) del, *s.*: whel, *s.* 1756/5.
(neuer a) del, *s.*: wel, *adv.* 2014/13.
stele (stiel), *s.*: wel, *adv.* 1450/49, 1484/3.
stiel, *s.*: wiel, *adv.* 2145/6.
stele, *s.*: wheel, *s.* 1150/49.
wel, *adv.*: whel, *s.* 1133/4.

-eld.
feld, *s.*: byheld, *pret.* 3873/4, 4262/1, 4468/7.
fe(e)ld, *s.*: she(e)ld, *s.* 2066/5, 2660/59, 3051/2, 4278/7, 4361/2.
byheld(e), *pret. sing.*: sheld(e), *s.* 1305/6, 2283/4.

-ēldis.
sheldys, *s. plur.*: feeldys, *s. plur.* 1531/2.

-ę̄lid.
asselyd, *pp.* (sealed): repelyd, *pp.* 3775/6.

-elle.
belle, *s.*: telle, *inf.* 85/6.
Capelle, *n. pr.*: telle, *inf.* 837/8.
compelle, *inf.*: telle, *inf.* 180/79, 1418/17.
dwelle, *inf.*: telle, *v.* 320/19, 532/1, 992/1, 2425/6, 2858/7, 3509/10, 4011/12, 4565/6.
dwelle, *inf.*: welle, *s.* 3097/8.
excelle, *inf.*: telle, *inf.* 570/69, 1561/2.
felle, *adj. plur.*: telle, *inf.* 3603/4, 4240/39, 4317/18.
(the) felle, *adj.*: welle, *s.* 4289/90.
helle, *s.* repelle, *inf.* 4034/3.
helle, *s.*: telle, *inf.* 854/3, 4060/59, 4163/4.
telle, *inf.*: welle, *s.* 3063/4.
telle, *pres. plur.*: welle, *s.* 3188/7.

-ēm, -ēme.
Ierusalem, *n. pr.*: rewme, *s.* 1741/2.
dyademe, *s.*: seme, *inf.* (to seem) 1805/6.
-ēmes.
bemes, *s .plur.*: reawmes, *s. plur.* 1767/8.
bemes, *s. plur.*: stremes, *s. plur.* 2299/300.
-ēn.
sen, *inf.*: merydyen, *s.* 4255/6.
-ēn, -ēne.
ben, *inf.*: quene, *s.* 765/6.
sen, *inf.*: quene, *s.* 4365/6.
-ę̄ne.
grene, *adj.*: kene, *adv.* 2222/1, 3494/3.
grene, *s.*: quene, *s.* 14/13.
grene, *adj.*: sene, *ger.* 3369/70.
grene, *s.*: shene, *adj.* 1052/1.
grene, *adj.*: shene, *adj.* 3026/5.
grene, *adj.*: sustene, *inf.* 661/2, 2258/7.
kene, *adj.*: shene, *adj.* 3220/19.
kene, *adj.*, *adv.*: sustene, *inf.* 4487/8, 4696/5.
kene, *adj. plur.*: tene, *s.* 3169/70.
quene, *s.*: (to) sene, *ger.* 4510/09.
quene, *s.*: tene, *s.* 3503/4.
quene, *s.*: wene, *s.* 1411/12.
sene, *pp.*: wene, *pres.* 2786/5.
sustene, *inf.*: tene, *s.* 478/7, 710/09, 2188/7.
sustene, *inf.*: wene, *s.* 1726/5.
O.E. ǣ[1]: ē.
clene, *adj.*: quene, *s.* 3628/7, 4712/11.
clene, *adv.*: sustene, *inf.* 1070/69.
vnclene, *adj.*: abstene, *inf.* 816/15.
vnclene, *adj.*: shene, *adj.* 538/7.
lene, *adj.*: grene, *s.* 74/3.
mene, *pres.*: grene, *adj.* 945/6, 2937/8.
O.E. ǣ[1]: ę̄.
clene, *adv.*: mene, *s.* 1346/5.
ę̄: ę̄.
grene, *adj.*: mene, *s.* (means) 3656/5.
tene, *s.*: mene, *s.* 638/7.
-ence.
absence, *s.*: violence, *s.* 3222/1.
apparence, *s.*: existence, *s.* 3843/4.
audience, *s.*: elloquence, *s.* 3812/11.
audience, *s.*: excellence, *s.* 1896/5.
audience, *s.*: offence, *s.* 3248/7.
audience, *s.*: presence, *s.* 4516/15.
audience, *s.*: prudence, *s.* 2968/7.
clemence, *s.*: reuerence, *s.* 4504/3.
conscience, *s.*: offence, *s.* 2853/4.
conscience, *s.*: reuerence, *s.* 1021/2.
credence, *s.*: resistence, *s.* 3704/3.
dyffence, *s.*: excellence, *s.* 2250/49.
diffence, *s.*: presence, *s.* 2833/4.
diffence, *s.*: prudence, *s.* 2200/199.
diffence, *s.*: resistence, *s.* 2748/7.
dyffence, *s.*: violence, *s.* 4233/4.
dylygence, *s.*: offence, *s.* 2363/4.
dyligence, *s.*: prudence, *s.* 1105/6.
diligence, *s.*: reverence, *s.* 3133/4.
eloquence, *s.*: excellence, *s.* 42/1.
eloquence, *s.*: influence, *s.* 215/16.
eloquence, *s.*: sapience, *s.* 842/1.
elloquence, *s.*: sentence, *s.* 2975/6.
elloquence, *s.*: violence, *s.* 287/8.
excellence, *s.*: presence, *s.* 255/6.
experience, *s.*: influence, *s.* 2815/16, 2940/39.
experience, *s.*: sentence, *s.* 793/4, 3636/5.
experience, *s.*: violence, *s.* 4689/90.
indygence, *s.*: offence, *s.* 2687/8.
influence, *s.*: reuerence, *s.* 348/7.
innocence, *s.*: offence, *s.* 811/12.
neclygence, *s.*: offence, *s.* 3237/8.
offence, *s.*: presence, *s.* 2019/20, 3513/14.
offence, *s.*: recompense, *s.* 3476/5.
pacience, *s.*: prudence, *s.* 3444/3.
pacience, *s.*: sentence, *s.* 198/7.
presence, *s.*: reuerence, *s.* 1396/5.
presence, *s.*: sapience, *s.* 2884/3.
presence, *s.*: sentence, *s.* 365/6.
-ende.
amende, *inf.*: condescende, *inf.* 3700/699.
amend, *inf.*: diffend, *inf.* 1607/8.
descende, *inf.*: wende, *pret.* (to ween) 644/3.
diffende, *inf.*: wende, *pret.* (to ween) 4080/79.
ende, *s.*: wende, *inf.* 3783/4.
ende, *s.*: wende, *pres. plur.* 4142/1, 4716/15.
-endyd.
conprehendid, *pp.*: condescendyd, *pp.* 1637/8.
comprehendyd, *pp.*: discendyd, *pp.* 549/50.
-ens.
physiciens, *s. plur.*: astronomyens, *s. plur.* 363/4.
-ent.
absent, *adj.*: entent, *s.* 846/5.
absent, *adj.*: parlement, *s.* 2095/6.
absent, *adj.*: serpent, *s.* 3272/1.
adiacent, *adj.*: assent, *s.* 4411/12.
adiacent, *adj.*: sent, *pp.* 3829/30.
amendement, *s.*: present, *adj.* 4714/13.
ascendent, *s.*: iugement, *s.* 370/69.
assent, *s.*: busshement, *s.* 2153/4.

assent, *s.*: entent, *s.* 2067/8.
assent, *s.*: parlement, *s.* 763/4.
assent, *s.*: present, *adj. plur.* 1114/13.
avisement, *s.*: evident, *adj. plur.* 957/8.
avisement, *s.*: expedient, *s.* 4111/12.
avisement, *s.*: iugement, *s.* 3661/2.
avisement, *s.*: prudent, *adj.* 3640/39.
avisement, *s.*: sacrament, *s.* 1137/8.
blent, *pp.*: entent, *s.* 1758/7.
Clement, *n. pr.*: Kent, *n. pr.* 83/4.
comaundement, *s.*: entent, *s.* 3339/40.
comaundemente, *s.*: iugemente, *s.* 928/7.
comaundement, *s.*: sent, *pp.* 408/7.
conuenyent, *adj.*: sent, *pp.* 2402/1.
discent, *s.*: entent, *s.* 333/4.
discent, *s.*: parlement, *s.* 4389/90.
enchauntement, *s.*: evidente, *adj.* 4100/099.
enchauntement, *s.*: serpent, *s.* 626/5.
entent, *s.*: expedient, *adj.* 2793/4.
entent, *s.*: present, *adj.* 825/6, 1715/16, 2083/4, 3148/7.
entent, *s.*: sent, *pp.* 1838/7, 2847/8, 3625/6.
excellent, *adj.*: sent, *pp.* 1649/50.
fraudulent, *adj.*: serpent, *s.* 689/90.
innocent, *adj.*: present, *adj.* 3670/69.
instrument, *s.*: prudent, *adj.* 222/1.
necligent, *adj.*: parlement, *s.* 2789/90.
parlement, *s.*: president, *s.* 2889/90.
parlement, *s.*: sent, *pp.* 2573/4.
potent, *s.*: spent, *pp.* 716/15.
present, *adj.*: sent, *pp.* 1455/6.
present, *adj.*: tornement, *s.* 565/6.
present, *adj.*: went, *pp.* 2521/2.
sent, *pp.*: sentement, *s.* 1904/3, 2468/7, 4400/399.
spent, *pp.*: tent, *s.* 4356/5.
tent, *s.*: went, *s.* 3740/39.

-ente.
assente, *inf.*: repente, *inf.* 1633/4.
assente, *pres. conj.*: brente, *pret.* 4271/2.
assente, *inf.*: wente, *pret.* 3162/1.
brente, *pp. plur.*: rente, *pp. plur.* 4495/6.
brent, *pp. plur.*: spent, *pp. plur.* 4569/70.
brente, *pret.*: wente, *pret.* 4556/5.
entente, *s.*: hente, *pret.* 4529/30.
hent, *pret.*: present, *inf.* 3497/8.
mente, *pret.*: repente, *inf.* 960/59.
ment(e), *pret.*: wente, *pret.* 1273/4, 3096/5, 4446/5.
bymente, *pret.*: wente, *pret.* 2828/7.
presente, *inf.*: wente, *pret.* 3135/6.

-entes.
instrumentes, *s. plur.*: oynementes, *s. plur.* 2393/4.

-ēp.
kep(e), *s.*: slep(e), *pret. sing.* 1284/3, 2405/6.
kep(e), *s.*: slepe, *s.* 3167/8.
kepe, *s.*: wepe, *pret. sing.* 1001/2.

-ēpe.
crepe, *inf.*: wepe, *inf.* 704/3.
depe, *adj. plur.*: kepe, *inf.* 2775/6.
depe, *adv.*: wepe, *inf.* 901/2, 3379/80.
kepe, *inf.*: slepe, *inf.* 1259/60, 2294/3, 3185/6.
kepe, *inf.*: slepe, *pret. conj.* 3579/80.
kepe, *inf.*: wepe, *pret. conj.* 457/8, 1798/7.

-ēr.
cheer, *s.*: massagere, *s.* 1897/8.
cher, *s.*: ȝer, *s.* 3719/20.
clyere, *adj.*: dynere, *s.* 153/4.
cler, *adv.*: orloger, *s.* 121/2.
cler, *adj.*: ryver, *s.* 3008/7.
comunere, *s.*: sqwyer, *s.* 1660/59.
fer, *s.*: ther, *adv.* 2320/19.
herber, *s.*: ner, *adv.* 3024/3.
messager, *s.*: ryver, *s.* 3102/1.

-ēre, ȩ̄ : ē.
appere, *pres. plur.*: chere, *s.* 944/3.
appere, *inf.*: clere, *adj. plur.* 1188/7.
chere, *s.*: clere, *adj. plur.* 3227/8.
chere, *s.*: dere, *adj.* 1458/7.
cheere, *s.*: here, *inf.* 175/6, 657/8, 3313/14.
chere, *s.*: matere, *s.* 1846/5.
chere, *s.*: preiere, *s.* 545/6.
chere, *s.*: yfere, *adv.* 3362/1, 3742/1, 4474/3, 4648/7.
clere, *adj. plur.*: here, *inf.* 4134/3.
clere, *adj. plur.*: manere, *s.* 1463/4.
dere, *adj.*: here, *inf.* 1899/1900, 3068/7.
dere, *adj.*: preyere, *s.* 3922/1.
here, *inf.*: matiere, *s.* 322/1.
here, *inf.*: requere, *inf.* 3344/3.
here, *inf.*: yfere, *adv.* 1103/4.
matere, *s.*: preyere, *s.* 3469/70.

ǣ[2] : ȩ̄.
there, *adv.*: enquere, *inf.* 1310/09.
were, *s.*: here, *inf.* 4304/3.

ǣ[1] : ē.
lere, *inf.*: enquere, *inf.* 522/1.
lere, *inf.*: frere, *s.* 36/5.
lere, *inf.*: here, *inf.* 196/5, 2551/2.
lere, *inf.*: matere, *s.* 2059/60.

-erd.
afferd, *pp.*: berd, *s.* 3905/6.
aferde, *pp.*: berde, *s.* 2928/7.
afferde, *pp.*: swerde, *s.* 2115/16.
afferd, *pp.*: swerd, *s.* 3637/8.
herde, *pp.*: swerde, *s.* 2535/6.
-erdys.
swerdys, *s. plur.*: berdys, *s. plur.* (beards) 4325/6.
-erk.
werk, *s.*: derk, *adj. plur.* 2667/8.
-erne.
discerne, *inf.*: gouerne, *inf.* 771/2.
gouerne, *inf.*: ȝerne, *adv.* 1123/4.
-ēris (-ērs).
cherys, *s. plur.*: ferys, *s. plur.* 3978/7.
cherys, *s. plur.*: prysonerys, *s. plur.* 4551/2.
cherys, *s. plur.*: ȝeeres, *s. plur.* 669/70.
feeris, *s. plur.*: ȝeeris, *s. plur.* 468/7.
banerys, *s. plur.*: lerys, *pres. sing.* 3. 1548/7.
ablasters, *s. plur.*: squyers, *s. plur.* 2592/1.
cheres, *s. plur.*: straungers, *s. plur.* 1467/8.
-erre.
differre, *inf.*: werre, *s.* 3802/1.
ferre, *adv.* (far): sterre, *s.* 1459/60, 2555/6.
ferre, *adv.*: werre, *s.* 3679/80.
ferre, *adv.*: Meleager, *n. pr.* 2609/10.
sterre, *s.*: werre, *s.* 4629/30.
-errid.
preferryd, *pp.*: erryd, *pp.* 4179/80.
-errys.
sterrys, *s. plur.*: werrys, *s. plur.* 2817/18.
-ĕrs.
dyuers, *adj. plur.*: pervers, *adj. plur.* 383/4.
-ērs.
fers, *adj.* (fierce): Pers, *n. pr.* 81/2.
-erse.
reherce, *inf.*: perce, *inf.* 427/8.
-ert.
desert, *s.*: pouert, *s.* (poverty) 4639/40.
-erte.
aduerte, *inf.*: experte, *adj. plur.* 2978/7.
aduerte, *inf.*: herte, *s.* 251/2, 679/80, 1818/17, 1993/4, 3916/15, 4268/7.
aduerte, *inf.*: smerte, *adj. plur.* 956/5.
aduerte, *inf.*: sterte, *pret. sing.* 1307/8, 4527/8.
aduerte, *inf.*: vpsterte, *inf.* 3394/3.
asterte, *pres. conj.*: herte, *s.* 2407/8, 2489/90.
asterte, *inf.*: herte, *s.* 2996/5.
asterte, *inf.*: dyuerte, *inf.* 3825/6.
dyuerte, *inf.*: herte, *s.* 2176/5.
herte, *s.*: smerte, *inf.* 2693/4.
herte, *s.*: smerte, *s.* 3376/5.
herte, *s.*: smerte, *adj. plur.* 4292/1.
herte, *s.*: sterte, *pret. sing.* 3. 2520/19.
sherte, *s.*: smerte, *adj. plur.* 2391/2.
-erved.
deserued, *pp.*: preserued, *pp.* 3255/6.
deserued, *pp.*: reserued, *pp.* 2227/8.
disserued, *pp.*: reserued, *pp.* 3716/15.
-ēs (ęs).
ches, *pret. sing.*: pes, *s.* (peace) 4706/5.
les, *s.* (lie): Ethiocles, *n. pr.* 1777/8.
rekkele(e)s, *adj.*: Ethiocles, *n. pr.* 1039/40, 3893/4.
rekkeles, *adj.*: pees (pes), *s.* 1447/8, 2343/4, 3864/3.
Aloes, *s.*: relees, *s.* 4572/1.
Cylmythenes, *n. pr.*: pees, *s.* 2602/1.
Diogenes, *n. pr.*: Socrates, *n. pr.* 2972/1.
disencrees, *s.*: pees, *s.* 2023/4.
encres, *s.*: Ethyocles, *n. pr.* 1680/79.
Ethiocles, *n. pr.*: pees, *s.* 1084/3, 2738/7, 3569/70, 3755/6.
Ethyocles, *n. pr.*: vnpes, *s.* 4259/60.
Ethiocles, *n. pr.*: relees, *s.* 3610/09.
pees, *s.*: prees, *s.* 575/6, 3712/11.
pres, *s.*: Polymytes, *n. pr.* 2435/6.
-ęse.
ap(p)ese, *inf.*: e(a)se, *s.* 2398/7, 3789/90.
appese, *inf.*: dissesse, *s.* 3277/8.
appese, *inf.*: dysesse, *inf.* 2532/1.
desese, *s.*: ese, *s.* 1335/6.
ese, *s.*: plese, *inf.* 1433/4.
ese, *s.*: plese, *pres. conj.* 1621/2.
-ēs (-ęs).
degrees, *s. plur.*: knees, *s. plur.* 3138/7.
degrees, *s. plur.*: sotyltees, *s. plur.* 1564/3.
degrees, *s. plur.*: trees, *s. plur.* 3539/40.
-ęse.
lēse, *inf.*: chese, *inf.* 1641/2.

-eseth.
leseth, *pres. sing.* 3: cheseth, *pres. sing.* 3. 4653/4.
-esse.
distresse, *s.*: gentillesse, *s.* 1314/13, 2348/7.
distresse, *s.*: feblenesse, *s.* 2255/6.
distresse, *s.*: hevynesse, *s.* 907/8, 3073/4.
distresse, *s.*: noblesse, *s.* 1987/8.
distresse, *s.*: prouesse, *s.* 2193/4.
dresse, *inf.*: hardynesse, *s.* 2324/3.
expresse, *inf.*: gentillesse, *s.* 3347/8.
expresse, *inf.*: hevynesse, *s.* 3862/1.
expresse, *inf.*: ydylnesse, *s.* 2442/1.
expresse, *inf.*: liklynesse, *s.* 1577/8.
expresse, *inf.*: worthynesse, *s.* 1736/5, 1902/1.
gentilles, *s.*: hevynesse, *s.* 511/12.
gentillesse, *s.*: holynesse, *s.* 23/4.
gentyllesse, *s.*: lowlynesse, *s.* 2461/2.
gentillesse, *s.*: noblesse, *s.* 3318/17.
gentyllesse, *s.*: redresse, *inf.* 4520/19.
humblesse, *s.*: worthynesse, *s.* 4589/90.
largesse, *s.*: goodnesse, *s.* 2418/17.
largesse, *s.*: noblesse, *s.* 2704/3.
largesse, *s.*: richesse, *s.* 4593/4.
oppresse, *inf.*: richesse, *s.* 2715/16.
oppresse, *inf.*: wytnesse, *s.* 4685/6.
processe, *s.*: hevynesse, *s.* 2874/3.
prouesse, *s.*: bysynesse, *s.* 572/1.
prouesse, *s.*: worthynesse, *s.* 752/1.
redresse, *inf.*: falsnesse, *s.* 2055/6.
redresse, *inf.*: rightwisnesse, *s.* 2074/3.
bysynesse, *s.*: kyndenesse, *s.* 3141/2.
bysynesse, *s.*: hevynesse, *s.* 2361/2.
doublenesse, *s.*: sikernesse, *s.* 2892/1.
doublenesse, *s.*: vnsicrenesse, *s.* 1747/8.
fayrnesse, *s.*: gladnesse, *s.* 1465/6.
fairnesse, *s.*: hevynesse, *s.* 420/19.
fayrnesse, *s.*: semlynesse, *s.* 3037/8.
falsnesse, *s.*: witnesse, *s.* 2100/099.
falssenesse, *s.*: sikernesse, *s.* 2499/500.
gladnesse, *s.*: holynesse, *s.* 168/7.
gladnesse, *s.*: siknesse, *s.* 2458/7.
gladnesse, *s.*: welfulnesse, *s.* 3214/13.
gredynesse, *s.*: sikernesse, *s.* 3114/13.
hevynesse, *s.*: sothfastnesse, *s.* 3249/50.
highnesse, *s.*: reklesnesse, *s.* 3455/6.
semlynesse *s.*: worthynesse, *s.* 1510/09.
wilfulnesse, *s.*: wrechednesse, *s.* 2957/8.
wittnesse, *s.*: worthynesse, *s.* 2086/5.
-essis.
duchessys, *s. plur.*: coñtessys, *s. plur.* 4413/14.
-est.
arest, *s.*: brest, *s.* 4225/6.
brest, *s.*: rest, *s.* 2177/8.
-este.
behest, *s.*: at the best, *adj.* 2046/5.
for the best: liklyest, *adj. superl. plur.* 2582/1.
for his best: in rest, *s.* 1707/8.
for the beste: reste, *inf.* 1261/2, 4002/1.
for the beste: at reste, *s.* 1588/7.
for the beste: in reste, *s.* 1108/7, 1615/16.
for the best: rest, *s.* 2291/2.
-ēte.
ẹ̄: ẹ̄.
mete, *inf.* (meet): swete, *adj.* 58/7.
mete, *pres. plur.*: vnswete, *adj.* 2915/16.
mete, *adj. plur.*: swete, *adj.* 230/29.
vnswete, *adj.*: quyete, *s.* 745/6.
ę̄: ę̄.
Crete, *n. pr.*: sete, *s.* (seat) 2612/11.
hete, *s.*: grete *adj. plur.* 1666/5, 2761/2.
ẹ̄: ē (?).
metè, *inf.*: hete, *s.* 4264/3.
quiete, *s.*: sete, *s.* 1712/11.
-ēth.
breth, *s.*: deth, *s.* 3367/8, 3931/2.
-et(t).
bette, *adj.*: lette, *s.* (delay) 172/1.
bet, *adj.*: set, *pp.* 145/6.
let, *s.*: whet, *pp. plur.* 4332/1.
besette, *pp.*: whette, *pp.* 2189/90.
-ette.
fette, *pret.*: sette, *inf.* 2534/3.
lette, *inf.* (hinder): mette, *pret.* 579/80.
lette, *inf.*: sette, *pret.* 2173/4.
lette, *inf.*: sette, *inf.* 2919/20.
lette, *inf.*: shette, *inf.* 601/2.
mette, *pret.*: sette, *pret.* 298/7.
mette, *pret.*: sette, *pret.* 2446/5.
mette, *pret.*: shette, *pret.* 4038/7.
mette, *pret.*: shette, *pp. plur.* 4475/6.
mette, *pret.*: smette, *pret.* 2179/80.
mette, *pret.*: whette, *pp. plur.* 3899/900, 4197/8.
-ēve.
ẹ̄: ẹ̄.
greve, *inf.*: reve, *s.* (O.E. geréfa) 27/8.

greve, *inf.*: releve, *inf.* 3077/8.
O.E. $\bar{æ}^2$: O.E. ēa.
eve, *s.* (evening): leve, *s.* 2721/2, 3965/6.
O.E. ēa: O.Fr. ẹ.
leve, *s.*: greue, *inf.* 1337/8.
O.E. $\bar{æ}^1$: O.Fr. ę̄.
leve, *inf.* (to leave): greve, *inf.* 2921/2.
-ę̄ved.
acheued, *pp.*: a-greued, *pp.* 3608/7.
achieuyd, *pp.*: vnrepreuyd, *pp.* 4151/2.
-ę̄we.
fewe, *adj. plur.*: hewe, *inf.* 4354/3.
fewe, *adj. plur.*: shewe, *inf.* 4109/10.
fewe, *adj. plur.*: shewe, *pres. plur.* 2456/5.
-ẹ̄we.
hewe, *s.* (hue): rewe, *inf.* 3071/2.
hwe, *s.*: newe, *adj. plur.* 2310/09.
knewe, *pret. plur.*: rewe, *inf.* 2918/17.
newe, *adj.*: trewe, *adj.* 1718/17, 2774/3.
newe, *adj.*: vntrewe, *adj.* 872/1, 2043/4, 2101/2, 2341/2, 2926/5.
renewe, *inf.*: rewe, *inf.* 4592/1.
-ewe (in Fr. words; cf. -ue).
dewe, *adj.*: eschewe, *inf.* 924/3.
eschewe, *inf.*: remewe, *inf.* 726/5.
-eye.
deye, *inf.* (to die): leye, *pret. plur.* 3012/11.
deye, *inf.*: withseye, *inf.* 739/40.
dreye, *adj.* (dry): seie, *inf.* (to say) 164/3.
leye, *pret. plur.*: disobeye, *inf.* 65/6.
seye, *inf.*: preye, *inf.* 3451/2.
seye, *inf.*: weie, *s.* (way) 61/2.
wiþsey, *inf.*: obey, *inf.* 1393/4.
weye, *s.* (way): conveye, *inf.* 3209/10.
hosteye, *inf.*: werreye, *inf.* 2991/2.
obeye, *inf.*: werreye, *inf.* 2730/29.
-eyed.
werreyed, *pp.*: conueyed, *pp.* 3963/4.
-ible.
invisyble, *adj.*: horrible, *adj.* 553/4.
odyble, *adj.*: invisible, *adj.* 4029/30.
-ice.
conseruatrice, *s.*: mediatrice, *s.* 1769/70.
-īde.
abide, *inf.*: besyde, *adv.* 415/16.
abide, *pres. plur.*: be-syde, *adv.* 3334/3.
abyde, *inf.*: be-syde, *adv.* 627/8.
abide, *inf.*: Cupide, *n. pr.* 1479/80.
abide, *inf.*: ryde, *inf.* 359/60, 1821/2, 2409/10.
abyde, *pres. plur.*: ryde, *inf.* 2586/5.
abyde, *inf.*: syde, *s.* 2717/18, 3103/4, 3584/3.
abyde, *inf.*: tyde, *pres. conj.* 4158/7.
abyde, *inf.*: wyde, *adj. plur.* 3912/11.
a-side, *adv.*: dyvide, *inf.* 3458/7.
a-syde, *adv.*: ouerslyde, *inf.* 1566/5.
a-syde, *adv.*: provyde, *inf.* 3356/5.
a-side, *adv.*: ryde, *inf.* 2148/7.
aside, *adv.*: tide, *s.* 3409/10.
be-side, *adv.*: guyde, *s.* 182/1, 610/9, 3082/1.
be-syde, *adv.*: ryde, *inf.* 534/3, 2275/6, 3300/299.
betide, *pres. conj. sing.*: syde, *s.* 1851/2.
glyde, *inf.*: side, *s.* 2185/6.
glyde, *inf.*: syde, *s.* 3495/6.
guyde, *s.*: side, *s.* 1292/1, 3947/8.
provide, *inf.*: side, *s.* 402/1, 2787/8.
ryde, *inf.*: side, *s.* 2732/1.
ryde, *inf.*: wyde, *adj. plur.* 2259/60.
syde, *s.*: wyde, *adj. plur.* 4644/3.
-īde (O.E. ȳd).
hide, *inf.*: abide, *inf.* 519/20.
hide, *inf.*: provide, *inf.* 2836/5.
hyde, *s.*: wyde, *adv.* 299/300.
pride, *s.*: abide, *inf.* 469/70, 1323/4, 3605/6.
pryde, *s.*: a-syde, *adv.* 259/60, 1731/2, 3647/8.
pride, *s.*: ryde, *pres. plur.* 1353/4.
pride, *s.*: side, *s.* 3490/89, 3567/8, 3901/2.
-ided.
provided, *pp.*: devyded, *pp.* 1601/2, 3760/59.
-ie.
alye, *s.*: deffye, *pres. sing.* 1. 2081/2.
allye, *s.*: specifie, *inf.* 2735/6.
armonye, *s.*: melodye, *s.* 830/29.
astronomye, *s.*: diffye, *inf.* 2930/29.
astronomye, *s.*: nigromancye, *s.* 4052/1.
certifie, *inf.*: occupye, *inf.* 4426/5.
chanpartye, *s.*: felonye, *s.* 2244/3.
chyvalrye, *s.*: companye, *s.* 2654/3.
chyvalrye, *s.*: Femynye, *n. pr.* 4507/8.
chyualrye, *s.*: guye, *inf.* 1120/19, 4374/3.
chyualrye, *s.*: hye, *inf.* 2135/6.
chyualrye, *s.*: iupartie, *s.* 3061/2.
companye, *s.*: curtesye, *s.* 178/7.

compenye, *s.*: denye, *inf.* 135/6.
companye, *s.*: espye, *inf.* 583/4.
companye, *s.*: gye, *inf.* 2163/4.
companye, *s.*: lye, *inf.* 4451/2.
companye, *s.*: ribaudye, *s.* 26/5.
conspiracye, *s.*: fantasye, *s.* 2172/1.
curtesye, *s.*: fantasye, *s.* 1643/4.
curtesie, *s.*: vileynye, *s.* 1329/30.
crye, *inf.*: hie, *inf.* 3224/3.
denye, *inf.*: lye, *inf.* 2861/2.
dye, *inf.* (die): replye, *inf.* 3467/8.
Emelye, *n. pr.*: espye, *inf.* 4511/12.
envye, *s.*: fantasye, *s.* 258/7.
envie, *s.*: surquedye, *s.* 1075/6, 4662/1.
envie, *s.*: trecherie, *s.* 861/2.
espie, *inf.*: fantasie, *s.* 903/4.
espie, *pres. conj.*: felonye, *s.* 2149/50.
espye, *inf.*: profecye, *s.* 4172/1.
fantasye, *s.*: flaterye, *s.* 1783/4.
fantasie, *s.*: folye, *s.* 1379/80.
fantasye, *s.*: modefye, *inf.* 3817/18.
fantasie, *s.*: signyfie, *inf.* 1523/4.
fantasye, *s.*: specifie, *inf.* 2663/4.
felonye, *s.*: malencolye, *s.* 2038/7.
fellonye, *s.*: tyrannye, *s.* 4493/4.
folye, *s.*: iupartie, *s.* 3975/6.
folye, *s.*: profecye, *s.* 2970/69.
Genologye, *s.*: verryfie, *inf.* 3538/7.
hye, *inf.*: specefie, *inf.* 1530/29.
ydolatrye, *s.*: mawmetrye, *s.* 4047/8.
iupartie, *s.*: regalye, *s.* 1860/59.
lye, *pres. plur.* (*mentiri*): specifye, *inf.* 3520/19.
magnyfie, *inf.*: occupie, *inf.* 1950/49.
Neemye, *n. pr.*: reedifie, *inf.* 1739/40.
Neemye, *n. pr.*: specyfie, *inf.* 1730/29.
occupie, *inf.*: specific, *pres. plur.* 762/1.
occupie, *inf.*: tragedye, *s.* 993/4.
philolegye, *s.*: skye, *s.* 833/4.
poysye, *s.*: specifie, *inf.* 214/13.
prophecye, *s.*: specifye, *pres. plur.* 2810/09.
ratefye, *inf.*: specifye, *inf.* 3349/50.
regalye, *s.*: specifie, *inf.* 3758/7.
remedye, *s.*: sorcerye, *s.* 4102/1.
surquedye, *s.*: tyranye, *s.* 282/1.
drye, *adj.*: malencolye, *s.* 2554/3.

-ied.
allyed, *pp.*: magnyfied, *pp.* 1682/1.
certefied, *pp.*: espied, *pp.* 2740/39.
certefied, *pp.*: hyed, *pp.* 557/8.
denyed, *pp.*: espied, *pp.* 3252/1.
denyed, *pp.*: y-occupied, *pp.* 1931/2.
denyed, *pp.*: tryed, *pp.* 3785/6.

-ies.
allies, *s. plur.*: espies, *s. plur.* 2754/3.
allies, *s. plur.*: remedyes, *s. plur.* 1702/1.
fantasies, *s. plur.*: specifies, *pres. sing.* 3. 1508/7.

-ieth.
espieth, *pres. sing.* 3.: hieth, *pres. sing.* 3. 3903/4.

-īf.
knyff, *s.*: liff, *s.* 2781/2.
lyff, *s.*: pensif, *adj.* 1215/16.
lyff, *s.*: prerogatiff, *s.* 1727/8.
lif(f), *s.*: strif(f), *s.* 1036/5, 1102/1, 1385/6.
lif, *s.*: stryf, *s.* 424/3, 1826/5, 2518/17.
lyff, *s.*: stryff, *s.* 678/7, 3439/40, 3930/29.
lyf, *s.*: strif, *s.* 886/5.
lif, *s.*: wif, *s.* 987/8, 2869/70.
lif(f), *s.*: wyf(f), *s.* 339/40, 3353/4.
lyff, *s.*: wyf, *s.* 795/6.
prerogatif, *s.*: strif, *s.* 1936/5.

-ight.
a-right, *adv.*: myght, *s.* 3433/4.
behight, *pp.*: ryght, *s.* 3986/5.
briȝt, *adj.*: knyght, *s.* 1658/7, 2618/17.
briȝt, *adj.*: myght, *s.* 345/6.
bright, *adj.*: sight, *s.* 1882/1.
bright, *adj. plur.*: nyght, *s.* 4583/4.
bright, *adv.*: lyght, *s.* 2169/70.
bright, *adv.*: nyght, *s.* 3992/1.
fight, *s.*: myght, *s.* 3888/7.
flight, *s.*: knyght, *s.* 4208/7, 4540/39.
fourtenyght, *s.*: knyght, *s.* 4505/6.
knyght, *s.*: myght, *s.* 769/70, 1629/30, 2422/1.
knyght, *s.*: nyght, *s.* 1316/15, 2161/2, 4216/15.
knyght, *s.*: right, *s.* 1331/2, 1785/6, 1856/5, 1934/3, 2063/4, 2507/8.
knyght, *s.*: sight, *s.* 753/4, 2316/15, 2463/4, 3040/39.
liȝt, *s.*: nyght, *s.* 1298/7, 3582/1.
light, *adj.*: nyght, *s.* 1370/69.
light, *adj.*: wight, *s.* 150/49.
light, *adj.* (easy): myght, *s.* 1978/7.
light, *adj.* (easy): nyght, *s.* 97/8, 1169/70.
liȝt, *adj.*: nyght, *s.* 144/3, 1576/5.
myght, *s.*: nyght, *s.* 895/6, 1328/7.
myght, *s.*: mydnyght, *s.* 119/20.
myght, *s.*: right, *s.* 719/20, 2237/8, 2571/2, 4397/8.
myght, *s.*: right, *adv.* 2877/8.

myght, *s.*: sight, *s.* 798/7.
nyght, *s.*: sight, *s.* 1225/6, 1383/4.
nyght, *s.*: riȝt, *s.* 1535/6.
nyght, *s.*: right, *s.* 3166/5.
ryght, *s.*: sight, *s.* 1606/5.
riȝt, *s.*: siȝt, *s.* 3283/4.
ryght, *adv.*: sight, *s.* 3752/1.
sight, *s.*: vnright, *s.* 3676/5.

-ighte.
alight, *pret.*: myght, *pret.* 1257/8, 1320/19, 1388/7.
fighte, *inf.*: myghte, *pret.* 3879/80.
fight, *inf.*: (be) nyght, *s.* 1364/3.
fight, *inf.*: sight, *s.* 1549/50, 3634/3.
highte, *pret.*: sighte, *s.* 4177/8.
hight, *pret.*: sight, *s.* 624/3.
behiht, *pret.*: myght, *pret.* 3275/6.
pyhte, *pret.*: sighte, *s.* 3128/7.

-igne.
assigne, *inf.*: benygne, *adj.* 233/4, 1656/5.
benygne, *adj.*: signe, *s.* 2369/70.
signe, *s.*: resigne, *inf.* 1839/40.

-īk.
rethorik, *s.*: lik, *adj.* 219/20.

-īle.
begyle, *inf.*: wile, *s.* 1671/2.
Cecile, *n. pr.* (Sicily): style, *s.* 3204/3.
compyle, *inf.*: while, *s.* 4611/12.
exile, *inf.*: while, *s.* 1986/5.
myle, *s. plur.*: while, *s.* 324/3.
style, *s.*: while, *s.* 2124/3.

-īled.
begyled, *pp.*: exiled, *pp.* 1279/80.
compyled, *pp.*: exiled, *pp.* 307/8.
exiled, *pp.*: reconcyled, *pp.* 1920/19.

-ill.
fil, *pret. sing.*: hil, *s.* 1043/4.

-ille.
fille, *s.*: ille, *s.* 107/8.
(at the) hille, *s.*: wille, *s.* 2525/6.
ille, *adv.*: stille, *adj.* 3813/14.

-ilt.
spilt, *pp.*: bylt, *pp.* 4635/6.

-īme.
pryme, *s.*: tyme, *s.* 124/3, 3734/3.
ryme, *inf.*: tyme, *s.* 2669/70.

-in: -īn.
chyn, *s.*: cherubyn, *s.* 33/4.

-īn.
cremysyn, *adj.*: hermyn, *s.* 1441/2.
declyne, *s.*: fyn, *s.* 2904/3.
engyn, *s.*: fyn, *s.* 4213/14.
fyn, *adj.*: wyn, *s.* 1500/1499, 3527/8.

-īne.
declyne, *inf.*: fyne, *inf.* 3690/89.
determyne, *inf.*: ruyne, *s.* 2550/49.
doctrine, *s.*: termyne, *inf.* 4183/4.
dyvyne, *inf.*: fyne, *inf.* 2811/12.
enclyne, *inf.*: fyne, *inf.* 3819/20, 3984/3.
fyne, *inf.*: vntwyne, *inf.* 733/4.
lyne, *s.*: ruyne, *s.* 4638/7.
lyne, *s.*: shyne, *inf.* 2167/8.
lyne, *s.*: termyne, *inf.* 2964/3.
nyne, *numer.*: shyne, *inf.* 828/7, 1050/49.
shyne, *inf.*: vndermyne, *inf.* 1766/5.
termyne, *inf.*: virgyne, *s.* 4707/8.

-īned.
fyned, *pp.*: enclyned, *pp.* 1627/8, 1795/6.

-īnde.
behynde, *adv.*: fynde, *inf.* 438/7.
bynde, *inf.*: fynde, *inf.* 2396/5.
fynde, *pres. sing.* 1.: Ynde, *n. pr.* 3839/40.
fynde, *pres. sing.* 1.: ynde, *adj.* 4465/6.
hynde, *s.*: lynde, *s.* 1275/6.
fynde, *pres. sing.* 1.: kynde, *s.* 614/13.
fynde, *inf.*: kynde, *adj.* 1981/2, 2367/8, 2849/50.
fynde, *inf.*: mynde, *s.* 43/4, 820/19, 3145/6.
mynde, *s.*: vnkynde, *adj.* 2563/4.
mynd, *s.*: vnkynd, *adj.* 3291/2.

-ing.
kyng, *s.*: thynge, *s.* 808/7.
kyng, *s.*: thyng, *s.* 974/3, 1631/2, 1722/1, 2719/20, 4064/3.
kyng, *s.*: thing, *s.* 2352/1, 3290/89, 4538/7.
kyng, *s.*: þing, *s.* 414/13, 1368/7.
kyng, *s.*: beeldyng, *s.* 1192/1.
kyng, *s.*: comyng, *s.* 3310/09.
kyng, *s.*: fighting, *s.* 1375/6.
kyng, *s.*: folowyng, *part. pres.* 2094/3.
kyng, *s.*: lesyng, *s.* 1404/3.
kyng, *s.*: lettyng, *s.* 1087/8, 4388/7.
kyng, *s.*: loggyng, *s.* 2672/1.
kynge, *s.*: menynge, *s.* 1912/11.
kyng, *s.*: rekenyng, *s.* 1804/3.
kyng, *s.*: spekyng, *s.* 245/6.
kyng, *s.*: taryng, *s.* 502/1, 776/5, 1255/6, 1940/39, 2106/5, 2452/1.
kyng, *s.*: vnsittyng, *part. adj.* 3650/49.
kyng, *s.*: wakyng, *part. pres.* 3574/3.
kyng, *s.*: weddyng, *s.* 803/4.
kyng, *s.*: wepyng, *s.* 589/90.
kyng, *s.*: werkyng, *s.* 1268/7.
kyng, *s.*: wyrchyng, *s.* 486/5.
kyng, *s.*: writyng(e), *s.* 241/2, 291/2, 1199/1200, 2600/599.

thinge, *s.*: biddynge, *s.* 174/3.
thyng, *s.*: comyng, *s.* 3342/1.
thing, *s.*: endyng, *s.* 2945/6.
thing, *s.*: knowlecchyng, *s.* 1503/4.
thyng, *s.*: liggyng, *part. pres.* 3892/1.
thyng, *s.*: loggyng, *s.* 3322/1.
thyng, *s.*: menyng, *s.* 4454/3.
þing, *s.*: tarying, *s.* 1391/2.
thyng, *s.*: werkyng, *s.* 1760/59.
bidding, *s.*: lettyng *s.* 1654/3, 2633/4.
comyng, *s.*: syttyng, *part. pres.* 2880/79.
compleynyng, *s.*: endynge, *s.* 996/5.
compleynyng, *part. pres.*: swyng, *part. pres.* 4357/8.
conveyinge, *part. pres.*: rydynge, *part. pres.* 4514/13.
hoom-comynge, *s.*: welcomynge, *s.* 2429/30.
in-comyng, *s.*: vprysing, *s.* 1462/1.
lyvyng, *part. pres.*: ryding, *part. pres.* 1264/5.

-inges.
kyngges, *s. plur.*: lettyngges, *s. plur.* (delays) 2575/6.
þingges, *s. plur.*: kyngges, *s. plur.* 3295/6.

-inis.
vynys, *s. plur.*: wynys, *s. plur.* 3531/2.

-inke.
drynke, *pres. plur.*: brynke, *s.* 3115/16.

-in(n).
inne, *adv.*: skynne, *s.* 303/4.

-inne.
bygynne, *inf.*: wynne, *inf.* 4651/2.
gynne, *pres. conj.*: wynne, *inf.* 2711/12.
twynne, *inf.*: wynne, *inf.* 280/79.

-ippe.
slippe, *inf.*: Menalippe, *n. pr.* 1277/8.

-īr.
desire, *s.*: fire, *s.* 608/7.

-īre.
a-fire, *adv.*: ire, *s.* 2036/5, 2560/59.

-iris.
desyris, *s. plur.*: ryverys, *s. plur.* 1617/18.

-irke.
wyrke, *inf.* (work): in the dyrke, *adj.* (dark) 2961/2.

-īs.
avis, *s.*: wis, *adj.* 1624/3.
avice, *s.*: wyce, *adj.* 2795/6.
avis, *s.*: wys, *adj. plur.* 3632/1, 3692/1, 4153/4.
devis, *s.*: hagys, *s.* 99/100.
devis, *s.*: paradys, *s.* 2279/80.
devys, *s.*: wis, *adj. plur.* 1782/1, 2015/6.
prys, *s.* (price): wys, *adj.* 4005/6.
pryse, *s.* (prize): wise, *adj.* 654/3.

-īse.
aryse, *inf.*: devyse, *inf.* 4682/1.
arise, *inf.*: wise, *s.* 1175/6, 1472/1.
arise, *pres. conj.*: wise, *s.* 1445/6.
chastyse, *inf.*: devyse, *inf.* 4659/60.
couetise, *s.*: devise, *inf.* 2710/09.
cowardys, *s.*: wyse, *s.* 2483/4.
cowardyse, *s.*: wise, *adj. plur.* 4118/17.
dispise, *pres. plur.*: devise, *inf.* 1004/3.
despyse, *pres. plur.*: guyse, *s.* 3996/5.
despyse, *inf.*: wyse, *adj. plur.* 264/3.
devise, *inf.*: guyse, *s.* 4567/8.
devise, *inf.*: iustice, *s.* 1206/5.
devise, *inf.*: suffise, *inf.* 3329/30, 3402/1.
devyse, *inf.*: wise, *adj. plur.* 361/2, 817/18.
devise, *inf.*: wise, *s.* 1311/12, 2648/7, 3795/6, 4020/19.
emprise, *s.*: wise, *s.* 3480/79.
emprise, *s.*: (the) wyse, *adj.* 4181/2.
ryse, *inf.*: wyse, *s.* 2054/3.
sacrifise, *s.*: wise, *s.* 344/3, 4188/7.
wise, *adj. plur.*: wyse, *s.* 3121/2.

-īsed.
devysed, *pp.*: solempnyzed, *pp.* 779/80.
devised, *pp.*: avised, *pp. adj.* 2887/8, 3944/3.

-īses.
guyses, *s. plur.*: devyses, *s. plur.* 2661/2.

-ist.
lyst, *pres.*: vnwist, *adj. plur.* 493/4.
vnwist, *adj. sing.*: trist, *s.* (trust) 4081/2.

-iste.
wiste, *pret. sing.* (knew): triste, *inf.* (to trust) 3623/4, 4107/8.

-ĭt.
wit, *s.*: qwyt, *adj.* (N.E. quit) 693/4.

-īt.
delit, *s.*: despit, *s.* 999/1000, 2923/4.
delyt, *s.*: opposit, *adj.* 4270/69.
despit, *s.*: respit, *s.* 3877/8.

-īte.
acquyte, *inf.*: respit, *inf.* 2103/4.
aquyte, *inf.*: visite, *inf.* 72/1, 3319/20.

Arcyte, *n. pr.*: whyte, *adj. plur.* 3525/6.
delyte, *pres. sing.* 1.: visyte, *inf.* 2353/4.
delite, *inf.*: white, *adj. plur.* 4444/3.
endite, *inf.*: (the) white, *adj.* 4481/2.
endite, *inf.*: whyte, *adj. plur.* 4501/2.
endyte, *inf.*: write, *inf.* 824/3.
(a) lyte, *adv.*: myte, *s.* 3358/7.
Polymyte, *n. pr.*: wite, *inf.* (blame) 1041/2.
Polymyte, *n. pr.*: write, *pres. plur.* 879/80.
white, *adj. plur.*: write, *inf.* 2434/3.

-īve.
alyue, *adv.*: blyve, *adv.* 2220/19.
alyve, *adv.*: descryve, *inf.* 4419/20.
Argyve, *n. pr.*: discryve, *inf.* 1210/09.
Argyve, *n pr.*: ryve, *inf.* 4484/3.
Argyve, *n. pr.*: (to) wive, *s.* 1646/5.
blyve, *adv.*: stryve, *inf.* 1342/1, 1915/16.
(al my) lyve, *s.*: stryve, *pres. plur.* 2009/10.
stryve, *pres. plur.*: thryve, *inf.* 4674/3.
vnthryve, *inf.*: (to) wyve, *s.* 781/2.

-ō.
-ǭ: -ǭ.
ago, *pp.*: mo, *adv.* 3990/89.
doo, *s.* (doe): roo, *s.* (roe) 3595/6.
fro, *adv.*: goo, *pp.* 2313/14.
fro, *adv.*: roo, *s.* 3867/8.
mo, *adj.*: so, *adv.* 912/11.
mo, *s.*: wo, *adj.* 3373/4.

Perhaps:
also, *adv.*: Iuno, *n. pr.* 352/1.
also, *adv.*: wo, *s.* 2515/16, 2906/5.
also, *adv.*: twoo, *numer.* 380/79, 708/7, 1208/7, 3190/89, 3242/1.
so, *adv.*: two, *numer.* 200/199.
ther-fro, *adv.*: two, *numer.* 2091/2.

-ọ̄: -ọ̄.
Possible cases:
also, *adv.*: do, *inf.* 459/60.
also, *adv.*: do, *inf.* 1038/7.
also, *adv.*: do, *pp.* 2627/8, 3403/4.
also, *adv.*: therto, *adv.* 1406/5.
so, *adv.*: do, *inf.* 3616/15.
so, *adv.*: ado, *inf.* 2034/3, 4266/5.
so, *adv.*: to, *adv.* 2494/3, 3800/799.
two, *numer.*: do, *inf.* 3151/2.
two, *numer.*: ado, *s.* 1343/4.
two, *numer.*: therto, *adv.* 1591/2.

-ọ̄: ǭ.
do, *pp.*: fro, *adv.* 3422/1.
do, *inf.*: wo, *s.* 892/1.
i-do, *pp.*: fro, *adv.* 676/5.
therto, *adv.*: fro, *adv.* 698/7.
ther-to, *adv.*: go, *pp.* 3418/17.
to, *adv.*: woo, *s.* 3445/6.

-oche.
roche, *s.*: approche, *inf.* 641/2, 2269/70, 3000/2999.

-ōd.
-ǭd.
abood, *pret. sing.*: rood, *pret. sing.* 4202/1.
abood, *s.*: rood, *pret. sing.* 4533/4.
abood, *s.*: rood, *pret. plur.* 3107/8.

-ọ̄d.
blood, *s.*: flood, *s.* 4279/80.
blood, *s.*: good, *adj.* 788/7, 2956/5, 4710/09.
blood, *s.*: good, *s.* 126/5, 1157/8, 1584/3, 1857/8, 4642/1.
blood, *s.*: hood, *s.* 89/90.
blode, *s.*: manhode, *s.* 1512/11.
blood, *s.*: mood, *s.* 2900/899.
blode, *s.*: stode, *pret.* 783/4.
blood, *s.*: sto(o)d, *pret.* 1218/17, 1428/7, 2267/8, 2321/2, 2475/6, 3398/7, 4574/3.
blood, *s.*: vnderstood, *pret. plur.* 3477/8.
blood, *s.*: wood, *adj.* 487/8, 868/7, 1014/13, 3664/3, 4273/4.
good, *s.*: stood, *pret.* 2846/5, 3243/4.
good, *s.*: wood, *adj. plur.* 3111/12.
mood, *s.*: wood, *adj.* 2480/79.
stood, *pret.*: vnderstood, *pret.* 3273/4.
stood, *pret.*: wood, *adj.* 2040/39, 2125/6.

ǭd: ọ̄d.
abood, *s.*: stood, *pret.* 525/6.
abood, *pret. sing.*: stood, *pret. sing.* 4222/1.
abood, *pret. plur.*: stood, *pret. sing.* 4035/6.
rood, *pret. sing.*: stood, *pret. sing.* 1880/79.

-ọ̄de.
goode, *adj. plur.*: woode, *adj. plur.* 275/6.
stood, *pret. plur.*: wood, *adj. plur.* 3875/6, 4322/1.

-ofte.
a-lofte, *adv.*: softe, *adj.*, *adv.* 208/7, 702/1, 1053/4, 1245/6, 2383/4, 4288/7.
ofte, *adv.*: softe, *adv.* 2329/30.

-ogh.
swogh, *s.* (swoon): drogh, *pret. sing.* 2333/4.

-oint.
poynt, *s.*: disioynte, *s.* 1077/8, 2477/8.

poynt, *s.*: **enoynt**, *adj. plur.* **4585/6.**
-oise.
froyse, *s.*: **koyse**, *s.* 101/2.
-ōk.
awoke, *pret.*: **shoke**, *pret.* 1358/7.
book, *s.*: **took**, *pret. sing.* 1528/7.
boke, *s.*: **woke**, *pret. sing.* 1505/6.
forsoke, *pret. sing.*: toke, *pret. sing.* 975/6, 4595/6.
loke, *s.*: toke, *pret.* 409/10, 1377/8.
look, *s.*: took, *pret.* 1885/6.
loke, *s.*: tooke, *pret. plur.* 4579/80.
-okis.
hokys, *s. plur.*: lokys (or crokys), *s. plur.* 1539/40.
lookes, *s. plur.*: hokes, *s. plur.* 1669/70.
-old.
bolde, *adj.*: housholde, *s.* 2138/7.
bold, *adj.*: old, *adj.* 3435/6.
cold, *adj.*: told, *pp.* 3016/15, 3119/20.
cold, *s.*: told, *pp.* 4194/3.
old, *adj.*: told, *pp.* 212/11, 1017/18, 4025/6.
-olde.
byholde, *inf.*: olde, *adj. plur.* 899/900.
beholde, *inf.*: tolde, *pret.* 1537/8.
byholde, *inf.*: colde, *adj. plur.* 2318/17.
colde, *adj. plur.*: olde, *adj. plur.* 596/5, 2542/1.
holde, *inf.*: olde, *adj. plur.* 1775/6.
hold, *inf.*: told, *pret.* 1698/7.
holde, *pp.*: tolde, *pret.* 2548/7.
holde, *pres. plur.*: tolde, *pret.* 2820/19.
holde, *inf.*: tolde, *pret.* 2990/89, 3642/1, 4432/1.
olde, *adj. plur.*· tolde, *pret.* 651/2.
tolde, *pret.*: vpholde, *pp.* 2251/2.
tolde, *pret.*: withholde, *inf.* 2911/12.
holde, *pp.*: wolde, *pret.* 3143/4.
olde, *adj. plur.*: wolde, *pret.* 355/6.
tolde, *pret.*: sholde, *pret.* 919/20.
ǭ: ō.
cold, *adj.*: gold, *s.* 4576/5.
many-fold, *adj. plur.*: gold, *s.* 2765/6.
tolde, *pp.*: (of) golde, *s.* 535/6.
-olle.
bolle, *s.*: nolle, *s.* 31/2.
-ombre.
nombre, *s.*: encombre, *inf.* 2143/4.
-ǭn.
anon, *adv.*: euerichon, *pron.* 77/8, 1705/6, 4470/69.
anon, *adv.*: echon, *pron.* 2584/3.
anon, *adv.*: non, *adv.* 509/10.
anon, *adv.*: non, *pron.* 3941/2.
anon, *adv.*: on, *numer.* 3140/39.
Creon, *n. pr.*: euerichon, *pron.* 4385/6.
echon, *pron.*: gon, *pp.* 897/8.
echon, *pron.*: ston, *s.* 2843/4.
euerichon, *pron.*: fo(o)n, *s. plur.* 4087/8, 4395/6.
euerychon, *pron.*: non, *pron.* 2473/4.
euerichon, *pron.*: on, *numer.* 59/60, 3557/8, 4175/6.
euerichon, *pron.*: oon, *numer.* 484/3.
euerichon, *pron.*: ston, *s.* 3306/5.
fon, *s. plur.*: gon, *pp.* 1609/10.
fon, *s. plur.*: to gon, *inf.* 1830/29.
foon, *s. plur.*: on, *numer.* 2195/6.
foon, *s. plur.*: ston, *s.* 2777/8.
goon, *inf.*: noon, *pron.* (*adv.*) 232/1, 466/5, 1214/13.
gon, *pres. plur.*: non, *pron.* 1501/2, 3001/2.
gon, *inf.*: on, *numer.* 616/15.
gon, *pp.*: on, *numer.* 2875/6, 4617/18.
non, *pron.*: Iohn, *n. pr.* 799/800.
noon, *pron.*: stoon, *s.* 239/40, 289/90.
on, *numer.*: ston, *s.* 951/2.
ouergon, *pp.*: ston, *s.* 3407/8.
shon, *pret.*: ston, *s.* 2272/1.
-ǫne.
allon(e), *pron.*: mon(e), *s.* (moan) 759/60, 1872/1, 2707/8.
-ōne.
bone, *s.* (N.E. boon): sone, *adv.* 353/4.
sone, *adv.*: to done, *ger.* 1819/20.
-ond.
bond, *s.*: londe, *s.* 2005/6.
brond, *s.*: hond, *s.* 1482/1.
hond, *s.*: lond, *s.* 209/10, 338/7, 1032/1, 1203/4, 1573/4, 2027/8, 2266/5, 2623/4, 2656/5, 4344/3.
-onde.
(on) honde, *s.*: (on) londe, *s.* 4138/7.
(on) honde, *s.*: stonde, *inf.* 737/8.
(on) hond, *s.*: vnderstond, *inf.* 1910/09.
(on) honde, *s.*: vnderstonde, *inf.* 4604/3.
stond(e), *inf.*: vnderstond(e), *inf.* 2029/30, 3777/8.
-onder.
wonder, *s.*: a-sonder, *adv.* 1373/4, 4324/3, 4499/4500.
ȝonder, *adv.*: thonder, *s.* 4313/14.
-ong.
euer-among, *adv.*: song, *pret. sing.* 2295/6.
longe, *adj. sing.*: wronge, *s.* 1812/11.

song, *s.*: strong, *adj.* 203/4.
song, *pret. sing.*: strong, *adj.* 3552/1.
stronge, *adj. sing.*: wronge, *s.* 1068/7, 1586/5, 3651/2.
strong, *adj. plur.*: wrong, *s.* 2733/4, 3533/4.
strong, *adj. plur.*: þer-among, *adv.* 4460/59.
-onge.
longe, *adv.*: stronge, *adj. plur.* 876/5, 4379/80.
-ǭnis.
atonys, *adv.*: nonys, *adv.* 970/69, 2214/3, 4276/5.
attonys, *adv.*: stonys, *s. plur.* 2949/50.
bonys, *s. plur.*: noonys, *adv.* 411/12.
noonys, *adv.*: stonys, *s. plur.* 311/12, 1251/2.
-onne (-unne).
begvnne, *pp.*: konne, *pres. plur.* 2562/1.
begonne, *pp.*: konne, *vrcs. conj.* 3546/5.
begonne, *pp.*: wonne, *pp.* 2008/7.
konne, *pres. plur.*: nonne, *s.* 138/7.
konne, *pres. plur.*: sonne, *s.* 3009/10.
ronne, *pret. plur.*: sonne, *s.* 3117/18.
ronne, *pp.*: sonne, *s.* 1802/1.
rvnne, *pret. plur.*: svnne, *s.* 2304/3.
sonne, *s.*: y-ronne, *pp.* 730/29.
yronne, *pp.*: ywonne, *pp.* 748/7.
-onnys.
gonnys, *s. plur.* (guns): tonnys, *s. plur.* (tuns) 2759/60.
-oppys (-oppes).
roppys, *s. plur.*: croppys, *s. plur.* 115/16.
-ǭr.
boor, *s.*: hoor, *adj.* 1546/5.
boor, *s.*: stoor, *s.* 3597/8.
boor, *s.*: 'mor, *adv.* 1521/2.
euermor, *adv.*: stor, *s.* 1983/4.
-ǭre.
hore, *adj. plur.*: more, *adj.* 4608/7.
hore, *adj. plur.*: sore, *adv.* 440/39, 2985/6.
lore, *s.*: restore, *inf.* 2403/4.
more, *adv.*: sore, *adv.* 905/6, 3518/17.
mor, *adv.*: sore, *adj. plur.* 2376/5.
more, *adj.*: sore, *adv.* 3781/2.
restore, *inf.*: (of) ȝore, *adv.* 2642/1.
rore, *inf.*: sore, *adv.* 1174/3.
-orche.
torche, *s.*: porche, *s.* 1299/1300.
-ord.
accord, *s.*: lord, *s.* 1082/1.
lord, *s.*: word, *s.* 1413/14.
-orde.
discorde, *inf.*: recorde, *inf.* 2088/7.
-orie.
glorye, *s.*: memorye, *s.* 46/5.
glorye, *s.*: victorye, *s.* 4598/7.
memorye, *s.*: victorye, *s.* 2240/39.
-orn.
aforn, *adv.*: corn, *s.* 4457/8.
a-forn, *adv.*: lorn, *pp.* 2943/4, 4165/6.
aforn, *adv.*: sworn, *pp.* 1937/8.
born, *pp.*: Capricorn, *s.* 392/1.
born, *pp.*: forsworn, *pp.* 2443/4.
born, *pp.*: sworn, *pp.* 664/3, 2233/4.
born, *pp.*: to-forn, *adv.* 404/3, 1401/2, 4521/2.
corn, *s.*: to-forn, *adv.* 2770/69.
forsworn, *pp.*: lorn, *pp.* 2503/4.
forsworn, *pp.*: to-forn, *adv.* 2048/7.
herto-forn, *adv.*: yborn, *pp.* 699/700.
horn, *s.*: toforn, *adv.* 1790/89.
lorn, *pp.*: sworn, *pp.* 2855/6.
lorn, *pp.*: to-forn, *adv.* 314/13, 1290/89, 3286/5.
sworn, *pp.*: to-forn, *adv.* 1325/6, 1695/6, 3644/3.
thorn, *s.*: to-forn, *adv.* 1016/15.
to-forn, *adv.*: yborn, *pp.* 1086/5.
-ors.
wors, *adj. comp.*: hors, *s.* 151/2, 3729/30.
cors, *s.* (body): remors, *s.* 2851/2.
-ort.
comfort, *s.*: disport, *s.* 2356/5, 3036/5, 3851/2.
comfort, *s.*: report, *s.* 1424/3.
disport, *s.*: port, *s.* 482/1.
disport, *s.*: sort, *s.* 647/8.
-orte.
conforte, *inf.*: resorte, *inf.* 3923/4.
disporte, *inf.*: resorte, *inf.* 2411/12.
reporte, *inf.*: resorte, *pres. plur.* 3803/4, 4150/49.
reporte, *inf.*: supporte, *inf.* 283/4.
-or(o)we.
borowe, *s.*: morowe, *s.* 3549/50.
borowe, *s.*: sorowe, *s.* 2914/13, 3474/3, 4687/8.
borowe, *inf.*: sorowe, *s.* 3384/3.
morowe, *s.*: sorowe, *s.* 106/5, 1443/4, 2509/10, 4491/2.
morow, *s.*: sorowe, *s.* 989/90.
-ǭs.
cloos, *adj.*: aroos, *pret. sing.* 1525/6 4013/14.
cloos, *adj.*: purpoos, *s.* 2837/8.
-ǭse.
purpose, *inf.*: disclose, *inf.* 3753/4.
-ǭsed.
disposyd, *pp.*: enclosed, *pp.* 2907/8.

-ǭst.
bost, *s.*: **host,** *s.* 80/79.
cost, *s.*: goost, *s.* 4340/39.
coste, *s.*: hoste, *s.* 2652/1.
cost, *s.*: host, *s.* 4061/2.
cost, *s.*: hoost, *s.* 2933/4.
host, *s.*: most, *adv.* 4078/7.
-ǭte.
bote, *s.*: (vnder) fote, *s.* 1007/8.
bote, *s.*: rote, *s.* 870/69.
(vnder) fote, *s.*: roote, *s.* 4333/4, 4677/8.
(on) foote, *s.*: vnsoote, *adj.* 573/4.
a-foote, *s.*: vnsoote, *adj.* 2192/1.
roote, *s.*: soote, *adj.* 3092/1.
roote, *s.*: vnsoote, *adj.* 3674/3.
-ǫth.
goth, *pres. sing.* 3.: loth, *adj.* 2118/17.
goþ, *pres. sing.* 3.: ooth, *s.* 1842/1.
goth, *pres. sing.* 3.: wroth, *adj.* 2557/8.
loth, *adj.*: ooth, *s.* 2050/49, 2859/60.
loth, *adj.*: wroth, *adj.* 389/90, 3710/09.
oth, *s.*: wroth, *s.* 2505/6.
-ǭthe.
bothe, *numer.*: wrothe, *adj. plur.* 4294/3.
both, *adj.*: loth, *adj. plur.* 3668/7.
-ǫth.
(in) soth, *adj.*: doth, *pres. sing.* 3, 4253/4.
-ǫthe.
the soth, *adj.*: smoth, *adj. plur.* 1793/4.
-other.
brother, *s.*: other, *pron.* 1115/16. 1714/13, 1952/1, 2502/1, 3702/1.
brother, *s.*: a-nother, *pron.* 1827/8, 3763/4.
-oude.
cloude, *s.*: shrowde, *inf.* 1761/2.
loude, *adj. plur.*: proude, *adj. plur.* 4338/7.
loude, *adj.*: proude, *adj. plur.* 4557/8.
-ought.
abouht, *pp.*: thouht, *s.* 2780/79.
boȝt, *pp.*: noȝt, *pron.* 1862/1.
bought, *pp.*: thought, *s.* 3859/60.
bought, *pp.*: wroght, *pp.* 2058/7.
brouht, *pp.*: nought, *pron.* 3389/90.
brouht, *pp.*: noght, *pron.* 3694/3.
brought *pp.*: sought, *pp.* 2400/399.
broght, *pp.*: thoght, *s.* 1966/5.
broght, *pp.*: wroght, *pp.* 1439/40.
nouȝt, *pron.*: thouȝt, *s.* 499/500.
noght, *pron.*: thoght, *s.* 592/1, 2692/1.
nouȝt, *pron.*: thoȝt, *s.* 1569/70.
nought, *pron.*: thouht, *s.* 2988/7, 4010/09.
noght, *pron.*: thouht, *s.* 3413/14.
noght, *pron.*: ybroght, *pp.* 2021/2.
-oughte.
aboughte, *pret.*: wroughte, *pret.* 3889/90.
abouht, *pret.*: wroght, *pret.* 1779/80.
besought, *pret.*: ought, *pret.* 3934/3.
-oun.
doun, *adv.*: champioun, *s.* 2210/09.
doun, *adv.*: compassioun, *s.* 3396/5, 4282/1.
doun, *adv.*: envyroun, *adv.* 1371/2.
doun, *adv.*: inspeccioun, *s.* 2282/1.
doun, *adv.*: lyoun, *s.* 1887/8.
doun, *adv.*: lamentacioun, *s.* 3382/1.
doun, *adv.*: Poliboun, *n. pr.* 435/6.
doun, *adv.*: regyoun, *s.* 4041/2.
doun, *adv.*: renoun, *s.* 890/89, 1687/8, 3485/6.
doun, *adv.*: resoun, *s.* 681/2.
doun, *adv.*: toun, *s.* 2644/3, 4296/5.
doun, *adv.*: vndiscreccioun, *s.* 3450/49.
renoun, *s.*: confusioun, *s.* 2492/1.
renoun, *s.*: envyroun, *adv.* 2184/3.
renown, *s.*: occisioun, *s.* 4203/4.
renoun, *s.*: regioun, *s.* 1269/70.
renoun, *s.*: Ypomedoun, *n. pr.* 2603/4.
soun, *s.*: Amphioun, *n. pr.* 202/1.
soun, *s.*: entencioun, *s.* 588/7.
toun, *s*: affeccioun, *s.* 2540/39, 3981/2.
toun, *s.*: Amphioun, *n. pr.* 310/09, 326/5.
toun, *s.*: conclusioun, *s.* 70/69, 3927/8.
toun, *s.*: condicioun, *s.* 3762/1.
toun, *s.* confusioun, *s.* 3824/3, 3969/70.
toun, *s.*: consolacioun, *s.* 4306/5.
toun, *s.*: conuencioun, *s.* 1694/3, 1930/29.
toun, *s.*: descripcioun, *s.* 3828/7.
toun, *s.*: destrucccioun, *s.* 186/5, 850/49, 1074/3, 1834/3, 4143/4, 4219/20.
toun, *s.*: domynacioun, *s.* 1096/5, 1974/3.
toun, *s.*: dongoun, *s.* 1293/4.
toun, *s.*: enviroun, *adv.* 1172/1, 1254/3, 2756/5.
toun, *s.*: exortacioun, *s.* 236/5.
toun, *s.*: lyoun, *s.* 4199/200.
toune, *s.*: mencioun, *s.* 1141/2, 4542/1.
toun, *s.*: occasioun, *s.* 2530/29, 3562/1.

toun, *s.*: opynyoun, *s.* 2459/60.
toun, *s.*: possessioun, *s.* 1160/59, 1787/8, 3696/5.
toune, *s.*: professioun, *s.* 131/2.
toun, *s.*: regioun, *s.* 755/6, 2745/6.
toun, *s.*: successioun, *s.* 4375/6.
toun, *s.*: suspecioun, *s.* 3617/18.
affeccioun, *s.*: regioun, *s.* 4577/8.
affeccioun, *s.*: sauacioun, *s.* 3087/8.
affeccioun, *s.*: trunchoun, *s.* 4285/6.
ambicioun, *s.*: domynacioun, *s.* 4675/6.
Amphyoun, *n. pr.*: conclusioun, *s.* 286/5.
Amphioun, *n. pr.*: envyroun, *adv.* 227/8.
Amphioun, *n. pr.*: fundacioun, *s.* 189/90.
Amphyoun, *n. pr.*: successioun, *s.* 332/1.
avisioun, *s.*: mencioun, *s.* 1519/20.
calculacioun, *s.*: disposicioun, *s.* 367/8.
calculacioun, *s.*: questioun, *s.* 2813/14.
Chaloun, *n. pr.*: Chysoun, *n. pr.* 1196/5.
champioun, *s.*: dragoun, *s.* 4665/6.
champioun, *s.*: Palamoun, *n. pr.* 3523/4.
collusioun, *s.*: conuencioun, *s.* 3997/8.
collusioun, *s.*: extorsioun, *s.* 2075/6.
collusioun, *s.*: questioun, *s.* 539/40.
comparisoun, *s.*: domynacioun, *s.* 1734/3.
conparisoun, *s.*: regyoun, *s.* 1941/2.
compassioun, *s.*: execucioun, *s.* 934/3.
compassioun, *s.*: occupacioun, *s.* 3079/80.
compassioun, *s.*: tresoun, *s.* 2379/80.
composicioun, *s.*: conuencioun, *s.* 1135/6.
conclusioun, *s.*: deliberacioun, *s.* 688/7.
conclusioun, *s.*: destruccioun, *s.* 3807/8, 4605/6.
conclusioun, *s.*: domynacioun, *s.* 3173/4.
conclusioun, *s.*: enviroun, *adv.* 2792/1.
conclusioun, *s.*: excepcioun, *s.* 3359/60.
conclusioun, *s.*: occasioun, *s.* 910/09.
conclusioun, *s.*: opynioun, *s.* 1853/4.
conclusioun, *s.*: pocessioun, *s.* 2110/09.
conclusioun, *s.*: regioun, *s.* 529/30.
conclusioun, *s.*: resoun, *s.* 1110/09.
conclusyoun, *s.*: Scorpioun, *s.* 387/8.
condicioun, *s.*: domynacioun, *s.* 3713/14.
condicioun, *s.*: excepcioun, *s.* 4646/5.
condicioun, *s.*: remyssyoun, *s.* 3472/1.
confusioun, *s.*: regyoun, *s.* 789/90.
conspiracioun, *s.*: opynyoun, *s.* 2160/59.
conspiracioun, *s.*: regioun, *s.* 3163/4.
constellacioun, *s.*: inspeccioun, *s.* 382/1.
contradiccioun, *s.*: pocessioun, *s.* 3798/7.
conuencioun, *s.*: pocessioun, *s.* 3774/3.
declaracioun, *s.*: exposicioun, *s.* 635/6.
declaracioun, *s.*: inspeccioun, *s.* 1534/3.
descripcioun, *s.*: lyoun, *s.* 619/20.
destruccioun, *s.*: domynacioun, *s.* 1752/1.
destruccioun, *s.*: regyoun, *s.* 2545/6.
deuocioun, *s.*: orysoun, *s.* 551/2.
digressioun, *s.*: regioun, *s.* 2466/5.
dilusioun, *s.*: regioun, *s.* 968/7.
discrecioun, *s.*: examynacioun, *s.* 2953/4.
discrecioun, *s.*: opynyoun, *s.* 3974/3.
discrecioun, *s.*: supportacioun, *s.* 2983/4.
disposicioun, *s.*: regioun, *s.* 2997/8.
domynacioun, *s.*: subieccioun, *s.* 2965/6.
domynacioun, *s.*: supportacioun, *s.* 270/69.
dongoun, *s.*: mancyoun, *s.* 1883/4.
dongoun, *s.*: relacioun, *s.* 3993/4.
dongoun, *s.*: tresoun, *s.* 3576/5.
dragoun, *s.*: penoun, *s.* 4364/3.
eleccioun, *s.*: successioun, *s.* 1202/1.
enviroun, *adv.*: mencioun, *s.* 3006/5.
envyroun, *adv.*: subieccioun, *s.* 2061/2.
exposicioun, *s.*: informacioun, *s.* 318/17.
fundacioun, *s.*: mencioun, *s.* 4624/3.
guerdoun, *s.*: mansioun, *s.* 4046/5.
haberioun, *s.*: lyoun, *s.* 1544/3.
inspeccioun, *s.*: lyoun, *s.* 1227/8.
intencioun, *s.*: regioun, *s.* 3515/16.
intencioun, *s.*: relacioun, *s.* 2229/30.
lyoun, *s.*: mencioun, *s.* 3836/5.
mansioun, *s.*: sesoun, *s.* 11/12.

mediacioun, *s.*: pardoun, *s.* 3505/6.
mencioun, *s.*: regyoun, *s.* 2577/8.
mencioun, *s.*: Ypomedoun, *n. pr.* 4246/5.
mocioun, *s.*: oposicioun, *s.* 5/6.
occasioun, *s.*: opynioun, *s.* 2882/1.
occasioun, *s.*: presumpcioun, *s.* 2026/5.
occasion, *s.*: vision, *s.* 1223/4.
opynyoun, *s.*: passioun, *s.* 113/14.
opynyoun, *s.*: regioun, *s.* 1613/14.
opynyoun, *s.*: tresoun, *s.* 2261/2.
Palemoun, *n. pr.*: regyoun, *s.* 2616/15.
Polyboun, *n. pr.*: regioun, *s.* 447/8.
possessioun, *s.*: regioun, *s.* 1595/6, 1991/2.
protеccioun, *s.*: sauacioun, *s.* 3430/29.
resoun, *s.*: tresoun, *s.* 2640/39.
supplicacioun, *s.*: transgressioun, *s.* 3257/8.
suspecioun, *s.*: tresoun, *s.* 1155/6.

-oune.
croun, *s.*: (out of) toun, *s.* 3780/79.
croune, *s.*: (out of) toune, *s.* 1145/6.
expowne, *inf.*: rowne, *inf.* 696/5.
frowne, *inf.*: rowne, *inf.* 254/3.

-ound.
ground, *s.*: rounde, *adv.* 2302/1.
hound, *s.*: pound, *s. plur.* 3855/6.

-ounde.
bounde, *pp.*: confounde, *pres. conj.* 4003/4.
bound, *pp.*: found, *pp.* 1816/15.
bounde, *pp.*: founde, *pp.* 2107/8, 4392/1.
confound(e), *inf.*: found(e), *pp.* 2208/7, 2728/7.
founde, *pret. plur.*: grounde, *pp.* 2538/7.
founde, *pp.*: (the) seconde, *numer.* 1212/11.
founde, *pp.*: wounde, *s.* 4238/7.
founde, *pret. plur.*: wounde, *s.* 4479/80.
founde, *pp.*: vnbounde, *pret. plur.* 445/6, 939/40.
founde, *pp.*: ybounde, *pp.* 527/8.
habounde, *adj.*: iocounde, *adj.* 3099/100.

-ounded.
forwounded, *pp.*: vnsounded, *adj.* 2437/8.

-ouned.
compowned, *pp.*: crowned, *pp.* 1604/3.
compowned, *pp.*: expowned, *pp.* 735/6.
crownyd, *pp.*: expownyd, *pp.* 1968/7.
drownyd, *pp.*: frownyd, *pp.* 4249/50.

-oundes, -ys.
boundes, *s. plur.*: woundes, *s. plur.* 2345/6.
stoundys, *s. plur.*: woundys, *s. plur.* 2895/6.

-ouns.
sowns, *s. plur.*: clarions, *s. plur.* 3578/7.
sownes, *s. plur.*: lyounes, *s. plur.* 1179/80.
sownys, *s. plur.*: lamentaciouns, *s. plur.* 4421/2.
touns, *s. plur.*: barouns, *s. plur.* 2580/79.
touns, *s. plur.*: rigiouns, *s. plur.* 4428/7.
champiouns, *s. plur.*: lyouns, *s. plur.* 1355/6.
champiouns, *s. plur.*: regiouns, *s. plur.* 2752/1.
condiciouns, *s. plur.*: excepciouns, *s. plur.* 3767/8.
coniurisouns, *s. plur.*: incantaciouns, *s. plur.* 4050/49.
constellaciouns, *s. plur.*: manciouns, *s. plur.* 4054/3.
dyvisions, *s. plur.*: regyouns, *s. plur.* 4683/4.
fracciouns, *s. plur.*: mansiouns, *s. plur.* 374/3.
habergons, *s. plur.*: sabatons, *s. plur.* 1438/7.
naciouns, *s. plur.*: regyouns, *s. plur.* 4701/2.

-our.
clamour, *s.*: socour, *s.* 4104/3.
conquerour, *s.*: flour, *s.* 4535/6.
conquerour, *s.*: gouernour, *s.* 2702/1.
dyvynour, *s.*: socour, *s.* 4096/5.
emperour, *s.*: shour, *s.* 3425/6.
errour, *s.*: honour, *s.* 541/2.
errour, *s.*: labour, *s.* 378/7.
favour, *s.*: socour, *s.* 2982/1.
flour, *s.*: werreyour, *s.* 2622/1.
gouernour, *s.*: socour, *s.* 757/8, 4384/3.
harberioure, *s.*: toure, *s.* 1498/7.
honour, *s.*: successour, *s.* 4191/2.
honour, *s.*: werreyour, *s.* 4124/3.
hour, *s.*: shour, *s.* 3405/6.
hour, *s.*: socour, *s.* 1186/5.
socour, *s.*: toure, *s.* 2866/5.
Tremour, *n. pr.*: werreour, *s.* 3895/6.

-oure.
deuoure *inf.*: loure, *inf.* 4072/1.

floure, *pres. conj.*: socoure, *inf.* 852/1.
-oured.
socoured, *pp.*: deuoured, *pp.* 2829/30.
-ourne.
soiourne, *inf.*: retourne, *inf.* 723/4.
soiourne, *inf.*: tourne, *inf.* 2113/14.
tourne, *inf.*: soiourne, *pres. sing.* 3231/32.
tourne, *inf.*: mourne, *pres. conj.* 3685/6.
-oures, -ours.
auctours, *s. plur.*: expositours, *s. plur.* 294/3.
colours, *s. plur.*: merours, *s. plur.* 3841/2.
conquerours, *s. plur.*: progenitours, *s. plur.* 4140/39.
flours, *s. plur.*: predecessours, *s. plur.* 1975/6.
floures, *s. plur.*: shoures, *s. plur.* 3216/15.
flours, *s. plur.*: sowdeours, *s. plur.* 2936/5.
herberiours, *s. plur.*: tours, *s. plur.* 3326/5.
houres, *s. plur.*: shoures, *s. plur.* 2893/4.
oures, *pron.*: werreoures, *s. plur.* 2495/6.
sowdeours, *s. plur.*: tours, *s. plur.* 2758/7.
sawdyours, *s. plur.*: werreyours, *s. plur.* 2630/29.
soudeoures, *s. plur.*: werreoures, *s. plur.* 2680/79.
-ous (Cf. -us).
hous, *s.*: contrarious, *adj.* 394/3.
bountevous, *adj.*: famous, *adj.* 2726/5.
contrarious, *adj.*: surquydows, *adj.* 472/1.
coraious, *adj.*: desyrous, *adj.* 567/8.
famous, *adj.*: plenteuous, *adj.* 1453/4.
odious, *adj.*: vngracious, *adj.* 821/2.
superstitious, *adj.*: vngracious, *adj.* 4057/8.
furius, *adj.*: Tydeus, *n. pr.* 3914/13.
furious, *adj.*: Tydeus, *n. pr.* 1961/2, 3265/6.
melodious, *adj.*: Mercurius, *n. pr.* 223/4.
pitous, *adj.*: Campaneus, *n. pr.* 4472/1.
vertuvs, *adj.*: Layus, *n. pr.* 916/15.
vertuous, *adj.*: Mercurius, *n. pr.* 835/6.
vertuous, *adj.*: Tidyus, *n. pr.* 1265/6.
vngracius, *adj.*: Campaneus, *n. pr.* 4348/7.
-oute.
aboute, *adv.*: doute, *s.* 728/7, 1513/14, 1813/14, 2750/49, 3613/14, 4069/70.
aboute, *adv.*: oute, *adv.* 1117/18, 1924/3, 3565/6, 3737/8.
aboute, *adv.*: route, *inf.* 109/10.
aboute, *adv.*: route, *s.* 1058/7, 1890/89, 2223/4.
doute, *s.*: loute, *pres. plur.* 262/1.
doute, *s.*: oute, *adv.* 4017/18.
oute, *adv.*: route, *s.* 4195/6.
oute, *adv.*: shoute, *inf.* 4091/2.
-outh.
kouth, *adj.*: south, *adj.* 2802/1.
mouth, *s.*: vnkouth, *adj.* 52/1.
mouth, *s.*: south, *adj.* 3014/13.
couth, *adj. sing.*: mouth, *inf.* 4408/7.
kouth, *adj.*: ȝouth, *s.* 706/5, 985/6, 1197/8, 1612/11.
-outhe.
routh, *s.*: slouth, *s.* 925/6.
slouthe, *s.*: trouthe, *s.* 1945/6.
slouth, *s.*: trouth, *s.* 3324/3.
-owe.
a-rowe, *s.*: knowe, *pp.* 2097/8.
blowe, *inf.*: lowe, *adv.* 112/11.
bowe, *s.*: lowe, *adv.* 3492/1.
bowe, *s.*: vnknowe, *pp.* 3962/1.
knowe, *inf.*: lowe, *adv.* 548/7, 721/2, 4350/49.
knowe, *pres. plur.*: lowe, *adv.* 814/13.
lowe, *adv.*: rowe, *s.* 3386/5, 4560/59.
lowe, *adv.*: sowe, *pp.* 4667/8.
lowe, *adv.*: throwe, *pp.* 1011/12.
lowe, *adv.*: vnknowe, *pp.* 492/1.
lowe, *adv.*: ythrowe, *pp.* 2031/2.
ouerthrowe, *pp.* : be rowe, *s.* 1754/3.
-ow (=ū).
howh, *adv.* (N.E. how): slogh, *pret.* 582/1.
howe, *adv.*: sclowe, *pret.* 1272/1.
howe, *adv.*: ynowe, *adv.* 2447/8.
-ude.
conclude, *inf.*: rude, *adj.* 29/30.
conclude, *inf.*: multitude, *s.* 2241/2.
-ue (Cf. -ewe).
due, *adj.*: salue, *inf.* 1893/4.
dwe, *adj.*: salwe, *inf.* 3601/2.
dwe, *adj.*: swe, *inf.* 2382/1.
eschwe, *inf.*: remewe, *inf.* 3788/7.
remwe, *pres. conj.*: swe, *inf.* 2140/39.
remwe, *inf.*: swe, *inf.* 3041/2.
hwe, *s.*: trwe, *adj.* 4447/8.
-ued.
eschewed, *pp.*: swed, *pp.* 2901/2.

-uge.
huge, *adj.*: refuge, *s.* 1183/4.
-ul.
dul, *adj.*: wonderful, *adj.* 183/4.
-ulle.
at the fulle: bulle, *s.* (Latin bulla) 3423/4.
-une.
contune, *inf.*: fortune, *s.* 2713/14.
contune, *inf.*: inportune, *adj.* 4116/15.
contune, *inf.*: opportune, *adj.* 140/39.
fortune, *s.*: importune, *adj.* 523/4.
-ure.
armure, *s.*: cure, *s.* 2665/6.
assure, *inf.*: auenture, *s.* 3083/4.
assure, *inf.*: endure, *inf.* 3794/3.
assure, *inf.*: pasture, *s.* 103/4.
aventure, *s.*: cure, *s.* 3281/2, 3822/1.
auenture, *s.*: endure, *inf.* 650/49, 1926/5.
auenture, *s.*: obscure, *adj.* 1242/1.
cure, *s.*: sepulture, *s.* 599/600, 4359/60.
disconfiture, *s.*: mysauenture, *s.* 2514/13.
nature, *s.*: scripture, *s.* 3832/1.
discure, *inf.*: auenture, *s.* 2360/59.
discure, *inf.*: creature, *s.* 3958/7.
recure, *inf.*: auenture, *s.* 1130/29.
recure, *inf.*: endure, *pres. conj.* 3415/16.
recure, *inf.*: endure, *inf.* 4126/5.
recure, *inf.*: eure, *s.* 4090/89.
-urid.
fyguryd, *pp.*: luryd, *pp.* 3954/3.
recured, *pp.*: assured, *pp.* 2453/4.
recured, *pp.*: endured, *pp.* 3124/3.
-urned (-ourned).
turned, *pret.*: soiourned, *pp.* 305/6.
-urys.
creaturys, *s. plur.*: auenturys, *s. plur.* 4433/4.
-us.
thus, *adv.*: Tydeus, *n. pr.* 2247/8, 3297/8, 3766/5.
vs, *pron.*: Campaneus, *n. pr.* 2608/7.
vs, *pron.*: Tydeus, *n. pr.* 1874/3.
Campaneus, *n. pr.*: Tydeus, *n. pr.* 3020/19.
Pyrrus, *n. pr.*: Tortolanus, *n. pr.* 2613/14.
-use.
accuse, *inf.*: excuse, *inf.* 3240/39.
excuse, *inf.*: muse, *inf.* 399/400.
excuse, *inf.*: vse, *inf.* 142/1.
-ust.
lust, *s.*: thrust, *s.* (thirst) 3109/10.
-ut.
refut, *s.*: destitut, *adj.* 4371/2.
-y.
by, *adv.*: cry, *s.* 441/2.

GLOSSARY

The Glossary is a good deal fuller than is usual in the publications of the Early English Text Society. It aims at giving all words used in *Thebes* and all the significations of each word. It gives full references for more rare words, but not all the passages in which the more common words occur. It is the first glossary of a Middle English text that may be termed complete also as regards the meanings of words. These latter are of importance as characterising the linguistic usage of the author. Many words or significations of words will be found to be evidenced earlier in *Thebes* than the first date given in the *Oxford Dictionary*.

The full lists of forms will render a comprehensive treatment of inflexion unnecessary, and much information generally given in the Notes in other editions will here be found in the Glossary.

A, *art.* 35, etc., 3926 (**a gret pas**); *numer.* 4450 (**out of a cuntrè**); *pron.* any 1077 (**in a poynt**). **An** 456 (**an norys**), 1790 (**an horn**), 2260 (**an esy pas**).

A, *prep.* 162 (**a twenty deuelway**).

A-bak, *adv.* back 2216.

Abasshe, *v. tr.* abash, confuse 3041.

Abide, *v. intr.* wait (*vpon*) 3334; lie in wait for (*vpon*) 4222; tarry, delay 359, 415; stay, remain 520, 1324, 1487 (*pret. sing.* **abood**); continue 470; stick to (*on*) 4158, 3606; hold one's ground 3912, 4202.

Ablaster, Arblast, *s.* arbalest, cross-bow 2592, 4315.

Abood, *s.* delay 3107; **with-out a.** 525, 1347; **w. more a.** 4533.

About (-e, -en), *adv.* around 4061, 562, 3397, 2385, 728 (**the wheel cometh a.** turns round); *prep.* around 1553, 2322 (postpos.); concerning 2044.

Aboue(n), *adv.* 1771 (**god a.**), 2073; *prep.* 834, 1544, 1721 (**a. alle thyng**).

Abrayde (Abraid), *v. intr.* call out, shout out 646, 1963, 479 (**vpon hym**); *pret.* **abrayd** 955, **abrayde** *plur.* 2925.

Absence, *s.* 3222.

Absent, *adj.* 3139; **absént** 846, 2095, 3272; *v. refl.* 1118 (**a. hym oute**).

Abstene, *v. intr.* abstain, refrain 815, 2920.

Abye, *v. tr.* pay for, suffer for; *pret.* **abouht** 1779, *plur.* **aboughte** 3889; *pp.* **abouht** 2780.

Acceptable, *adj.* acceptable, pleasing 788 (*to-for*), 1943 (*vnto*), 4386 (*to*).

Accepted, *pp.* favourably received, heard 354; *pp. adj.* approved 2804, acceptable, satisfactory 275.

Accord(e), *s.* harmony 829; agreement, convention 1082, 1141, 2096, 4399; **be on a.** 2705; **of oon a.** 2731, 3128.

Accorde, *v. intr.* agree 1592 (*therto*); **be accorded** 3297 (with *to* and inf.), 775 (with *that*-clause), 3711.

Account, *s.* account, reckoning 3677.

Account, *v.* reckon 4622.

Accuse, *v.* accuse 3240 (*of*).

Acheue (Achieue), *v. tr.* achieve, perform 3608, 4151.

Acomplyssh, A-complisshen, *v. tr.* accomplish, perform 1140, 3192.

Adawe, *v.* awake 2333 (see *Notes*).

Adiacent, *adj.* 563, 931 (*vnto*), 2750 (**a. aboute**), 3829 (**besyden a.**).

Admit, *v. tr.* allow 27, 179.

Ado, *inf.* to do 2033 (**haue eny thynge ado**); *s.* business, trouble 1344 (**haue a.**); combat, encounter 4265 (**han a.**).

A-doun, *adv.* down 890.

Adrad, *pp.* afraid, frightened 1177 (*therof*).

Aduersitè, *s.* misfortune 847, 1318, 1746, 2885.

Adverte (Aduerte), *v. intr.* pay attention, take heed 251, 1993, 1067 (*to*), 1940 (*that*-clause), 3284 (*how*); *tr.* notice, consider 679, 956, 1307, 1818, 3394, 4268. A favourite word of Lydgate's.

Afer(e)d, Affered, Afferd(e), *pp. adj.* afraid, frightened 1888, 2115, 3905, 2262 (*of*), 1154 (*to* + inf.).

Affeccioun, *s.* affection, love 3087, 3982.

Afferme, *v. tr.* affirm, maintain, assert 718, 1029, 1449, 3511, 3973; declare 520, 1379, 3766.

Affiaunce, *s.* faith, trust 893, 1703, 4056, 4083.

Affray, *s.* consternation 963, 2340; alarm, fright 1232, 3265; disturbance 1296, 3372, 4114.

Affrayd (Affrayed), *pp.* frightened, afraid 2350, 3044.

A-fire, *adv.* afire 2036.

Aforn, Afore, Afor, *adv. temp.* 296, 707, 1145; *prep. temp.* 124; *adv. loci* 438 (: *behynde*); *prep. loci* 1427, 3562, 3587.

After, *adv. temp.* afterwards 148, 305, 309; *prep. temp.* 72, 108, 462; **after that** afterwards, then 432, 704, 1353; **after this** hereafter 2058; according to 544 (**a. custome**), 1782 (**a. her devys**); *conj. temp.* 1214.

Afterward, *adv.* 938; **-es,** *adv.* 665.

Age, *s.* age 93, 665, 1399; old age 714, 1194, 2798.

Ageyn, Aȝeyn, *adv.* again, once more 517 (**eft a.**), 604, 671; in return, in response 1092, 3954.

Ageyn, Agayn, Ageynes, *prep.* against 262, 402, 592, 2066; *temporal* 778 (**a. a certeyn day**). **Aȝeynst,** *prep.* 758 (**a. her foon**).

Ageynward, *adv.* in return, on the other hand 4270, 4396.

Ago, *v.* depart; *pp.* 3990 (**grekys ben a.**). **Agon,** *adv.* ago 210.

Agrè, *v. intr.* be agreeable, suit 1622.

Agreable, *adj.* pleasant 1468 (*to*).

A-greued, *pp.* annoyed, vexed 3607 (*ther-with*).

Al, *adj.* all, whole 33, 749, 3401 (**al a day**), 67 (**on and all**), 49 (**noght at al**); *adv.* altogether, quite 89, 1092 (**al opynly**), 444 (**all at onys**).

Al be that, *conj.* although 574, 809, 1273. **Al be** *id.* 799, 1016.

Alder-, Alther-, *gen. plur.* of all 668 (**alderlast**), 712 (**alther-last**), 1143 (**alderfirst**).

Ale, *s.* ale 110.

Alegge, *v.* allege, urge as a reason 1085 (*that*-clause).

Algate, *adv.* nevertheless, after all 3712.

Alighte (Alyghte), *v. intr.* alight (from a horse); *pret. sing.* **alight** 1257, 1320; **alighte doun** 4282, 2282.

Allas, *interj.* 947, 1101, 4216 (**O. allas**), 1747 (**a. that**), 1184 (**a. the while**), 3365 (**a. the whyl**).

Allay, *s.* admixture with water 3532 (see *Note* 3520–21); *figur.* alloy, deteriorating element 4461.

Allaye, *v. tr.* dilute (wine) with water 4460 (MSS. Ar. G. **laye**).

Al(l)iaunce, *s.* union, common bond 1071 (*of brotherhode*); union by marriage 844, 1218, 1516, 1590.

Al(l)one, *adj.* alone 759, 1152, 2866 (**al a.**).

Allure, *s.* garden walk 2313.

Allye, *v. tr.* ally, unite; **allyed,** *pp.* 1682 (*with*).

Allye, *s.* kinship 2081 (see *Notes*); a relative, kinsman 1702, 2735, 2754.

Almost, *adv.* almost 1186, 3371, 4219.

Aloe, *s.* aloe; *plur.* **aloes** the fragrant resin of the plant 4572 (: *relees*).

Alofte, *adv.* up, on high 208, 702, 1053; in (to) an upper storey 1245, 2383.

A-lowde, *adv.* aloud 3364.

Also, *adv.* 6, 24, 4069; **a. ek** 573, 3824; **ek a.** 32.

Al-thoh, Althogh, *conj.* although 3651, 4389.

Alway, Alwey, *adv.* always 45, 792, 1523.

Alyve, *adv.* alive 2977, 4346 (**be a.**), 4419 (**man a.**).

Amaat, *adj.* overwhelmed, utterly defeated 741.

Amased, *pp.* amazed, confounded 2216.

Ambassyat, *s.* embassy 3728.

Ambicioun, *s.* ambition 4675.

Ame, Hame, *v. intr.* aim 4326 (*at*).

Amende, *v. tr.* repair, make amends for 3700; improve 1607.

Amendement, *s.* amendment, correction (of sins) 4714.

Amerous, *adj.* amorous 1669.

Amervaylyd, *pp.* astonished 4467 (*v.l.*).

Among, *prep.* 256, 423; *adv.* all the while 819, 2295 (**euer a.**).

Amonges, *prep.* 615.

And, *conj.* and 3, 5, etc.; if 489, 2980, etc.

Angelik, *adj.* angelic 3979.

Angre, *s.* anger 2036.

Angre, *v. tr.* make angry, vex 35.

Anguysshous, *adj.* full of anguish, sore distressed 2263 (see *Notes*).

Annys, *s.* anise 118.

Anon, Anoon, *adv.* at once, forthwith 77, 82, 146; soon, in a short time 357, 694, 2093; **a. as** as soon as 128, 150, 3309; **a. ryght** immediately, straightway 3752.

Another, *pron.* 1828, 3655, 3989; *adv.* differently, otherwise 3764 (**thouhten al a.**).
Anoy, *s.* annoyance, discomfort 1287.
Answer, *s.* answer 540, 1311, 3478.
Answer, *v.*; *pret.* **answerd(e)** 92, 688, 1313.
Antiquytè, *s.* olden time 187, 4024, 4128; old age (of human life) 2803.
Any, *adv.* 4565 (**a. lenger**); see **eny.**
Anyghtes, *adv.* by night 2406.
Apayd, Apeyde, *pp.* satisfied, pleased, content 1636 (*wel*), 2127 (*euel*), 3697, 4498.
Ap(p)ese, *v. tr.* appease, relieve 2398, alleviate 3277.
Apoint, Apoynt, *v. tr.* arrange, put in order and connexion 498; settle, decide 2793 (**vp tapoynt**).
Apoynt, *s.* decision, resolution 3805 (see *Notes*).
Appaire, Apeyre, *v. intr.* become worse or weaker, weaken 1034, 4097 (**is apeyryd**).
Appallen, Apalle, *v. intr.* become pale or dim, fade 44, 4159.
Apparayled, *pp.* apparelled, adorned 2385; prepared, equipped, fitted up 4146.
Apparaylle, *s.* preparation, array 3612.
Apparceyve, *v. tr.* discern, discover 1838.
Apparence, *s.* appearance, outward look 3843 (**fals a.**).
Appartene, *v. intr.* appertain, belong 490.
Appere, *v. intr.* appear 944, 1188.
Appetit, *s.* desire 3110.
Apport, *s.* bearing, demeanour 248, 1464, 2039.
Approche, *v. tr.* approach 642; *intr.* 1190 (**a. to**).
Aprille, *s.* April 2.
Aquyte, Aqwite, *v. tr.* discharge, fulfil 72; *refl.* acquit oneself, discharge one's duties, perform one's part 1816, 1934, 4435; *pret. plur.* **aquytte** 29.
Araied, *pp.* attired, dressed 91.
Aray, Array, *s.* array, attire, outfit 1307, 3312.
Arest, *s.* stop 4225.
A-right, *adv.* rightly, properly 3433.
Arise, *v. intr.* rise 1445 (*the sonne*): get up (in the morning) 1526 (**vp aroos**); rise from a seat 1472; rise in hostility 4682 (*agayn*); begin 4299; rise, increase 1175 (of wind).
Arm, *s.* arm (of body) 1259, 3030.
Arme, *v. tr.* arm; *pp.* **armed** 1150, 3040, 4300 (**armyd foot and hed**), **y-armed** 1306, 1346; *refl.* 1864, 4015.
Armes, *s. plur.* arms, weapons; feats of arms 1267.
Armonye, *s.* harmony 203, 830.
Armure, *s.* arms 2665; defensive armour, mail 4332.
Armyng, *s.* arms, armour 2662.
Arow(e), Arwe, Harowe, *s.* arrow 3493, 1277, 3963, 1484.
As, *adv., conj.* 28 (**lich as**), 36, 176, 174 (**so as**); *pleonastic* 454 (**as in that langage**), 1989, 4046, 2219 (**as blyve**); *temp.* as, while 1274, 1276 (**so as**); as if 159 (**as it were**), 486 (**lik as thow were sone**); *relative* 260 (**swich as**), 363.
Ascende, *v. intr.* ascend 834 (*vp*), 1132.
Ascendent, *s.* ascendant 370 (astronomical and astrological term).
A-side, *adv.* 132, 260, 3458.
A-sonder, *adv.* asunder 1374 (**put a.**, separate); in pieces 4323.
Aspecte, *s.* aspect (astrological term) 383; *plur.* **aspectes** 218 (**a. glade**), 275 (**a. goode**), 4054 (**diuerse a.**).
Assay, *s.* trial 4462.
Assaye, Asseye, *v. intr.* try 3304, 3984; *tr.* 2617.
Assaylle, *v. tr.* attack 3882, 3919, 4309.
Assele, *v. tr.* attest by seal; *figur.* 3775.
Assemble, *v. intr.* assemble 60, 2660, 4068.
Assemblè, *s.* assembly 4431.
Assent, *s.* consent, accord 238 (**be on a.**), 777 (**by ful a.**), 1114 (**of on a.**).
Assente, *v. intr.* consent, agree 1633 (*to*), 3162 (*to* with inf.), 4271.
Asshe, *s.* ash; *plur.* **asshes** 596, 2542, **asshen** 602.
Assigne, *v. tr.* assign, appoint 1656, 2651; direct, appoint 64, 139, 233.
Asstonyed, *pp.* stupefied 2484 (rubric).
Assuraunce, *s.* assurance 2645.
Assure, *v. tr.* pledge 103 (*myn hede*); guarantee 3794; *refl.* be so bold as, venture 3083; *pp.* **assured,** pledged 871 (**a. othes**), 2252 (**knyght sworn and a.**); *adj.* confident, bold 680, 2175.
As(s)wage, *v. tr.* assuage, mitigate 2398, 3016; *intr.* abate, diminish 2874, 3499.
Astat, *s.* 1029 = **Estat** q.v.
Asterte, *v. intr.* be absent, lacking 2407; *pret. sing.* **asterte** escaped 2489; *tr.* escape, avoid 2996, 3825 (**it to telle may me not a.** I cannot escape telling it).

Astouned, *pp.* confounded, bewildered 2115, 3358, 3892.
Astronomye, *s.* astronomy, astrology 2930, 4052.
Astronomyen, *s.* astrologer 364.
A-swoune, *adv.* in a swoon 3386 (**a. she fille**).
At, Att, *prep.* at 19, 60, 131.
Attempré, *adj.* temperate, mild 1056.
Attendance, *s.* attention 1620.
Attendaunt, *adj.*; **be a. on** wait upon 2390, 3952.
Atteyne, *v. tr.* reach, arrive at 1678, 1883; gain, accomplish 4173; *intr.* (*to, vnto, into*) arrive at, reach 560, 714, 1582, 2264; suffice, be sufficient 3331.
Atteynt, *pp.* convicted 2069 (*of thy promys*); overpowered 2253.
Attones, -ys, *adv.* at once 4451, 2732 (**al a.**), 4517.
A-twen(e), *prep.* between 655, 990, 1515.
Atwixe, *prep.* between 1591, 4684; **atwixt** 1591 (*v.l.*).
Auctour, *s.* author 199, 225, 294. **Autour,** *s.* 877, 1266, 3511.
Auctorité, *s.* authority 2804; authorization 3335.
Audience, *s.* hearing 1896, 2968, 3812 (**he had but lytyl a.**).
Augrym stoones, *s.* stones or counters for calculation 376.
Avail, *s.* advantage, benefit 3707.
Avail(l)e, *v. intr.* be of value or advantage, avail 244, 1111, 2980; be efficacious or able, suffice 2077 (MS. Ar. **vaile**); *tr.* profit, benefit 1861, 2001, 3345.
Avale, *v. intr.* fall down 8; *pp.* **availled** (*doun*) defeated, discomfited 4296.
Avaunce, *v. tr.* help, aid 278.
Auauntage, *s.* advantage 1144, 3599, 3791.
Avenge, *v. tr.* avenge 3880; **be avenged** take vengeance 2055, 2132 (*vpon*), 3254 (*on*).
Avengyng, *s.* 3932.
Aventaylle, *s.* ventail of a helmet 4328.
Aventure, *s.* adventure 650, 2359, 2372; fortune, experience 4434; misfortune, accident 3281, 3822; risk, peril 3084; chance 1129, 1926; **of a.** by chance, fortuitously 580, 1263, 1284; **be a.** *id.* 1242.
Auenturous, *adj.* perilous 3480.
Avis, *s.* consideration, deliberation 632; forethought, prudence 683, 1106; opinion, judgment 1624; counsel, advice 3632.
Avisé, *adj.* prudent, circumspect 3940 (see *Notes*).
Avised, *adj.* deliberate, judicious 2083, 2888; with mind made up, determined 3943, 4009.
Avisement, *s.* consideration, deliberation 957, 1137, 3661.
Avisioun, *s.* vision, dream 1519.
Avowe, *v. tr.* declare, vow 3960.
Avoyde, *v. tr.* leave, depart from 1947; clear away, do away with 3504; *intr.* withdraw, depart 3721.
Awake, *v. tr.* awaken 1303 (*pp.* **awaked**); *intr.* awake 4698, 1358 (*pret.* **awoke**).
Awapyd, *pp.* amazed, utterly confounded 741.
Away *adv.* 191 (**his fame neuere shal a.** die).
Awayt, Aweyte, *s.* ambush 692, 1764, 4215; snare 1672; watch, guard 2294, 3572.
Awhile, (for) a short while, (for) a little 2123 (Ar., **a while** Bo, etc.).
Axe, *v.* ask 1400.
Ay, *adv.* always 577; continually 605, 875, 905.
Ayr, Eir(e), *s.* air 1053, 1056, 2297 (in MS. Ar. always with *h-*).

Badde, *adj.* bad 2955.
Bak, *s.* back 4226; **at the b.** behind 4307.
Bal, *s.* ball 597 (**vessel mad as a bal**); round stone used as a missile 4312.
Balaunce, *s.* uncertainty, suspense 1515 (**hangyng in b.**), 3682.
Baner, *s.* banner 4362, 1548 (**banerys: lerys**).
Banishe, *v. tr.* banish 1280 (MS. Ar. **banshed**).
Banke, *s.* bank (of river) 3491.
Barayn, Bareyn, *adj.* barren, childless 342; dry, poor 183 (*wit*).
Barbyd, *adj.* wearing a barb 4440.
Barbykan, *s.* barbican 2774.
Bare, *adj.* bare, naked 4438 (**on foote b.**), 4561; laid waste, desolate 873, 4692; defenceless, unprotected 4372; simple, unambiguous 631 (**wordes pleyn and bare**).
Barfote, -foot, *adj., adv.* barefoot 4445, 4469.
Baronage, *s.* the barons, nobles 1651.
Baroun, *s.* baron 1081.
Barre, *s.* bar 4352.
Barrer, *s.* palisade 2775.
Batailled, *pp. adj.* battlemented, crenelated 4145.
Batayl(l)e, *s.* battle, fight 2078, 3659, 3920.

Bathe, *v. tr.* bathe 3119, 4258.

Bawme, *s.* balm, fragrance 17.

Be, *v.*; *inf.* 218, 349, 683, **ben** 765 (: *quene*), 45, 1757, **bene** 249; *pres. ind.* 1. **am** 178; 2. **art** 489; **artow** 481; 3. **is**; *plur.* **arn** 2244, **are** 1586, **ar** 494, **be** 701, **ben** 818, 1732; *pres. conj.* **be** 488, 406; *pret. ind.* 1. 3. **was** 39; 2. **wer(e)** 492, 2558; *plur.* **weren, were** 872, 146, *conj.* **were** 159, 484; *imp.* **be** 143, *plur.* **beth** 1774, 3043 (to one person); *part. pres.* **beyng** 565; *pp.* **be** 103, **ben** 789; with **ne** : *pres. ind.* **nys** 603; *pret.* **nas** 870.

Beautè, *s.* beauty 421, 884, 1209.

Because, *conj.* 1249, 3631, 4025.

Bed, *s.* bed 149, 906.

Beer, Bere, *s.* bear 3596, 1180.

Be(e)st, *s.* animal 659, 1177, 431.

Begyle, *v. tr.* beguile, deceive 1279, 1671.

Begynne, *v. tr.* begin 1046, 4651; *pret. sing.* **began** 296, 329; *pp.* **begonne** 187, **-gvnne** 2562, **bygon** 4142.

Bygynnyng, *s.* beginning 4524.

Beheest, *v. tr.* promise 2421.

Behest, Bihest, *s.* promise 2046, 1775.

Beholde, Byholde, *v. tr.* behold, see 451; regard, look on 899, 1531, 1661; *pret. sing.* **beheeld, -held** 512, 4261, 4467; *plur.* **beheelden** 420, **beheld** (: *felde*) 3874; *intr.* 1537, 1171 (**b. environn** look round).

Behote, *v. tr.* promise 3143; *pret. sing.* **behiht** 3275, *plur.* **biheght** 3150; *pp.* **behight** 3986.

Behynde, *adv.* behind 438.

Bekke, Bek, Beeke, *s.* nose 169 (see *Notes*).

Belle, *s.* bell 85.

Bem, Beem, *s.* beam, ray 1767, 2299, 4134, 4700.

Bende, *v. tr.* bend 3492 (**he bent a bowe**).

Benygne, *adj.* benign 234; humble, meek 1655.

Benygnely, Benignely, *adv.* 3344, 506, 3060.

Berd(e), *s.* beard 2927, 4326, 3906 (**met hem in the berd** face to face).

Beerdlees, *adj.* beardless 33.

Bere, Bern, *v. tr.* bear 337 (*the Croune*), 265 (*hym vp*), 3654 (*witnesse*); carry 702, 654 (**b. away the pryse**); *refl.* conduct o. s. 247, 492; *pres. ind.* 3. *sing.* **berth** 4686; *pret. plur.* **bar(e)** 447, 4212; *pp.* **born** carried 664, born 392, 404, **yborn** 700, 1085.

Berer, *s.*; **b. vp** upholder, supporter 269, 1769.

Bereyne, *v. tr.*; **bereyned** drenched with rain 1237; streaming with tears 3264.

Beseche, *v. tr.* beseech 86, 347; *pret.* **besoughte** 351, **bysoughte** 505, 3983.

Bysechyng, *s.* 4711.

Besette, *v. tr.* invest, surround 3565 (*pp.* **besette about**), 3586, 3871; assail on all sides 2189.

Beseyn, Byseyn, *pp.* looking, appearing, with qualifying adv. 1285 (**hidously b.** in a dreadful state, especially as to dress), 1558 (**halle wel b.** well appointed, furnished), 1658 (**many knyght ful wel b.** well appointed, dressed).

Beside, -syde, *adv.* by the (one's) side 182 (**her b.**), 534 (**ther b.**), 610 (**fer b.** far out of his way), 3829 (**besyden** adiacent); *postpos.* 2318 (**hym b.**); past 628 (**passeden b.**).

Best, *adj.* 4231; **at the b.** in amplissima forma, outright 2045 (see *Notes*); **for the beste** for the best 1108, 1588; for good, finally 1261, 2291.

Bestaylle, *s.* cattle 3592.

Bet, Bette, *adj.* better 145, 2833; **bet and wors** higher or lower in rank 151; **nouther for bet nor wors** 3729 (on no condition); **it wolde be no bette** 172 (there was no help for it).

Bete, *v. tr.* beat, strike; *pret. sing.* **bete** (*doune*) 4556; *plur.* **bete** 4544; *pp.* **bete** 4147, 1237 (*with the tempest*); beat off, repel 4312 (**betyn** of *pp.*); emboss 1548 (**bete** *pp.*), 4364 (**of gold I-betyn**); *intr.* fall violently 1176 (of rain; **bete** *pret. sing.*).

Betide, *v. intr.* happen 1851.

Better, Bettre, *adj.* 1345 (**no b. mene**), 4123 (**b. it wer**), 2024 (**he b. were to ha ben in pes**).

Betwixe, *prep.* between 1719 (**b. tweyn**).

Bid, *v. tr.* bid, order; *pres. p.* **biddyng** 404; *pret.* **bad** 555, 924, **badde** 2389; pray, exhort 1419, 1785 (*pret.* **bad**).

Bidding, Byddyng, *s.* command 65, 2730, 1654, 3569.

Bigge, *v. tr.* build 236 (T_2.; the other MSS. **bylde**).

Bilde, Bylde, *v. tr.* build 236, 302; *pret.* **bylt(e)** 204, 287; *pp.* **bilt, bylt, belt** 1252, 187, 2269.

Bieldyng, Beeldyng, *s.* building 4624 (**the b. of gret Rome**); structure, construction 1191; buildings 297.

Bille, *s.* bill, petition 3257.

Binde, *v. tr.* bind, tie 528 (**ybounde** *pp.*); bind by oath, promise 174 (**bonde** *pret. sing.*), 130 (**bounde**

pp.), 2646 (**bounde of lygeaunce**), 3283 (**bound** *pp.*).
Bisshop, *s.* 2798.
Bitter, *adj.* 1867 (*teeres*), 3420 (*rage grief*).
Blak, *adj.* black; *plur.* **blake** 857, 3548; *s.* 73, 4469 (**clad in b.**).
Blame, *s.* reproof, censure 1419; blameworthiness, fault 4132, 4155.
Blede, *v. intr.* bleed 451.
Bledyng, *s.* bleeding 2254.
Blende, *v. tr.* blind, deceive 1758 (**blent** *pp.*).
Blew(e), *adj.* blue 3093, 3494.
Bleyk, *adj.* pale, wan 2332.
Blody, *adj.* bloody 2185 (*swerde*).
Blood, *s.* blood 89, 126; family 487, 494; race, nationality 2905.
Blowe(n), *v.* blow 1790 (*in an horn* **figur.** whistle for it); break wind 112.
Blowing, *s.* 1054.
Blunt, *adj.* curt, unpolished 3635.
Blynd(e), *adj.* blind 1017; temporarily deprived of sight 1297; ignorant, unconscious 810 (*of*).
Blyve, *adv.* at once 1342, 1915; **as b.** speedily, quickly 2219.
Body, *s.* body 620; person 1860, 4394; corpse 4495, 4569.
Bold, *adj.* bold 3350, 3435.
Boldēly, *adv.* arrogantly, audaciously 2020.
Bole, Boole, *s.* bull 299, 3526; Taurus, a sign of the zodiac 2.
Bolle, *s.* bowl 31.
Bon, *s.* bone 411, 4563.
Bond, *s.* bond 1230, 1695; agreement, covenant 1789, 2000, 2005.
Bone, *s.* prayer, petition 353.
Book, Boke, *s.* book 200, 880; prayer-book 1528.
Boor, *s.* boar 1180, 3597.
Boos, *s.* stud on bridle 85 (see miniature in Plate 2).
Bore, *v. tr.* bore, pierce 454.
Borned, Boornyd, *pp.* burnished 537, 2169.
Borowe, *s.* pledge, security 2914, 4687, 3474 (**lay his hed to b.** pledge, *i.e.* lose its head); 3549 (**with seynt Iohn to b.** as security, to speed).
Borowe, *v. tr.* borrow 3384.
Bost, *s.* loud, tall talk, boasting 80.
Bote, *s.* remedy 870; relief 1007.
Both(e), *adj.* 199, 494, 707; *adv.* **both(e) . . . and** 151, **bothen . . . and** 2801, 4491.
Bough, *s.* bough, twig 16 (**braunch and b.**), 429 (*plur.* **bowes**).
Bound, *s.* limit, boundary 298, 2345.
Bountė, *s.* goodness, worth 3206.
Bountevous, *adj.* bounteous, munificent 2418, 2726.
Bowe, *s.* bow 157 (**a b. draught**), 3492, 3962 (**Cupides b.**).
Boystously, *adv.* rudely, coarsely 30.
Brake, *s.* winch of crossbow 4224.
Brasyn, *adj.* of brass 3578 (*hornys*).
Braunch, *s.* branch 16.
Braunche, *v. tr.* arrange in branches 3540.
Brede, *s.* breadth 2387, 4699.
Breefly, *adv.* briefly 1902.
Breke, *v. tr.* break 155 (**b. our faste**), 1352 (**brak** *pret. sing.*); *intr.* 4526 (**felt his herte b.**); break out into passionate words 970 (**he brak out vnto the queene**), 1963 (**he out-brak**).
Brekyng, *s.* breaking 2505.
Brenne, *v. intr.* burn; **brente** *pret.* 1075 (**the hatred b.**), 2560 (**the Citė b.**); **brennyng** *part.* 607, 868 (*Ire*); *tr.* **brent(e)** *pret.* 596, 3589, 4272; **brent(e)** *pp.* 2542, 4495.
Brest, *s.* breast 1306, 4476.
Breste, *v. intr.* burst 902 (**brast out for to wepe**).
Breth, *s.* spirit, life 3367, 3931.
Brigge, *s.* bridge 4248.
Bright, Briȝt, *adj.* shining 1, 1365, 1767; fair, beautiful 1658 (**lady b.**); *adv.* brightly, brilliantly 1150, 3992.
Bringe, *v. tr.* bring 1242, 2022 (*pp.* **ybroght**), 813 (**brought lowe** abased, disgraced); lead, put 541, 1232 (**which broght his herte in affray**); prevail upon, persuade 1114 (*pp.* **broght**).
Bristel, *s.* bristle 1546.
Broke, *v. tr.* 96 (see *Notes*).
Brond, *s.* torch 1482.
Broode, *adv.* broadly, openly 1549 (**banerys displaied b.**).
Brose, *v. tr.* bruise 2951.
Brother (**Broder** not in rhyme), *s.* brother 1041, 1115, 1278, 1642 (a very dear friend); *genit. sing.* **brother** (**broder**) 796, 1847, **brotheres** 2064, 2080 (brother-in-law); *plur.* **bretheren** 1136, 3937.
Brother(h)ede, *s.* brothership 1452, 1989; **Brotherhode,** *s.* 1071.
Brotherly, *adv.* in the spirit of a brother 4283.
Brow, *s.* eyebrow 857, 3548.
Brydel, Bridel, *s.* bridle 75, 85.
Brynke, *s.* brink, margin of river 3116.
Buk, *s.* buck 3595 (**b. and doo**).
Bulle, *s.* papal bull 3424.
Bulwerk, *s.* rampart, bulwark 2774.
Burlyd, *pp. adj.* striped 3219.

Burnet, *adj.* of a dark brown colour 4441.

Burye, *v. tr.* bury 1061, 4163.

Busshement, *s.* ambuscade 2154.

But, *conj.* 45 (= sed), 117; but, except 226 (**no thyng b.**), 4055 (**bot**); than 4606 (**no mor b.**); unless 1585; **but ȝif** 4459; **but ȝif that** unless 664; **but that** unless 284; *adv.* only 1575 (**b. now**), 2023.

By, Be, *prep.* by 367, 57; near, close to 3489, 3496; **on be on** 60; *adv.* 3049 (**her faste by** here close by); **by and by** one after another, in due order 441, 652, 3193, 4420.

Byble, *s.* the Bible 4660.

Bye, *v. tr.* buy, pay the penalty of, pay for; *pp.* **bouht, boȝt, bought** 1862, 3782, 2058.

Byfalle, *v. intr.* happen, occur; *pret.* **byfil, byfel** 70 (**me b. to entren**), 3822, 4028 (**bifyl a cas**); *pp.* **befall** 2488.

Byloued, *pp.* beloved 2464.

Bymene, *v. tr.* lament 2828 (**bymente** *pret.*).

Byrth(e), Birth(e), Berthe, *s.* birth, parentage 494, 920, 1079.

Bysy, *adj.* active, eager, diligent 599, 1425, 4685; **bysiest** 4027.

Bysily, *adv.* 1105.

Bysynesse, *s.* diligent endeavour 572, 2361; trouble, labour 3141.

Bywaylle, *v. tr.* bewail 4434.

Bywelde, *v. refl.* use one's limbs, move about freely 2413.

Caarte, *s.* paper or treatise, spec. astrological 376.

Calculacioun, *s.* computation 367, 4052.

Calke, *v. tr.* calculate 372 (rubric).

Kalkyng, *s.* calculation 2930.

Calle, *v. tr.* call, name 452; call, consider 68; call in 456; summon 1359, 2012; *pp.* **called** 303, **y-called** 227, 561.

Can, *v.* can 36, 283; be able 63 (**I can**); know 953; *pres. sing.* 2. **canst** 3690; *pres. ind. plur.* **konne** 138, 2561, **can** 4074; *pres. conj.* 1. **konne** 3545, 2. **can** 740; *pret.* **couth** 1993, **coude** 941, **cowde** 2811, **kowde** 1720.

Cankered, *pp.* cankered, envenomed 4273.

Capricorn *s.* a constellation of the zodiac 391.

Capteyn, *s.* captain, commander 2771.

Care, *s.* anxiety, trouble 3065; sorrow, grief 4562.

Carect, *s.* mark, scar 900.

Carye, Karye, *v. tr.* carry, convey 2994, 3598.

Cas, Caas, *s.* event, occurrence 1282, 4028; case, condition 3280; state of matters 3691; **in cas** in fact 3671.

Cast, *s.* throw 4547 (*of ston*).

Caste, *v. tr.* throw, cast 2170, 1007 (*at*), 4667 (*doune*); consider, ponder 682, 1523, 1687 (**castyng vp and doun**); design, purpose, intend 1699; determine 423, 501; *refl.* purpose, intend 1985, 2569, 3805; determine 4167; *pret. sing.* **cast(e),** *plur.* **cast(en),** *pp.* **cast.**

Castel, *s.* castle 561; **castel gate** 981.

Casuelly, *adv.* accidentally, by chance 897, 1250.

Cause, *s.* cause 190, 789; matter in dispute 1910, 3679; *conj.* **by cause** 919; **for cause** 2850, 2968.

Cause(n), *v. tr.* 251, 847, 1752.

Causer, *s.* causer, origin 4260 (*of venyes*).

Caue, Kave, *s.* cave 1182, 4073.

Celestial, *adj.* heavenly 1470.

Centre, *s.* centre, fixed middle point 1724.

Cerchen, *v. tr.* 374 = **serchen** (q.v.).

Ceriously, Cereously, *adv.* in uninterrupted succession 333; from beginning to end 526, 957.

Certefie, *v. tr.* inform certainly 557, 2740; declare certainly 4426.

Certes, *adv.* certainly 2043, 3075.

Certeyn, *adj.* sure 936; certain, some particular 412, 778; *adv.* with certainty 341; certainly 1024; **in certeyn** certainly 980, 2831.

Cessen, *v. tr.* cease, leave off 3920; see **Sesen.**

Chaf, *s. figur.* chaff, worthless matter 55.

Chalaunge, *v. tr.* challenge, lay claim to 1824.

Chamberleyn, *s.* chamberlain 1359.

Chambre, *s.* chamber 898, 1245.

Champioun, *s.* champion, warrior 1355, 4665.

Chanon, *s.* canon, a cathedral clergyman 137.

Chanpartye, *s.* field (of battle) 2244 (see *Notes*).

Char, Chaar, *s.* chariot 345, 536, 3526.

Charge, *s.* order, command 2631, 2698; charge, custody 3076; burden, trouble 4602; injunction, ordinance 1281.

Charge, Charche, *v. tr.* charge, command 120, 459, 653; care about, trouble oneself about 1972.

Charitė, *s.* Christian love 4671, 4699.

Chas, *s.* pursuit 3925.

Chastyse, *v. tr.* chastise, punish 4659.
Chaunce, *s.* chance, hazard 3681; accident, mischance 810, 4084.
Chaunge, *s.* change 1749 (**ch. of word** violation of promise).
Chaunge, *v. tr.* change 497 (*cheer and contenaunce*); *intr.* 1718.
Cheke, *s.* cheek 3264, 3400.
Cher, Cheere, Chier, *s.* face, countenance 175, 743; *plur. for sing.* 669; mien, look 234, 246; **make chere** give a kindly welcome 1458.
Cherissh, Chershe, *v. tr.* cherish, affectionately care for 1028.
Chershing, *s.* nursing, fathering 974.
Cherubyn, *s.* a cherub 34.
Chese, *v. tr.* choose 1642; see, perceive 4654; *intr.* have a free choice, do as one likes 133; *pret.* **ches** 4706 (: *pes*); *plur.* **chosen** 4167 (rubric); *pp.* **chosen, chosyn, ychosen** 1198, 2655.
Chevysaunce, *s.* remedy, shift 4106.
Cheyne, *s.* chain 1744, 2775.
Chief, *adj.* chief 48, 190, 1244; *s.* chief, ruler 1200; chief part, sum and substance 2327; **in chief** 3715 (**the domynacioun in chief**).
Child, Chyld, *s.* child 344, 368.
Chilyndre, *s.* a kind of portable sundial of cylindrical form 1048.
Choys, *s.* choice, election 4180, 4390; choice company 2137 (MS. Ar. **Chooce**); see, however, *Notes.*
Chyn, *s.* chin 33.
Chyualrye, *s.* chivalry, knighthood 1120; *coll.* chivalry 2654, 4374.
Circuete, *s.* the action of moving round, circumvolution 730.
Circumspect(e), *adj.* discreet, cautious 2797, 2888.
Circumstaunce, *s.* circumstance 1579; detail, particular 37; formality, ceremony 1555.
Citè, Cytè, *s.* town 296, 204, *plur.* **cities** 4428.
Citezeyn, *s.* citizen 1080.
Clamour, *s.* clamour, outcry 2933, 4115.
Clarion, *s.* a shrill-sounding trumpet 3578.
Clemence, *s.* 4504 (**the goddesse C.**).
Clene, *adj.* free from treachery, innocent 3628; pure 4712 (**a mayde c.**); *adv.* entirely, wholly 1070, 1346 (**in steel y-armed c.**).
Cler, Cleer, Clier, Clyere, *adj.* bright, shining 153, 1187; splendid, beautiful 3228; pure 3008 (*water*); clear, evident, distinct 636, 793, 958; *adv.* bright 121; clearly 214 (*expownyng*).
Clerly, *adv.* brightly 1766; plainly, distinctly 4426; thoroughly, completely 374.
Clerk, *s.* learned man, writer 283, 396 (astrologer).
Clernesse, *s.* brightness 2271.
Cleyme, *v. tr.* claim 2002, 3722.
Clipse, *v. tr.* eclipse, obscure 1763 (*trouthe*).
Clok, *s.* clock 1050.
Cloos, *adj.* hidden, secret 1525; concealed 2837; confined 4013 (to the camp); reticent, discreet 2844.
Close, *v. tr.* enclose 598; *intr.* close, shut 4037.
Cloth, *s.* piece of woven stuff 1441, 109; *plur.* **clothes** dress, garments 4417.
Clothe, *v. tr.*; *pp.* **clad** 14 (**the soyl clad in grene**), 4469 (**c. in blak**).
Cloude, Clowd, *s.* cloud 1188, 1761.
Coarte, *v. tr.* enforce 3666; coerce, restrain 2699 (MS. Ar. **coherten**).
Cokkyl, *s.* darnel 4668 (rubric **lollium**).
Cold, *adj.* 596, 3119; *s.* 4194.
Collecte, *adj.* 380 (**the ȝeeres c.** collected years; see *Oxf. Dict.*).
Collik, *s.* colic 114.
Collusioun, *s.* fraud, deceit 539, 2075.
Colour, *s.* colour 3841; false pretext, outward show 1720, 1958.
Comaunde, *v. tr.* command 1361, 3152.
Comaundement(e), *s.* command, order 408, 928; command, disposal 3339.
Combust, *adj.* burnt up 2554 (see *Notes*).
Come, *v. intr.* come 154, 160 (*imp.*); *pret. sing. plur.* **cam, kam** 2, 438, 2196; *pp.* **come, y-come** 94, 1512; **come aboute** come round 1117; **come out** come to an end, run out 1125.
Comyng, *s.* 950, 1296; **comyng out** 4268.
Comendacioun, *s.* 1721 (rubric).
Commoditè, *s.* convenience 3126.
Comowner, Comunere, *s.* commoner 1660; *plur.* commoners, the common people 4380.
Company(e), **Compenye,** *s.* company, party 26, 125, 135.
Comparisoun, Conparisoun, *s.* 1734 (**in c.**), 1941.
Compas, *s.* circumference, circle; **be c.** round about 2183; in the form of a circle or with regularity, regularly 298; **in c.** around 2223; *prep.* about, round 3127, 3585.
Compassioun, *s.* compassion 934, 4281.
Compelle, *v. tr.* compel, constrain 180, 1418, 2856.

Compendeously, *adv.* briefly 4526 (rubric).

Complet, *adj.* complete 19; ended 1807, 3796.

Compleyne, Conpleyne, *v. intr.* complain, lament 3225, 4633, 3671 (*for*), 4357; *tr.* bewail 4367; pity 2487 (*of* for).

Compleynyng, *s.* 996.

Compleynt, -playnt, Conpleynt, *s.* lamentation 590, 865, 4422, 3070.

Composicioun, *s.* agreement 1135.

Compowne, *v. tr.* put together, form 735; settle, agree upon 1604.

Comprehende, Conprehende, *v. tr.* summarize, sum up, describe summarily 549, 1637.

Compyle, Conpile, *v. tr.* compose, tell 307, 4611, 3207.

Comyn, *s.* caraway 118.

Concelen, *v. tr.* conceal 2838.

Conceyte, *s.* thought 1957; idea, opinion 2891, 3641.

Conceyue, *v. intr.* become pregnant 357; understand 691, 959; *tr.* understand, comprehend 1911; observe 907, 2038.

Conclude, *v. intr.* end, terminate 792; come to a conclusion, decide, resolve 765, 1099; demonstrate 839; **shortly to c.** 29.

Conclusioun, *s.* final arrangement or agreement 1110, 2792; end, purpose 3173; **in c.** after all, finally 69, 285, 387.

Concord, *s.* 4703.

Concours, *s.* concourse, crowd 3750.

Condescende, *v. intr.* consent, agree 768, 1110, 1638 (**they ben condescendyd**).

Condicioun, *s.* condition, proviso 3472, 3713; condition, social position 4646.

Conduit, *s.* safe-conduct 3969.

Conferme, *v. tr.* confirm, ratify 3349; ratify the election of 4189.

Conforme, *v. refl.* conform, act in conformity 4003.

Confort, Comfort, *s.* comfort, pleasure 3036, 3851; relief, consolation 1424, 3279; mental support, reliance 4083, 4095.

Conforte, *v. tr.* comfort, relieve 3923, 4529.

Confounde, *v. tr.* defeat 2728; ruin 4004.

Confusioun, *s.* confusion 789, 3823; utter defeat, discomfiture 2492, 3970.

Coniure, *v. tr.* conjure, beseech 518.

Coniurisoun, *s.* magical invocation, conjuration 4050.

Conpassed, *pp.* planned 2160.

Conquerour, *s.* conqueror 4140, 4535.

Conquest, *s.* conquest 3192; **war of conquest** 2569; victory 4598.

Conscience, *s.* conscience 1021, 2853; conscientious scruples 2862.

Conseruatrice, *s.* conservatrix 1769.

Consider, Consydre, *v. tr.* consider, take into consideration 708, 381.

Consolacioun, *s.* 4305.

Conspiracioun, *s.* conspiracy 2160, 3163.

Conspiracye, *s.* 2172.

Constable, *s.* 2135.

Constellacioun, *s.* constellation 382, 4054.

Constreyne, *v. tr.* force, compel 2695; urge 962; urge onward 559; oppress, distress 1518.

Constreynt, *s.* constraint, compulsion 1318; oppression, affliction, distress 3377; pang, agony 4487.

Contagiously, *adv.* perniciously 1916.

Contek, *s.* strife, dissension 1035, 2818, 4628.

Contenaunce, Countenaunce, *s.* countenance, mien 277, 497, 623.

Contesse, *s.* countess 4414.

Contradiccioun, *s.* contradiction 3798.

Contrarie, *adj.* self-willed, contrarious 482; opposed 1854, 3806; *s.* **the** opposite 3971, 3988.

Contrarye, *v. tr.* contradict, argue against 1800.

Contrarious, *adj.* adverse, hostile 393; self-willed, perverse 472.

Contrarioustè, *s.* antagonism, hostility 2897.

Contrayr(e), *adj.* contrary, unlike 1960; opposed 3178; hostile, unfriendly 1033; perverse, wrong 3165.

Contrè, Cuntree, *s.* region 87, 611; country 237, 1399.

Controover, *s.* contriver, inventor 2926.

Contune, *v. tr.* continue, persist in 140 (: *opportune*), 4116; *intr.* continue 2713 (: *fortune*).

Conuencioun, *s.* convention, agreement 1136, 1693.

Conuenyent, *adj.* suitable, appropriate 2402; convenient, fit 1893, 3453.

Conuersa(u)nt, *adj.* dwelling habitually 614, 3840.

Conveye, *v. tr.* accompany, escort 3210, 3738; lead, conduct 1475, 2878; transmit 332 (*doun*); convey, communicate 3450 (*doun*).

Cook, *s.* cook 28.

Co(o)st, *s.* region, quarter 361, 748, 941.

Cop, *s.* cup 1500.
Cope, *s.* cope (of a monk) 73.
Corage, *s.* mood, disposition 646; mind 1222; heart, soul 3245; courage 3500.
Coraious, *adj.* courageous 567.
Coriandre, *s.* coriander 118.
Corn, *s.* corn 2770, 4458.
Corps, *s.* corpse, dead body 596.
Correcte, *adj.* correct 378.
Corrupt, *adj.* corrupt, depraved, bad 2564 (*blood*).
Cors, *s.* body, *i.e.* person 2851; corpse 3391, 3408.
Cost, *s.* cost, expense 3293.
Cosyn, *s.* cousin (used by a sovereign in addressing another) 3315, 3320.
Couche, *v. tr.* lay down, lay to sleep 3091.
Counsail, -sayl, -sale, -sell, *s.* counsel, advice 773, 1780; plan, scheme 685, 953; purpose, intention, design 2044; council 1715, 2012; *coll.* councillors 4107.
Counsaille, Conseyle, *v.* advise 4002, 1108.
Count, *v. tr.* value, estimate (*at*) 3357.
Cours, *s.* course, orbit 729, 1124; course, dish 1562.
Courser(e), *s.* war-horse, charger 4282, 4528.
Court(e), *s.* court-yard 1320, 1363; court, palace 1360, 1557; the members of a court 1466.
Couth, Kouth, *adj.* known 985, 706, 1612.
Couenant, *s.* covenant, agreement 1696, 1929.
Couertly, Couartly, *adv.* secretly, in a hidden manner 1720, 2154.
Couetise, Coveytise, *s.* covetousness 1072, 1158, 4675.
Coward, *s.* coward 2928, 4125; *adj.* cowardly 2490.
Cowardyse, *s.* cowardice 4118.
Coy, *adj.* quiet, still 587 (**kept hym c.**).
Crabbe, *s.* Cancer, the fourth sign of the zodiac 10.
Craft, *s.* skill, ingenuity, art 209, 219, 2453, 1670.
Crafty, *adj.* clever, ingenious 57; artful 226.
Craftyly, Craftely, *adv.* skilfully 15, 3207, 2396.
Craggy, *adj.* craggy, steep and rugged 1166 (*roches*), 3000.
Creature, *s.* human being 3957, 4433.
Credence, *s.* credence, belief 3704 (**ȝiue c. to**).
Cremysyn, *adj.* crimson 1441.
Crepe, *v. intr.* creep 704, 722.
Crest, *s.* crest, top line of a fortified tower or wall 2273.
Crestyd, *adj.* furnished with a crest 4145.
Cristalyn, *adj.* clear as crystal 3127 (*ryuere*).
Cristene, *adj.* Christian 160 (*name*).
Crok, *s.* crooked claw 1540 (MSS. Bo. M., etc.).
Croked, *adj.* crooked, bent 866 (*age*); *figur.* 2079 (**wrong is c.**).
Crop, *s.* throat 116.
Crop, *s.* top of a plant; *figur.* **c. and root** completely, thoroughly 965.
Croun(e), Crowne, *s.* crown 337, 315, 3780.
Crowne, *v. tr.* crown 808, 4043.
Cruel, *adj.* cruel, pitiless 864, 3427; merciless, severe 2053; fierce, savage 622, 638.
Cruelly, *adv.* 479, 581.
Cruelté, *s.* fierceness, ferocity 1012, 3907.
Cry, *s.* cry, crying 442, 4338; outcry, shout 4299.
Crye, *v. intr.* cry, wail, weep loudly 703, 3224, 4370 (*pret. plur.* **cryden**); cry out, proclaim 3364.
Crying, *s.* 4557.
Cure, *s.* care, attention; **do one's busy c.** give one's care, apply oneself diligently 599, 2666, 3821.
Cursid, *pp. adj.* cursed 1014.
Curtesye, *s.* courtesy 177, 1329, 1643.
Curteys, *adj.* courteous 1265.
Cusshewes, *s. plur.* cuisses 1437.
Custom(e), *s.* custom 135, 544; **of c.** by habit, as a matter of habit 2861.

Dagger, *s.* 4291, 4325.
Daliaunce, *s.* light conversation, chat 1478.
Damage, *s.* loss, detriment 1686, 4656; trouble, inconvenience 1287, 2358; hurt, injury 1322, 2822.
Damask, *s.* a rich silk fabric 2766.
Dar, *v.* dare; *pres. sing. plur.* **dar** 103, 3347; *pret.* **durst(e)** 474, 616, 3513.
Dar(r)eyne, *v. tr.* settle, decide 656, 3659; vindicate, maintain 3786.
Date, *s.* date, time 947.
Daun, Dan, *s.* dominus, master, sir 82, 83, 96, 160.
Daunce, *s.* dance 1664.
Daunger, *s.* liability to punishment 3507; haughtiness 282.
Dawe, *v. intr.* dawn 129.
Day, *s.* day 434; daylight 128; lifetime 462, 531; *plur.* **daies, dayes** 651, 467; **dawes** 543 (: *lawes*).

Debat, *s.* strife 3529, 4628; struggle 732, 1928; combat 1350, 1398; **at d.** hostile, contrarious 385.
Debate, *v. intr.* quarrel, wrangle 475, 1064; fight 577.
Debonayr(e), *adj.* gracious, affable 248, 1959; gentle, kind, courteous 1025, 3177.
Deceyt(e), Disceyte, *s.* deceit, fraud 1750, 1763; wile, stratagem 4021.
Deceyue, Disceyue, *v. tr.* deceive, trick 692, 3842.
Deceyveable, *adj.* deceitful 2048.
Declaracioun, *s.* explanation 635, 1534.
Declare, *v. tr.* explain, expound 632, 678; set forth, state 3048, 4568; tell 508, 874, 941.
Declyne, *s.* decline, decay 2904.
Declyne, *v. tr.* turn aside, avert 3690.
Dede, *s.* deed, act 1451 (**in word and d.**); *plur.* **dedys** acts of bravery 1121; **in dede** indeed 418, 1060, 2059.
Ded(e), *adj.* dead 406, 686; deadly pale, livid 743, 4423.
Dedly, *adj.* deathlike, very pale 2332, 2439, 3227; mortal 2896; exceedingly painful 3377 (*peyne*).
Defaute, *s.* fault 3241.
Deffye, Diffye, *v. tr.* challenge 2082; despise, disdain 2929.
Defrauded, *pp.*; **be defrauded of** be disappointed of, fail to get 353; be left without the help of 2707.
Degrè, Degree, *s.* rank 21, 1564; high rank 4415, 3743; a step in direct line of descent 3539; (astron.) the ninetieth part of a right angle 371.
Deiecte, *adj.* dejected (astrol. term; see *Oxf. Dict.*) 393.
Del, Dell, *s.* part; **euery del**(l) wholly 1421, 4531; **neuer a del** not at all 1756, 2014, 3905.
Delay, *s.* delay 964, 1875.
Delay, *v. tr.* 415, 2070; *intr.* 1625.
Deliberacioun, *s.* 687.
Delit, Delyt, *s.* joy, pleasure 999, 2923, 4270.
Delyte, *v. refl.* take great pleasure 2353, 4444.
Delyuere, *v. tr.* deliver, give up 1694, 3326, 3780.
Deme, *v. intr.* deem, judge 255, 818 (*imp. plur.* **demeth**); *pret.* **dempt(e)** 3628, 4099; *tr.* consider, think 4006 (*pret.* **dempt**).
Demur, *adj.* grave, serious 1552, 2041.
Denye, *v. tr.* deny, gainsay 3252; deny, withhold 3785; say "no" to, refuse (cum acc. personæ) 136.
Dep, *adj.* deep 2775.
Departe, *v. tr.* decide, settle 1382 (*her querel*); *intr.* depart, go away 3085, 3549.
Depe, *adv.* deep, deeply 869, 1488.
Depende, *v. intr.* be in suspense 3682.
Depeynt, *pp. adj.* painted, coloured 16, 2305.
Depressed, *pp. adj.* 394 (astrol. term; see *Oxf. Dict.*).
Dere, *adj.* dear, beloved 1457, 3068; always post-positional and in rhyme.
Dere, *adv.* dearly 1862, 3889.
Derk, Dirk, *adj.* dark 1315; obscure, hard to understand 214, 2668; ignorant 810; **in the dyrke** in darkness, blindly 2962.
Derke, Dyrke, *v. tr.* darken, *figur.* 1763, 4136.
Derknesse, *s.* darkness 1369; blindness 866.
Descende, Discende, *v. intr.* come down, go down 644, 1361; come (of), spring (from) 487 (*of royal blood*), 550.
Discent, Dissent, *s.* lineage, descent 333, 1401, 1201.
Descripcioun, *s.* description 619, 3827.
Descryven, Discryve, *v. tr.* describe 1673, 1209. **Discryving,** *s.* 73 (rubric).
Desert, *s.* wilderness 4639.
Desert, Decert, *s.* desert, merit 2072, 3236.
Deserue, Disserue, *v. intr.* deserve, merit 3255, 3716.
Desese, *s.* trouble, inconvenience 1335; suffering, misery 2348.
Desire, Desyr(e), *s.* desire 525, 608, 774, 1617.
Desire, *v. tr.* desire, wish 3756.
Desirous, Desyrous, *adj.* desirous, eager 4263, 568.
Desolat, *adj.* depopulated 873, 4692; forlorn, wretched 4627.
Despit, *s.* scornfulness 473; contempt 1000, 2924; anger 2037; malice, spite 3877, 4093; **in d. of** 2011, **d. of** 2777 in spite of.
Despitous, Dispitous, *adj.* scornful 657, 2130.
Despyse, Dispise, *v. tr.* despise 264, 1004; reject with scorn 3996.
Destinè, *s.* destiny, fate 1233; **Destanye** 921.
Destitut, *adj.* lacking 757; helpless, unprotected 4372.
Destruccioun, *s.* destruction 185, 849; ruin, downfall 1752.
Determyne, *v.* declare, state 2550.
Deth, *s.* death 592, 617; (personified 864.

Devel, *s.* devil 4039.
Deuelway ; a twenty d. an imprecation or exclamation of petulance 162. Cf. *Notes.*
Deuer, Devoyre, *s.* duty 460, 3821, 4359.
Devis, Devys, *s.* opinion 2015; direction 1782; arrangement, plan 2097; pleasure, fancy 99, 2279.
Devise, Devyse, *v. tr.* appoint 779; order, direct 2648; arrange 2709, 4020; relate, tell 361, 817.
Deuocioun, *s.* devotion 551.
Deuoure, *v. tr.* devour 2830, 4072.
Deuout, *adj.* devout 347.
Deuoutly, *adv.* 1528.
Devoyde, Devoide, *adj.* free 378 (*of*), 885; destitute (*of*), wanting 89, 1009.
Devoyde, Devoide, *v. tr.* cast out, expel 1330; remove 1070; *refl.* withdraw 3779; *intr.* go away, withdraw 1342, 3696.
Devyde, *v. tr.*; *pp.* **devyded** divided 1602; taken away 3759 (*fro hym*).
Dewe, *s.* dew 1052.
Dewe, *v. tr.* bedew, wet 1867.
Dey(e), Dye, *v. intr.* die 739, 3012, 3467.
Deyntee, *s.* dainty 1561, 2402.
Difface, *v. tr.* mar the brightness of, dim 4136; deface, disfigure 4447.
Diffence, *s.* defence 2200, 4103.
Diffend(e), Defende, *v. tr.* 1608, 759.
Differre, *v. tr.* defer, delay 3802.
Diffiaunce, *s.* defiance 2130.
Dignytè, *s.* honour, dignity 1127.
Digressioun, *s.* digression 2466.
Diligence, Dyligence, *s.* exertion, diligent effort 3133, 189, 1105.
Diligent, *adj.* 377.
Dilusioun, *s.* delusion, false impression 968.
Directe, *pp.* addressed, dedicated 3203.
Disamayed, *pp.* dismayed, appalled 742; utterly astonished 1367.
Disapere, *v. intr.* disappear 4032.
Disarme, *v. tr.* disarm 1436.
Discerne, *v.* discern, understand, see 771.
Disciple, *s.* pupil, disciple 4183.
Disclose, *v. tr.* make known, declare 3754.
Disconfiture, *s.* defeat 2514.
Disconfort, *v. refl.* distress oneself, be disheartened 2351.
Disconsolat, *adj.* disconsolate 742, 4430.
Discorde, *v. intr.* deviate, be at variance 2088 (*from*).
Discrecioun, *s.* discretion, prudence 2953, 2983.
Discure, *v. tr.* discover, disclose, reveal 2360, 2846, 2859; *refl.* 3958 (**hym d.** betray himself, confess his love).
Disdeyn(e), Desdayne, *s.* scorn, haughtiness 250, 264; indignation 3883.
Disdeyne, *v. intr.* be indignant or angry 1897.
Disencrees, *s.* decrease, loss 2023.
Disespeyre, *v. intr.* despair 4098; *pp.* **disespeyred** in despair 4306; hopeless 3212 (*of alle ioye*).
Disioynt(e), *s.* strained relation 1078; mental conflict 2478; difficulty, peril 3273.
Dismay(e)d, *pp.* dismayed, terrified 2349, 3043.
Disobeye, *v. tr.* 65.
Disobeysaunt, *adj.* disobedient 232.
Dispeir, Dyspeyr, *s.* despair 516, 1593.
Dispeire, *v. refl.* despair 4085.
Displaie, *v. tr.* display 1549.
Displese, *v. tr.* displease, offend 3044.
Disport, Desport, *s.* merriment, pleasantry 22; amusement, entertainment, pleasure 163, 647; sport, game, pastime 482.
Disporte, *v. refl.* divert, enjoy 2411 (*hym*).
Dispose, *v. intr.* ordain, appoint 2907, 4648.
Dispocicioun, *s.* ordering, appointment 2997; the fortune of a person as determined by the situation of the planets at the time of his birth 368.
Dissesse, *s.* trouble, distress 3278.
Disseuer, *v. intr.* separate, part from each other 1386.
Dissimule, *v. intr.* dissemble 514, 1958.
Distaunce, *s.* discord, dissension 1072.
Disteyne, *v. tr.* stain, discolour; **disteyned** *pp.* 3263.
Distille, *v. intr.* trickle down 4477 (*the teerys*).
Distracte, *adj.* distracted, confused in mind 3265.
Distrauht, *pp. adj.* distracted 3382.
Distresse, *s.* distress, trouble 907, 1314, 1987.
Distroie, *v. tr.* destroy 1777.
Diuers(e), Dyuers, *adj.* divers, various 51, 613; different, differing 383, 669, 1715.
Diuersytè, *s.* variety 2942.
Do, Don, *v.*; *pres. ind. sing.* 1. **do,** 3. **doth,** *plur.* **do** ; *pres. conj.* 3. *sing.* **do,** 2. *plur.* **do** ; *pret. sing.* **did, dide, dyd, dede,** *plur.* **did, dyden, deden** ;

ger. **done**; *pp.* **don, done, do, I-do**; *v. tr.* do 969; make, perform 94; make 2030 (**I do the vnderstond**); do 108 (**slepe wil do non ille**), 125 (**shal do ȝou good**), 1820 (**what was best to done**); render, pay 542 (*honour*), 1556; end, finish 676, 3404, 3422; as auxiliary 58, 284, 703; as substitute 1289.

Doctrine, *s.* instruction, teaching 4183.

Doghter, *s.* daughter; *plur.* **doghtren** 858, **doghtres** 881, **doghters** 1457.

Dome, Doom, *s.* judgment, decision 395, 402; opinion 4454.

Domynacioun, *s.* 270, 1095.

Dongoun, *s.* the great tower or keep of a castle 1294, 1883, 3576.

Doo, *s.* doe 3595.

Dool, Dooel, *s.* sorrow, grief 996, 4499, 590.

Doolful, *adj.* sorrowful 2995.

Dotage, *s.* imbecility 998.

Dotard, *s.* an imbecile, a fool 2928.

Double, *adj.* double 4648; false, deceitful 1757.

Double, *v. tr.* double 4492.

Doublenesse, *s.* duplicity, deceitfulness 1747, 1778; double meaning, ambiguity 2892.

Doun(e), *adv.* down 332, 435 (**vp and d.**); to the end 1753 (**redeth the story d.**).

Doune-cast, *pp.* downcast 743.

Doute, *s.* doubt 262, 936; hesitation 1514; fear 2326, 2749; **out of d.** doubtless; **no d.** 727.

Doute, *v. tr.* doubt 1569, 3253.

Douteles, *adv.* doubtless 4654.

Dragoun, Dragon, *s.* dragon 4364, 625, 690; Satan, the "Old Serpent" 4666 (see *Notes*).

Draught, *s.*; **a bowe d.** a bowshot 157; drawbridge 4248.

Drawe, *v. tr.* draw 4442; *refl.* betake oneself 1162; *intr.* go, proceed 750, 1182; approach, draw near 1050, 1170 (*to nyght*); tend, incline 170, 2904; *pret. sing.* **droh** 3734, **drogh** 1182, **drowe** 1170, *plur.* **drowe** 444; *pp.* **drawen.**

Dred(e), *s.* dread 862, 3053; deep awe or reverence 1009, 1027; doubt 1980 (**with-oute d.**).

Dred(e), *v. tr.* fear, dread 1685, 2014, 1205 (*pp.* **drad**); *intr.* be afraid (*of*) 2841.

Dredful, *adj.* 554, 641, 2566.

Dreme, *s.* dream 1525.

Drenche, *v. tr.* drown; *pret. sing.* **dreynt** 3535; *figur.* drown, plunge; *pp.* **dreynt** 3262 (*in sorow*).

Dresse, *v. refl.* proceed, move, go 2324, 4470.

Drinke, *v. tr.* drink; *pret. plur.* **drank** 3122; *intr. pret. sing.* **drank** 3057, *plur.* **dronk** 3111; *pp.* **dronken** 31.

Drope, *s.* drop 1051.

Drouht, *s.* drought 3005.

Drowne, *v. tr.* drown 4249; *figur.* 3446 (*in woo*).

Drye, Drey(e), *adj.* dry 3003, 164.

Dryve, *v. tr.* drive; *pret. sing.* **droff** 4210; *pp.* **dryve** 3687; constrain 1316 (*pp.* **dryven**); carry through, effect 2792; spend, pass 1490 (**d. forth the day**).

Duchesse, *s.* duchess 4413.

Due, Dwe, Dewe, Dieu, Diew, *adj.* due 1893, 924, 1022, 1395.

Duely, *adv.* duly 3933, 4599.

Duk, *s.* duke 3425, 2063.

Dul, *adj.* dull, obtuse 183 (*wit*).

Dure, *v. intr.* continue, hold out 4379.

Duryng, *prep.* during 339, 1147.

Dwelle, *v. intr.* dwell, live, reside 309, 2858; tarry, stay 532, 2425; remain 4011; spend time, dwell 320, 992, 4565.

Dwellyng place, *s.* 302.

Dyademe, *s.* diadem 1805.

Dych, Dich, *s.* ditch 3484, 2775.

Dynere, *s.* dinner 154.

Dysemol, *adj.* dismal, unlucky, unpropitious 2893 (*daies*).

Dysesse, Discese, *v. tr.* expel, dispel, remove 2531 (see *Notes*).

Dyuerte, *v. intr.* turn aside out of one's course 2176; *tr.* turn (one's pen) to another subject 3826.

Dyvide, *v. tr.* divide, split up 3457.

Dyvision, *s.* dissension, discord 4683.

Dyvynaylle, *s.* divination, soothsaying 4170; riddle, problem 630.

Dyvyne, *v. tr.* divine 2811.

Dyvynour, *s.* diviner, soothsayer 362, 919.

Ebbe, *s.* ebb 3422.

Ech(e), Ecch, *pron.* each 53, 237, 1068, 1450.

Echon, *pron.* every one 38, 182, 897.

Eclipse, *v. tr.* eclipse, obscure, *figur.* 4132; cf. **Clipse.**

Eer, *s.* ear 231.

Effecte, *s.* result, consequence 170; purport, gist 1903, 1953.

Effectuely, *adv.* in effect, in fact 2937.

Eft, *adv.* a second time, again 517 (**eft a-geyn**).

Egally, *adv.* equally 1605.

Eilen, *v. tr.* ail, pain 911 (**what her eileþ**).

Either, Eyther, *pron.* either 3790, 3939, 4653.

Ek(e), *adv.* also, besides 381, 383, 1235, 1719; **ek also** 32, 459.

Elat, Ellat, *adj.* proud 1349, 3530.

Eleccioun, *s.* election 1202.

Ellys, Ellis, *adv.* else 385, 678, 1024.

Eloquence, Elloquence, *s.* 42, 215, 287; personified 842.

Emperour, *s.* emperor 3425.

Emprente, Enprente, *v. tr.* imprint, impress (*figur.*) 901, 4267.

Emprise, *s.* enterprise, undertaking 1849, 2957, 3480, 4181.

Enarched, *pp.* arched over 1253.

Enbassyat, *s.* embassy 1849.

Enbrace, Embrace, *v. tr.* embrace 3392, 2434; cover 1542.

Enchace, *v. tr.* chase, pursue 3872, 3898.

Enchauntement, *s.* enchantment, witchcraft 626, 4100.

Enclose, *v. tr.* enclose, shut up 602, 4577; surround 1243; swallow up 2908.

Enclyne, *v. tr.* incline, bow 1628, 2987; induce (*to do*), dispose 3984; *intr.* be inclined, disposed 3819.

Encombre, *v. tr.* overcome, overpower 2144 (see *Notes*).

Encres, *s.* increase, growth (in prosperity) 1680, 1977.

Encres(e), -cresse, *v. intr.* increase 1871, 2714.

Ende, Eende, *s.* end, termination 4055, 848; completion 4142 (**make an e. of** accomplish); death 1018, 4061; agreement, settlement 3724, 3942.

Endynge, *s.* end 995.

Endure, *v. intr.* endure, continue 3416, 4125; *tr.* support, sustain 649, 1925; undergo, suffer 3123.

Endyte, *v. tr.* describe, put into words 824, 4481.

Enforme, *v. tr.* inform, tell 2253.

Enforse, *v. refl.* exert oneself, strive 578, 1424.

Enforth, *adv.* uniformly, uninterruptedly 2009.

Engendre, *v. tr.* produce, cause 114.

Engroce, Engrose, *v. tr.* write out in legal form 3999, 2098 (*vp*).

Engyne, *s.* craft, cunning, trick 1764, 2243, 3690.

Enhaste, *v. refl.* hasten, hurry 605, 1471, 1536.

Enlumyne, *v. tr.* illumine, illustrate 56.

Enmytè, *s.* enmity 4093.

Ennemy, Enemy, Enmy, *s.* enemy 2208, 2715, 1609.

Enoynt, *pp.* rubbed with oil (in preparation for wrestling) 4586.

Enquere, *v. tr.* ask, request to be told 502, 908, 1309; *intr.* inquire, make investigation 521, 1397 (*of* about).

Enrolle, *v. tr.* write upon a roll or parchment, engross; *pp.* 1141, 2099, 4000, 1930 (*vp*).

Ensample, *s.* example 807, 2236.

Entaille, *s.* shape, construction 243.

Entencioun, Intencioun, *s.* intention, purpose; **of e.** on purpose 587, 3515.

Entent(e), *s.* intention, purpose 1615, 1838; **of e.** intentionally, purposely 334, 825; determination, resolution 2083, 3755; opinion, view 1715, 3625; thought, meaning 1757, 1960; heart 3148.

Entre(n), *v. intr.* enter 70, 178, 1891 (*inne*); *tr.* 1300, 4319.

Entrè, *s.* entering 1469; entrance, gate 4295.

Entryng, *s.* 3981.

Entrechaunge, *v. intr.* interchange, alternate 1131.

Enterchaungyng, *s.* alternation 1926.

Entrete, *v. intr.* negotiate, debate 3361.

Entryke, *v. tr.*; *pp.* **entryked** (*with*) enveloped in, complicated by 2892.

Envious, *adj.* malicious, spiteful 1101, 3901, 4272.

Enviously, *adv.* 4092.

Envye, Envie, *s.* envy, malice 258, 861.

Envye, *v. intr.* envy, grudge 4673.

Envyroun, Environ, *adv.* around, round about 228, 2170; **al e.** 2203; **be compas e.** 2183; *prep.* round about 3482.

Eny, *pron.* 134, 209, 607 (**hoot as eny fire**).

Equytè, *s.* equity, justice 1604, 3283.

Er(e), Ar, *conj. temp.* ere, before 642, 1284; **er that** 805.

Erly, *adv.* early 123.

Erraunt, *adj.* travelling 1316 (*knyght*).

Erre, *v. intr.* err, be mistaken 4180.

Errour, *s.* error, mistake 378; false belief 541; wrong-doing 814, 4011.

Erst, Arst, *adv.* not long ago, a little while since 2028; **not arst** not before, not till then 3787.

Erth(e), *s.* earth 4669; dust 724 (**to e. retourne**); ground 1011, 4034.

Erthly, *adj.* earthly, worldly 894, 1858.

Eschewe, *v. tr.* avoid, escape 804, 923; *pp.* **eschewed** 2901.

Eschewyng, Eschuyng, *s.* 1907, 2913.

Ese, Ease, *s.* ease, comfort 1433, 2397, 1336 (**do me ese** give me assistance).

Eskape, *v. intr.* escape 166, 633; *tr.* 1234, 3233.
Especial, *adj.*; **in e.** especially, in particular 1469, 2823.
Espie, *s.* spy 2753.
Espie, *v. tr.* find out, discover 584, 4172 (**out e.**); see, perceive 903, 4512.
Est, *s.* east 129, 153; *adv.* 2801.
Estat, Estaat, Astat, *s.* degree, condition, rank (especially high rank) 20 (see *Notes*), 731 (**hegh and lowe e.**), 3727, 1397, 1029; **chambres of estat** 1432.
Ete, *v. tr.* eat 117.
Eternal, *adj.* 4715.
Eure, *s.* destiny, fate 4089.
Eurous, *adj.* prosperous, successful 1267.
Eue, *s.* evening 2166, 2509, 3965.
Euel, Euyl, *adj.* wretched, miserable 942, 2470; unpleasant, painful 2987; *adv.* ill 2127 (**e. apayd** ill pleased), 4498.
Euen(e), *adv.* exactly, just 356, 1964, 3116; quite, fully 2520.
Euer, *adv.* ever, always 482; ever, at any time 606; **euere in oon** always, continually 483, 2876, 4116.
Euerich(e), *pron.* every 21; every one, each 1182, 1102, 1603.
Euery, *pron.* 37, 64, 271.
Euerychon, Euerichon, Euerechon, *pron.* every one 4068, 59, 2924.
Euermore, *adv.* always 1983, 2712.
Evidence, *s.* 549.
Evident, *adj.* evident, obvious 958, 4099.
Example, *s.* example 4139; pattern 3308.
Examynacioun, *s.* examination 2954.
Excelle, *v. intr.* excel, be pre-eminent 1561; *pres. p. adj.* **excellyng** 3748 (*of bewtè*); *tr.* surpass 570.
Excellence, *s.* 41, 255, 1895.
Excellent, *adj.* prominent, distinguished 219; supreme, exceptionally great 421, 3037.
Excepcioun, *s.* exception 3360, 3768, 4645.
Except(e), *pp.* excepted 2228, 2251, 3998; **exceptid** 3352; *prep.* except 2498.
Exceptyng, *prep.* 1029 (**e. non astat**), 3057.
Excus, *s.* excuse 3252.
Excuse, *v. tr.* excuse 142, 3239; prevent 399.
Execucioun, *s.* putting to death 933.
Execute, *v. tr.* execute, perform 414, 1892; *pp.* **executed** 349, **execut(e)** 1255, 2071.
Exil(e), *s.* exile 1098, 3419, 4706.
Exile, *v. tr.* banish, expel 308, 1280.
Existence, *s.* actuality, reality 3844.
Exorcisme, *s.* exorcism 4050.
Exortacioun, *s.* exhortation 235.
Expance, *adj.* separate 380 (**the ȝeeres e.,** astrol. term; see *Oxf. Dict.*).
Expectaunt, *part. adj.* expecting, waiting for 1954.
Expedient, *adj.* expedient, fit 2794.
Experience, *s.* 706, 793, 2815 (*in*), 3636 (*of*).
Expert(e), *adj.* experienced, skilled 364, 2952; tried, proved by experience 3630.
Exposicioun, *s.* explanation, interpretation 318, 636.
Expositour, *s.* narrator, writer 293.
Expowne, *v. tr.* expound, interpret, solve 214, 630, 696, 736; set forth, state 964, 1967; **expounded** 696 (rubric).
Expresse, *v. tr.* declare, state 1577, 1736, 3347.
Extorsioun, *s.* wrongful intrusion, usurpation 2076.
Eye, *s.*; *plur.* **eyen** eyes 1002, 1463.

Face, *s.* face 3, 34, 410, 4202.
Fader, *s.* father 398, 922; *figur.* originator, contriver 4493; *genit. sing.* **fadres** 3195.
Fage, Phage, *s.* idle talk, lie 453 (cf. 430), 2051, 2821.
Faile, Faille, Faylle, *v. intr.* be without, lack 609 (*of*); fail, be absent or wanting 2678; fail, not succeed 629, 1585, 3660; fail, be wanting at need, disappoint 2717, 3153.
Fair(e), Feir(e), *adj.* fair, beautiful 461, 797; bright, fine 1055; equitable, right 787.
Faire, *adv.* courteously, kindly 247, 1339, 3917.
Fairnesse, *s.* beauty 420, 3037.
Fal, *s.* fall, downfall 1132.
Fallas, *s.* deceit, guile 1832.
Falle, *v. intr.* fall 517 (*doune on knees*), 2181, 516 (*in dispeir*), 998 (*into dotage*); pass suddenly into, rush into 1350 (*at debat*); rush upon, attack 2182 (*vpon*); happen, turn out 3800; become of, happen to 938, 1043; accede 774 (*to*); *pret. sing.* **fille** 904, **fil** 812, *plur.* **fille** 2204; *pp.* **falle** 2798.
Fals, *adj.* false, wrong 539, 689, 1072.
Falshed(e), *s.* falseness, deceitfulness 1755, 1815.
Falsly, *adv.* falsely 1794; wrongfully 795.

Falsnesse, *s.* 2056, 2100.
Fame, *s.* celebrity, renown 191, 748, 4131; report, rumour 1674.
Famous, *adj.* 295, 363.
Fantasie, *s.* imagination, mind 1523, 1783; fancy, speculation 904; inclination, liking 1644.
Fare, *s.* condition, fortune, hap 2470, 4404; state of mind 942.
Farwel, *interj.* farewell to, no more of 270.
Faste, *s.* fasting 155.
Faste, *adv.* firmly, closely 4351; close, very near 534; quickly, rapidly 417, 1347.
Fat, *adj.* fat 3597.
Fatal, *adj.* fatal 397, 650; mortal 4237.
Fate, Faate, *s.* fate 923, 4647.
Faute, *s.* fault, defect 2367.
Fauour, *s.* favour 2982, 4178.
Fauourable, *adj.* agreeable, winning favour 230; well-disposed, partial 3620.
Fauoured, *adj.*; **wel f.** good-looking, comely 754.
Fede, *v. tr.* feed; *pp.* **fed** 104.
Feeld, Feld, *s.* field 3866, 4458; battle-field 3899, 2078; ground 4278; *plur.* fields of a shield in a heraldic sense 1532 (**feeldys**).
Feeste, Feste, *s.* feast 1454, 594.
Feith, *s.* promise 2001.
Feithful, *adj.* faithful, true 1071, 1982.
Feithfully, *adv.* 4446.
Felawe, *s.* fellow, companion 1161.
Fel(l), *adj.* fierce, savage, cruel 622, 2480, 4259.
Felly, *adv.* fiercely 480; eagerly 500.
Fel(l)onye, *s.* treachery, perfidy 2150, 2243; anger, fury 2038.
Felyn, *v. tr.* feel 4656; *pret. sing.* **filt** 1287.
Fend(e), *s.* fiend, demon 553; a grisly monster (the Sphinx) 745.
Fenel, *s.* fennel 117.
Fer, Ferre, *adv.* far 416, 3023 (**fer and ner**), 1459, 3679.
Fer, Feer, *s.* fear 866, 1099.
Ferdful, *adj.* fearful, frightened 3085.
Fere, Feere, *s.* companion, comrade 3977, 4666, 468 (**pleying feeris**).
Fere, *s.*; **in f.** in company, together 3560.
Feren, *v. intr.* behave, act; *pret.* **ferde** 911.
Ferforth, *adv.* far; **as f. as** as far as 2366, 3959.
Fers, Feerce, *adj.* fierce 81, 620, 1543.
Feruence, *s.* heat 1482.
Feruent, *adj.* hot, ardent 1666; fierce, burning 2559; eager, ardent 3112.
Fette, *v. tr.* fetch 2106, 2394, 3335; *pret. plur.* **fette** 2534.
Feturis, *s. plur.* features 3956.
Fewe, *adj.* few 1166; **a f.** 1876, 2456, 4354 (**a grekys f.**).
Feyn(e), *v. intr.* speak falsely 39, 667; be false 4456; invent a story, indulge in fiction 242, 292; *pp.* **feyned** fictitious 50; **yfeyned** false 1677.
Feynt, *adj.* weak, wanting in nutritive power 104; faint, exhausted 2254.
Fiche, *v. tr.* fix; *pp.* **yfiched** 1488.
Fight, *s.* fight, battle 3888.
Fight(en), *v. intr.* fight 4018, 1364, 1549; *pret. sing.* **faught** 4247.
Fightyng, *s.* 1376, 4253.
Fille, *s.* fill, heart's content 107.
Fille, *v. tr.* fill 116.
Fire, Fyr, *s.* fire 607, 3582, 2036 (**set a-fire**), 4272 (**envious fyr**).
First, *adj.* 1721, 3488; *adv.* 59.
Firy, *adj.* fiery, burning 1482.
Fissh, *s.* fish 2770.
Flatarer, *s.* flatterer 1785 (rubric).
Flater, *v. tr.* flatter 1794.
Flaterye, *s.* 1784.
Flaumbe, *s.* flame, fire 4570.
Flee, *v. intr.* flee 684, 3516, 4205 (*pret. plur.* **fledde**); *tr.* 3181 (**fledde þe contrè**).
Flessh, *s.* flesh 411; meat 2770.
Flete, *v. intr.* float, hover (in the air) 17.
Flight, *s.* flight 4208, 4540.
Flood, *s.* flood, flood-tide 3422; stream 4280.
Flour(e), *s.* flower 15, 2309; the best, chief 40 (**f. of Poetes**); brightest example or embodiment 2622; *coll.* 2654 (**f. of Chyvalrye**); *plur.* **flours** prime of life 2936; state of great prosperity 1975.
Floure, *v. intr.* flourish 192, 852.
Fodder, *s.* fodder 3600.
Folk, *s.* people 872; men, retainers 897, 4035; **folkes** people, persons 568, 692; kinds of people 1716; peoples, nations 4659.
Fol(o)we, *v. tr.* follow, pursue 1617; *intr.* come after 2093; result 3681.
Foly(e), *s.* folly 1380, 2965.
Fool, *s.* fool 2869, 4094.
Fooman, *s.* enemy; *plur.* **foomen** 2191, 2728.
Foon, Fon, *s. plur.* foes 758, 1917, 1830.
Foot, Fot, *s.* foot 1008, 4300 (**armyd foot and hed**); **on foote** on foot 573;

a-foote 2192; *plur.* **feet(e), fete** 428, 454, 663, 666 (**on foure fete**); a measure 2006.

For, *prep.* for, for the purpose of 75; in quest of 362; by reason of 1789; on account of 589; in spite of 144, 255; during 3720, 3920; **for to** + inf. 55, 195.

For, *conj.* because 27, 124; since 3674; **for that** because 140, 524, 609.

Forage, *s.* forage, fodder 3600.

Forbern, *v. tr.* bear with, tolerate 1078.

Forby, *prep.* past, by 617.

Force, *s.* force, compulsion 798, 1342; bodily strength 570, 1511; **I do no f.** I care not, attach no importance to 2489.

Forest, *s.* 416, 437, 491.

Forey, *s.* hostile or predatory incursion, raid 3589 (rubric).

Foreyn, *s.* foreigner, stranger 1079.

Forraye, *v. intr.* forage, pillage 3588.

Forsake, *v. tr.* leave, withdraw from 3897; depart from 4595; give up 4120, 4138.

Forsworn, *pp. adj.* forsworn, perjured 2048, 2503.

Forth, *adv.* forth 160, 1862; away 124, 930, 940; further 335, 1060; **and so f.** and so on, etcetera 973.

Forther, *v. tr.* further, assist 3276.

Forthwith, *adv.* immediately, at once 1597.

Fortunat, *adj.* fortunate 2806; auspicious, favourable 272.

Fortune, *s.* fortune, chance 69, 648, (personified) 887; **of f.** by chance 77, 434, 978.

Fortune, *v. tr.* regulate the fortune or issue (of something) 1483.

Forwounded, *pp.* sorely wounded 2437.

Forȝete, *v. tr.* forget 49; *pret. sing.* **forgat** 499; *pp.* **forȝete** 373.

Foster, *v. tr.* nourish 457.

Foul, *adj.* foul, vile 690.

Four(e), *numer.* 537, 666, 672.

Fourtenyght, *s.* fortnight 4505.

Foyne, *v. intr.* foin, make a thrust with a pointed weapon 4325.

Fraccioun, *s.* fraction 374.

Franchemole, *s.* a sort of haggis 101.

Fraternal, *adj.* 869 (*hate*).

Fraude, *s.* deceit 539, 694; wile 3843.

Fraudulent, *adj.* deceitful 689.

Fraunc encence, *s.* frankincense 4572.

Fraunchyse, *s.* freedom from arrest secured to fugitives in certain privileged places 3430.

Fre, Free, *adj.* free, unfettered 1202, 2700; generous, liberal 2685.

Fredam, Fredom, *s.* generosity, liberality 2418, 2704, 2711, 4592.

Frend, *s.* friend 2011.

Frere, *s.* friar 35.

Fressh, Freessh, *adj.* fresh, refreshing 12; fresh, vivid 45, 1570; blooming, youthful 1659; untarnished, bright 2169.

Fresshly, *adj.* blooming, youthful 3956 (see *Notes*), 3307.

Fresshly, *adv.* in a flourishing, magnificent manner 1975.

Fresshnesse, *s.* brightness, beauty 1467.

Frete, *v. intr.* gnaw at, prey on; *pret. sing.* **frat** 2517 (*on*).

Frett, *pp.* adorned, set 1440 (MSS. Bo. T_1. S. **freyt**, MS. Lb. **freight**).

Fro, *prep.* from 8, 58, 61, 605; **fro when** from where 967 (MSS. Lb. M., etc. **fro whens**); *adv.* **to and fro** 3421.

From, *prep.* 156, 331, 890.

Frosty, *adj.* cold 3 (see *Notes*).

Froward, *adj.* perverse, refractory, naughty 483, 1340; adverse, unfavourable 1033, 2895, 4629; antagonistic, opposed 3178, 3710.

Frowardly, *adv.* ill-humouredly, adversely 892.

Frowne, *v. intr.* look displeased or gloomy 254, 4071; frown, be hostile 4250.

Froyse, *s.* a kind of pancake 101.

Ful, *adj.* full, filled 80, 473; complete 1630; **at the fulle** in the state of fullness 3423.

Ful, *adv.* (intensive) very 210, 425, 1312; quite 1099, 153; completely 3339 (**f. and hol**).

Fulfille, *v. tr.* fulfil, perform 1639.

Fully, *adv.* fully, quite 154, 358, 825.

Fulsom, *adj.* full, plentiful 2676.

Fundacioun, *s.* foundation, founding 190, 4624.

Funeral, *adj.* 594 (**the feste called F.**).

Furious, Furius, *adj.* wrathful 390; furious, mad with anger 1961, 3914; mad, deranged in mind 3265.

Furred, *pp.* trimmed with fur 1442.

Fury, *s.* 1356.

Fy, Fye, *interj.* fie (*on, vpon*) 2238, 2490.

Fyfty, *numer.* 93.

Fygure, *v. tr.* picture in the mind 3954.

Fyle, *v. tr.* file, smooth 3493.

Fyn, *adj.* fine 1500 (*gold*), 3527.

Fynal, *adj.* final, ultimate, conclusive 395, 3475, 4644.

Fynaly, Finaly, Fynally, *adv.* at last 2218, 3726; definitely 779; after all 268.
Fynde(n), *v. tr.* find, find out, discover 43, 200, 437; **fynden out 366, 984**; *pret. sing.* **fond(e)** 987, 2198; *plur.* **founde** 388, 574, **fond(e)** 2191, 1368; *pp.* **founden** 491, **founde** 445, 1212, **found** 1815; *intr.* **fynde ful vnsoote** find it very grievous 574, 2191, 3673.
Fyn(e), *s.* end, final issue, result 608, 792, 871; death 4214; purport, meaning 495; aim, object 1892; purpose 3171; decision, resolution 3808; final agreement 3799 (see *Notes*); fine, penalty 651 (see *Notes*).
Fyne, *v. intr.* cease, stop 3983; come to an end, die 733; terminate, result 2812; *tr.* bring to an end, finish 1627, 1795.
Fynysshe, *v. tr.* finish 552.
Fyret, *s.* ferret 3838 (see *Notes*).

Gadere, Gadre, *v. tr.* gather 2066, 2756.
Gadryng, *s.* gathering 2435.
Game, *s.* game, sport 4336; jest 159; game, animals hunted 437.
Gape, *v. intr.* 2225, 3911, 3013.
Gardyn, *s.* garden 2275.
Gate, *s.* gate 578, 981; **ȝate** 3964.
Gendre, *v. tr.* engender, cause 258.
Genologye, *s.* genealogy 3538.
Gentil, Gentyl, *adj.* gentle, worthy 1331, 1629.
Gentilles(se), *s.* gentleness, courtesy 23, 1313; kindness 511, 2347.
Gery, *adj.* changeable, capricious 2899 (*mood*).
Geseran, *s.* a light coat of armour 4329.
Get(e), *v. tr.* get 571, 301, 654; *pret. sing.* **gat** 1740; *pp.* **geten** 303.
Geyn, *s.* expedient, resource, help 2832.
Geyne, *v. intr.* avail, help 732, 1341, 3253.
Geynpath, *s.* short cut 2148 (see *Notes*).
Gift, Gyft, *s.* gift, present 3343, 1665.
Gild, *v. tr.* gild; *pret. sing.* **gilte** 2300; *pp.* **gilte** golden 3228, 4258 (*tresses*).
Gilt, *s.* guilt 3239.
Give, *v. tr.*; *imp.* 2. *plur.* **gif** 1626; *pret. sing. plur.* **gaf** 540, 929, 2762, 3635.
Ȝiue, ȝive, ȝeue, ȝeve, *v. tr.* give 1819, 369, 4516, 1896; *imp.* 2. *sing.* **ȝiue** 3704; *pret.* **ȝaf** 216, 636; *pp.* **ȝoue** 46, 224.
Glad, *adj.* glad, joyous 97, 105; delightful 3202; favourable, propitious 218.
Glade, *v. tr.* gladden, cheer 1461.
Gladnesse, *s.* 168, 1466.
Glas, *s.* glass, mirror 3844.
Glasy-eyed, *adj.* with glassy, lifeless eyes, dull-eyed 34.
Glede, *s.* live coal 1667.
Glorye, *s.* glory 46.
Glyde, *v. intr.* pass swiftly 2185, 3495.
Go, Gon, Goon, *v. intr.* 616, 1829, 466, 697; *pres. ind.* 3. *sing.* **goþ** 668, **goth** 149; *pret. plur.* **went** 236, 436; *pp.* **gon, go** 898, 3417; go walk, pass, depart.
God, *s.* god 215, 518, 1756.
Goddes(se), *s.* goddess 350, 4649.
Gold, *s.* gold 281, 536; textile material embroidered with or partly consisting of gold thread 2766.
Gommes, *s.* gums employed as incense 4570.
Gonne, *s.* gun, cannon 2759.
Gonne-shot, *s.* gunshot (*coll.*) 4315.
Good, *adj.* 148, 275, 787; *s.* 125 (**do ȝou g.**).
Good, *s.* property, wealth, riches 1158, 2693, 3355, 4394; *plur.* **goodes** property, possessions 3151.
Goodlihed, *s.* goodness, kindness 245.
Goodly, *adj.* comely, graceful 881, 1464; courteous 1655; kindly, gracious 1896, 2369; pleasant 2283.
Goodly, *adv.* kindly 1456, 2389; courteously 1472, 3135.
Goost, *s.* ghost, life 4339.
Gouernaile, Gouernaylle, *s.* government, rule 2002; guidance 4381; management 1112; *coll.* commanders, leaders 3881.
Gouernaunce, *s.* government 1614; charge, care 1704; management 148; control 1390; demeanour, conduct 1580, 2959.
Gouerne, *v. tr.* govern, control 772, 2947; *refl.* regulate one's actions 2932.
Gouernour, *s.* ruler, leader 79, 181; king 757, 4384.
Goyng, *s.* going 131.
Grace, *s.* grace, favour 3046, 3935; God's grace 806, 1238.
Gracelees, *adj.* graceless, wanting God's grace, unfortunate 1037, 2493.
Gracious, *adj.* charming, attractive 3031.
Graciously, *adv.* kindly 3060.
Gras, *s.* grass 2288.
Graunt, *s.* grant 639; favour 2809; promise 3349.

Graunt(e), *v. tr.* grant 348, 3506; allow, permit 3719.
Grave, *s.* pit, trench 3484.
Graue, *v. tr.* bury; *pp.* **graue** 1061, 1599, **grauen** 3408; engrave (*figur.*); *pp.* **graue** 3245.
Gray, *s.* a grey-haired man 2879.
Gredynesse, *s.* greediness, avidity 3114.
Grek(e), *s.* Greek 3149, 3886; *plur.* **Grekes** 3146; **Grekes lond** 210, 1204, 2054, etc. Greece.
Grene, *adj.* green 1276; fresh, new 946, 3656, 2304 (*woundes*); unripe, tender, young 411, 661; early 986; *s.* verdure 14; grass-field 1052; green cloth 73.
Gret(e), *adj.* great, large, big 346, 1500, 100; **the grete** the chief part, sum and substance 3270.
Gretely, Gretly, *adv.* greatly, much 1684, 3041, 1042 (MS. Ar. alone **gretlich**).
Greuaunce, *s.* distress 2839; trouble 3270; heaviness of heart, lowness of spirits 3857.
Greue(n), *v. tr.* grieve 2853; trouble 1173, 1338; offend 27; *refl.* grieve, be distressed 2922; *intr.* feel bodily pain 115.
Greues, *s. plur.* greaves 1437.
Greuous, *adj.* heavy, grievous 2362, 4695.
Greyhound, *s.* greyhound 3837.
Greyn, *s.* grain, corn 56.
Grisly, *adj.* grim, ghastly 1176.
Ground, *s.* ground, origin, cause 791, 943; fundamental facts, principal points 316, 508; foundation 297; earth, ground 2908, 3386.
Grounde, *v. tr.* found 2238; bring to the ground, compel a knight to descend from his horse and fight on foot 2193; *refl.* rely on, have for one's authority 294 (*vpon*).
Grow(e), *v. intr.* grow 1016, 4458.
Gruche, Groc(h)he, *v. intr.* grumble, be dissatisfied 1799, 1139, 3443; moan 2295.
Grynde, *v. tr.* grind, sharpen; *pp.* **grounde** 2537, 4275, 4331.
Grype, *v. tr.* gripe, grasp, seize firmly 3393.
Guerdon, *s.* reward 4046.
Guyde, *s.* guide 181, 609, 1153.
Guye, Gwye, Gye, *v. tr.* guide 1298, 2164; *refl.* get along, manage one's affairs 1119.
Guyse, *s.* manner 3995, 4568; style, fashion 2661.
Gynne, *v. intr.* begin 704, 1064; as auxiliary verb 336, 417, 428; *tr.* begin, commence 129, 168, 658, 4630; *pret. sing.* **gan, ganne,** *plur.* **gonnen, gonne, gan**; *pp.* **gonne** 3657.
Gynnyng, *s.* beginning 2958, 4604; origin 3674, 4678.
Gypon, *s.* a short doublet 1545.

Habergoun, Haberioun, *s.* a sleeveless coat or jacket of mail or scale armour 1438, 1544.
Habounde, *v. intr.* be rich 2692.
Habounde, *adj.* abounding, abundant 3099 (*of*).
Habundaunce, *s.* abundance 1583, 1969, 2676.
Hagys, *s.* haggis 100.
Half, *adj.* half 1596; *s.* side 2189, 3744.
Halle, *s.* hall 80, 455, 1890.
Halt, *adj.* limping 2079 (**h. and lame**).
Hand, Hond, *s.* hand 1690, 209; side 4471 (**vpon his hand** at his side); **of his hond** in his actions, in valour 2266 (**manly o. h. h.**); **took on honde** undertook 737; *plur.* **handys** 3226; **hondes** 707.
Handle, *v. tr.* handle 4287.
Hange, Honge, *v. tr. and intr.* hang 932; *pret. plur.* **henge** 427 (**they h. hym vp**); *pp.* **hanged** 2485; *pres. p. tr.* **hangynge** 1258, *intr.* 443, **hongyng** 3496.
Hap, *s.* chance 69, 523; good luck, success 806.
Happe, *v. intr.* happen 1758, 3667; *pret.* **happed** 3488.
Happy, *adj.* fortunate, favourable 386.
Harberioure, Herberiour, *s.* purveyor of lodgings 1498, 3326.
Hard, *adj.* difficult 1234, 3663, 4126; difficult to bear, cruel 4653.
Hardy, *adj.* bold 65, 1834, 1888.
Hardynesse, *s.* courage 2323.
Harm, *s.* injury 4519.
Harneys, *s.* harness 1438, 2222.
Harpe, *s.* harp 206, 223.
Hast(e), *s.* haste 158, 407, 433.
Haste, *v. intr.* hasten 3926; *refl.* 1146, 2151, 2416.
Hasty, *adj.* swift, speedy 559, 3279; rash, inconsiderate 477, 2957; requiring haste 3691.
Hate, Haate, *s.* hate 476, 4273.
Hate, *v. tr.* hate 4266.
Hatful, *adj.* full of hate, malignant 3605; odious, hateful 824.
Hatrede, *s.* hatred 252, 855.
Hauberk, *s.* coat of mail 4697.
Hauke, *v. intr.* hawk, hunt with a hawk 1618.

Haunte, *v. refl.* busy oneself, occupy oneself 1121.

Haue, *v. tr.* have 925, 1062, 3105; *inf.* **haue** 2072, **han** 229, 424, **ha** 2024 (**to ha ben**), 918 (**tabene**); *pres. ind. sing.* 1. **haue, ha** 3255; 2. **hast** 2022; 3. **haþ** 648, **hath** 1037, **haueth** 2982; *plur.* **han** 1910, 103, 116; *imp. plur.* 2. **hath** 819; *pres. conj.* **haue** 85, 921, 2033, 1585; *pret. sing.* **hadde, had** 41, *plur.* **hadde(n), had** 3004, 1555, 1000; *pp.* **had** 3004.

Hay, *s.* hay 3600.

He, *pron.* 96; **his** 3, 21, **him, hym** 39; **hym-silf, hymsilve, hymseluen** 402, 3136, 710.

Hed(e), *s.* head 10, 90; **sperys hedes** spear-heads 3015; commander, ruler 4378; **of hede** headlong, rashly 2949 (MSS. Ra. Ba. P. **on hede**).

Hede, *v. tr.* put a head on, fit with an arrow-head; *pp.* **heded** 4223 (**a quarel sharpe h.**).

Hede, *s.* heed, care, observation 463, 489, 1913; only in **take(n) h.** pay attention, have a care 698, 2931 (*to, of*).

Hegh, High, Hih, Hie, *adj.* high 271, 1106, 1154 (**the heghe way**), 3727, 1221; *adv.* 834, 1222, 425, 2485 (**highe**).

Heghly, *adv.* 1681.

Highnesse, *s.* highness 3455.

Heghte, *s.* height 194 (**on h. reised**).

Heir(e), Hair, Hayr, *s.* heir 1594, 761, 918, 462.

Helle, *s.* hell 854, 4034.

Helme, *s.* helmet 4363.

Help(e), *v. tr.* help 352, 3276; remedy 399.

Helpe, *s.* help 1980, 3261.

Hennys, Hennes, *adv.* hence 3784; from this life 4715.

Hente, *v. tr.*; *pret. sing.* seized, grasped 2519 (*a swerd*), 3376 (**the . . . smerte . . . hent hym by the herte**); drew out 3496 (*a swerde*); caught up, took up 4530 (**in his armys he hem all vp hente**).

Hepe, *s.* heap 4497.

Her, Here, *adv.* here 182, 244, 330, 4335 (**her . . . and ther**), 4313 (**her . . . ȝonder**); in this world 723, 3418.

Her-after, *adv.* 1582.

Herof, *adv.* hereof, of this 1039, 3676.

Herto-forn, *adv.* before this time, before now 313, 699, 1696.

Her-vpon, *adv.* upon this matter 677.

Herb, *s.* herb 2290, 2317, 3026.

Herber(e), *s.* garden 3024, 2279, 3370 (**therber**).

Herbygage, *s.* lodging, abode 1301.

Here(n), *v. intr.* hear 176, 557; *pp.* **herde** 812; *tr. pret.* **herde** 442.

Heritage, *s.* heritage, inheritance 1089, 1333, 3792.

Hermyn, *s.* ermine 1442.

Hert(e), *s.* hart 3595, 1275.

Hert(e), *s.* heart 144, 471.

Hertly, *adj.* hearty, heartfelt, sincere 2924, 3035, 3263; *adv.* heartily 3317.

Heste, Heeste, *s.* promise 1699, 2089, 3643.

Hete, *s.* heat 3118; ardour, passion 1666; excitement, eagerness 2761; heat of the battle, fury 4263.

Heuene, *s.* heaven 4661; sky 8, 1188.

Heuenly, *adj.* heavenly, belonging to heaven 216, 373, 4665; divine 830; divinely beautiful 3978.

Heuy, Hevie, *adj.* heavy, big 169; *figur.* heavy, sad 952; sorrowful, despondent 943, 2863; weary, sleepy 2289; heavy, distressful 2691.

Hevy-chered, *adj.* gloomy, mournful 389, 4430.

Hevynesse, *s.* sadness, grief 419, 512, 591.

Hewe, *v. intr.* hew 4353.

Hewe, Hwe, *s.* colour 3071, 2310, 3841; hue, complexion 4447.

Hide, *v. tr.* hide, conceal 519, 2836; *pp.* **hid** 1525.

Hidous, *adj.* dreadful, horrible 1545, 3489; **hydouser** 4314.

Hydous-chered, *adj.* 859.

Hidously, *adv.* 1175, 1285.

Hie, Hye, *v. intr.* hie, hasten 3223, 1530, 3904; *refl.* 558.

Hight(e), *v. intr. pret.* was named 624, 882, 4177; *pp.* promised 95.

Hil(l), Hyl, *s.* hill 440, 1044, 641, 627.

Historial, *adj.* historical 50.

Hok, *s.* hook 1539; fish-hook 1670 (*figur.*).

Holde, *v. tr.* hold, keep 113 (*wynde*), 566 (*a tornement*), 1775 (*ȝour bihestes*), 1884; persist in, continue 2820 (*her iournè*), 4432; think, consider 2051, 2970 (*pp.* **holden**); *pret.* **helde** 1240, 767; *pp.* **holde** bound, obliged 3143; *refl.* adhere to, stick to 3799 (*to*).

Holt, *s.* wood, copse 440.

Holy, *adj.* holy 71, 794.

Holynesse, *s.* holiness 24, 167.

Hom, *adv.* home 106, 447, 3598.

Hoom-comynge, *s.* home-coming 2429.

Homward, *adv.* homewards 141, 1530.
Honestè, *s.* honour, respect 1027.
Honour, Honur(e), *s.* honour, dignity 1727, 46, 3758; worship 542, 1022.
Hood, *s.* hood (worn by monks) 90.
Hool, *adj.* whole, entire 54, 975, 1057; well, restored to health 460, 2457; true, unimpeachable 1724, 3629; *adv.* wholly, entirely 1795, 3665, 3339 (**ful and hol**).
Hoolsom, *adj.* wholesome, healthful 1056, 3027; healing 3092.
Hoolsomnesse, *s.* wholesomeness 2307.
Hooly, Holy, *adv.* wholly, completely 1390, 746, 3160.
Hoor, Hor, *adj.* grey 1545; grey from absence of foliage 440; grey-haired with age 2985.
Hoot, *adj.* hot 2554.
Hoot(e), *adv.* hotly 607, 1075.
Hope, *s.* hope 1217. **Hope,** *v. intr.* 1588.
Horn, *s.* horn, an instrument 3578; **blowen in an horn** get nothing for one's pains, fail conspicuously 1790 (see *Notes*).
Horrible, *adj.* horrible, dreadful 554, 3490.
Hors, *s.* horse 152, 559; *genit.* 2285 (**his horses hede**).
Hors-bak, *s.* 573 (**on h.**), 3904 (**to h.**).
Horsed, *pp. adj.* mounted on horseback 2659 (**wel h.**); **yhorsed** 2146 (**wiel y.**).
Host(e), Hoost, *s.* host (of an inn) 79, 152, 158.
Host, Hoost, *s.* army 3891, 4536.
Hosteye, *v. intr.* make a warlike expedition 2991, 2998.
Hound, *s.* hound, dog 435, 3855.
Hour(e), *s.* hour 372, 382.
Hous, Hows, *s.* house 4556, (in astrology) 394.
Houshold(e), *s.* household 2137, 2587.
How, Howh, *adv. interrog. indirect* 194, 201, 244, 582, 972; *conj.* that 685, 2088; **how that** 978, 1404, 983 (**how . . . that**); **how as** as if 1079 (MSS. Ar. Bo. a. o. Cf. Du. Ad_1. Ra. a. o. **As though**).
Howsyng, *s.* house accommodation 3330.
Huge, *adj.* large 2211; great, violent 1183 (**tempest h.**).
Humanytè, *s.* courtesy, politeness 3744.
Humble, *adj.* 277, 545, 3816.
Humblesse, *s.* humility 4589.
Humbly, Humblely, *adv.* 1388, 1631, 3746.
Hundred, *numer.* 4623.
Hungre, *s.* hunger 4194.
Hunte, *v. intr.* hunt 1618.
Hunte, *s.* huntsman 436, 939.
Huntyng, *s.* 1274 (**they on h. wente**).
Hurte, *v. tr.* hurt; *pp.* **yhurt** 2221.
Hurte, *s.* hurt, wound 2375, 2438.
Hurtle, *v. intr.* dash together, collide 1357; strike against, come into collision with 2950 (**h. ageynes harde stones**).
Husbond, *s.* husband 3168.
Hyde, *s.* hide 299, 1543.
Hynde, *s.* hind 1275, 3595.
Hynder, *v. tr.* hinder 2358.
Hyndryng, *s.* disparagement, discredit 4122.

I, *pron.* 63, 68; **me** 70, 159; **my-silf** 122, 1577; *plur.* **we** 124, 140; **vs** 161, 170; *poss.* **myn** 103, 942, 2083, **my** 44, 648, 676; **our** 140, 155; *absol.* **oures** 2495.
If, ȝif, *conj.* if 667, 811; **ȝif that** if 635; **but ȝif that** unless 664, 1693.
Ignoraunce, *s.* ignorance 809.
Ignoraunte, *adj.* ignorant 640, 784.
Ile, *s.* isle 1195.
Ille, *adv.* ill 3813; *s.* harm 108.
In, *prep.* in 4, 6, 158, 220; **into** 1232; **in al that euere** as much as ever 606; *adv.* 301 (**to get inne londe**), 1299 (**he cam inne**), 3868 (**rennyng in and oute**).
Incantacioun, *s.* incantation, magic, sorcery 4049.
Incomyng, *s.* incoming, entrance 1462.
Indigence, *s.* poverty, destitution 2687; (personified) 863.
Indisposicioun, *s.* unfavourable disposition 387 (rubric).
Indurat, *adj.* stubborn, obstinate 4007.
Infeccioun, *s.* infection 2565 (**Bynfeccioun**).
Influence, *s.* 216, 720, 1738.
Informacioun, *s.* the action of telling something 317.
Infortunat, *adj.* unfortunate 386, 1030, 3058.
Infortuned, *adj.* unfortunate 822, 4366.
Iniquytè, *s.* 887.
Iniurie, *s.* injury, wrongful act 3675.
Inly, *adv.* inwardly, in heart 471, 647, 1685; fully, quite 884.
Inne, *s.* quarters, lodgings, inn 77.
Innocence, *s.* 811.
Innocent, *adj.* 3670.
Inportable, *adj.* insufferable, unendurable 2516 (*wo*), 2734 (*wrong*), 3010, 3375 (*smerte*).
Inportune, *adj.* persistent, pertinacious 524, 4115 (**clamour i.**).
Inspeccioun, *s.* careful scrutiny, close

examination 381; **of i.** of sight, to see, to look at 2281 (**heuenly of i.**); **by cleer i.** by clear sight, in plain view 1227, 1533.

Instrument, *s.* 222 (of music), 2393 (of surgery).

Intencioun, *s.* see **Entencioun.**

Interrupte, *v. tr.* interrupt, disturb 1991 (see *Notes*), 3176.

In-to, *prep.* 2, 70, 305, 596, 1073.

Invisible, *adj.* 553, 4030.

Inward, *adj.* heartfelt 280 (*loue*); mental 1226 (*sight*); *adv.* inwardly, in heart 1961, 4453.

Inwardly, *adv.* inwardly, deeply 1871.

Ire, *s.* anger 868, 1308, 2035 (see **Yrously**).

It, Hit, *pron.* 68; *genit.* **his** 190, 3474.

Ialous, *adj.* ardently amorous 1671.

Iambisons, *s. plur.* a pair of jambs, *i.e.* armour for the legs, greaves 1438 (only in MSS. Ra. Ba.).

Iape, *s.* jest, joke 634; laughing matter 165 (see *Notes*).

Iocounde, *adj.* jocund, cheerful 3100.

Ioly, *adj.* joyous, gladsome 12.

Iournè, *s.* journey 559, 4438; expedition 2820.

Ioye, *s.* joy 171, 852, 4715.

Ioyne, *v. tr.* join 769 (*be way of mariage*), 844.

Ioyneaunt, *adj.* adjoining 2274 (*to*).

Ioynyng, *adj.* adjoining, adjacent 1163 (*to*).

Iuellis, *s. plur.* jewels 2765.

Iuge, *s.* judge 1366, 3663.

Iugement, *s.* judgment, sentence 395; decision 3662; conviction, punishment 927.

Iuparte, Iupard, *v. tr.* jeopard, risk, imperil 1381, 1826, 3086, 2869; *intr.* risk, hazard 3968.

Iupartie, *s.* jeopardy, risk 1860, 3062, 3976.

Iust, *s.* joust, tournament 1664.

Iust, *adj.* just, equitable 2096; correct 1803.

Iustice, *s.* 1205.

Iustly, *adv.* rightfully 1065; accurately 379.

Kache, *v. tr.*; *pret.* **kaught** 2323 (**k. hardynesse** took courage).

Kalendys, *s. plur.* beginning 2544, 4687; prelude, first taste 3601.

Kene, *adj.* keen, sharp 274, 3169, 3220, 4487.

Kene, *adv.* sharply 4696.

Kepe, *v. tr.* take care of, guard 457, 772, 2294; keep, retain 53, 1259, 2007; continue to follow 1154 (*the heghe way*); keep, stand to, abide by 1939 (*ȝour oth*), 3986; *refl.* maintain oneself, continue 587 (**kept hym coy**), 4013.

Kep(e), *s.* heed, care; **taken k.** 2405, 3167; **take eny (no) k.** 1284, 1001.

Kerve, *v. tr.* cut, carve 3378 (*pp.* **koruen**); *intr.* 4353.

Knaue, *s.* man-servant, man of low condition 137.

Kne, *s.* 505; **knees** 517, 547.

Knette, *v. tr.* knit, tie 430 (*pret.* **they knet hym vp**); conclude 1137 (**conuencioun ful knet vp** *pp.*).

Knotte, Knot, *s.* knot, bond, tie 1452; spec. bond of marriage 815, 844, 1590.

Knowe, *v. tr.* know 317, 608, 2013; *pret.* **knewe** 1422; *pp.* **knowe** 2098; *intr.* 325, 548; *pret.* 1842, 3309.

Knowlecchyng, *s.* knowledge 1504.

Knyff, *s.* knife 2781; *plur.* **knyves** 3169.

Knyght, Knight, *s.* 137, 753, 2063; *plur. genit.* **knyghtes** 1448, 1485, 1491, 1531.

Knyghthood, *s.* chivalrousness 23, 3288; bravery, prowess 310, 4129.

Knyghtly, *adj.* brave, bold 1377, 1885; chivalrous 1471; *adv.* bravely 1608, 4151; chivalrously 3133.

Kok, *s.* in the oath **by kokkis blood** by God's blood 126.

Konnyng, *s.* skill 2455.

Konnyng, *adj.* clever, wise 2977.

Konnyngly, Konyngly, *adv.* politely, courteously, comme il faut 1894, 1474.

Koyse, *s.* body, person 102 (see *Notes*).

Kylle, *v. tr.* kill 2186 (**kylleth** *pres.* 3. *sing.*).

Kynd(e), *s.* nature 262, 2554, 3833, 3848; kind, sort 613; **of kynde** in accordance with what is natural, according to the established order of things 728; cf. **naturely** 729.

Kynde, *adj.* kind 1982.

Kyndely, *adj.* natural, founded in nature 1021; *adv.* naturally 674; cf. **naturely** 671.

Kyndenesse, *s.* kindness 3142.

Kyndle, *v. tr.* kindle 3582.

Kyndle, *s.* the young (of a tiger) 3845 (**kyndles** *plur.*).

Kyng(e), *s.* king 189, 224.

Kyngdam, -dom, *s.* kingdom 314, 1768.

Kyngly, *adj.* royal 1895.

Kynne, *s.* kindred 1422.

Kynrede, *s.* family, stock 490, 550; kindred 856, 984.

Kysse, *v. tr.* kiss 3747.
Kytt, *v. tr.* cut 3170.

Labour, *s.* labour, trouble 377, 3142; toil, painful labour (personified) 861; exertions 3474.
Lady, *s.* 835, 841, 1462.
Lak(ke), *s.* lack, want 1565, 2267, 4680; fault, crime 2547.
Lame, *adj.* crippled, lame 4335, 2079.
Lamentacioun, *s.* 3381, 4422.
Lang(u)age, *s.* 47, 454.
Lappe, *s.* lap 3089.
Large, *adj.* large, great 301, 930, 1187, 4625; **at l.** at liberty, free 3075, in the open country 2121, 2643; **at his l.** freely, unrestrained (by wounds) 2413; **at her l.** freely, according to their own hearts 2697.
Largely, *adv.* 3330.
Largesse, *s.* liberality, bountifulness 2418, 2704, 4593.
Larke, *s.* skylark 2296, 3552.
Last, *adj.* last 1575; **at the laste** at last 1766, 2042.
Laste(n), *v. intr.* last, continue 323, 2876, 483; hold out, stand the test 4352.
Late, *adj.* 982, 1249; *adv.* late 91; lately 104; not long since 948, 1697.
Laugh, Lawgh, *v. intr.* 1797, 3686.
Laughter, *s.* 26.
Launce, *s.* lance 1487.
Laurer, *s.* laurel 4597 (**with l. crownyd**); **laurer tre** laurel tree 3029.
Lawe, *s.* law 130, 544, 1088.
Laye, *v. tr.* temper, mix 4460 (MS. Ar. G.); see **Allaye.**
Leche, *s.* physician 459, 2395, 2450.
Leche-craft, *s.* art of medicine, remedy 4228.
Led, *s.* lead 2289.
Lede, *v. tr.* lead, conduct 1430; *pret.* **ladde** 1554, 3949; *pp.* **lad** 978, 1494; carry, convey 940; *pp.* **lad** 3526; lead 1727 (*his lyff*), 886.
Lene, *adj.* lean 74.
Lenger, *adj.* longer 171; *adv.* 320, 532 (**no l.**), 4565 (**any l.**).
Length, *s.* 2387, 4699; **be length of** after the lapse of 670.
Lere, *v. tr.* teach, tell 36, 196, 1547 (**lerys : banerys**); learn 522, 2059.
Lerne, *v. tr.* learn 4181.
Les, *s.* lie, falsehood 1777.
Lese, *v. tr.* lose 678, 1788, 4218; *pret.* **lost(e)** 801, 999, 1102; *pp.* **lorn** 314, 4166; **be lorn** 1290, 2855, 3286.
Lesyng, *s.* loss 2141.
Lesyng, *s.* lie 1403.
Lest, *adv.* least 4079.
Lest, *conj.* lest 806, 1830, 3575; **lest that** 1691; **List** 3988; **list that** 3619, 4072; **Lyst** 4004.
Let, Lette, *s.* delay 171; hindrance, obstruction 4332.
Lete, *v. tr.* let, permit, cause (with infin.) 1790; *imp.* **lat** 161, 1945, 2013; *pres.* 1. *sing.* **lat** 466, 1565; *pret. sing.* **lete** 1277, 2185.
Lette(n), *v. tr.* hinder, prevent 579, 645, 2004; *intr.* tarry, delay 601.
Lettyng, *s.* hindrance, objection 1088; delay 1653, 4387, 2576 (*plur.* **lettyngges**).
Lettre, *s.* letter 2574.
Leue, *v. tr.* believe 2070.
Leve, Lieve, *s.* leave, permission 1337; **take leve** bid farewell 533, 2587.
Leue, *v. tr.* leave 334, 2123; leave off, cease 1109; abandon, forsake 1783, 2921; *pret.* **lefte** 935, 2232; *pp.* **left** 2220, 4375, 4561; *intr.* leave off, cease 445.
Leyn, *v. tr.* lay 132, 2154 (*a busshement*); *pres. conj.* 3. *sing.* **lay** 3474; *pret. sing.* **leyde** 2116; *pp.* **leyd** 1670; *refl.* 1260 (**leyde hym doune**).
Leyser(e), *s.* leisure 1476, 2412, 4264.
Liberal, *adj.* liberal, generous 2726, 1559.
Libertè, *s.* liberty 3508.
Licence, *s.* permission 1740.
Lie, *v. intr.* lie; *pres. ind.* 2. *sing.* **lyst** 692; 3. *sing.* **lith** 2366, 3370; *pres. conj. plur.* **lye** 111; *pret. sing. plur.* **lay** 1246, 2205, *sing.* **ley** 2148, *plur.* **leye** 66; *pp.* **leyn(e)** 2213, 3371; *pres. ind.* 3. *sing.* **lyggeth** 3388; *pres. p.* **liggyng** 1764, 3891.
Lief, *adj.* glad, willing 2050 (**l. or loth**), 2117.
Lif(f), Lyf(f), *s.* life 424, 339, 656, 678; *genit. sing.* 735 (**lyves thred**); *plur.* **lyves** 1381; **al my lyve** 2009; see **Lyven.**
Lifte, *v. tr.* lift 105 (*up*), 2165; *pret.* **lift** 954.
Light, *adj.* light 150; shining, burning, bright 1370.
Liȝt, Lyght, *s.* light 1298, 3582.
Light, *adj.* lighthearted, cheerful 97, 1978 (**glad and l.**), 144 (**of herte l.**), 1169, 1576.
Lighte, *v. intr.* alight 1393, 1887 (**lighte doun** *pret.*).
Lightly, *adv.* easily, quickly 1489, 3955.
Lik, *adj.* like 220, 289, 621; **Lich** 81, 239, 1052.
Lik, *adv.* 21, 1567, 4125; **Lich** 722,

1316, 1940; **lik, lyk** according to 135, 1798; **lich** 257, 1701; **lik as** like 1126; **lik (lich) as** even as 119, 307, 1460, 1541, 28, 64, 1295, 3644; **lik as** just as if 486, 515.

Like, *v. intr.* like, please (as an expletive) 1003, 4437.

Likly, *adj.* fit, suitable 771, 2581 (**the moste liklyest**); likely (with *to* + infin.) 1290, 1582, 2711, 3054; *adv.* probably 3660.

Liklynesse, *s.* comeliness, handsomeness 1578.

Lippes, *s. plur.* lips 164.

Liste, *v. intr.* please 233 (**list** *pres. conj.*), 489, 3447; like 196; choose 827 (**list** *pret.* 3. *sing.*), 1771; wish, desire 43, 1700, 1954; as a kind of auxiliary verb 213.

Lit, *adv.* little; **lit or noght** 592, 3431; **a lyte** a little 3358.

Litil, Lytyl, *adj.* little 1350, 1992, 2040; *adv.* 1338, 4382; **a litil** 313, 3410.

Lo, Loo, *interj.* lo 2034, 4628–30, 676.

Logge, *v. intr.* lodge, dwell 1325; *tr.* lodge 67; encamp, place in tents 3051, 3333.

Logging, Loggyng, *s.* lodging 1497, 1319.

Lok, *s.* lock of hair 2985.

Lokke, *v. tr.* lock, shut 2851 (**lokked vp**).

Lombe, *s.* lamb 3847.

Lond(e), Land, *s.* land, country 210, 301, 1689; **on see and lond** 1031.

Long(e), *adj.* 74, 993, 323; *adv.* 2849, 3693; see **Lenger.**

Longe, *v. intr.* belong 1089, 2665; belong, be fitting 1722, 1912.

Look, Loke, *s.* look, countenance 622, 409, 3031; *plur.* **lookes** astrological aspects 383.

Looke, *v. intr.* look 89, 126; look, consider 4532.

Loos, Los, *s.* loss 3447, 4644; **loos of deth** loss by death 3415.

Lord, *s.* lord 1081, 773; master, ruler 484, 1413; husband (of rank) 4436.

Lordship, *s.* lordship, sovereignty 270, 1096.

Lore, *s.* teaching, direction 2403.

Loth, *adj.* hostile 389; sorry, displeased 3667 (**glad or l.**), 2050 (**lief or l.**), 3710; unwilling 1417.

Lothsom, *adj.* hateful, shocking 4029; very unpleasant 1167.

Loud, *adj.* loud 4338; shrill 3578.

Loud(e), *adv.* loudly 4298, 4557.

Loure, *v. intr.* be depressed or mournful 4071.

Loute, *v. intr.* bow, make obeisance 261.

Loue, *s.* love 23, 280, 1667 (**louys folk** enamoured persons).

Louer, *s.* lover 1503.

Lowe, Lowh, Lowgh, Lough, *adj.* low 731, 4646, 3055, 2680.

Lowe, *adv.* low 111, 722, 813, 4041; low, humbly 261, 1628.

Lowly, *adj.* humble, modest 1265; *adv.* humbly 505, 1394.

Lowlynesse, *s.* humility, modesty 2462.

Lownesse, *s.* lowliness, humility 245 (MSS. Ar. G.; **lowlynesse** Bo. and the rest).

Lugge, *v. tr.* lug, worry 4587.

Lure, *v. tr.* allure, entice 3953.

Lust, *s.* pleasure, delight 229; inclination, bent 1617; vigour, lustiness 715.

Lusty, *adj.* pleasant, delightful 12, 222, 1055; vigorous, strong 1511, 1657, 3567.

Lye, *v. intr.* lie, tell a lie 2862, 3520, 4452.

Lyege, *s.* subject 247.

Lygeance, Lygaunce, *s.* allegiance 2090, 4392.

Lym, *s.* limb 3535, 701 (leg).

Lym, *s.* mortar 240, 290.

Lynage, *s.* lineage, descent 556, 1400; consanguinity, relationship 2524.

Lynde, *s.* lime-tree 1276.

Lyne, *s.* line, rope 2964; fishing-line 1670; line of descent 330; lineal descent, direct line 464; **lyne-right** in a straight line, in a direct course 750, 2167 (**riȝt as eny line**).

Lyneal, *adj.* direct 333.

Lynealy, *adv.* in the direct line of descent 3158, 3539.

Lynke, *v. tr.* link, join together 1744.

Lyoun, Lyon, *s.* lion 620, 1180, 4200 (**pleyeth the lyoun**).

Lyvely, *adv.* in an active manner, briskly 1348.

Lyven, Leue, *v. intr.* live 2690, 1098, 2423.

Maat, *adj.* tired, exhausted 1170, 1257, 2255.

Mace, *s.* mace, club 3428.

Mad, *adj.* beside oneself, out of one's mind 1178.

Magik, *s.* magic 2815.

Magnyfie, *v. tr.* magnify, praise 1950; *pp.* **magnyfied** exalted 1681.

Make(n), *v. tr.* make, cause 462, 115, 161; *pres.* 3. *sing.* **makeþ, maketh** 666, 952; *pret.* **maked** 546, **made** 8, 206, 1055, 1142, **maad** 4558; *pp.*

maked 3609, 4062, **mad(e)** 75, 99, 240, **maad** 2096, **y-made** 2001.
Making, *s.* poetical composition, poems 43.
Male, *s.* bag, wallet 76.
Malencolik, *adj.* melancholy 5, 389; gloomy, morose 472.
Malencolye, *s.* sullenness, gloomy anger 2037, 2553.
Malice, Malys, *s.* ill-will, hatred 734, 1008, 1156, 1273.
Malle, *s.* mall, big hammer 4543; cf. RE a marteaulx.
Man, *s.* man 64; human being 816; man-servant 76; *genit. sing.* **mannys** 209, 754; *plur.* **men** men, people 3573, 115.
Manace, *v. intr.* menace 3427, 4694; *tr.* 805, 3586.
Manacyng, *s.* 2014.
Maner(e), *s.* manner 582; manner, behaviour 1464; sort, kind 413 (**al m. þing**), 149, 161, 1514 (**a m. doute**), 1709 (**in a m. drede**), 2852 (**a m. of remors**); **in maner** in a manner 514 (**in m. feyne**), 1959 (**in m. debonayre**).
Manful, *adj.* manful, brave 1891.
Manfully, *adv.* 1822.
Manhode, *s.* manliness, courage 752, 1608, 4075.
Mankynde, *s.* mankind 4710.
Manlihede, *s.* manliness 3308.
Manly, *adj.* manly, brave 339, 1193, 1267; *adv.* 2055, 4124, 4247.
Mansioun, Mancyoun, *s.* abode 4045; residence 1884; (astrological term) "each of the twenty-eight divisions of the ecliptic, which are occupied by the moon on successive days" (*Oxf. Dict.*) 11, 373, 4053.
Mantel, *s.* mantle 1439.
Many, *adj.* 8 (**m. shour**), 1657, 2781 (**m. a man**); **m. on** 4196.
Many-fold, *adj.* of many kinds, numerous 2765 (**Iuellis m.**).
Marcyal, *adj.* martial, warlike 1121 (**dedys m.**), 2273 (**crestes m.**).
Mariage, *s.* marriage 768, 1221; wedding 1652.
Marke, *v. tr.* hit, wound 3428, 3962, 4224; mark, stain 4155; *pp.* **markyd** noticed, observed 1881.
Maskowe, *v. tr.* machicolate 2757.
Massage, *s.* message 1823, 2018.
Massagere, *s.* messenger 1898, 360, 2574; **Messager** 3102.
Mater(e), Matiere, *s.* matter, subject 319, 321; affair, business, dispute 3753, 3656, 3665; cause 4633.
Maugrè, *prep.* in spite of 579, 1328, 2697, 2864; 2010 **Maugre of hem** Ar. G. against all the other MSS.
Mawe, *s.* stomach 134, 116.
Mawmetrye, *s.* idolatry 4048.
May, *v.* may, can; *pres. ind. 2. sing.* **maist** 718; *pret.* **myght(e)** 1159, 300.
Mayde, *s.* maiden, girl 621; virgin 4712.
Mayle, Maile, Maylle, *s.* coat of arms, mail 1864, 2145, 1365, 4310.
Maylle, *s.* one of the metal rings or plates of which mail-armour was composed 4327.
Maylle, *s.* halfpenny 4076.
Mayster, Maister, *s.* leader, commander 2181; master, teacher 4182, 4501; model of excellence 2623.
Mede, *s.* meadow 3564.
Mede, *s.* reward 2072, 3259, 3885.
Mediacioun, *s.* mediation 3505.
Mediatrice, *s.* mediatrix 1770.
Medle, *v. intr.* meddle, interfere, interpose (*in*) 2060 (MSS. Ar. L_2. Ap. **medle of** against all the others).
Meke, *adj.* humble 1655.
Mekely, *adv.* humbly 1389.
Melodious, *adj.* sweet-sounding, tuneful 202 (*soun*), 223 (*harpe*).
Melodye, *s.* sweet music 829.
Memorye, *s.* memory 45 (MS. Ar. alone **memoyre**).
Mencioun, *s.* mention 1142, 4623.
Mene, *adj.* middle 3936 (**some m. way** middle course); mean 1675 (**this m. while**).
Mene, Meene, *s.* means, way 637, 1345, 1219 (**by m. of**); *plur.* **menys** means 3817; **meenys** mediators, intermediaries 1919.
Mene, *v. tr.* mean, refer to 181, 960 (*pret. sing.* **mente**); signify 945; purpose 1273.
Menyng, *s.* thought, mind 4453; meaning 1911.
Menge, *v. tr.* mix, mingle; *pret.* **meynte** 3533; *pp.* **meynt(e)** 2306, 4461, **y-meynt** 15.
Mercy, *s.* mercy 405, 1744, 3046.
Mercyles, *adj.* 2206.
Mervaile, Mervaylle, Merveil, *s.* wonder, astonishment 1366, 1965; wonderful thing, marvel 195, 4457.
Mervaille, *v. intr.* wonder, marvel 3611, 4467.
Merveilous, Mervaillous, *adj.* marvellous 659, 3849.
Mery, *adj.* merry 127, 886.
Merydyen, *s.* meridian, zenith 4256.
Meschaunce, *s.* misfortune, disaster 791, 3622, 2217 (**wente to m.** came to grief).

Meschief, -cheef, Mischief, *s.* misfortune 1770, 2488, 4085; sorrow, grief 996, 2905; trouble, distress 2690, 3012, 4194; harm, damage 2567, 3789.
Mesur, *s.*; **out of m.** immoderately 3115.
Mesurable, *adj.* moderate 3122.
Metal, *s.* 598, 2778.
Mete, *s.* meal, repast 1456, 1566.
Mete, *adj.* meet, apt, suitable 230.
Mete, *v. tr.* meet 580, 3311, 4264 (in combat); *intr.* come together, come across 58, 4038 (*with*), 4197; *pret.* **mette, met** 2179, 3906.
Metyng, *s.* meeting 2430, 1483; encounter, fight 2233.
Meue, *v. tr.* move; *pp.* **ymeued** 2640.
Mevyng, *s.* movement 2817 (*of the sterrys*).
Meynè, *s.* retinue, retainers 1372, 2590.
Meynten, *v. tr.* maintain, secure 4398.
Milk, *s.* 458, 4574.
Millere, *s.* miller 28.
Mirre, *s.* myrrh 4572.
Mo(o), *adj.* 912 (**withoute wordes mo**), 3688 (**moo delayes**); *s.* 3373; *adv.* 3989.
Moche, *adj.* great 2242 (**m. multitude**); *adv.* 3083, 244 (**myche**).
Mocioun, *s.* movement 5; proposal, suggestion 4110.
Modefie, *v. tr.* modify, lessen 3818 (*ire*).
Moder, *s.* mother 664, 702.
Moderly, *adj.* motherly 405 (*pytè*).
Mon(e), *s.* moan, complaint 760, 2708; grief 1871.
Mone, Moone, *s.* moon 7, 121, 3992.
Monk, *s.* 93, 102, 126.
Monstre, Monster, *s.* monster 618, 613, 644.
Monstre, *v. intr.* muster 3560; see **Mostren.**
Mood, *s.* disposition, temper 2899.
Moral, *adj.* 995, 2972 (**m. Senek**).
Moralitè, *s.* morality, moral lesson 22.
Mordre, *s.* murder 3178.
Mordre, *v. tr.* murder 3414.
Mor(e), *adj.* more 817, 501; **withoute more** without further ceremony or trouble 88, 1321; **mak therof no more** make no more ado about it 3781; *adv.* 278, 3639 (**moor**); **mor and mor** 516.
Morow(e), *s.* morning 989, 4014; the following day 1526, 3733.
Mortal, *adj.* deadly 2517, 3221; implacable 1063, 1609; terrible, awful 618, 1540, 2346, 3577; fatal 1279; deathlike, pale as a corpse 3391.
Mortally, *adv.* in a deadly or destructive manner 3890, 4218.
Mosel, *s.* muzzle 3837.
Most, *adj.* greatest, most 266, 2824, 4178; *s.* 41 (**m. of excellence**); *adv.* most 223, 889, 1111.
Mostren, *v. intr.* muster 2596; see **Monstre.**
Mot, *v.* must; *pres.* 1. 3. *sing.* **mot** 3236, 3269, 3436, 3681 (**moot**); 2. *sing.* **most** 738; *pret.* **most** 712, 781, 1133.
Mounteyn, *s.* mountain 612, 979.
Mourne, *v. intr.* mourn 3686; **mournyng,** *part. adj.* 1869.
Mournyng, *s.* 4440.
Mouth, *s.* 52.
Mouth, *v. tr.* utter, tell 4407.
Moyst, *adj.* causing rain 7 (cf. 8).
Muet, Mwet, *adj.* mute 743, 2844.
Multitude, *s.* great number 4381.
Muse, *v. intr.* meditate, ponder 400, 500, 677, 1508.
Muse, *s.* 828 (**the musys nyne**).
Musycal, *s.* musical instrument 222.
Mutabilitè, *s.* changeableness, inconstancy 1749.
Myd, *adv.* in the middle (*of*) 2 (**m. of Aprille**), 210, 3955, 4028; *prep.* **myd(de)** in the middle or centre of 2651, 3899 (**myd the feld**).
Mydnyght, *s.* 120, 1186.
Myght, *s.* physical strength 661, 2877; power 119, 3465.
Myghty, *adj.* physically strong, vigorous 2410; mighty, great 13, 186, 1355; massive, bulky 312.
Myghtily, *adv.* vigorously 3495; strongly 1253 (**myghtely**).
Myle, *s.* mile 324 (**vii. myle : while**).
Mynde, *s.* memory 44; remembrance 819; **make m.** call to mind 2563, 3146, 3291.
Myne, *v. intr.* penetrate 3379.
Mynistre, *v. tr.* furnish, administer 3603.
Mynut, *s.* the sixtieth part of a degree (q.v.) 371.
Myrk, *adj.* dark 1241.
Myrour, Merour, *s.* mirror 3842; pattern, model 2623, 2723, 3038; warning, example 1040.
Myrth, *s.* mirth, joy 134, 161, 168, 3036.
Mysauenture, *s.* misadventure 2513.
Mystery, *s.* ministry, profession 4170.
Mysty, *adj.* dark, obscure 630 (*dyvynaile*).
Myte, *s.* mite, thing of no value 3357.
Mytred, *adj.* mitred 4186.

Nacioun, *s.* nation 4701.
Naked, *adj.* 3117, 4586.
Name, *s.* name 87, 160, 305, 2080; renown 2605, 2763; reputation 4122, 4127.
Name, *v. tr.* name, call; **ynamed** 837, 1211, 915.
Namely, *adv.* especially, in particular 767, 893.
Narow, *adj.* narrow 2198.
Narowe, *adv.* precisely, strictly 1281; close 3687 (**n. to the stake**).
Nat, *adv.* not 75, 249, 520, 732, 458 (**nat ne**); *s.* naught, nothing 4055 (**is nat bot sorowe**).
Natiuitè, *s.* birth 217, 372, 660.
Nature, *s.* 720 (**naturys right**), 3832.
Naturely, *adv.* 671, 729.
Nay, *adv.* no (with the verb **sey**) 127 (**who so that sey nay** whoever may object to it), 777, 1598, 1767, 1799.
Ne, *adv.* not 1673, 458 (**nat ne**); *conj.* nor, or 137, 828, 1564, 85 (**neither . . . ne**); unless, if not 268.
Necessitè, *s.* necessity 1317.
Necligent, *adj.* negligent 2789.
Neclygence, *s.* 3237.
Nede, *s.* need, necessity 112, 1317, 3654; want, destitution 863 (personified).
Nede, *v. intr.* need, be necessary; *pres. ind.* 3. *sing.* **nedeth** 1522 (**it nedeth nat to** + infin.), 2676; *pret.* **neded** 3384.
Nedes, *adv.* needs, necessarily 712, 738, 781.
Neet, *s.* cattle 3593.
Neither, *pron.* 1384; *conj.* **neiþer . . . ne** 85, 787, 1172; **neither . . . nor** 212, 831.
Nekke, Nek, *s.* neck 4330, 2284.
Ner, *adv.* near 3023 (**fer and ner**).
Neuer(e), *adv.* never 44, 309, 191.
Newe, *adj.* new 14, 130, 990; **of n.** (**nwe**) anew, once more 1718, 2341, 3776; **n. and n.** again and again 4116.
Newly, *adv.* recently, lately 84, 1682; anew, afresh 3700.
Next, *adj.* next 2093, 3550, 4358; nearest (in relationship) 1702, 2081 (**n. of his alye**); *adv.* 1572 (**after n.**), 3543, 4206.
Nigromancye, *s.* necromancy 4051.
No, *adj.* 95, 163, 171; *adv.* 532 (**no lenger**).
Noble, *adj.* 13, 289, 3896.
Noblesse, *s.* nobleness, generosity 1988; nobility (coll.) 2904.
Nodde, *v. intr.* nod 169.
Nolle, *s.* head 32.
Nombre, *s.* number 832; great number 3558.
Non, Noon, None, *pron.* no one 27, 231, 464, 828; nothing 936 (**in non certeyn**); **non other** nothing else, no more 4239; not otherwise 406 (**it may non other be**), 672, 3701; **non other but** nothing else than 1951; *adj.* no 167, 637 (**non oþer mene**), 685, 1213, 4229 (**non delayes**); *adv.* not 510, 1502.
Nonne, *s.* nun 137.
Nonys, Noonys; for the n. for the nonce, for this occasion, expressly, on purpose 1251, 311, 412, 4275; on the spur of the moment, with no special meaning 969.
Nor, *conj.* nor 50, 133, 399, 817, 3002 (**hors nor man**).
Norys, *s.* nurse 456.
Not, *adv.* 39, 111, 133, 142.
Not, *pres. sing.* for **ne wot** know not 68.
Note, *v. tr.* note, take note of 3698.
Note, *s.* note, song (of birds) 2297.
No-thing, *adv.* not at all, in no respect 489, 1169, 2349, 3363.
Notty, *adj.* nutty, tasting like nuts, high-flavoured 110.
Nought, Noght, *pron.* nothing 49, 499, 592 (**lit or noght**), 1164; **al for n.** all in vain 2414; *adv.* not, not at all 1067, 1569.
Now, *adv.* 143, 325; nowadays 4673; *conj. temp.* now that 4166.
Nowher, *adv.* nowhere 239, 289, 1185.
Nowther, Nouther, *pron.* neither 1077, 4654; *conj.* neither 2003 (**n . . . nor**), 4137 (**n . . . ne**); nor 4443, 4495.
Noyeng, *s.* annoyance, molestation 1322.
Noys(e), *s.* crying 442; outcry 588; noise, racket 1363; din 4314; loud discussion 2522; clamour 2933; rumour 4063.
Nutritif, *adj.* nutritive, nutritious 2403.
Nye, *v. intr.* neigh; **Nyinge,** *s.* neighing 1304.
Nygh, Nyȝ, Nye, Ny, Negh, *adv.* near 642, 93, 2479, 3385, 1178.
Nyght, *s.* night 117, 1506, 1444 (**her nyghtes sorowe**).
Nyne, *numer.* nine 828, 1050.

O, *interj.* 4216 (**O. allas**), 4288.
Obeye, *v. tr.* obey 1027; comply with, perform 408; *intr.* obey 1133, 173 (*vnto*).
Obscure, *adj.* obscure, dark 1241.

Obsequies, *s.* 4567.
Obseruaunce, *s.* homage, respectful attentions 1474; customary rite or ceremony 1556, 4582.
Obstynat, *adj.* obstinate 4008.
Occasioun, *s.* opportunity of attacking, quarrel 2026 (see *Notes*); cause 909, 2529, 3561.
Occisioun, *s.* killing, slaughter 3603 (see *Notes*), 4204.
Occupacioun, *s.* occupation 3080.
Occupie, *v. tr.* hold 762, 1949; take up, occupy 993; engage, busy 4425; *intr.* hold possession, be in possession 1932 (**y-occupied**).
Odyble, *adj.* hateful, odious 4029.
Odyous, *adj.* odious, hateful 623, 821, 3247.
Of, *prep.* of 2, 7, etc.; out of 31; of, from 87; of, in respect of 5; concerning 3536; by 211, 664; by, through 177; after, on account of 304.
Of, *adv.* off 3497 (**smoot of**).
Offence, *s.* hurt, injury, damage 2364; wrong, fault 2688, 3238; sin 812, 2854; breach of etiquette 2019.
Offende, *v. tr.* wrong, injure 3455.
Officer, *s.* domestic official 1430, 2627.
Offre, *v. tr.* offer 1435; offer up to a deity, present as an act of devotion 4362 (*vp*).
Ofte, *adv.* often 251, 706, 1290; **ofte sith** often 1759, 1868, 3229.
Old, *adj.* 3, 187, 212 (**ȝong nor old**), 2959 (**the olde** the old man); **eldest** 1210, 1937; **of olde** long since, formerly 3700, 3775, for a long time 3630.
On, *prep.* on 17, 74, 400; in 115.
On, Oon, One, O, *numer., pron.* one 832, 60 (**on be on**), 951 (**all this . . . rekned into on**), 4492 (**O thyng ther was**), 4313 (**on . . . another**), 4176 (**the ton . . . the tother**); **euere in oon** continuously, without ceasing 483, 2876, 4116; **on and all** 67.
Only, *adv.* 171, 205, 463.
Onys, *adv.* once 260; **at onys** at once 2105, 2208 (**attonys**), 444 (**all at onys**).
Open, *adj.* open, evident 2074.
Openly, Opynly, *adv.* clearly 36, 632, 697; openly, unreservedly 1092, 3347, 3754.
Opne, *v. intr.* become open, open 4034.
Oposicioun, *s.* opposition (astronomy) 6.
Opportune, *adj.* fit, suitable 139, 503.
Opposit, *s.* opposite side 4269.
Oppresse, *v. tr.* subdue, conquer 2715, 4685; *pp. adj.* **oppressyd** downcast, sad 4551 (*of her cherys*).
Opynyoun, *s.* opinion 113, 1613; view 1854; mind 2261; good opinion, esteem 2460 (*in*).
Or, *conj.* or 100, 168, 488.
Or, *conj.* before 899, 2041, 3657, 3783, 3785, 2140 (**toforn or**); **or that** 2867.
Ordeyne, *v. tr.* arrange, make ready 4360; marshal, array 4027; appoint 412; ordain 4658; command 627; *intr.* arrange, make preparation 593 (*for*).
Ordinaunce, *s.* arrangement, preparation 2741.
Ordre, *s.* order; **be (in) o.** in order, one after the other 2371, 2664.
Orloger, *s.* a proclaimer of the hours 122.
Orygynal, *adj.* original 2565.
Orysoun *s.* prayer 552.
Oth, Ooth, Hoth, *s.* oath 1138, 1841, 2645.
Other, *pron.* the other 27, 1116; *plur.* others 1719 (**other ek**), 4579; *adj.* 401, 1007; **non other** in no other way 672, 922, 1147, 3701.
Other-wise, *adv.* otherwise, on any other condition 3724.
Otys, *s.* oats 3600.
Ought, *pron.* anything 2041; *adv.* at all 740.
Ought, Oght, *v.* 1909, 1086; *impers.* 1395.
Out(e), *adv.* out 4018 (**yssen o.**), 3566; *prep.* **out of** out of, from 610, 891, 1270; outside 1097; without, beyond 4017 (**out of doute**).
Out-breke, *v. intr.* break out, burst out; *pret.* **out-brak** 1963 (cf. 970 **brak out**).
Outher, *pron.* either, each 3902, 4633; *conj.* or 2426, 4455; **o. . . . or** either . . . or 282, 825.
Out-korve, *pp.* cut out 299 (*of a bodys hyde*).
Out-mete, *v. tr.* measure out, stake out 298 (**out-mette the boundes** *pret.* 3. *sing.*).
Outrage, *s.* violent injury, harm 1321; gross offence 4039.
Outraunce, *s.* the last extremity; **bringe to o.** put to death, kill 2218.
Outrayed, *pp.* gone beyond, broken away from 2069 (*of thy promys*); *pret.* 2172 (rubric).
Outre, *adj.* entire, whole 4056; extreme, exceedingly great 4122.
Outrely, *adv.* altogether 1710; absolutely, quite 4009 (**outtrely avised** quite determined).

Out-ringe, *v. intr.* resound 4316 (**out-ronge** *pret. sing.*).
Outward, *adv.* outwardly 234, 250, 1839.
Ouer, *prep.* 4677.
Ouergo, *v. intr.* pass away 3407 (**ouergon** *pp.*).
Ouerlade, *pp.* overwhelmed 4547 (*with cast of ston*).
Ouerleyd, *pp.* overpowered 2256 (*of verray feblenesse*).
Ouermore, *adv.* moreover, furthermore 2764, 3324.
Ouerslyde, *v. intr.* pass unnoticed 1565.
Ouerthrowe, *pp.* overthrown, ruined 1754.
Owne, *adj.* own 500, 1899, 3414.
Oynementes, *s. plur.* ointments 2394.
Oyther, (MS. Ar.) for **outher** either 282, 1825, 2955; or 3680.

Pacience, *s.* patience 198, 3444.
Paciently, *adv.* 1129, 1925.
Paganysme, *s.* heathendom 544.
Pale, *adj.* 7, 175, 496, 3363.
Paleys, Palays, *s.* palace 1244, 1191; (astron.) place (see l. 4), mansion 11.
Palfrey, *s.* palfrey 74, 4443.
Palm, *s.* victory, triumph 654 (**gete the p.**); palm-branch 4598 (as a sign of victory).
Panter, *s.* panther 3840.
Parbrake, *v. tr.* break thoroughly, shatter 2951 (see *Notes*).
Parcel, *s.* part, portion 942; used attributively 913, 2504 (**p. cause**); *adv.* somewhat, a little 124, 3499.
Pardè, *interj.* by God! verily, indeed 125, 1335.
Pardoun, *s.* pardon 3506.
Pardowner, *s.* pardoner 33.
Parfit, *adj.* perfect 24; complete 4714.
Parforme, Parfourme, *v. tr.* perform, fulfil 418, 933, 3810; **vp. p.** complete (the building of Thebes) 311.
Parforn, *v. tr.* perform, fulfil 3643.
Parlement, *s.* parliament 2573, 2889, 4390; formal council or conference 764.
Part, *s.* part 1084, 3150; part, portion 2824; region, quarter 523; party, side 3790, 4633; **on no part** in no respect 4159.
Parte, *v. intr.* depart 4143, 4600; give part of something (*of*) to somebody (*with*), share something with somebody 4594; break, burst 4490 (*on tweyne* in two).
Party, *s.* part, portion 1600; party, side 1068 (**partie**), 4097, 3941; point, particular 3176; **in p.** somewhat 3620, 3864.
Pas, *s.* step, gait 2118; pace 2260 (**ryde an esy pas**); speed 3279, 3926.
Passage, *s.* passage, place where to pass 617, 2155; passage, the action of passing 645, 1675, 3437 (from life to death); journey 1288; going onward, movement 666.
Passe, *v. intr.* pass, get away (*from*) 156; pass, go by 1610; vanish 3955, 4617; **pass-ouer** pass by in silence 825, 2670; *tr.* pass 1045 (**we ben ypassed the vale**), 1 (**phebus passed was the ram**).
Passyng, *adj.* extreme 419; *adv.* extremely, exceedingly 469, 770, 1208, 3914.
Passingly, *adv.* exceedingly, pre-eminently 1216, 2355, 2802, 3345.
Passioun, *s.* illness 114.
Pasture, *s.* 104 (*figur.*).
Pasture, *v. refl.* graze 2288.
Patere, *v. intr.* recite the paternoster 163.
Pay, *s.* pay 2584, 2684.
Pay, *v. tr.* 4040 (**paied hym his wages**).
Peerle, *s.* collect. and without a plur. 1440; **peerlys** 1052 (of dewdrops).
Pees, Pes, *s.* peace 470, 1083, 3863.
Penoun, *s.* pennon 4363.
Pensif, *adj.* thoughtful, sad 1216, 3860.
Peraunter, *adv.* fortuitously, by chance 1248.
Perce, *v. tr.* pierce 428, 932, 1485 (*pp.* **Iperced**), 3220 (**the Venym was so persyng**).
Perceyue, *v. tr.* perceive, observe 358.
Peryl, *s.* peril, danger 1290, 2855.
Perilous, *adj.* dangerous 643, 3221.
Periur, *adj.* perjured 2049 (*of thyn oth*).
Perpetuel, *adj.* perpetual 4121.
Perpetuelly, *adv.* 3416, 4046.
Person, *s.* person 1579.
Persshe, *v. intr.* perish 3678.
Perteynent, *adj.* appertaining, belonging 564 (not in *Oxf. Dict.*).
Perturbaunce, *s.* perturbation 4105.
Perturbe, *v. tr.* disturb, throw into disorder 3824.
Pervers, *adj.* adverse, unpropitious 384.
Pes, *s.* piece 2665; part, fragment 4328 (**peces** *plur.*).
Pessibly, *adv.* in peace 2784.
Peyne, *s.* penalty 927, 1385; pain 1486, 4291; sorrow, grief 1220, 3377, 4549; endeavour, pains 1425.
Peynte, *v. tr.* paint 1532 (**peynted** *pp.*).

Phage, *s.* see **Fage.**
Philolegye, *s.* Philologia 833.
Phisik, *s.* physic, the science of medicine 2403.
Physicien, *s.* physician 363.
Phylosophre, *s.* philosopher 362.
Piked, *adj.* picked, cleared of husks 56 (*greyn*).
Pikkeys, *s.* pickaxe 4543.
Pilgrimage, *s.* 20, 48, 3419.
Pilgrym, Pylgrim, *s.* 59, 66.
Pillage, *s.* 3590.
Pitè, Pytè, *s.* pity 405, 422, 4303.
Pith, *s.* substance, essential points 318.
Pitous, *adj.* piteous, sad 409, 4472; pitiful 442, 3234.
Pitously, *adv.* 2225.
Place, *s.* place 4, 426; dwelling-place 3316; position (on the battle-field) 3897.
Plates, Platys, *s. plur.* plate-armour 2169, 1365, 1864, 4277.
Platly, *adv.* flatly, plainly 196, 1328; certainly, decidedly 453, 634, 3972.
Play, *s.* pastime, fun 161, 1491; game, sport 575; play (iron. for fight) 4336.
Playe, Pleye, *v. intr.* play 3852, 4200 (**pleyeth þe lyoun** fights like a lion); *refl.* amuse oneself 2411.
Plee, *s.* plea, lawsuit 1254.
Plentè, *s.* plenty, abundance 1035, 1970.
Plenteuous, *adj.* plentiful 1454 (**a feeste p.**).
Plesaunce, *s.* pleasure, wish 2675; delight 3036; inclination 1619; satisfaction 147.
Plesaunt, *adj.* pleasant 230, 797.
Plese, *v. intr.* please 1434, 1622, 1756.
Pleying feeris, *s. plur.* playmates 468.
Pleyn, *v. intr.* complain, lament 961.
Pleyn, *s.* plain 3560, 3003, 1166.
Pleyn, *adj.* plain, clear 631, 877; honest, straightforward 673, 1724; *adv.* level 4148 (**with the erthe p.**), 4638.
Pleynly, *adv.* fully, plainly, clearly, openly 423, 1736, 3649, 2495; fully, in plenty (?) 1499.
Plonge, *v. tr.* plunge, thrust 890 (*adoun*).
Poete, *s.* poet 840, 40.
Pollex, *s.* pole-axe 2781, 3052.
Pompous, *adj.* arrogant, haughty 1076, 1349, 3530.
Pope, *s.* pope 3424.
Porayle, *s.* poor people 268.
Porche, *s.* porch 1252, 1300.
Pore, Poor, *adj.* poor 1992, 2680.
Port, *s.* external deportment, bearing, behaviour 234, 469, 3816, 4453.
Porter, *s.* porter, gatekeeper 854, 1250.
Portoos, *s.* breviary 162.
Possede, *v. tr.* possess 1066, 1229, 2693.
Possessioun, Pocessioun, *s.* possession, holding, occupancy 1159, 1810, 1991.
Possible, *adj.* 2886.
Posterne, *s.* back gate 2147.
Potent, *s.* staff 716.
Pound, *s.* pound (of money) 3856 (**many hundred p. : hound**).
Pourpartie, *s.* proportion, share 1604.
Pouert(e), *s.* poverty 4640, 863.
Pouertè, *s.* poverty 1098, 1987.
Power, Pouer, *s.* 1630, 1688, 3078 (**to my pouer** to the best of my power).
Poynt, *s.* point 413 (**from p. to p.**), 4585 (**p. be p.**); position 3694; sharp point 1488.
Poysye, *s.* poetry 214.
Preche, *v. intr.* preach 167.
Predecessour, *s.* predecessor 1976.
Preef, *s.* trial, experiment 649; examination 2328.
Prees, Pres, *s.* throng in battle, the thick of the fight 576, 580, 4249; dense throng 2435, 3750; great crowd of courtiers 3711.
Prees, Presse, *v. intr.* press forward 4319, 4311.
Preferre, *v. tr.* prefer, favour 3458, 4179.
Preise, *v. tr.* praise 193, 1950.
Prerogatif(f), *s.* precedence 1728; prerogative 1936.
Presence, *s.* 256, 365, 2834.
Present, *adj.* 565, 826, 1652, 3439.
Presente, *v. tr.* present, introduce 3135 (*to*); present, endow 3498 (*with*), 4236.
Preserve, *v. tr.* save 431, 1745, 3180, 3256.
President, *s.* president (of parliament) 2890.
Prest, *s.* priest 137.
Presume, *v. intr.* behave arrogantly, be presumptuous 485; presume, venture 2019.
Presumpcioun, *s.* presumption 2025.
Preue, *v. tr.* try, test 569, 2630; prove, demonstrate 2067, 2342, 2571; *pp.* **ypreued out** computed, figured out 377; **so wel a preued knyght** such a well-proved, acknowledged k. 1856.
Preye, *v. tr.* pray 98, 3917; *intr.* 1528 (*to the goddes*), 4709.
Preyere, *s.* prayer 546, 3459 (**preier**).

Pride, Pryde, *s.* pride 281, 259; daring, gallantry 3567; ferocity 3490, 3605.
Priket, *s.* small wax candle 1299.
Principal, *adj.* chief 1244.
Pris, *s.* glory, renown 747; praise 46; price, value 4005.
Prison, *s.* 801.
Priuely, *adv.* privately, secretly 253.
Problem, *s.* riddle 631, 736.
Procede, *v. intr.* proceed, go on 328, 1059, 3752, 3809 (**forth p.**); act 1640.
Process, *s.* narration, tale 824, 971; **by p.** in course of time 336, 708, 467 (*of dayes*), 665 (*of age*).
Professioun, *s.* profession, calling 132.
Profit, *s.* profit, advantage 3126.
Profre, *s.* offer 1632, 3997.
Progenitours, *s.* forefathers 4139.
Prolixitè, *s.* prolixity 1907.
Promys, *s.* promise 2069, 4605.
Pronounce, *v. tr.* pronounce, express 2889.
Prophecye, *s.* prophesy, prophesying 2810, 2969, 4171.
Prophete, *s.* prophet 4096.
Propoos, *s.* purpose, intention 461 (MS. Ar.).
Proscript, *adj.* proscribed, prohibited 4693.
Prosperitè, *s.* prosperity 888, 1772.
Proteccioun, *s.* protection 3430.
Proude, *adj.* proud 481; high-mettled, spirited 1304; stately, magnificent 4558.
Proudly, *adv.* valiantly, bravely 1069, 3882, 4211.
Prouesse, Prowesse, *s.* courage, bravery 571, 752, 3500.
Proue, *v. tr.* 2609 (**proued ful wel** well tried, reliable); see **Preue.**
Prouerbe, *s.* 51.
Provide, *v. intr.* provide, prepare 402, 2787, 2945, 3088; stipulate 3855, 3760.
Prouidence, *s.* foresight, care for the future 2982.
Provynce, *s.* province 4411.
Prudence, *s.* 682.
Prudent, *adj.* wise 201, 221.
Prudently, *adv.* 766, 1835.
Pryme, *s.* prime (of day) 124 (6 o'clock), 3734 (9 o'clock).
Prynce, *s.* prince 254, 803.
Pryse, *s.* prize 654 (**bere away the p.**).
Prysoner, *s.* prisoner 4552.
Pryvè, *adj.* secret, privy 1666 (*sighes*).
Pryvetè, *s.* secret counsel, secrets 2808.
Puddyng, *s.* pudding 100.
Pulle, *v. tr.* pull, pluck 4286 (*out*).
Punishe, Punshe, *v. tr.* 813.
Puple, *s.* people 252, 541, 4067.
Pur, *adj.* pure 4708; guiltless, innocent 3628.
Purchace, *v. tr.* contrive, devise 3936, 3301; procure, obtain, get 4167.
Purpo(o)s, *s.* purpose 154; proposal 1588, 4087; matter in hand, point at issue 329; **in purpos** minded, intending 1698, 3879; **of purpoos** purposely, designedly 3021, 3739; **to purpos** with regard to the matter or point at issue 1541.
Purpoose, Purpose, *v. intr.* mean, intend 2008; *tr.* set forth, state 3753.
Pursue, *v. tr.* pursue 3909, 4211; *intr.* pursue 1157.
Purtraie, *v. tr.* portray, picture 3954.
Purueaunce, Purvyaunce, *s.* providence 843 (**by heuenly p.**); provision, pre-arrangement 2742 (cf. 2769), 2840; foresight 3462, 3999.
Purveie, *v. refl.* provide oneself 2769 (*of* with).
Put, Putte, *v. tr.* put 1477, 1860, 3662; *pret.* **put** 576, 2335 (**put vp**), 4208 (**putte**), 1374 (**put a-sonder** separated); *pp.* **put** 38, **put out** turned out, exiled 1927.
Pycche, *v. tr.* pitch; *pret. plur.* **pyhte** 3128 (*tentys*), 3563 (**pight**).
Pyler, *s.* pillar, mainstay 267, 1726.
Pylled, *adj.* bald 32.
Pylow, *s.* pillow 111.
Pypen, *v. intr.* play on a pipe 1791 (*in a red*).
Pyrat, *s.* pirate 3182.
Pytte, *s.* pit, hole 1011.

Quake, *v. intr.* quake, tremble 3260 (**quaking** *pres. p.*).
Quarel, *s.* square-headed crossbow-bolt 4223.
Quarte, *s.* the sixtieth part of the tierce (astron.) 375 (see Littré, *Dict.* p. 1404; not noted in *Oxf. Dict.*).
Quene, Queene, *s.* queen 13, 766, 3627, 357, 404.
Querel(e), Quarel, *s.* quarrel, altercation 1382; contest, cause of contention 1069, 2498, 3657.
Questioun, *s.* 540.
Quod, *pret. sing.* quoth, said 96, 177, 481, 1329, 3340.
Quyete, *s.* quiet, tranquillity 746, 1712, 4703.
Quyk, *adj.* alive 2831.
Qwyte, *v. tr.* pay 3885; repay, requite 694; *refl.* acquit oneself 1946 (**quyteth ȝour-silf of ȝour trouthe**); do one's duty 3285 (*pret. sing.* **qwit**), 4207 (*pret. sing.* **qwitte**), 1952 (*pp.* **quytt**).

Race, *v. tr.* tear away 1006; pull out, eradicate 1489.

Rage, *s.* madness 1380, 2017; furious passion 1302, 2523, 3246; violence, fury 618, 1229, 4655; violent grief 865, 913, 3420; furious fight 2374.

Rage, *adj.* wild, savage 431, 1168, 1291, 1540.

Ram, *s.* Aries, the first sign of the zodiac 1; the golden ram (fleece) of Colchos 3192.

Rampaunt, *adj.* rampant 2197 (**a lyoun r.**).

Rancour, *s.* ill-will, malice 477, 2929, 3893.

Rasour, *s.* razor 3169.

Ratefie, *v. tr.* ratify 3349.

Rather, *adv.* 575, 1100, 1990.

Ravyn, *s.* rapacity, greediness 3590.

Rayle, *v. tr.* array, adorn 2386 (**yrayled** *pp.*).

Raylle, *v. intr.* flow, gush 2202, 4280.

Rebuke, *v. tr.* treat lightly, despise 1004.

Receyve, *v. tr.* receive 751, 1127, 3742.

Reche, *v. tr.* seize, take or lay hold of 158 (*pp.* **rauht**).

Recomfort, *s.* comfort, consolation 1221.

Recompense, *s.* reparation, atonement 3475.

Reconcile, *v. tr.* 1919, 3502.

Record, *s.* witness, evidence, proof 263, 286, 3831.

Recorde, *v. tr.* call to mind, remember 3653; tell, state orally 2087; record, tell 794, 4679.

Recur, *s.* succour, remedy 3105, 4074, 4637.

Recure, *v. tr.* recover, win back 1130, 2572, 3415; restore to health 2453; cure, restore 3124 (*of*); *intr.* recover what one has lost, win back lost ground 4090.

Recurlees, *adj.* incurable, beyond remedy 3931.

Red, *s.* reed, rustic musical pipe 1791.

Red, Rede, *adj.* red 9, 117, 3363; *s.* red colour 16.

Red(e), Reed, *s.* advice, counsel 685, 1792, 2744; plan, expedient, means 3235, 4227.

Rede, *v. intr.* advise 2103, 1019; *tr.* 802, 1844.

Rede(n), *v. tr.* read 43, 994, 1753; *pp.* **rad** 1407.

Redresse, *s.* redress, remedy 3692.

Redresse, *v. tr.* redress, repair, set right 2055, 2074.

Redy, *adj.* ready 577, 3145, 4015.

Reedifie, *v. tr.* rebuild 1740.

Reenge, go over, go along (searching) 441.

Reforme, *v. tr.* restore, re-establish 4702; redress, remedy 2076, 2362.

Refresshe, *v. tr.* refresh 3124; *refl.* 3008.

Refresshyng, *s.* 3149.

Refreyne, Reffreyn, *v. refl.* restrain, curb 1997, 2948; *tr.* keep back, keep secret 1957.

Refuge, *s.* 1184.

Refut, *s.* place of refuge, refuge 1181; remedy 4371; expedient, help 3009.

Regaly(e), *s.* royal power, royalty 1095, 1859, 3770.

Regestres, *s.* registers, records 2100.

Regioun, *s.* country, region 448, 756, 4042, 4427 (**rigions**).

Registrer, *s.* registrar, recorder 48.

Regne, *s.* kingdom 1984.

Regne, *v. intr.* reign 327, 1712, 1948, 4376 (*vpon* over); be thriving, flourish 1975, 2936 (**lordes regnyng in her flours**).

Rehersaile, *s.* recital, narration 52, 3154.

Reherse, Reherce, *v. tr.* repeat, relate, tell 63, 427, 1477, 4232.

Reise, *v. tr.* raise, build up 194, 208, 241.

Reioyse, *v. tr.* enjoy, have the use of 1606 (*his ryght*), 2006, 3706; *refl.* rejoice, be delighted 4089 (*of* at).

Rekke, *v. intr.* reck, care 2486 (*of*).

Rekkeles, *adj.* heedless, careless, rash 2343, 3864, 3893; negligent 1039 (**reklees** Ar. Bo. a. o.), 1447.

Reklesnesse, *s.* heedlessness 3456.

Rekne, *v. tr.* stretch out 707 (**yrekned** *pp.*).

Rekne, *v. tr.* reckon, count 1944; *pp.* **rekned** 951; enumerate, mention 2278.

Reknyng, Rekenyng, *s.* reckoning 987, 1803.

Relacioun, *s.* relation, report 3994.

Rele(e)s, *s.* release, relief 3129, 4562, 4571 (see *Notes*); cessation 3609.

Reles, *v. tr.* release, relieve 1220, 4549.

Releve, *v. tr.* relieve, ease 3078.

Remedy(e), *s.* remedy 403, 1701, 3261, 4102.

Remedyen, *v. tr.* 4113, 3289.

Remembrance, *s.* memory, remembrance 38, 498, 1488, 4581.

Remembre, *v. intr.* remember, consider 493, 4522, 2860 (*on*); *tr.* 193.

Remewe, Remwe, *v. tr.* avert, put off 725; *intr.* move off, run away 3041; go away 2140, 3787; set off, march off 3555.

Remnant, Remenaunt, *s.* rest 1046, 2552.
Remors, *s.* remorse 2852.
Remyssyoun, *s.* remission, pardon 3471.
Rende, *v. tr.* rend, tear 3228; *pret. plur.* **rent** 4328; *pp.* **rent** 864, 4496.
Renewe, *v. tr.* renew 725; give fresh proof of 4592.
Renne, *v. intr.* run 2948; *pret. sing.* **ran** 330, 1674, 3866, 4614, *plur.* **ronne** 3117, 3876, **rvnne** 2304, **ran** 4330; *pp.* **ronne** 1802, 1124, 1194, **y-ronne** 729, 748, 4064.
Renomed, *adj.* renowned 4130 (: *hed*; see *Notes*), 2615, 4175, 4024 (**renomyd**).
Renoun, *s.* renown, fame 889, 1269, 4134; bravery, valour 2184, 2491.
Repair(e), Repeir(e), *s.* resort, habitual going 2308 (**maked her repeyr**); return (home) 937, 1551; return journey 2427; the right to return 1125; gathering, crowd 3750.
Repelle, *v. tr.* repel, ward off 4033.
Repelyd, *pp.* repealed 3776.
Repente, *v. intr.* repent 1634, 3668; sorrowfully reflect on 959.
Repleveshed, *pp.* filled = **repleneshed** 3440 (see *Oxf. Dict.* replevish v.[2]).
Replie, *v. tr.* reply 1092, 3468.
Report, *s.* report, statement 1423, 1677; report, rumour 4137.
Reporte, *v. intr.* report, tell 283, 1362, 4150.
Repreef, *s.* reproach, shame 2689.
Requere, *v. tr.* require, ask 1933, 2085; demand 3692; request 3343, 1895 (*pres. p.* **requiring**), 3631; ask, inquire of 2857.
Request(e), *s.* request 349, 506, 3459.
Rescus, *s.* rescue, help 3846.
Resemble, *v. tr.* 3836.
Reserue, *v. tr.* reserve 3715, 3757, 3769.
Resigne, *v. tr.* resign 1840.
Resistence, *s.* resistance 2747, 3703.
Resorte, *v. intr.* return 935 (**hom r.**), 1134, 2738, 3721 (**resoort**).
Resoun, Reson, *s.* reason 1094; mind 682; **be r.** reasonably, justly 1806; **be r. of** because of 1143; **of r.** reasonably, fairly 740, 1086.
Respit, *s.* respite, delay 3254, 3878.
Respite, *v. intr.* delay, put off 2104.
Rest, *s.* rest 2178 (**cast his spere in the r.**).
Rest(e), *s.* rest, sleep 1445, 1502; peace 1107; quiet, repose 1616; tranquillity, comfort 1708; **sette at reste** satisfy, assure 1587.
Reste, *v. intr.* rest, repose 107, 1262; take one's stand upon, rely on, trust to 4001 (*vpon*); *refl.* 3129, 3991.
Restore, *v. tr.* restore 2642, 3508, 4564.
Restreyne, *v. tr.* restrain, keep back 3399; restrict, retrench 2685; prevent 3683, 4657.
Retenue, *s.* retinue, train 2588.
Rethorik, *s.* rhetoric, eloquence 42, 219; **rethorikes glade** eloquent and delightful discourses 3202.
Retourne, *v. intr.* return 604, 724, 2034.
Reve, *s.* reeve, bailiff 28.
Reuel, *s.* revelry, sport 1491, 1664.
Reuerence, *s.* 347, 1022, 3922.
Reuerently, *adv.* 1495.
Reuolue, *v. tr.* turn over and over mentally 1513 (**r. aboute**).
Reward, *s.* regard, consideration 1734, 1969.
Reward, *v. tr.* regard, look at, take notice of 261.
Rewe, *v. intr.* have pity (*on, vpon*) 2339, 4519, 4591; *tr.* rue, regret, grieve for 2917.
Rewme, *s.* realm 1742, 1768 (**reawmes**).
Reyn, *s.* rain 1176, 1286, 3004.
Reyn, *v. intr.* rain, fall like rain 3400.
Reyne, Rene, *s.* rein 2696, 2947, 1258.
Ribaudye, *s.* ribaldry, coarse language, irreverent jesting 25.
Riche, *adj.* rich 239, 243, 1193; precious 1440 (*stonys*).
Richely, *adv.* richly, splendidly 601, 1442, 4022.
Richesse, *s.* riches 281, 1944, 4594.
Ride, Ryde, *v. intr.* ride 91, 106, 360, 521 (**ryden**); *pret. sing.* **rode** 1293, **rood** 1880, *plur.* **rood** 3881; *pp.* **ryden** 2609; *refl.* 2264 (**he rode hym forth**), 1150.
Right, Riȝt, *adj.* straight 1527, 1886, 3556; *adv.* quite, very 97; very 916, 1208; straightway, at once 1536; altogether, at all 499, 2692; just 1251, 1761.
Right, Riȝt, *s.* right, justice 720, 1067, 1786, 3283, 3985.
Rightful, *adj.* lawful 1405 (*heir*), 1824, 3773.
Righwisnesse, *s.* righteousness 1912, 2073.
Rigour, *s.* rigour, severity 3461.
Rise, *v. intr.* rise 153 (**the sonne roos**); rise, get up from sleep 120; rise, revolt, take up arms 2054 (*vpon* against), 2527 (*pp.* **ryse**).
Robbe, *v. intr.* rob, plunder 3591.

Roche, *s.* rock 641, 2269, 3491 (**rocche**).
Rody, *adj.* ruddy, rosy 2298 (**morowe r.**).
Roo, *s.* roe 3596.
Roose, *s.* rose 1016.
Roote, Rote, *s.* root 3092, 4334 (**herte rote**); *figur.* 869; origin, source 791, 3674; an astrological term 370 (see Chaucer's *Astrolabe* II, § 44).
Rooted, *pp. adj.* rooted, deep-seated 1994 (**scorn r. in his herte**), 2562.
Roppys, *s. plur.* entrails, intestines 115 (see *Oxf. Dict.* rope, *s.*[2]).
Rore, *v. intr.* roar 1174.
Rouncy, *s.* horse, esp. riding-horse 166.
Round, *adj.* 100, 597, 4312; *adv.* around 2301; **rounde aboute** 109, 1058, 2223; *prep.* (postpos.) 1802, 3613.
Route, *s.* company, crowd 1057, 1889, 2224.
Route, *s.* rout, precipitate retreat 4196.
Route, *v. intr.* snore 110.
Routh, *s.* pity 925, 2347, 3395.
Rowe, *s.* row; **a-rowe** in a line 2097; **be r.** in order, one after another 1753; **vpon a r.** in succession, one after another 3385, 4559.
Rowne, *v. intr.* whisper 695; talk privately 253.
Royal, *adj.* 186, 315, 487, 593, 850, 1148.
Rubrich, *s.* rubric, heading of a chapter, chapter 3205.
Rude, *adj.* rude, uncivil 30.
Rumour, *s.* clamour, loud and violent talk 2522, 2531, 4062.
Rusty, *adj.* 75.
Ruyne, *s.* ruin, destruction 850, 1074, 4637.
Ryal, *adj.* royal, magnificent 1152, 3305, 4625.
Ryally, *adv.* royally, splendidly 781, 4621.
Ryaltè, *s.* royalty, royal state 1948; royal pomp, magnificent display 1661.
Ryme, *v. intr.* make rhymes or verses 2669.
Rytys, Ryytys, *s. plur.* rites, ceremonies 543, 355, 1556.
Ryve, *v. intr.* break, burst 4483, 4500 (*a-sonder*); *tr.* pierce, stab; *pret. sing.* **rove** 2520 (**he rove hym-silf**), **roof** 3915, 4278.
Ryver, *s.* river 3007, 1618.
Ryver-side, *s.* 3489.
Sabaton, *s.* broad-toed armoured shoe 1437.
Sacrament, *s.* eucharist 1138 (**oth of s.** oath confirmed by taking the sacrament upon it).
Sacrifise, *s.* 344, 4188.
Sad, *adj.* grave, serious 1408, 1552, 2041, 3940.
Sadyl, *s.* saddle 3730.
Sage, *adj.* wise 767, 840, 3705.
Sake, *s.*; in **for . . . sake,** as 800 (**for her s.**), 1491 (**for the knyghtes s.**), 3678 (**for þi s.**).
Sale, *s.* sale 75.
Salue, *v. tr.* salute, greet 1894, 3602 (**salwe**).
Same, *adj.* 79, 1737, 3848 (**myn autour writ the same** = this).
Sapience, *s.* wisdom 841 (personified), 2283.
Sauacioun, *s.* rescue, preservation 3088, 3429.
Sauage, *adj.* wild 3594, 3870; ferocious 3833.
Saue, *v. tr.* save 1181, 2833 (*his lif*), 4396.
Saue, *adj.* safe, assured, secured 3717; *conj.* save that, except that 939; *prep.* except 870, 2228 (**s. on excepte**); **sauf** except 2474, 4611.
Sauffecondit, *s.* safe-conduct 3432.
Saw, *s.* saying, speech 2979; story, tale 57.
Sawdyour, Soudeour, *s.* soldier 2630, 2680, 2758.
Sayllyng, *s.* attack, assault 4341.
Scarmosshe, *v. intr.* skirmish 3567.
Scarshed, *s.* parsimony, stinginess 2710.
Sceptre, *s.* 315, 338, 391, 1805.
Scorn, *s.* derision, mockery 1994.
Scorpioun, *s.* a constellation of the zodiac 388.
Scripture, *s.* written composition, passage in one 3831.
Seche, *v. intr.* seek (*for*) 2449. **Seke,** *v. tr.* seek 2026, 3817; *pp.* **sought out** 371, **soght** 379; *intr.* 439 (**serch and seke**), 4078.
Second, *numer.* second 1211; *s.* the sixtieth part of a minute of arc 375 (see Skeat, *Works of Chaucer*, Vol. III, p. 353).
Secrè, Sykrè, *adj.* secret 504, 1568; confidential, familiar 2807.
Secrely, *adv.* secretly 903, 2149.
Sede, *s.* seed 118.
See, Se, *v.* 426, 449, 2312 (**sen**); *imp.* 2. *plur.* **seth** 1754, *pres.* 3. *sing.* **seeþ** 1760; *pret. sing.* **saugh** 172, 503, **sauhe** 2988, **segh** 961, *plur.* **saugh**

1364, **sawh** 755, **segh** 591, 753; *pp.* **seyn** 2336, 2595, **seie** 793, **yseyn** 212, **sene** 2786; *ger.* **to sene** 3370.

See, *s.* sea 612, 1031, 4137 (**se**).

See, *s.* royal seat, throne 1122, 1240, 2131; seat of a bishop 4189.

Sege, Siege, *s.* siege 3604, 185, 4401.

Seke, *adj.* sick, ill 103, 2404 (**syk**).

Selde, Seeld, *adv.* seldom 2963, 3441, 4458.

Sely, *adj.* poor, wretched 4444.

Seme, *v. intr.* seem 272 (**me semeþ**), 1626, 1331; *pret.* **sempte** 1179 (**as it s.**), 1261 (**as hym s.**).

Semly, *adj.* handsome, elegant 753.

Semlynesse, *s.* handsomeness, elegance 1510; gracefulness, beauty 3038.

Sende, *v. tr.* 1954, 1837 (*pp.* **sent**); *intr.* 1829; *pret. sing.* **sente** 1702 (*for*); *pp.* **sent** 407, 1456 (*for*), 1650.

Sentement, *s.*; **as in s.** in substance, in its essentials, in its general meaning 1903, 2467, 4399. Equivalent to **in sentence**; the two phrases are characteristically Lydgatean, see *Oxf. Dict.*

Sentence, *s.* sense, significance 54; opinion 3635; **in s.** 197, 366, 794, 2976; see **Sentement.**

Sepulture, *s.* burial 4360; tomb 600.

Serche, Cerche, *v. intr.* 439, 681; *tr.* search 3006; examine 2393 (*his woundes*); *pp.* **cerched** sought out 374.

Serpent, *s.* 625, 690, 1765; Satan 4663.

Serue, *v. intr.* serve 2092; *tr.* furnish, supply 147, 2681 (*of* with; *pp.* **Iserued**), 2684 (**serued of her pay**).

Servise, *s.* service 3953.

Sesen, *v. intr.* cease 1376 (*of fighting*); cf. **Cessen.**

Sesoun, *s.* season (of the year) 12.

Sete, *s.* seat 1711 (**royal s.**), 2611.

Setten, *v. tr.* set, put 1083, 3577; lay 297 (*the ground of the bieldyng*); fix, appoint 733 (*pp.* **his tyme sette**), 1694; beset, surround 1291; **be set** be decided, resolved 1612, 1827; 2174 (**of al that he no thyng ne sette** did not care or trouble about it at all), 4005 (**he set it at no prys** put no value upon it), 1984; *pret.* **sette, set**; *pp.* **sette, sett, set.**

Seuere, *v. intr.* part, withdraw 4143.

Sew, *s.* pottage, broth 1563 (**straunge sewes**).

Seyn, *v.* say 55, 603, **seye** 61, **saye** 2086, **sey** 1598; *pres. ind.* 3. *plur.* **seyn** 295, **sayn** 4545; *pret.* **seide, saide**; *pp.* **seid, sayd.**

Seynt, *s.* saint 71; *adj.* 800 (**s. John**).

Shadowed, *pp.* shadowed 3025 (*with* by).

Shake, *v. tr.* 4587, 4697; *intr.* 1357 (**shoke** *pret.*).

Shal, *v.*; *pres. ind.* 1. 3. *sing.* **shal** 39, etc.; 2. *sing.* **shalt** 127; 1. 2. 3. *plur.* **shal** 656, 99, 1131; 2. 3. *plur.* **shul** 1607, 1024; *pret.* **shulde, shuld** 1549, 637, **sholde** 920 (: *tolde*).

Shalle, *s.* shawm (a musical instrument) 4298 (**loud as eny s.**).

Shame, *s.* shame 95, 1414; disgrace 2497, 4121.

Shame, *v. tr.* put to shame, disgrace 4126.

Shamfast, *adj.* full of shame, humiliating 2516.

Shape, *v. tr.* devise, contrive 403, 1701, 3655; ordain 1233, 3234; *pret.* **shope** 1082 (*a way*); *refl.* make preparations, get ready to start 1865 (**shope hym forth vpon his iournè**); *pp.* **shape** 1233, 3234.

Sharp, *adj.* sharp, keen 145, 1354; prickly 1545; shrill, loud 205; intense, vehement 955; violent, painful 3406, 2894.

Sharpe, *adv.* sharply 274, 2190 (**sharpe whette**).

She, *pron.* 408, 797; *genit.* **her** 703, **hir** 2422; *dat. acc.* **her** 799, 911, **hir** 968, 2421, **hur** 799 (MS. Ar.); **her-self** 2315 (**h. allone**), **hir-silf** 2853.

Sheding, *s.* shedding 2475 (*of his blood*).

Sheede, *v. tr.* shed 3477; *pret.* **shadde** 4710; *pp.* **shadde** 2900, **shad** 3939, 4643 (**shad out**).

Sheld, *s.* shield 2065, 1531, 1537.

Shene, *adj.* shining, bright 537, 730, 2303; glistening 1051.

Shep, *s.* sheep 3593.

Sherte, *s.* shirt 2391.

Shete, *v. tr.* shoot; *pp.* **shette, shett** 4311.

Shette, *v. tr.* shut, close 162 (*imp.* **shet**); *pret. plur.* **shet** 4351; *pp.* **shet vp** 2865; enclose 602, 4476 (*pp.* **shette**); *intr.* close 4037 (*pret.* **togydre shette**).

Shewe, *v. tr.* show 1767, 248; prove 2016; set forth, offer 4110; explain, state 963 (*out*); *pp.* **shewen** 2555, **shewed** 1225, 3844.

Short, *adj.* 1985, 1231.

Shorte, *v. tr.* shorten 4615.

Shortly, *adv.* briefly, in short 29, 88, 231, 474.

Shortnesse, *s.* 1036 (*of liff*).

Shour, *s.* shower of rain 8; attack, fit, conflict 3215, 3406, 3426, 2894.
Shoute, *v. intr.* shout, scream 4303; assail with shouts of derision, shout at 4092 (*on*).
Shrowde, *v. tr.* hide, conceal 1762; *refl.* shelter 1185 (**schrowde**), 3426.
Shyne, *v. intr.* shine 121, 827, 1049, 1766; *pret. sing.* **shon** 889.
Shynyng, *s.* splendour, lustre 4131.
Shyuere, *v. intr.* split, fly in pieces 4323.
Side, Syde, *s.* side 1291 (**on euery s.**), 3948 (**be her s.**); *plur.* **sydes** bodies, men 2783 (**ther shal many s. blede**).
Sigh, *s.* sigh 955, 1666.
Sighe(n), *v. intr.* sigh 906, 2986, 3380.
Sight, *s.* sight, view 1384, 3865, 1762, 1226; view, opinion, judgment 1605, 3633; aspect, look 623, 3127; **han a siȝt (how)** take into consideration 3284, 3676.
Signe, *s.* sign, token 548, 959, 1990; *plur.* **the twelve signes** the twelve divisions of the zodiac 1802.
Signyfie, *v. tr.* mean, refer to 221; import, portend 1524.
Sikerly, *adv.* certainly 2015.
Sikernesse, *s.* certainty 2500, 2891, 3113.
Siknesse, *s.* illness 72, 2457.
Silf, *adj.* same 1249, 3218 (**þe selue place**); **the silfe houre** the very hour 372.
Siluer, *s.* silver; *adj.* silvery 1051, 2301.
Siluer-shene, *adj.* shining as silver 3219.
Singe, *v. intr.* sing; *pret.* 3. *sing.* **song** 830, 3552.
Syngyng, *s.* singing 241.
Sinke, *v. intr.* sink; *pp.* **sonken** 4060, 4080.
Sir, *s.* sir 1901; **Sirs** gentlemen 177.
Sith, *adv.* afterwards 672; *conj. caus.* since, because 177, 322, 1088, 2733, 4128; *conj. temp.* since 1803; **sith that** since, as 1856.
Sith, *s.* in **ofte sith,** see **Ofte.**
Sitten, *v. intr.* sit 2097; *pret. sing. plur.* **sat** 896, 1564; *impers.* be suitable, proper 843 (**it sat wel hem to be ioyned**).
Sitting-place, *s.* seat 1475.
Skalis, *s. plur.* scales (of a serpent) 3219.
Skye, *s.* sky 834.
Skyn, *s.* skin, hide 3839, 304 (**skynne**).
Slauhter, *s.* slaughter 3916, 4261; killing 589, 3874.
Sleen, Slee, Sle, *v. tr.* slay, kill 628, 922, 2507, 925; *pret. sing.* **sclowe** 1271, **slogh** 581, 2196, **slough** 980, 4557, *plur.* **slowe** 3594; *pp.* **slawe** 398, 749, 785, **yslawe** 2536, 4294, **slayn** 2473, **slayen*** 948, 3873, 3877, **islayen*** 4243, 4342, 4361.
Sleght, Sleight, Sleyht, Scleight, *s.* craft, trickery 3845, 4213, 1759, 2243.
Sleghty, *adj.* wily, cunning 693.
Slender, Sclender, *adj.* thin, lean, "scraggy" 74, 102.
Slepe, *v. intr.* sleep 1260; *pret. sing.* **slep** 2406, **slepe** 1283, **slepte** 1246, **slept** 1227.
Slepe, *s.* sleep 108, 3168.
Slippe, *v. intr.* slip 1277.
Slouth(e), *s.* sloth, laziness 3237, 3241; tardiness, delay 926, 1945, 2108.
Slowgh, Slouh, *adj.* slow 5, 3223.
Smal, *adj.* slender, thin 429; narrow 2277; small 374, 2331, 2923.
Smerte, *v. intr.* suffer, be in distress 2694.
Smerte, *s.* pain 3375.
Smerte, *adj.* painful 2392; keen 4291; bitter 955.
Smete, *v. tr.* smite; *pret. sing.* **smette** 2180, 4278.
Smite, *v. tr.* smite; *pret. sing.* **smote** 744 (*of* off), **smoot** 3497 (*of* off); stabbed 4292.
Smoth, *adj.* pleasant, calm 1055; smooth, insinuating, deceitful 1794.
So, *adv.* so 65, 136; thus, in this way 451, 3800; *intens.* so 345, 3551, 3957.
Sobbe, *v. intr.* sob 3380.
Socour, *s.* succour, help 758, 1185, 3235; support 2981.
Socoure, *v. tr.* succour, help 851, 2829, 3047.
Sodeyn, *adj.* sudden, unexpected 891, 913, 3892; immediate 3680.
Sodeynly, *adv.* suddenly 644, 898; quickly, swiftly 4036, 4281.
Softe, *adj.* soft, mild 1054, 3816; tender, feeble 701; *adv.* softly 207, 4287; sweetly 1246.
Soget, *s.* subject 3763; *adj.* 1690.
Soiour, *s.* continuance, stability 3424.
Soiourne, *v. intr.* remain, reside 306; remain, stay 723, 3232.
Solempne, *adj.* solemn 1560.
Solempnely, *adv.* solemnly 2540.
Solempnytè, *s.* solemnity 4621; solemn festival 848, 1662.
Solempnyze, *v. tr.* 780.
Soleyn, *adj.* sullen, morose 249.
Soleyntè, *s.* distant haughtiness, moroseness 259.

Solier, *s.* shoe 1437 **MSS. Ra. Ba.** (Fr. *soulier*; not in *Oxf. Dict.*).
Somdel, *adv.* somewhat 1194.
Some, *pron. s.* 22, 438, 4302, 1837 (**s. other** some one else); *adj.* 161, 293, 4213.
Somer, *s.* summer 3118 (**s. sonne**).
Somwhat, *pron. adv.* in some measure 3407.
Sonde, *s.* dispensation, ordinance 3444 (*of goddes*).
Sondry, *adj.* different 19, 1668, 1672, 670 (**many s. ȝeeres**); several 880.
Sondy, *adj.* sandy 3000.
Sone, *adv.* soon 148, 354.
Sone, *s.* son 410, 464, 1004, (disyllabic) 917, 1213, 1404, 878, 4367; son-in-law 2735.
Song, *s.* song 203, 225.
Sonne, *s.* sun 153, 1049, 2303 (**svnne**).
Soor, *s.* wound 2438.
Soort, *s.* sort, species 3592 (**al maner soortes**).
Soote, *adj.* sweet, delightful 273, 2280, 3091; see **Swete**.
Soper, *s.* supper 108.
Sor, *adj.* grievous 2375.
Sorcerye, *s.* sorcery 4101.
Sore, Soore, *adv.* deeply, intensely 400, 906, 1173; eagerly 439; grievously 1779; tightly, closely 3393.
Sorow(e), *s.* sorrow 105, 849, 858.
Sorowe, *v. intr.* sorrow 3413.
Sorowful, *adj.* 2863, 4433 (**sorwful**), 4476 (**sorful**).
Sort, *s.* destiny, fate 397, 2895 (**soort**); divination (by drawing lots) 4171; lot 3685 (**soort**); power, authority 648.
Sory, *adj.* sorry 3967.
Soth, *s.* truth 634, 727, 522, 1793; **in s.** in truth, really 18, 25, 4253.
Sothfast, *adj.* true, just 1770.
Sothfastnesse, *s.* truth 3250.
Sothly, *adv.* verily, indeed 41, 59, 3694; truly, with truth 55.
Sotyl, *adj.* subtle, wily 1670 (*craft*).
Sotyltee, *s.* elaborately dressed and highly sugared dish 1563.
Soude, *v. tr.* enlist 2583 (MSS. T_1. M. a. o.).
Sowde, *s.* pay 2683 (rubric).
Soul, Sool, *adj.* sole, alone 97, 2163 (**sool by hym-silf**).
Soule, *s.* soul, life 3417.
Soun, Sown, *s.* sound, noise 1179; cry, scream 588, 4421; rumour 1678.
Soupe, *v. intr.* take supper 98.
Sours, *s.* source, origin 4290.
South, *s.* south 4257; *adv.* 2801, 3013.
Souereyn, *adj.* supreme, pre-eminent 884, 4705; excellent, exquisite 3203; *adv.* supremely 1649 (**s. excellent**).
Souereyntè, *s.* supremacy, pre-eminence 2974; sovereignty 3717.
Sowe, *v. tr.* sow; *pp.* **sowe** 4668.
Sowpowayle, *s.* support 267.
Soyl(e), *s.* soil, ground 14, 303.
Space, *s.* extent of time 993, 1187, 3405; time 503 (**opportune s.**); room 3585; extent 301; distance, range, stretch 157, 324.
Spare, *v. intr.* forbear, refrain from 112, 507, 2371, 3641.
Spech(e), *s.* speech, language 3411, 226.
Special, *adj.*; **in s.** especially, in particular 396, 1093, 3769.
Specially, *adv.* particularly 350, 246 (**specealy**).
Specifie, *v. tr.* relate in detail 2664; state explicitly 213, 761, 1507 (**specifies : fantasies**); explain, interpret 1529.
Sped(e), *s.* good fortune, success 4161; advantage 1836.
Spede, *v. intr.* succeed, fare (well, ill) 2231 (*pp.* **sped**), 3645; succeed, be able 2246 (**s. tendure longe**); *refl.* hasten 417, 1875 (*pret. sing.* **spedde hym**), 2122 (*pret. sing.* **sped hym forth**).
Speke, *v. intr.* speak 396, 4537 (**spekyn**); *pret. sing. plur.* **spak** 1236, 699, 82, 3640.
Spekyng, *s.* 246.
Spende, *v. tr.* spend, pay away 2762 (*pret.* **spent**); consume, waste 4356 (*pp.* **spent**); use up 715.
Spere, *s.* spear 1352, 1487, 3052 (**speer**).
Spere, *s.* sphere 2557.
Sperkle, *s.* sparkle 2555.
Spice, *s.* spice 1499.
Spille, *v. tr.* spill, shed 4635.
Spirit, *s.* spirit, spiritual being 538; animating principle 2810.
Spotte, *s.* blot, stain 4132 (*of blame*).
Spotted, *adj.* spotted, speckled 3494.
Spousale, *s.* marriage 816.
Spoyle, *v. tr.* plunder, ravage 3591.
Sprede, *v. intr.* open, expand 2312; *tr.* spread 4700, 4468 (*pp.* **sprad**); spatter 2322 (*pp.* **sprad**).
Spryng, *s.* spring, well 3064.
Sprynge, *v. intr.* grow up, shoot up 4459 (*vp*).
Squar, *adj.* square-hewn 312, 1252; four-cornered 2211.
Sqwyer, Squyer, *s.* squire 1659, 2591.

Stable, *adj.* stable, firm 1724, 3777; reliable 3630, 2047 (**s. of** true to).
Staf, *s.* staff, stick 710, 713.
Stage, *s.* stage, distance travelled between two places of rest 19.
Staire, *s.* staircase 1495.
Stake, *s.* stake (at each end of the lists) 3687 (**dryve so narowe to þe s.** to the last extremity, to the last shift; see Skeat, *Works of Chaucer*, Vol. V, *Notes*, p. 89).
Stalke, *s.* stalk 2312.
Stalle, *s.* stall, bishop's seat in a choir 4186.
Stalled, *pp.* placed, ranking 3542; installed 4189; **ystallyd** enthroned 4043.
Stark, *adv.* rigidly, stiffly 4481.
Statly, *adj.* stately, dignified 1239; splendid 1497.
Statue, *s.* 536.
Staunche, *v. tr.* quench, slake 3110 (*her thrust*); stop the flow of blood from 2396 (*woundes*).
Stede, *s.* steed 1152, 1887; horse 4442.
Stede, *s.* stead; **stonde s.** be of use, profit, avail 4051; **in sted of** 4162.
Stele, Steel, Stiel, *s.* steel 1150, 1450, 1346, 1484.
Stele, *v. tr.* steal; *pp.* **stole** 1669.
Stere, *v. tr.* stir 2956 (*pp.* **stered**); see **Styring.**
Sterne, *adj.* stern, harsh 81; firm 2118; fierce, wild 3490.
Sterre, *s.* star 1460, 1187.
Sterte, *v. intr.* start; *pret. sing.* **stert** 1302 (*vp*), 2334, **sterte** 1308 (*vpon his hors*), 4528; move suddenly 2519 (*a-side*).
Stille, *adj.* still 3814 (**be s.** hold one's peace).
Stille, *adv.* quietly 4609; motionless 3388; continually, always 798; habitually, constantly 2587.
Stody, *v. intr.* study, meditate 143.
Stok, *s.* stock, race, family 332, 1401, 3158.
Ston, Stoon, *s.* stone 240, 952, 2844; tombstone 3408.
Stond(e), *v. intr.* stand 742, 738 (*to the lawe* abide by); *pres.* 3. *sing.* **stondeth** 2720 (*in* consists of), **stont** 3048; *pret.* **stood** 526, **stod** 1078; *plur.* **stoode** 1396; *pres. p.* **stonding** 80.
Stoor, *adj.* stern, surly 81 (MSS. Ra. Ba.).
Stoppe(n), *v. tr.* stop, block, bar 645, 2152.
Stor, Stoor, *s.* store, supply of food 3598; **set lityl stor of** set little store by, value little 1984.
Storm, *s.* violent outburst 3406 (*of wepyng*).
Story, *s.* one of the Canterbury Tales 36; the story of Thebes (esp. le Roman de edipus 341, 361, 427, etc.; Boccaccio's Genealogia deorum 193, 307), 2550 (**the s.**: 2551 **my tale**); history 3194 (**the s. hool of this ysyphylè**).
Stound, *s.* time, hard time 2895.
Stoundemele, *adv.* at intervals, from time to time 2304, 3387.
Straunge, *adj.* distant, reserved, unfriendly 249; curious, extraordinary 1563, 2661; unknown 1364, 1431.
Straunger, *s.* stranger 1468.
Strecche, *v. intr.* stretch, reach 300; be sufficient or adequate 3331.
Streght, *adv.* straightway, directly 1294, 1501, 1880.
Streite, *adj.* narrow 2155; **streght** (*adv.*) closely, tightly 1542.
Strem, *s.* stream (of blood) 4279; ray 2556; bright look 1463 (*of her eyen*), 2300.
Streng, *s.* string 207 (of a harp).
Strengthe, *s.* force, validity 3777.
Strok, *s.* stroke, blow 4234.
Strong, *adj.* strong 110, 204, 4460; potent, powerful 3651.
Strongly, *adv.* 4146.
Stryf, *s.* quarrel, dispute 423, 3662, 4671; strife, contest 2566, 4634; violence, vehemence 2517.
Stryve, *v. intr.* contend 1916, 2010, 4674; dispute, argue 1341.
Stuff, *s.* military force, body of soldiers 2772.
Stuffen, *v. tr.* man, garrison 2758; *refl.* provide oneself with troops 2590.
Stumble, *v. intr.* stumble 2962.
Sturdy, *adj.* strong, stout 3492.
Style, *s.* pen 2124, 3826 (**styell**); style, manner of expression 3203.
Stynge, *v. tr.* sting 3368 (**stonge** *pp.*).
Stynke, *v. intr.* stink 745 (*adj.* **stynkyng**).
Stynten, *v. tr.* stop 2532, 3277; *intr.* cease 1386 (*of her strif*), 3925, 3919; stop 3561, 4463.
Styring, *s.* impulse, influence 235; see **Stere.**
Subieccioun, *s.* subordination, bondage 2966; obedience 2062.
Substaunce, *s.* substance, matter 3451; **in s.** substantially, essentially 53.
Succede, *v. intr.* succeed, follow after 336, 1065, 1594.

Successioun, *s.* 331, 1201.
Successour, *s.* successor 918, 4192.
Sue, Swe, *v. intr.* ensue, follow 989, 3422; follow 3042 (*after*); *tr.* follow, pursue 2139, 4219; follow up, prosecute 2902; accompany, come with 2381.
Suffisaunce, *s.* abundance 1970.
Suffise, *v. intr.* suffice, be sufficient 3330, 3401.
Suffraunce, *s.* permission, leave 3763.
Suffre, *v. tr.* suffer, permit, put up with 1100, 1338, 2690, 4494.
Sugred, *pp. adj.* sugared, honeyed 52 (**his sugrid mouth**); sweet-sounding 273 (*harpe*).
Superfluytè, *s.* superfluity, unnecessary supply (of words) 1908.
Supersedyas, *s.* writ to stay legal proceedings or to suspend the powers of an officer 3432.
Supersticious, *adj.* 4057.
Supplicacioun, *s.* supplication, petition 3257.
Support, *s.* support, countenance 198.
Supportacioun, *s.* support, prop, stay 269, 2984.
Supporte, *v. tr.* support, uphold 284.
Suppose, *v. intr.* 324, 626, 1332, 1983.
Supprise, *v. tr.* overtake, seize suddenly, affect violently 2017, 2510, 3094.
Sur, *adj.* sure, certain 2013, 509 (**sure**); sure, trusty, not liable to break 1864 (*platys*).
Sured, *pp.* pledged 2234 (**he s. was and sworn**), 4395.
Suretè, *s.* surety, guarantee 2000; security, safety 3441 (**suertè**).
Surly, *adv.* surely 1561, 2851 (**seurly**).
Surmounte, *v. tr.* surpass, excel 1976.
Surplus, *s.* rest, remaining part 1996, 3357.
Surplusage, *s.* = surplus 3987.
Surquedye, *s.* arrogance 282, 1076, 4661.
Surqwydous, *adj.* arrogant, overbearing 471, 1353 (**surquedous**), 2018.
Suspecioun, *s.* suspicion 1155, 3618.
Suspecte, *adj.* suspected, suspicious 1831.
Sustene, *v. tr.* sustain, bear 478, 4488; support 266, 1726; maintain 1069; *intr.* hold out 2188; *refl.* hold up (oneself) 662, 2257.
Suster, *s.* sister 3068, 3043 (**sustir**), 2432 (**sustre**), 832 (**sustren** *plur.*); sister-in-law 2432.
Swalowen, *v. tr.* swallow 4073.
Swerd, *s.* sword 274, 3638, 1378.
Swere, *v. tr.*; *pret.* **swoor** 2779; *pp.* **sworn** 663, 1325, 1938 (**ȝe are s.**), 2641, **I-sworn** 1695.
Swete, *adj.* sweet, pleasant 57, 203; *compar.* **swetter** 4571.
Swetnesse, *s.* 202.
Sweuen, *s.* dream 1224.
Swich, Such, *pron.* such 260, 1793, 363, 542; *adj.* 2074, 4686, 229, 2075.
Swift, *adj.* swift 1675, 3832.
Swogh, *s.* swoon 2333.
Swow, *s.* sigh, groan 4338.
Swowne, *v. intr.* swoon 1868, 4517.
Swounyng, *s.* swooning 4423, 4478.
Swyn, *s.* swine 3597.
Syngulerly, *adv.* singly 4265.
Synne, *s.* sin 4659.
Syyt, *s.* site, situation 563, 1164, 3027.

Tables, *s. plur.* tables for astrological calculations 378.
Taile, *s.* tail 3219.
Taken, *v. tr.* take 555, 265 (**take**); *pret.* **took** 77, 533, **toke** 152, *plur.* **token** 432, **tokyn** 4377, **tok** 1001; *pp.* **take** 11, **taken** 4, **y-taken** 370, **I-take** 3556; **t. vp** levy 2590.
Tale, *s.* tale, narrative 35, 4424; statement 1955; speech, discourse 1568; 18 (**Canterbury talys**); **my tale** 176, 4716 etc. refers to Lydgate's own poem The Siege of Thebes; a mere story, idle tale 430.
Tame, *adj.* tame, domesticated 3847, 3868.
Tansey, *s.* pudding flavoured with the juice of tansy 101.
Tarye, *v. intr.* tarry, linger, stay 1140, 2993; *tr.* delay, detain 321.
Tarying, *s.* delay 501, 1392, 1939.
Teche, *v. tr.* inform 225; admonish 3412; direct 2864 (*pret.* **taught**).
Tedious, *adj.* 991.
Teer, *s.* tear 1867, 3384.
Telle, *v. tr.* tell 86, 138, 170; *intr.* 3545 (**telle forth of her iournè**), 4012; *pret. sing.* **tolde** 313, 652, *plur.* **tolden** 937, *pp.* **told** 19, 211.
Tempest, *s.* 1175, 1237, 2876.
Temple, *s.* 534, 1554, 4365.
Ten, *numer.* 2215.
Tender, Tendre, *adj.* tender, delicate 411, 451, 661, 14; immature, youthful 705, 914; fine, slender 429.
Tene, *s.* anger, wrath 477 (**hasty t.**), 2480; hate, hostility 638, 709, 2187.
Tent, *s.* tent 3740, 4355, 3128.
Terme, *s.* appointed time 2595 (**t. sette**); pay-day 2683 (**terme-day**); *plur.* expressions, words 30, technical terms 2668.

Termyne, *v. tr.* declare, state 2963, 4184.
Than, *adv.* then 711, 1323, 3721; *conj.* than 274, 575, 625.
Thanke, Thonke, *v. tr.* thank 1631, 3148, 4590; *intr.* give thanks, thank (*to, vnto*) 3317, 2417 (**thonkyng**).
Thar, *v. intr. pres.* 3. *sing.* need 2841.
That, *conj.* that 86, 295; in order that 111, 458, 1159; so that 239, 4038; (so) that 231, 989, 4202.
That, *pron. demonstr., plur.* **tho,** *s.* 599, 579, 628, 1100, 4351 (**tho of the toun**); *adj.* 401, 1462, 2586, 4308.
That, *pron. relat.* 8, 49, 230, 89, 180, 568; = that which 1623, 3451, 4003, 4151.
The, *v. intr.* thrive, prosper 1024.
The before a comparative 145 (**þe sharper and the bet**), 1339.
The, þe, th-, *defin. art.* 1, 6, 7.
The ton—that other, *pron.* 882, 1132, 4176 (**the ton—the tother**).
Thenke, Thynke, *v. intr.* think 1800 (*pret.* **thoght**), 1812, 1828; consider 1776, 1785, 1938, 3462 (**thynk**); intend, mean 1321.
Thennys, *adv.* 308 (**from t.** from there, from that place).
Ther, þer, there, *adv.* there 306, 155, 1310; *relat. adv.* where 2302, 2322, 4464 (**þer as**).
Ther-ageyn, *adv.* against or in opposition to that 1799, 3972, 2010 (**therageynes**).
þer-among, *adv.* among that 4459.
Ther-at, *adv.* there, at the feast 1455; at that, on the occasion of that 1797.
Therby, *adv.* by that, through that 4090.
Therfor, *adv.* therefore, for that reason 466, 1039, 4383.
Ther-fro, *adv.* from that 697 (**go t. shuffle** out of it), 2091.
Ther-in(ne), *adv.* therein, in that place 2384, 3028, 4364.
Ther-of, *adv.* thereof, of that, of it 95, 823, 4424.
Therto, *adv.* to that, to it 698 (**tak hede t.**), 1598, 1405 (**heir t.**); in confirmation of this 2027, 3323.
Ther-vpon, *adv.* on that (matter, question, business) 253, 636, 992, 1928.
Ther-with, *adv.* thereat, on account of that 3607, 3697.
Ther-with-al, *adv.* besides 1168, 2146; therewith, with it 3498.
They, Thei, þei, *pron.* 138, 58, 31, 4320 (**they of Thebes**); *genit.* **her** 2587, 2588, **theyr, their, ther** 3590, 2594, 1429; *dat. acc.* **hem** 990, 2010, **ham** 990 (MS. Ar.), **them** 990 (MS. Ra.); **hem-silf, -self, -silue** 256, 760, 4013.
Thider, *adv.* thither, there 1657, 1880, 2271.
Thikke, *adj.* thick 1365, 2145.
Thilke, *adj. demonstr.* that, this, the same 1240, 3570, 1841, 434 (**t. same day**).
Thing, Thyng, *s.* thing, matter 400, 226, 2678, 4138; creature, being 1470, 3295 (**þingges**), 1743; **in al maner þing** 413, 807.
Thirst, Thrust, *s.* thirst 3016, 3110, 4194.
This, *pron., plur.* **thise, thies,** *s.* 144, 334, 430, 951; *adj.* 48, 468, 741, 872 (**thise folk weren**), 396, 4433 (**thys creaturys**); **this** = this is 453, 634, 1953.
Tho, *adv.* then 1113, 2257, 3822; **as tho** then 3029, 3976.
Thonder, *s.* thunder 1286, 4314.
Thong, *s.* thong 299.
Thorgh, *prep.* through 437; by means of 235 (**t. his styring**), 798; on account of 1297 (**t. derknesse**); throughout, all over 749, 4669; *adv.* 428 (**his feet t. they gan to perce**).
Thorgh-girt, *pp.* pierced through 4480.
Thorgh-out, *prep.* 40, 271, 1650; *adv.* 3378, 4311 (**was shette t.**).
Thorn, *s.* rose-bush 1016.
Though, Thogh, *conj.* although, though 4380, 85, 97, 1336, 582 (**thow**); **thogh that** though 183; **as thow** as if 1079.
Thought, Thouȝt, *s.* thought 2700; mind 500, 1570, 4009; melancholy, heavy-heartedness 591, 3414, 4614.
Thoghtful, *adj.* thoughtful, pensive 1507.
Thousand, *numer.* 3671 (**many t.**), 4455.
Thow, Thou, *pron.* 127; **the** 142, 492; **þi-silf** 133; *plur.* **ȝe** 176, 1503, one person 84, 96; **ȝow, ȝou** 1600, 1623, one person 120, 86; **ȝour-silf** 818, 1915; *poss.* **thyn** 169, 2049, **thy** 132, 696, *plur.* **ȝoure** 85, 90, *absol.* **ȝoures** 3331.
Thre, *numer.* three 350, 1716.
Thred, *s.* thread 735 (**lyves t.**).
Thredbar, *adj.* threadbare 90.
Thries, *adv.* thrice 832.

Thrifty, *adj.* provident, prudent 4019.
Throp, *s.* hamlet, village 1047, 3589 (**thorpes**).
Throte, *s.* throat 3170.
Throwe, *v. tr.* throw; *pp.* **throwe** 1012, **ythrowe** 2032.
Thryve, *v. intr.* prosper 4673.
Thus, *adv.* thus, in this manner 240, 303 (**þus**); as follows, in these words 480, 658, 688.
Thynke, *v. impers.* seem 3601 (**thynke** *pres.* 3. *sing.* for **thynketh**); *pret. sing.* **thoght(e)** 1470, 924 (**as hym t. dewe**), 1855, 1893, 3716, 3957.
Tide, *s.* time 3409.
Tiers, *s.* the sixtieth part of a second (q.v.) 375 (astron. term).
Tigre, *s.* tiger 1013, 867 (**tygre**).
Til, *prep.* till 1336 (**t. to morowe**); *conj.* till, until 460, 475, 670, 1710, 4144; **til that** until 1919, 4464; **til tyme** until 522.
Time, *s.* time 12, 79; **twenty tyme** 3385.
Title, *s.* right, just claim 799, 1090 (**be t. of age**), 4389 (**t. by discent**).
To, *prep.* 21, 82, 130, 3947 (**hauyng to hyr guyde**), 855 (**fader to hatrede**); **to** + *infin.* 94, **for to** + *infin.* 91, 279 (**forto**).
To, *adv.* **to and fro** 3421, 3867; also, besides, too 3445; too 249 (**to straunge**), 1209, 4602.
Tofor, *prep.* before, in the sight of 787, 3913; previously to 4624.
Toforn, *adv.* before, in front 76, 1762, 1086 (**go t.** take precedence); *adv. temp.* 403, 1289; **toforn that** *conj.* before 4141.
To-gider, *adv.* together 1351, 2660 (**to-gydre**), 3899 (**to-gyder**).
Token, *s.* sign 1989, 4099.
To-morowe, *adv.* 106, 123, 128.
To-nyght, *adv.* to-night, this evening 98, 143.
Tonne, *s.* tun, barrel 2760.
Torche, *s.* torch 1299, 1370.
Torment, *s.* torment, suffering 3420, 3446.
Tornement, *s.* tournament 566.
Touch, *s.* touch 1669.
Touche, *v. tr.* touch, come into contact with 788; strike, play upon 207; concern 3353.
Touchyng, *prep.* with regard to, touching, concerning 185, 1400, 2514.
Tough, *adj.* tough 429.
Toun, *s.* town 70, 873 (**towne**).
Toure, *s.* tower 1172; *plur.* **toures** 1877, **towrys** 4558, **tourres** 4145.
Tourn, *s.* turn 1134 (*of the whel*), 1924 (**tourne**).
Tourne, Turne, *v. intr.* turn 3231, 3685; followed by *to, vnto*: turn, result, lead 1686, 2955, 3988; *tr.* 902, 1962, 4482 (**tournyd vp**).
Touard, *adj.* favourable, auspicious 385.
Toward, *prep.* toward 433, 1962, (time) 117, 150; with regard to 3619; **towardes,** *prep.* 606, 982, 3319; **to meward** toward me 1982.
Tragedye, *s.* 994.
Transgressioun, *s.* offence 3258.
Trappe, *v. tr.* entrap, ensnare 1830.
Traunce, *s.* trance, state of stupor 3388.
Travaylle, *s.* labour, pains 3293.
Trayn, *s.* trickery, guile, deceit 3271 (**traynys**), 3575 (**treynys**).
Trayssheu, *v. tr.* betray 1671.
Tre, *s.* tree 425, 3029; genealogical tree 3540 (**trees**).
Trecherie, *s.* treachery 862.
Trede, *v. tr.* tread, trample 4677; *pret. plur.* **trad** 1008; *pp.* **troden** 4333.
Trench, *s.* path or track through a forest 441.
Tresoun, *s.* treachery 863, 1156; dereliction of duty 3096 (**treson**), 3240.
Tresour, *s.* treasure, riches 1742, 1942, 3859.
Trespace, *s.* trespass, fault 2338, 3670.
Tresse, *s.* braid of hair 3228; ray of the sun 4258.
Trete, *v. intr.* treat, negotiate 766, 3689; argue, debate 1845, 3664; *tr.* treat 1026.
Tretè, *s.* treaty 3938; negotiation 3731.
Trewe, Trwe, *adj.* true 508, 3960; rightful 2094; honest, loyal, trustworthy 1717, 1781; reliable, trusty 1450; genuine, real 56.
Trewly, *adv.* truthfully 4660; correctly 371.
Trist, Trest, *adj.* sad, sorrowful 1216, 1956, 4498, 4627 (**trest**).
Trist, *adj.* self-confident, rash 2345 (**tryst in himself**).
Tristy, *adj.* trusty, reliable 4103 (**t. diffence**).
Trompet, Trumpet, *s.* trumpet 3553, 4066.
Trouble, *s.* trouble, grief, distress 3439, 4707.
Trouble, *v. tr.* trouble, disturb, perplex 1223.
Troubly *adj.* tempestuous, stormy 1241.

Trouth(e), *s.* truth 43, 519, 1735 (**trouthes myght**); truthfulness 801; troth, solemn promise 3323, 1946; faith, loyalty 4435.
Trowe, *v. intr.* believe 2657.
Trunchoun, *s.* fragment of a spear 4286.
Trust, Trist, *s.* trust, reliance 894, 1217, 4082.
Truste, Triste, Treste, *v. intr.* trust, be sure, firmly believe 693; rely on 1979 (*to*), 3624 (*vpon*); be confident 3660 (**tresteth** *pres.* 3. *sing.*); *tr.* trust, rely on 4108, 2053.
Trye, *v. tr.* try, determine 1344 (**trie**), 3638, 3786.
Tusshy, *adj.* tusked 3597.
Twelue, *numer.* 1802, 3540.
Twenty, *numer.* 162.
Tweyn(e), *numer.* two 655, 668, 878.
Two, *numer.* 199, 881, 1603.
Twynne, *v. intr.* pass away, cease 280.
Tyde, *v. intr.* betide, happen 4157.
Tyding, *s.* piece of news 2022; **tydinges** tidings 1309 (see *Notes*).
Tyrannye, *s.* tyranny 4494, 281 (**tyranye**).
Tyraunt, *s.* tyrant 4385.

Vggely, *adj.* ugly, horrible 859.
Vnarm, *v. tr.* disarm 2391.
Vnavysed, *adj.-adv.* inconsiderately, rashly 4651.
Vnbinde, *v. tr.* untie, set free 446 (*pret. plur.* **vnbounde**), 940.
Vnbrace, *v. tr.* untie the armour of 4284.
Vnclene, *adj.* unclean, impure 538, 816.
Vnder, *prep.* 198, 1276, 3762, 4677.
Vndermyne, *v. tr.* undermine 1765.
Vnderstonde, *v. tr.* understand, know 1909, 3778, 3274 (*pret. sing.* **vnderstood**).
Vndertake, *v. tr.* undertake, take in hand 1848, 2952, 4119.
Vndiscreccioun, *s.* indiscretion, imprudence 3449.
Vndiscret, *adj.* imprudent 3114.
Vngracious, *adj.* graceless, wanting God's grace 822, 4058; unfortunate 4348.
Vnhap(pe), *s.* ill luck, misfortune 791, 2495, 3460.
Vnhappy, *adj.* unfortunate, unhappy 821, 1036, 4029.
Vnknowe, *adj.* unknown 491, 3961, 4081 (**vnknowen**).
Vnkouth, *adj.* unusual, strange, curious 51, 2662, 4114, 4454.
Vnkynde, *adj.* unnatural 868 (*blood*), 1157; ungrateful 3292.
Vnnethys, *adv.* scarcely, with difficulty 4350, 4670.
Vnperturbed, *adj.* undisturbed 1714.
Vnpes, *s.* warfare 4260.
Vnrepreuyd, *adj.* irreproachable, blameless 4152.
Vnreste, *s.* strife, contention 4260.
Vnright, *s.* wrong 3675.
Vnsicrenesse, *s.* unreliableness 1748.
Vnsittyng, *adj.* 3649.
Vnsoote, *adj.* bitter, painful 574, 2191, 3673.
Vnsounded, *adj.* not probed 2438 (*of wounds*).
Vnstabiletè, *s.* inconstancy, fickleness 1750.
Vnstable, *adj.* inconstant, unreliable 3619.
Vnsupported, *adj.* 2985.
Vnswete, *adj.* bitter, dreadful 2916; noisome 745.
Vnthryve, *v. intr.* be unprosperous, fail of success 781.
Vnto, *prep.* 147, 149, 192, 365, 486.
Vntrewe, *adj.* false, treacherous 2044; falsely broken 871 (*othes*).
Vntrouth, *s.* deceit, faithlessness 2056.
Vntwyne, *v. tr.* untwist 734 (*his lyves thred*).
Vnwarly, *adv.* unawares 1300, 2144, 4214.
Vnweldy, *adj.* impotent, too weak to support (a man's body) 719; decrepit 997.
Vnwist, *pp. adj.* unknown 494, 783, 3961; unknowing, unwitting(ly) 811.
Vnytè, *s.* unity, concord 4703.
Vp, *adv.* up 126, 427, 681 (**vp and doun**); *prep.* upon 927, 2141.
Vpholde, *pp.* upheld, uplifted 2252.
Vpon, *prep.* on, upon 90, 294, 323, 425 (*a tre*), 3131, 1259 (**vppon**); against 2054.
Vpright, *adj.* upright, erect 668.
Vprightys, *adv.* lying on one's back 3911, 4481.
Vprist, *s.* rising 2303 (*of the sonne*).
Vprysing, *s.* rising 1461.
Vpsterte, *v. intr.* start up, spring to one's feet 3393.
Vpward, *adv.* upwards 3013.
Vrne, *s.* urn 4575.
Vse, *v. tr.* use 141, 543.
Vtter, *adj.* utter, complete 850; full, entire 3475.
Vttrely, *adv.* completely, altogether 2834, 3996; fully, very well 493; decidedly, positively 1343, 1847, 2989.

Vale, *s.* valley 1045, 17, 2909.
Valewe, *s.* value, 4076.
Vapoure, *v. tr.* evaporate 1053.
Variable, *adj.* changeable, inconstant 1723, 3629.
Variant, *adj.* different 3646 (*fro*).
Varia(u)nce, *s.* variation 54; variableness 894; inconstancy 1748; disagreement 1589; dissension 3621.
Varye, *v. intr.* disagree, depart, swerve 1139, 1699 (*from*), 3805.
Vayle, *v. intr.* avail 592, 4053.
Veluet, *s.* velvet 1441, 2766.
Vengeaunce, *s.* vengeance 805; punishment 792, 4065.
Venqwisshe, *v. tr.* vanquish, conquer 4666.
Venym, *s.* venom 3220, 4690.
Verrely, *adv.* verily, in truth 515, 584, 2059.
Verrey, Verray, *adj.* true, real 634, 510, 1313, 4290, 4526; *adv.* really, quite 2281.
Verryfie, *v. tr.* verify, confirm 3537.
Vertue, *s.* power, magic influence 205; **by v. of** by the authority of, in consequence of 2884.
Vertuous, *adj.* 835, 3069, 916 (**vertuvs**).
Vessel, *s.* 597.
Veyn, *adj.* idle, useless 320, 1800, 2376; **in v.** to no purpose 1905, 3722.
Veyne, *s.* vein 3378.
Viage, *s.* journey, expedition 2357, 2826; way 432, 555.
Victorye, *s.* victory 4597, 2239.
Vilage, *s.* village 3589.
Vileynye, *s.* rudeness, discourtesy 1330.
Violence, *s.* violence 3221; force 288, 796.
Virgyne, *s.* virgin 4708; Virgo, one of the signs of the zodiac 4.
Visage, *s.* face 4440.
Vision, *s.* vision, prophetic appearance in sleep 1224.
Visite, *v. tr.* visit 71.
Vitayle, *s.* victuals, provisions 3336, 3591 (**vitaille**).
Voide, *adj.* empty 76, 3585.
Voiden, Voyden, *v. tr.* evacuate, quit 1128, 1808; relinquish, leave 713; take off 1438, 2284; remove, banish 4693; remove, clear away 55, 1188 (*pp.* **voyde**); avoid, remove 1908 (*pp.* **voyde**), 2100; omit 3287 (*pp.* **voide**); *intr.* leave, go away 1923 (**voyden oute**).
Vois, *s.* voice 554.
Voluntè, *s.* will ; **of v.** of free will, gratuitously 3657.
Vow, *s.* vow, solemn promise 72, 2776 (**vouh**).
Vowen, *v. tr.* declare solemnly 2045.
Vyle, *adj.* vile, horrid, disgusting 690 (MSS. Ar. G. L_2. Ap.).
Vyne, *s.* vine 3531.
Vyser, *s.* visor 4326.

Waast, *adj.* waste, desert 611 (*contrè*).
Waast, *s.* waste, destruction 1034 (*of his good*).
Wacche, *s.* watch 3579.
Wages, *s. plur.* wages, reward 4040.
Wake, *v. intr.* lie awake 1506 (*pret. sing.* **woke**); watch 3573.
Wake-playes, *s. plur.* games at a lichwake, funeral games 4584.
Wal, *s.* wall 1243; *plur.* **walles, wallys** 208, 194.
Walke, *v. intr.* walk 713.
Walle, *v. tr.* furnish with walls 562.
Want, *s.* 3054.
Wante, *v. intr.* want, lack 3195 (*of*).
War, *adj.* aware 642, 899, 2212, 3610; careful, cautious 143, 653, 804, 1774, 4650.
Warde, *s.* guard, watch, watching 3580; body of men on watch 3550, 4020, 4027.
Warly, *adv.* warily, carefully 2739, 3167.
Warne, *v. tr.* warn 2918, 3553.
Wasshe, *v. tr.* wash 2392.
Waste, *v. tr.* consume, spend 715, 4356.
Water, *s.* water 3002, 3113; tears 3399.
Wawe, *s.* wave, *i.e.* the sea 4258.
Way, Weie, Weye, *s.* way 610, 62, 976; means 1333; expedient 403.
Wayle, *v. intr.* wail, lament 3224.
Wayte, *v. intr.* wait on, watch 2406 (*on*); look out for, expect 3801 (*after*).
Wed, *s.* pledge 2232 (see *Notes*), 4206.
Wedde, *v. tr.* wed 835, 842 (**I-wedded**).
Weddyng, *s.* wedding 780, 786.
Wede, *s.* weed, noxious plant 4459.
Wede, *s.* garment, dress 864, 1668; weeds 1869, 4441.
Wedere, *s.* weather 1055.
Weie, *v. tr.* weigh 951 (*pp.* **yweied**).
Wel, Wiel, *adv.* well 67, 109, 751, 2146; much 31; fitly, appropriately 91.
Welcom, *adj.* 84.
Welcomynge, *s.* 2430.
Welful, Wilful, *adj.* prosperous, propitious 386, 1850.
Welfulnesse, *s.* happiness 3213.
Welle, *s.* well, spring 3007, 3098; origin, source 4290.

Wel-seyinge, *s.* eloquence 47.
Wende, *v. intr.* go 4715, 1274 (*pret. sing.* **wente**), 2522 (*pp.* **went**); return 3784, 4141.
Wene, *v. tr.* suppose, imagine 2785, 3869, 3877, 643 (*pret. sing.* **wende**); expect 4079; hope 4090.
Wene, *s.* doubt 1412, 1725 (**withouten eny w.**).
Went, *s.* passage, way 3739.
Wepe, *v. intr.* weep 703, 902, 458 (*pret. conj.* **wepe**), 3224; *tr.* cry (one's eyes) out (*out*) 1002 (*pret. sing.* **wepe**); shed tears for, bewail 2828 (*pret. sing.* **wepte**).
Wepyng, *s.* weeping 590, 4421; tears 3264.
Wepnys, *s. plur.* weapons 4331.
Werble, *s.* tune, melody 205.
Were, *s.* doubt, fear 4304.
Were, *v. tr.* wear 1145 (*a croune*).
Werk, *s.* work 2667 (*plur.* **werk**), 4057 (*plur.* **werkes**).
Werken, Wirke, *v. intr.* work 1843, 2795, 2961.
Werkman, *s.* workman 2773.
Werkyng, *s.* doings, actions 1267, 1759; action, operation 1573 (**workyng**).
Werre, *s.* war 677, 1035, 4645.
Werreye, *v. tr.* make war on 2729, 2992; wound, hit 3963.
Werreyour, Werreour, *s.* warrior 2621, 2629, 3896.
Wers, *adj.* worse 1013 (**werre** in MSS. Ar. G. E_1.); **wors** 151, 625, 3645, 3729 (see **bet**).
Wery, *adj.* weary 823, 1170, 1257.
Werynesse, *s.* weariness 2293.
Westre, *v. intr.* pass to the west 4349 (**Titan westryd was**).
Westward, *adv.* to the west 4257.
Wexe, *v. intr.* grow, become 496, 985, 1178; *pret. sing., plur.* **wex** 2203, 4240.
Whan, *conj.* when 1, 9, 107; **whan that** 13, 420, 1305; **whan so euer** whenever 1619.
What, *pron.* 814, 1626; why 4565; whatever 1023; *interj.* 126.
Wheel, Whel, *s.* wheel 537; figur. of fortune 890, 1755, 1134; of human life 728.
Whelp, *s.* whelp, puppy 3853.
When, *adv.*; **fro when** whence, from where 967 (**fro whens** in MSS. M. Lb. a. o.).
Whennys, *adv.* whence, from where 1310.
Wher, *relat. adv.* where 78, 556, 1239; and there 576; wherever 4208; **where as** where 1245, 1884, 4135; **wher that** where 613, 979, 1791; **wher so that** wherever 1319, 4201; **wher so euere** to whatever place 233; *interrog.* 1879.
Wherby, *relat. adv.* 208, 228, 747.
Wherfor, *relat. adv.* 272, 1945, 4650.
Wherof, *relat. adv.* 1550, 1978, 4498.
Wherthorgh, *relat. adv.* through which 3499, 4097, 4227.
Wherto, *interrog. adv.* why, wherefore 481, 1581, 2433.
Wher-vp-on, *relat. adv.* 302.
Wherwith, *relat. adv.* 496.
Whete, *s.* wheat 3599.
Whether that whether 465; **wher that** 1840, 3667, 3697; **wher** whether 385, 1502, 1516; **wherso** whether 803; **wher so be** whether 488; **wher so be that** 2050; **wher soeuer that** whether 1641, 3813.
Whette, *v. tr.* whet, sharpen; *pp.* **whetted** 274, **whette** 2190, 3900, **whet** 2537, 4331.
Which, *pron.* who, which 41, 77, 44, 191, 211, 221, 1644, 1742; **which that** 322, 675; **the which(e)** 660, 1689, 1173, 4668.
Whider, *adv.* whither, where 3231.
Whil, While, *s.* time 66, 323; long space of time 723; short space of time 4612; **allas the while** *exclam.* 1184.
Whil, While, *conj.* while 1845, 2027, 2737; **whilis** 3361, 3131; **whil that** 3656, 4026; **whilys that** 2124, 2131.
Whilom, *adv.* once upon a time, formerly 204, 304, 1413, 2975.
Whisper, *v. intr.* whisper 695.
Whit, *adj.* white 376, 3526; *s.* white colour 16; the white of the eyes 4482.
Who, *pron.* who 570, 1927; whoever 43, 1737; *genit.* **whos** 536, **whoos** 1070, 1576; **of whom** 820; **to whom** 46; **who so** whoever 265, 1771; **who so euer** 1797; **who that** whoever 251, 1767; **who so that** whosoever 127.
Why, *adv.* 911, 975; **why that** 965, 4674.
Wichecraft, *s.* witchcraft 4101.
Wif, Wiff, *s.* wife 465, 857, 796, 340; *dat.* **wive, wyve** 1645, 782.
Wight, *s.* person, creature, man 149, 474, 583, 1322.
Wil, *v.*; *pres.* **wil** 328, 323, 86, 2414 (**he wil hom**); **wol** 122, 110, *plur.* 124; *pret.* **wolde** 356, 401, 993, **wold** 501; **nolde** 1858.
Wylde, *adj.* wild 1228, 611.

Wildely, *adv.* freely, unrestrainedly 3866.
Wyldernesse, *s.* wilderness 4639.
Wile, *s.* guile, trickery 1672.
Wilful, *adj.* headstrong, self-willed 4007.
Wilfully, *adv.* purposely, intentionally 3456; gratuitously, unnecessarily 1381.
Wilfulnesse, *s.* inconsiderateness, rashness 3975.
Will(e), *s.* will 418, 3755.
Wymple, *s.* wimple, a kind of head-covering 4502.
Wympled, *adj.* wearing a wimple 4441.
Wis, *adj.* judicious, prudent 263, 818, 4077, 2796 (**wyce**).
Wisdam, *s.* wisdom, prudence 1109, 1205, 3815 (**wisdom**).
Wise, *s.* wise, way, manner 343, 976, 3479, 3448 (**in no wise**).
Wisely, *adv.* 1537, 1844, 3699.
Wisse, *v. tr.* guide, direct 2164.
Wisshe, *v. tr.* wish 4490.
Wit, *s.* wit, understanding 145, 183, 693; wisdom 1197, 1607; mind 681; **lost his wit** went out of his mind 999.
Wite, *v. tr.* know 910; *pres.* **woot** 945, 1480, 1674 (**wote**); **not** know not 68; *pret.* **wiste** 1428, 3623, 4107.
Wite, *v. tr.* blame, reproach 1042, 3390.
With, Wiþ, *prep.* 15, 16, 475; by 4442; *adv.* therewith, withal 35.
Withdrawe, *v. tr.* withdraw, remove 2834; revoke, cancel, avoid 397, 2825 (*pp.* **withdrawe**); snatch out of, save from 3180 (*fro*); *intr.* get out of doing something 133; *refl.* withdraw, go away 586.
Withholde, *v. tr.* retain, engage the service of 2752 (*pp.* **withhold**); relinquish, give up 2912.
With-in, *adv.* within 538, 1011, 553 (**with-innen**); *prep. loci* 764, 1825; *prep. temp.* 1231.
With-out, *adv.* without, outside 4304; *prep.* **with-out, -oute, -outen** 3664, 54, 88, 1292, 3844; **with-oute that** *conj.* unless 3348.
Withseyn, *v. tr.* gainsay, contradict 474, 718; refuse 1393; object to, urge as an objection to 740.
Witnesse, *s.* witness, testimony 2099, 3654, 2086 (**wittnesse**).
Wode, *s.* wood, forest 1618.
Woman, *s.*; *plur.* **wymmen** 1732, 2389, **wymen** 4455; **wommen** 2843, 3202.
Wommanhede, *s.* womanly feeling 2842, 4435; womanly kindheartedness 2388, 3063, 3184.
Wommanly, *adj.* 341, 1464, 1647; *adv.* 2419, 2837.
Wonder, *s.* wonder 195, 1373, 3374; *adj.* wonderful, strange 1363, 3822; *adv.* wondrously, greatly, very 81, 90, 164, 439, 3552.
Wonderful, *adj.* 184, 669.
Wonderly, *adv.* extremely 1960.
Wonte, *adj.* wont 892 (**as she is w. to do**).
Woo, *s.* grief 849, 3215; *adj.* sad, grieved 3374 (**wo**).
Wo(o)ful, *adj.* sorrowful, doleful 409, 810, 2897, 3230.
Wo(o)fully, *adv.* 3226, 4551.
Wood, *adj.* furious, fierce 276, 390, 1961, 4274; vehement, frantic 3438; mad, demented 2039; mad (after) 3112 (*vppon*).
Worchen, *v. intr.* act 1782, 1073, 809 (*pret.* **wroght**); do execution on 3890; *tr.* make; *pp.* **wroght** 1440 (**w. of cloth**); commit 2057; cause 2380; plan 2173.
Word, *s.* word 37, 499, 1451; promise 1749, 2047; **at a w.** in one word 3338.
World, *s.* 220, 700, 4135.
Worldly, *adj.* worldly, earthly 999, 2846, 3035.
Worship, *s.* honour, dignity 4124, 4152.
Worthe, *v. intr.* get up, mount 2259 (**worthed vp** *pret.*).
Worthy, *adj.* worthy, deserving 814, 1204; distinguished, illustrious, noble, famous 186, 188, 1428, 2597, 2755.
Worthynesse, *s.* worthiness, nobleness 1509, 2622; high character, moral excellence 2085; goodness 4590; **ȝour w.** used by Tydeus as a term of address to king Ethiocles, your Majesty 1901.
Wounde, *s.* wound 450, 900, 3369.
Wounde, *v. tr.* wound 973, 4402, 2221 (*pp.* **ywounded**).
Wrak, *s.* ruin, destruction 2215 (**wenten vnto w.** were killed), 4308.
Wrappe, *v. tr.* wrap 109, 1443, 3090.
Wrastlyng, *s.* wrestling 4585.
Wrath, *s.* 2897.
Wrech, *s.* wretch 3230, 3463.
Wrecched, *adj.* miserable 1018.
Wrechednesse, *s.* misery 865, 2958.
Wreth, *s.* wreath 3527.
Writ, *s.* Scripture 794 (**holy w.**).
Write, *v.* write 823; *pres.* 3. *sing.* **writ** 199, 582, 877; 3. *plur* **write** 880; *pp.* **writ** 1716, **ywrite** 38.

Writyng, *s.* writing 57, 1200; poems 242.
Wrong, *s.* wrong, injustice 1067, 1585, 2074, 3534.
Wroth, *adj.* angry 390, 488, 2558, 3697; *s.* wrath, anger 2506 (: *oth*).
Wryng, *v. tr.* wring 3226 (*her handys*).
Wyd, *adj.* wide 3911.
Wyde, *adv.* wide, widely 300.
Wyn, *s.* wine 1732, 3528; *plur.* **wynys** 3532, 4460.
Wynde, *s.* strong wind 1175, 1286; wind on the stomach, flatulence 113; inflated language, bombast 80.
Wynne, *v. tr.* win, gain 279, 2028; *pp.* **wonne** 2007, **ywonne** 747; *intr.* win 1641, 4652.
Wyrching, *s.* working; **in w.** in thy doings 485.

Ydolatrie, *s.* idolatry 4047.
Ydylnesse, *s.* idleness, useless waste of time 2441.
Yfere, *adv.* together 3361, 4473, 1104 (**al y.**), 3741, 4647 (**both y.**).
Ymagyn, *v. tr.* imagine 2171.
Ynde, *adj.* indigo-blue 4466.
Ynowe, *adv.* enough 2448, 3336 (**ynoh**).
Yren, *s.* iron 3016.
Yrously, *adv.* angrily, wrathfully 1355, 4289.
Yssen, *v. intr.* issue out (*oute*) 4018, 4195 (**issen**), 3566 (**yssyd oute** *pp.*).
ȝeer, *s.* year 2003; **ȝeer be ȝeer** 1117; *genit.* **a ȝeeres space** 1921; *plur.* **ȝere, ȝeer** 93, 4623, **ȝeeris** 467.
ȝelde, *v. tr.* yield 2344; *pret. plur.* **ȝolden** 4339; *pp.* **ȝolden** 3367.
ȝerne, *adv.* quickly, soon 1124.
ȝif, *conj.* if 39, 112, 992, 635 (**ȝif that**); whether 510, 649.
ȝit, *adv.* yet, even 192; however 293, 1335, 1222.
ȝonde(r), *adv.* yonder 4313, 4334.
ȝong, *adj.* young 212, 410, 567.
ȝore, *adv.* formerly, long ago 210 (**ful ȝoor agon**), 3987; **of ȝore** 2641.
ȝouth(e), *s.* youth 705, 715; youthfulness 1511.

Zephyrus, *s.* 1054.

PROPER NAMES

Adrástus 1192, 1212, etc. **Ádrastus** 1239, 1358, etc. King of Argos.
Albumasar 2973. See *Notes.*
Allecto 861. Alecto, one of the Furies.
Amphiorax 2800, 2994, 3806, 4023. Amphiaraos, a Greek.
Amphioun 189, 227, 310. **Amphyoun** 201, 286, 325, 332. Amphion, founder of Thebes.
Antygone 882, 3736. **Antigone** 3747, 3949. **Antigonee** 4369. Antigone, daughter of Oedipus.
Apollo 345. **Appollo** 535, 546, 977. Apollo.
Archadye 448, 3950. **Archada** 2600. Arcadia.
Arcyte 3525. A Theban knight.
Arge 1190, 1199, etc. Argos.
Argyve 1210, 1646, 4409. The eldest of Adrastus' daughters.
Athenes 3524, 4552. **Athenys** 4507. Athens.
Aurora 9. The dawn.
Autropos 734. Atropos, one of the Moiræ. See *Notes.*

Bachus 3528, 3534. Bacchus.
Bellona 4649. Bellona, the goddess of war.
Bery 93. Bury St. Edmunds.
Boece 304. Bœotia (but according to Lydgate the ancient name of Thebes).
Bochas 199, 213, 1541 (: *was*). **Bochas decertaldo called** 3541. **Iohn Bochas** 3201, 3510. Boccaccio.
Bowtoun on þe ble 1047. Boughton under Blean. See *Notes.*
Breteyne 40. Britain.

Cadmvs 295. **Cadmus** 306, 314. Cadmus.
Calydonye 1269. **Caledoyn** 1406. **Calcedoyne** 2625. Calydon (Greece).
Calyope 831. Calliope, one of the Muses.
Campaneus 2607, 3020, 4347, 4471, 4546. Capaneus, a Greek king.
Canterbury 18 (*talys*), 62, 67, 131, 156.
Cecile 3204. Sicily.
Cerberus 854 (*Chief porter of helle*).
Chaloun 1196. A king, father of Adrastus.
Chaucer 39 (rubric), 4501.
Chysoun 1195. An island.
Clement 83.
Cloto 735. Clotho.
Clyo 831. Clio, one of the Muses.
Colchos 3191. Colchos.
Creon 4385, 4489 (rubric), 4493, 4538. **Creaunt** 4385 (rubric). King of Thebes.
Crete 2612.
Crist 4679. Christ.
Cupide 1480. **Cupides** (*bowe*) 3962. Cupid.
Cylmythenes 2602. A Greek king.

Depforth in the vale 4523. Deptford.
Deyfyle 1211. **Deyphylee** 1648, 4409 etc. **Deyphyle** 1866. Deipyle, the second of Adrastus' daughters, wife of Tydeus.
Diogenes 2972.
Domynyk (**daun D.**) 83. Dominic.
Dyane 352. Diana, the goddess.

Edíppus 452, 496, 513, 532 etc. **Edýppus** 545, 551, 576, etc. **Édippus** 744, 1914. **Édyppus** 468, 586, 808. Oedipus.
Egipte 3830. Egypt.
Emelye 4511. Sister-in-law of Theseus.
Esdre 1729, 1736. Ezra.
Ethýocles 879, 4259, etc. **Ethíocles** 1040, 1084, etc. **Ethiócles** 1956. **Ethiócle** 1803, 1839. Eteocles, son of Oedipus.

Femynye 4508. The country of the Amazons.
Flora 13. The goddess of flowers.

Genor 2611. King of Crete.
Godfrey (**dan G.**) 83.
Grece 1200, 1950. Greece.

Thoante 3196. Father of Isyphile.
Tholomee 2973. Ptolemy, the geographer.
Tidyus 1266. **Tydeus** 1312 etc. **Tideus** 2620, etc. Tydeus.
Tortolanus 2614. A Greek king.
Trace 3521. Thrace.
Tremour 3895. A king who fought on the side of the Thebans.
Tullius 2974. Cicero.
Tytan 4014. **Titan** 4349. Titan, the sun god.

Venus 393. The planet.
Vermes 3197. According to some the father of Isyphile.

Ymeneus 826. Hymenæus, the god of marriage.
Ymeyne 883, 3736, 3748, 3952. Ismene, daughter of Oedipus.
Ynde 3840. India.
Ypolita 4510. Hippolyta, wife of Theseus.
Ypomedoun 2604. Hippomedon, a Greek king.
Ytaille 3542. Italy.

APPENDIX

Ch. = Christchurch Library, MS. 152, Oxford.

This MS. was overlooked by Professor Erdmann. It is mentioned by Miss Hammond in her *Chaucer Manual*, p. 456, where the text of *Thebes* is stated to be a fragment. This is a mistake. The *Thebes* text is complete, except for the accidental omission of six lines.

(a) *Description of the MS.*

Paper, 342 leaves, $11\frac{1}{8} \times 8\frac{1}{4}$ inches. The volume contains Chaucer's *Canterbury Tales* and a fragment of *The Tale of the Churle and his bryd.* The title on the back is "Chaucer." The date of the MS. is stated in the catalogue of Christchurch Library to be the fifteenth century. The volume is bound in calf.

The *Thebes* part, which is in the list of contents described as "The monk of Buryys tale of the Sege of Tebes," fills the last 60 leaves. The last leaf is turned inside out. The text of *Thebes* is written in single columns of 40 to 44 lines, but in the last few leaves the writing grows smaller and the number of lines to a page increases. No ruling. A mark of cæsura is found only in a very few places. Occasionally *y* for *th* in pronominal words. Red initials at the beginning of the Prologue and the three Parts (W six lines, S 4 lines, P 2 lines, O 3 lines). Rubrics in red, usually in the text column. No colophon.

The paper is in a few places somewhat damaged, so that some words or parts of words have become illegible.

(b) *The Place of MS. Ch. in the Genealogy.*

Ch. belongs to the class P. E_2. C. T_2. L_2. Ro. Ap. It shows all the characteristic readings of this class enumerated in Chap. VI, § 19. Likewise it shares in all the readings common to this class and Bo.-M., as well as those common to P.-Ro. and Bo-M. given in § 20. It shows all the characteristic readings common to (Lb.) P. E_2. C. T_2.

L_2. Ro. enumerated in § 17, except for 3890, where Ch. has " Tideus " as against "Thebans" in the said MSS., clearly an individual mistake, and 3904, where Ch. has " lion " as against " a lyon."

Ch. goes with the branch (Lb.) P. E_2. C. T_2. It shows all the characteristic readings of this branch mentioned in § 15, except 345, where Ch. has " so bright," as against " full bright " in the said branch, evidently a negligible deviation. In the cases where P.-T_2. agree with Bo.–M. (§ 20), Ch. shows the same reading, except in 43 and 294 (see *infra*). In 191 the MS. is damaged, so that of " fame " or " name " only " me " can be read.

Ch. is more nearly related to P. E_2. than to C. T_2. It is true Ch. seems sometimes to go with C. T_2. against P. E_2., but the agreements are of small value as evidence. In 833 Ch. has " Philoloye "; cf. " Philoloy " C. T_2., " Philolaic " E_2., " philolis " P. In 1269 Ch. has " Calcidoyne " (=C. T_2.; cf. " Callidoyne " E_2., " Calcydoun " P.). In 1273 Ch. C. T_2. have " on hym " instead of " to hym," while P. has " at hym " and E_2. " to hym." Cf. also 42 and 308 *infra, d.*

Far more striking are the coincidences with (Lb.) P. E_2. See *e.g.* 967, 2090, 3380, 3660, 3674, 4051 *infra, d.* Particularly important are, *e.g.* 2612. Crete] Grece. 3072. her] his. 3312. ful] *om.* 3670. Innocent] verrey Innocent. 3684. this tweyne] yow tweyne. 3879. in purpos] purposed. 3920. day] tyme. In all these Ch. goes with (Lb.) P. E_2. against C. T_2.

But Ch. deviates from (Lb.) P. E_2. in many cases, showing the correct reading against this group, *e.g.* 1028. And] And hem P. E_2. 1099. Ful] Fully Ch. *om.* P. E_2. 1286. wynde] *om.* P. E_2. 1306. vpon] and on P. E_2. 2717. loue] but loue P. E_2. 4145. Crestyd] crested Ch. crestes Lb. P. and crestes E_2. and batailled] Enbatayled P. E_2.

Where (Lb.) P. and E_2. disagree, Ch. goes with E_2. more often than with (Lb.) P. An exception is 4427, where Ch. Lb. P. have " all(e) Grece " against " Grece " E_2. Ch. agrees with E_2. in the following cases: 2517. frat] was. 2648. Redy] Lowly E_2. Lowely Ch. 3628. were] that were. 3686. euer] euer ther-at E_2. euer ther atte Ch. euer therof Lb. P. 4390. in] a. 4694. swerd] swerdes.

The agreements between Ch. and E_2. are hardly strong enough to point to a sub-group Ch.–E_2. as against (Lb.) P. Some of them are rather striking, it is true (*e.g.* " was " for " frat " 2517), but it is quite possible that the faults common to Ch. and E_2. were in the immediate source of Ch. P. E_2., though they were corrected by the scribe of P. (or in the common source of Lb. and P.). Some at least of these faults are comparatively easy to correct. Thus in 2648 Low(e)ly Ch. E_2. comes directly after " in ful lowly wyse " in the preceding line, a fact that would attract the notice of an observant copyist. The plural " swerdes " in 4694 instead of " swerd " would be easily corrected in conformity with the singular " spere " in the next line. For the matter of that the *-es* of Ch. and E_2. might be due to misreading a meaningless tag for an abbreviation for the plural *-es*.

At any rate it is evident, in view of the many special faults of E_2. and Ch., that neither MS. is derived from the other. The probability seems to be that the position of Ch. in the group is correctly indicated by the following diagram.

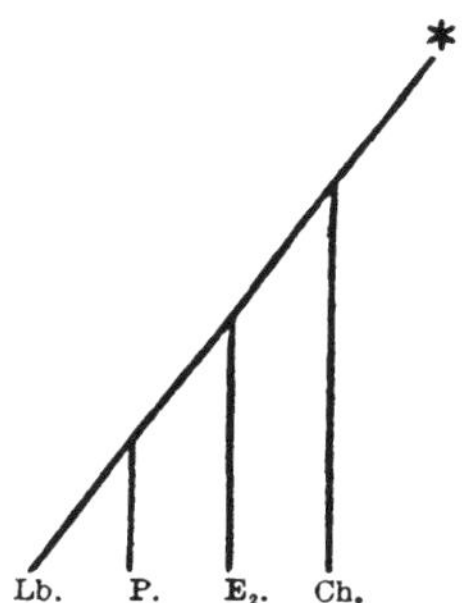

(c) *Special Faults of Ch.*

Ch. has many special faults due to careless copying. Frequently the order of words is inverted. Only six lines are omitted, viz. 1001–4 (the omission being due to the similar ending of 1000 and 1004, " despit " and " dispise "), 1636, 1670. Only a select list of special faults can be given here.

5. of] in. 34. and] with. 43. Rede] Seke. 48. Chief] The. 93. ȝere] wynter. 112. ȝif] If it. 141. wil] shall. 162. a] in. 210. myd of] a mydde the. 216. the myght] myght. 229. lust] lustes. 252. puples] puple. 263. That eny] The. 272. mor is] is more. 289. lik was nowher] nowher like was ther. 316. of] *and*. 324. space] space in soothnesse. 330. lyne] lyfe. 347. deuout] so deuote. 355. ryytys] rightes (=543). 386. welful] welthfull. 427. They] There. 492. therfor] ther. 571. hegh] *om.* 578. entren] entre in. 582. the maner] *om.* 586. in hast gan hym] gan hym haste to. 602. dide they] they dede. 642. gan ful nygh] full nye gan. 643. platly] plainly. 667. After on] And than vppon. 720. naturys] naturell. 736. fully is] is fully. 771. likly] hool. 781. which] that. 802. Therfor] Wherfore. 803. Prynce,

lorde] lorde prince. 804. That he eschewe *and* beware of suche wowyng. 828. Ne ther was] Neyther was there. 859. hydous-chered] hidous chier. 895. For] And. 924. me in hast] men haste. 936. in non certeyn] vncerteyn. 939. han] hadde. 942. evel] cruell. 952. hevy] as heuy. 961. And whan the kynge sawe in man*er* pleyn. 991. tedious] petous. 993. occupie] yow occupie. 1001–1004 *om.* 1018. ȝou pleynly] pleynly yow. 1030. first be] be first. 1075. envie] of enuye. 1112. That] And. 1114. They] *om.* 1137. Ful] Fully. 1141. enrolled] rolled. 1182. drogh] draweth. 1199. alle] *om.* 1200. Chief] Ther. 1224. Of] And of. 1233. þing] thenke. 1235. Eke] And. 1237. bete] wete. 1286. With] Be. 1287. anoy] anoied. 1290. peryl] parcell. 1304. his] the. 1307. his aray] this ray. 1311. bad] *om.* 1400. I-axed] And askynge. 1422. he knewe þe ground] the grounde he knewe. 1429. ther] her. 1446. than] whan. 1452. bounde] ther bounde. 1474. konyngly] knyghtly. 1480. god] good. 1484. arowes] arowe. 1489. raced] reised. 1498. hem] to hem. 1529. his] of his. 1538. tolde] hym tolde. 1550. wherof] Where fore. 1554. the] his. thys] the. 1557. resort] retorn. 1572. next] next it. 1582. likly be] be lyke. 1602. it shal be] it be shall be. 1616. in] *and.* 1617. lust] lustes. 1620. attendance] entendaunce. 1636 *om.* 1638. On eu*er*y part fully is he condescended. 1665. the gyftes] yeftes. 1666. pryvè sighes] paynfull sightes. 1668. devyses] deuyse. sondry] sodeyn. 1670 *om.* 1671. traysshen] betraien. 1695. by bond] *om.* 1701. desire] desires. 1720. colour] cou*er*t. 1728. whilom] som tyme. 1758. world] worde. 1759. ofte] of. 1774. ȝe kyngges] the kynge. 1779. That with his puple sore after boght. 1799. sey] sayth. gruche] gruccheth. 1804. was crowned] crowned was. 1811. due] trewe. 1812. in soth] forsoth. 1815. ther] *om.* 1822. manfully] manly. 1838. apparceyve] p*er*ceyve. 1840. his croune wil] wille his crowne. 1851. what so that] what that so. 1861. auayled] availleth. 1890. rounde] *om.* 1924. kam] comyth. 1938. eke] *om.* 1948. Ryaltè] roial See. 1989. token as of] token of no. 1990. a signe] assigne. 1998. platly] pleynly. 2075. of] by. 2082. I shortly] shortly I. 2104. no tyme lenger ȝou] not tyme lenger hau*e*. 2127. In] And in. 2194. gret] hie. 2202. Raylle] traile. 2212. er that] or. 2216. amased] amanassed. 2218. And] Thus. 2223. The] *om.* 2240. Therfor ech] For eu*er*y. 2242. nor moche] or grete. 2244. Chanpartye] a champ*er*tie. 2249. which] What. 2264. rode] ridde. 2302. ground] colde ground. 2311. hadde] had she. 2325. a manere] in man*er*. 2330. touched] toucheth. ful] *om.* 2345. he] that he. 2363. hool] hold. 2377. her] it. 2386. yrayled] railede. 2396. staunche] chaunge. 2406. he slep] that he did slepe. 2438. soorys] sorowes. 2444. falsly was] was falsly. 2455. konnyng] comynge. 2458. Tho was ther] Ther was thoo. tho] than. 2502. And the] With thyn. 2505. was fals brekyng] Fals brekyng was. 2506. almost mad] mad almost. 2510. Supprised] Suppressed. 2513. meschief] grete myschief. 2522. That] And. 2550. shal clerly] clerly shall. 2574. lettres and] *om.* 2583. As of] Of her. 2584. pay] paiement. 2606. excellyng] excellent. 2621. noble] worthy. 2640. Ymeued] Yment. 2655. Ychosen] And chosen. 2660. sothly] lightly. 2670. only] *om.* 2680. poore] proude. 2685. hym list] he lyste. 2688. f. *much altered*: But all thyng redy was to here p*re*sence And in a prince it is full grete repref. 2693. good] body. 2702. euery] iche. 2716. gold or] *om.* 2772. strong] stondynge. 2774. newe] stronge *and* newe. 2796. on] *om.* 2804. acceptid] accepte. 2821. this] it is. 2824. parte of the] blode parte of. 2839. trust] truste is. 2849. Thogh it was long] Soughten longe. 2897. contrariouste] curiouste. 2898. in] *and.* 2936. regnyng] reignes. 2998. hosteying] hasteyng. 3000. A] And. 3012. man] men. 3042. after gan to] gan after. 3171. Vnto] but. 3194. hool] helde. 3255. as] *om.* 3273 *and* 3274 *transposed.* 3341. cause] *om.* 3360. excepcioun] recepcioun. 3463. doth] hath. 3468. agayn] aȝein routh. 3523. same] son *and.* 3596. beer] dere. 3637. nat ben] be not. 3647. neyther] nor. 3666. his] oure. 3673. And] *om.* 3683. no man] thow ne. 3693. now] it. 3724. wil] wolde. 3797. To hym] Than. 3800. ȝif it] so. 3801. but only] only but. 3826. my styell I mot] I mote my stile. 3831. the whiche beest] whiche. 3876. ful] as. 3881. out] forth. 3890. the Thebans] Tideus. 3900. speres sharpe] sharp speres. 3924.

hom] hem hoom. 3939. party] part. that] *om.* 3967. sory] loth. 3981. from] for. 4016. han] bene. 4017. out of] with oute. 4031. char and hors] hors and chare. 4053. vaylled] vaileth. 4069. To-fore] For. aboute] hym aboute. 4080. hym not] not hym. 4096. prophete] profite. 4110. mocioun] moue. 4165. shal falle] sholde fine. 4173. And] *om.* 4217. enchace] chace. 4264. at good leyser] in the felde. 4293. al her lyf hadde] hadde alle her lyfe. 4366. infortunyd] fortunat. 4379. may] *om.* 4443. nowther] other. 4453. Both] But. *second* in] *om.* 4494. his] her. 4518. preiden] bysought. 4531. reherseth] rehersyng. 4572. As] Of. 4595. ek] hem. 4607. shortly] *om.* 4697. Nor] For. 4698. in hertys shal] shall in hertes. 4713. her in this lyf] in this lyfe here. 4715. hennes] shull hens.

(d) *Collation.*

The following list does not claim completeness. It chiefly aims at including readings that are of importance for determining the place of MS. Ch. in the genealogy of MSS. For the special faults of Ch. see preceding list. The readings of the printed text are added only when this seemed necessary for the sake of clearness.

1. bri**ȝ**te] *om.* 2. the bole. 3. olde. 8. mony a. 20. the] thaire. 23. gentilesse. 25. also] eke. 29. Aquite. 42. Bothe in. 43. whoo. 46. ȝoue] yeue. 53. in] the. 66. in this. 74. longe sclender. 78. logged were. 85. ne] nor. 97. sool. 98. this nyght. 101. franchemoile. 114. Collys. 117. rede. 118. coliander. 120. to ryse. 125. that shall. 127. who that seyth. 133. nor] ne. 136. noon is. 144. right lyght. 152. oure] the. 154. Full. 165. a] no. 170. effekke. 171. and make. 183. be barreyn. 191. shal neu*er*. 197. shortly] platly. 204. whilom] somtyme. 212. nor] ne. 214. Clerly. 215. Seith that. 220. to] vnto. 224. yeuen. 230. fauorable plesaunt. 233. tassigne. 249. to be nat. 255. And shortely. 263. That eny] The. 266. hym susteneth. 269. beryng. 274. whet. 284. That but. 294. Groundynge. 298. oute be compas. 302. Ther vppon. 306. hath noght longe there. 308. from thennys] thens. 311. rich, *corrected from* right. 316. vnto] to. 318. pith] path. 323. oure] youre. 324. as] *om.* 327. And reigned. 345. tapollo. 346. to Iubiter. 358. conseyued. 360. for to ride. 400. sore muse] to muse. 402. to p*ro*uide. 403. a forn. 407. al] *om.* 416. fer] ther. 420. that] *om.* 425. ful] *om.* 426. a] *om.* it se. 428. they gan thorgh perce. 444. drewe hem. 449. the childe first. 466. I late. 469. his] *om.* 479. to brayde. 489. and thow] if the. 493. remembre the. 514. in a man*er*. 517. An doun ayein ofte on knees. 532. wolde. 535. it is. 539. illusiou*n*. 562. ywalled. 563. syyt] sight. 564. appertenet. 568. folke. 574. that] thought. fond it. 584. it verely aspie. 592. availeth. 617. forth by. 632. opynly] pleynly. 634. platly] pleinly. 647. Seide I. 676. *second* is] *om.* 690. foule. 699. herto-forn] byforn. 723. here no while. 733. y-sette. 740. But] For. ought] not. 741. so] tho. 742. alle dismaide. 743. hevy as any lede. 744. the] his. 746. holy] only. 748. in eu*ery* coste is ronne. 749. that the monstre was slawe. 752. grete] hie. 762. scepter *and* corone to. 796. brothers. 799. title hadde he. 814. ar] er. 832. On] Noon. 833. Philoloye. 837. And as. de] be. 839. this] his. 882. that oon. 894. hertly trist. 898. his] *om.* 918. Lyke. 922. myght. 931. vnto] to. 932. Persyng. honge hym] hengyng. 935. resorted hom. 967. Fro whens. 970. brast. 1001–1004 *om.* 1016. a] the. 1051. þe] of. 1064. to] forto. 1067. ne] nor. 1079. as thow] lyke as. 1082. make hem accord. 1092. gan to. 1095. Both Regalie. 1099. Fully. and] or. 1117. ȝeer] There. 1128. that other. 1145. a] the. 1177. was. 1195. chifoun. 1196. whylom] somtyme. Choloun. 1203. He helde. 1216. passyng. 1221. comfort. 1222. high] ofte. 1241. trouble. 1254. the plees. 1255. the lawes. 1259. sure. for to. 1264. Oon the. in this] of the. 1269. Calcidoyne. 1273. to] on.

1280. banshed. 1289. hadde do] haddo. 1300. entred into. 1309. Tideous. 1310. or] and. 1314. that] *om.* hegh] his. 1318. hym constreyned. 1322. menyng no. 1338. but litell. 1348. take] bestryde. 1352. Either. 1357. And] *om.* 1373. ful] *om.* 1384. no] a. 1393. light] hie. 1404. to] vnto. 1405. Calcedoyne. right heire. 1406. soth] cause. 1414. not] neu*er*. 1438. voide. 1439. Twey. 1458. make hem. 1504. fully knowelecchynge. 1515. in a. 1520. made is. 1522. mor] nomore. 1535. in] on. 1538. Wher as. 1539. honkyng. 1540. crokys. 1565. it] *om.* 1578. likenesse. 1591. Betwene. 1596. this] my. 1599. that] *om.* 1636 *om.* 1641. Whether so eu*er* they. 1648. than] *om.* 1657–1660, 1668, 1672. mony a. 1670 *om.* 1677. feyned. 1686. after tyme turn to. 1707. his] the. 1715. this] his. 1724. countre. 1738. Be] *om.* 1776. thenketh. 1800. he] hym. 1834. the tou*n*. 1836. were. 1850. welfull. 1856. wele appreued. 1871. encres gan. 1872. ridynge. 1882. armed. 1887. a doun. 1888. a lyoun. 1895. kyngly] knyghtly. 1901. Sir] *om.* 1903. only] holy. 1913. that] *om.* 1922. to] into. 1932. occupied. 1934. lik] as. 1952. han quytt] acquite. 1987. *and* in. 1997. nat no] not. 2000. nys. 2003. neither . . . ne. 2005. his bonde. 2007. all] *om.* 2010. wil strife. 2017. suppresses. 2022. tydinges. 2030. pleynly. to vnderstonde. 2042. seide. 2045. vowe it. 2073. of] *and.* 2077. vaile. 2081. his next. 2090. thynke on. 2119. Thorgh. 2123. ridyng. 2132. wolde. 2137. choos. 2138. Suche. *second* most] *om.* 2139. to] forto. 2165. at laste. 2174. ne] *om.* 2187. *and* in. 2192. light on fote. 2193. ful] *om.* 2204. fallen. 2220. was] *om.* 2224. valey. lay] *om.* 2229. this entenciou*n*. 2257. thoo hym selfe. 2270. fast he. 2274. ioynyng. 2276. gan to. 2282. adou*n*. 2296. til] to. 2305. was] *om.* 2322. al] on. 2331. Where. 2334. He vpstert. *second* he] *om.* 2349. be no thyng. 2368. so] *om.* 2371. will. 2374. wody. 2421. Byhotyng. 2422. trewe knyght. 2423. wille. 2435. and] nor. 2436. of] *om.* grete sorowe. 2437. sore wounded. 2480. in his felle. 2485. highe] *om.* 2492. into] to. 2500. sothnesse. 2504. A] And. 2517. frat] was. 2519. He hente. 2523. Thorghoute] Thorgh. of] *and.* 2539. and of. 2540. the tou*n*. 2556. þi] the. 2581. And to. 2586. tho] the. 2590. stuffen] susteyne. 2592. alabastres. 2602. Gilmychenes. 2612. Grece. 2613. loeris. the] *om.* 2614. tortolonus. 2616. Palamou*n*. 2618. armed. 2622. the flour. 2648. Redy] Lowely. 2661. myght. 2699. cohert. 2713. contynue. 2735. Don to] Vnto. *and* to. 2756. the toun. 2780. bene yboght. 2784. Or that. 2796. on] *om.* right] *om.* 2838. conselyng. 2846. Diskeueren. 2893. disemal. 2902. executed. 2916. so] *om.* 2923. ful] *om.* 2932. after] be. 2935. poure saudeoures. 2942. couetynge. ful] *om.* 2944. by] in. 2951. Bruseth. 2987. evyl] heuy. 2988. stand. 3026. herbes *and* of floures. 3028. which] that. 3052. speer] *om.* and with. 3062. stont] stonde. 3072. vpon] of. her] his. 3076. which I haue in. 3107. enhasted. 3160. alle the hole. 3161. why] how. 3168. husbondes. 3186. she lefte allone to. 3194. of Isiphile. 3206. hegh] *om.* 3213. wilfulnesse. 3229. she] *om.* 3231. may] shall. 3238. so] to. 3251. quene] kynge. 3286. whan] That. forto] to. forlorn. 3298. worthy] with hem. 3312. and] *om.* ful good array] a good raye. 3328. assigned shall. 3330. largely may. 3334. ententifly. 3341. No noo parte. 3346. oure . . . we. that] *om.* 3348. wille. 3351. what thyng euer. 3361. trete. 3364. And loude. 3366. forto] to. 3372. That] And. 3374. was. 3380. sobbe sigh *and* wepe. 3383. the] *om.* 3385. ny] *om.* 3386. to the erthe. 3394. this thynge gan. 3399. water] teeres. 3415. Aȝeinst deth may be no recur. 3425. *first* nor] *om.* 3433. loketh. 3442. as it. 3447. ȝif that] *and.* 3460. bifalle. 3473. þis] *om.* 3474. her] his. 3479. Of oon accorde. 3496. And hent. 3499. her sorowe] *om.* tassuage. 3501. this P*ar*tholonope. 3507. that] *om.* 3512. this] the. 3519. me a forn. 3521. called was. 3526. I ladde. 3556. take. 3560. *sec.* in] on. 3567. lusty] hasty. 3582. kynled. 3594. slayn. 3601. thoght. 3602. The Grekes. 3603. occasions. 3612. that] *om.* 3615. the] *om.* 3622. which] That. 3628. Siche. that were. 3633. better. 3660. ful likly] lightly. 3665. ȝif] *om.* 3666. the] his. 3667. wroth. 3670. verrey Innocent. 3674. gynner. 3684. this] yow. 3686. ther atte laugh.

either morne. 3693. Forto. 3716. it wele. 3722. nat] *om.* 3748. excellent. 3749. were passyngly. 3754. to disclose. 3778. platly so. 3784. is ther. 3785. which] that. 3824. also] *om.* 3838. fire. 3858. that did. 3859. not] *om.* 3879. purposed. 3897. make. 3901. *sec.* of] *om.* 3913. this] *om.* 3915. Thebans. vnto] to. 3917. prey gan. 3920. day] tyme. 3940. avised. 3972. pleynly. 3983. thilke] that. 4022. armed. 4036. that he on stode. 4051. What stode in stede. 4071. frowne] sorowe. 4101. fals] *om.* 4117. *second* most] *om.* 4122. vnto] to the. 4176. Menalippus. 4177. Tredimus. that other. 4204. occasioun. 4229. Ther of may. 4230. he was. 4262. out] *om.* 4265. to do. 4273. with] Which. 4278. the felde. 4282. adoun. 4292. roof. 4310. Grekes. 4314. more hidous. 4323. in sonder. 4326. at berdes. 4330. nekke *and* breste. 4334. yonde. 4338. swowys] shoutes. 4351. Of the toun they. 4376. vpon] on. 4380. it so. 4382. it may. 4390. a parlement. 4427. alle Grece. þe] *om.* 4456. noon] oon. 4464. as] *om.* 4467. And gretly. 4481. vpright. 4485. gan. 4490. koruen. 4532. loke it. 4549. may. 4553. I can. 4563. bodies. 4585. tellyng. 4604. At gynnyng. 4630. begynne. 4638. any lyne. 4659. sinfull. 4679. luke. 4684. atwene. 4693. voide. 4694. swerdes. 4702. a twene. 4704. *second* and] *om.* 4710. Which] That. 4712. a] *om.* 4716. And of.

ERRATA

(IN PART I)

p. vii, l. 11 from bottom. *For* 3999 *read* 3399.
p. ix, l. 4 from bottom. *For* 13 *read* 31.
l. 98. *For* soupë *read* soupe.
l. 106. *Exchange mark of exclamation at the end of the line for comma.*
l. 107 (vv. ll.). *For* restid han *read* rested han.
l. 114 (vv. ll. Wil). *For* T *read* I.
l. 191 (vv. ll. Which). *Omit* Ad_1. Ad_2. I. Ra. L_2.
l. 318 (vv. ll. thexposicioun). *Omit* T_2.
l. 379. *For* bothe* *read* bothë*.
l. 410 (vv. ll. childe). Insert Bo. T_1. L_1. Lb.
l. 488 (vv. ll. so be). *After* Di. *add* T_2.
l. 507. and not spare *should be between commas.*
l. 553 (vv. ll.). *For* Ed_1. *read* E_1.
l. 564. *For* Thebes *read* Thebës.
l. 626. *For* enchauntement *read* enchauntëment.
l. 660. *For* natiuyte *read* natiuytè.
l. 915. *For* I-named *read* I-namëd.
l. 970 (vv. ll.). *Insert* brak] brast C. T_2. E_2. P (brest).
l. 978 (vv. ll.). *Between* I. *and* E_1. *insert* Ra. Ba.
l. 1082 (vv. ll.). *For* E_2. L_1. *read* E_2. L_2.
l. 1145 (vv. ll.). *For* crowne *read* croune.
l. 1178. *For* ferë *read* fer (as in Ar.).
l. 1195 (vv. ll. þat). *Between* Ad_2. *and* Ra. *insert* I.
l. 1222 (vv. ll.). *For* right *read* riȝt.
l. 1254 (vv. ll. and). *Omit* Di.
l. 1300. *For* entred *read* entered*.
l. 1384 (vv. ll.). *For* myghte *read* myght.
l. 1393. *For* light *read* light*.
l. 1400. *For* I-axed (Ar. G.) *read either* He axed *or* And axed *with other MSS.*
l. 1448 (vv. ll.). *For* set *read* sett.
l. 1488. *For* yfichëd *read* yfiched.
l. 1561. (vv. ll. deyntees). *Insert* 1561.
l. 1619. *For* hauë *read* haue *or* ha.
l. 1671 (vv. ll.). *For* this original *read* his o.
l. 1755. *For* fortunes *read* fortunës.
l. 1773. *For* afferme *read* affermë.
l. 1841. *For* thilke* *read* thilkë*.
l. 1876. *For* fewe *read* fewë.
l. 1876 (vv. ll. in space). *Omit* L_2.
l. 1918. *For* shulde* *read* shuldë*.
l. 1961 (vv. ll.). *For* in herte *read* his herte.
l. 2000 (vv. ll.). *For* no bond *read* no bonde.
l. 2005 (vv. ll.). *Insert* no bond] his bond C. T_2. P. E_2.
l. 2033. *For* Thebës *read* Thebes.
l. 2053. *Delete the full-stop at the end of the line.*
l. 2077. *For* availe *read* (with Ar.) vaile.
l. 2099–2294 (vv. ll.; p. 87, l. 16 from bottom). *For* four *read* three.
l. 2102. *For* sayë *read* say.

l. **2145**. *For* Armed *read* Armëd.
l. **2274** (vv. ll. Ioyneaunt). *Between* Ar. and L_2. *insert* G.
l. **2305**. *Delete* was*.
l. **2331**. *For* hondes *read* hondës.
l. **2430** (vv. ll.). *Between* L_1. and M. *insert* Lb.
l. **2437** (vv. ll.). *After* Du. *insert* T_1. L_1. Lb., *after* E_1. *insert* Ra. Ba. C. T_2.
l. **2502**. *For* vntrouthe* *read* vntrouth.
l. **2604** (vv. ll. Epymedon). *Delete* I.
l. **2608**. *For* Argë *read* Arge.
l. **2711** (vv. ll.). *After* begynne *insert* Lb.
l. **2951** (vv. ll.). *Insert* parbraketh] pbraketh Ar. Bo. Lb. P. parbrakith T_1. M. Di. Ad_1. I. Ra. Ba. S. pbrakith C. T_2. perbraketh E_2. pbrakyth L_1. L_2. parbrakethe Ro.
l. **3011** (vv. ll.). *For* 3010–3210 *read* 3011–3210.
l. **3078** (vv. ll.). *For* 3378 *read* 3078.
l. **3218** (vv. ll.). *For* Ap. *read* Ra.
l. **3224**. *For* wepe *read* wepë.
l. **3246** (vv. ll.). *For* falle *read* fallen.
l. **3253**. *For* doutë *read* doute.
l. **3295** (vv. ll.). *For* his *read* hir.
l. **3440**. *For* Repleneshëd *read* (with Ar.) Repleveshëd.
l. **3619** (vv. ll.). *For* Ra. Ra. *read* Ra. Ba.
l. **3645** (vv. ll.). *For* to make *read* to mak.
l. **3678**. *For* alle *read* allë.
l. **3798**. *Exchange full stop at the end for comma.*
l. **3901**. *Delete* of* *and note* 3901 *in* vv. ll.
l. **4048** (vv. ll.). *After* Ar. *add* G.
l. **4081**. *For* vnknowen *read* vnknowën.
l. **4084** (vv. ll. myschaunce). *For* Ba. *read* Ra.
l. **4096**. *For* false *read* falsë.
l. **4104**. *For* herde* *read* herdë*.
l. **4175** (side-note). *For* Melanippus *read* Menalippus.
l. **4334**. *For* ȝonder* *read* ȝonde.
l. **4422** (vv. ll. and her lamentacions). *Omit* her.
l. **4499** (vv. ll.). *For* 4999 *read* 4499.
l. **4710** (vv. ll. Which). *Omit* Ro.

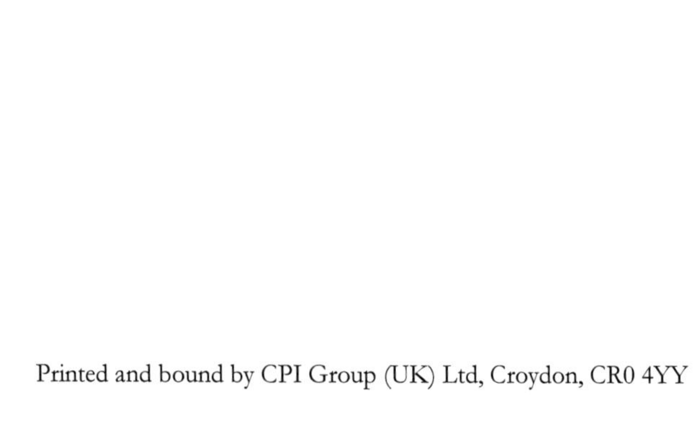

Printed and bound by CPI Group (UK) Ltd, Croydon, CR0 4YY